We hereby initial in Token
of our acceptance, this
" 27th day of April 1914

A..........
British Plenipotentiary
Tibetan Plenipotentiary

The Fate of Tibet
When Big Insects Eat Small Insects

The Fate of Tibet

When Big Insects Eat Small Insects

CLAUDE ARPI

HAR-ANAND
PUBLICATIONS PVT LTD

HAR-ANAND PUBLICATIONS PVT LTD
D-9, Anand Niketan, New Delhi-110 021
E-mail: haranand@mantraonline.com
Website:www.har-anandpublications.com

Cover design by Auroville Press

PRINTED IN INDIA

Published by Ashok Gosain and Ashish Gosain for Har-Anand Publications Pvt Ltd
and printed at Nice Printing Press, New Delhi.

To

Tara, the Mother

Thou who saviest, arise and save!
Mother, to thee I bow.

OM TARE TU TARE TURE SWAHA

Abbreviations

CPR	=	Chinese People's Republic
DIIR	=	Department of Information & International Relations (Dharamsala)
GOI	=	Government of India
IB	=	Intelligence Bureau
KMT	=	Kuomintang
NEFA	=	North East Frontier Agency
PLA	=	People's Liberation Army
PRC	=	People's Republic of China
SWJN	=	Selected Works of Jawaharlal Nehru
USFR	=	Foreign Relations of the United States

Acknowledgements

The issue of Tibet has been 'pursuing' me for nearly thirty years now, more than half my life, and if I had to express my gratitude to all those who have helped me during this research, or should I say 'discovery', it would take too many pages.

However, I am grateful to the Tibetan people who showed me that the saying of Shantideva can be put into practice and become a living reality:

> *If it can be remedied*
> *There is no need to be unhappy.*
> *If it can't be remedied*
> *What is the use to be unhappy?*

To discover this is certainly more important than writing a book.

Above all others, I am grateful to the one who represents so well the genius of his people: His Holiness the Dalai Lama. Perhaps more than the enlightened insights on Tibetan history and the issue of Tibet that he gave me during several interviews, I am grateful to 'Kundun' for his 'presence'.

I had the good luck to meet him when Tibet was not yet a fashion, and one of the most remarkable features of this man who calls himself a 'simple monk' is that in spite of all the noise, the heavy security and media around him, he has not changed, he has still kept the same simplicity, the same warmth, the same friendliness for all.

I always also remember what the Mother of the Sri Aurobindo Ashram said when he visited her in 1973, she said: "His physical body is compassion, there is nothing which can be called 'ego' in this man, even in his physical body."

Thank you for being here during these difficult times for the planet. At the dawn of the new millennium, the earth will need more compassionate beings like you, if it is not going to explode under the pressure of hatred, violence and egoism.

I would like to associate with His Holiness, Tenzin Geyche Tethong, his Private Secretary since more than two decades who has always helped and encouraged me. I still remember a long meeting with Tenzin Geyche-la in 1978, in which he told me that when he leaves his job, he would like to come and live in Auroville. But I am happy that he has kept his 'job'.

One of the first people who triggered this research was a man whom I greatly admired, Sir C.P.N. Singh, former Indian Ambassador and Governor of Uttar Pradesh.

Some twenty years ago in the course of an informal conversation about Tibet, he kept mentioning 'that man in Peking'. I discovered later that he was speaking of K.M. Pannikar. Ever since I have been interested to know more about this 'hidden' aspect of recent Indian history. Sir C.P.N. Singh was very clear that the path of appeasement was not the path that the newly independent India should follow — at least not vis-à-vis China. India should be strong and self-reliant.

I have to say 'un grand merci' to my friend François Gautier, the Correspondent for *Le Figaro* for the countless times he shouted at me: "Put your research in writing, why do you want to keep it only for yourself, why are you so egoistic?" Without his (friendly) admonishments, this book would not have been published. His wife Namrita was associated with him in the battering and now she is associated in my thanks.

I should not forget François' (and my) friend, Tiziano Terzani and his gentle wife Angela. Having been for many years Correspondents for *Der Spiegel* in China and perfectly fluent in Chinese, Tiziano with his great love for the people of China has greatly enlightened me on certain aspects of the Chinese mentality.

My gratitude to all my Tibetan friends and all the Tibetan officials who readily accepted to be interviewed. I shall specially mention Mr Rinchen Sadutshang with his sharp memory of the events of the early fifties, Mrs Rinchen Dolma Taring who has played a major role in the rehabilitation of the first refugees with her husband Jigme Taring; Kasur Kundeling; Late P.T. Takla for his information on the 17-Point Agreement and the 1954 visit to China and Kalon Tashi Wangdi with his great knowledge not only of Tibetan history, but also the political scene in India and China.

I want also to mention Gyatso Tshering, the previous Director of the Tibetan Library of Works and Archives who whole-heartedly helped me to find some rare books and documents in the Tibetan archives and Ven. Amchok Rinpoche, his successor, for his enlightening interview on the 'Karma of Tibet'.

Mɲ Tempa Tsering, Secretary of the Department of International Relations for his help and for giving me permission to use the Department Library and photocopy whatever documents I needed.

Thanks also to my old (not in age) Tibetan friends, Thubten Samphel, Phuntsok T. Atisha, and Tsering Tsomo for their remarks, corrections of the manuscript and encouragement.

I am grateful to Mr Robert Ford to have accepted to discuss with me in detail the situation in Eastern Tibet when the Chinese entered Chamdo. I share many of his perceptions.

I want also to thank all the retired Indian diplomats and Generals who have enlightened me with their first-hand knowledge of the Tibetan issue and the Sino-Indian relations. They may not always accept my conclusions, but I am grateful to them. I should particularly mention Mr N.B. Menon, former Political Officer in Sikkim and Ambassador of India and Lt. Gen. Zoru Bakshi who visited Tibet on a secret mission during the crucial months of 1949.

I must also mention the charming interview with Mrs Malini Menon, daughter of K.P.S. Menon, the first foreign Secretary of independent India and wife of P.N. Menon, who was the Indian Consul General in Lhasa in the mid-fifties.

My gratitude to the management of *The Hindu* in Madras for allowing me to consult old issues of their paper.

Thanks to Mangalam and Uday for their sweet hospitality each time I had to visit Delhi for this research. Their home has been a refuge of peace in the midst of the great city.

A very special mention should go to my father-in-law, Maj. Gen. K.K. Tewari (Retd.) who had the bad (or good) karma to spend seven months in Tibet as a POW after the debacle of October 1962. He and his colleagues, officers and *jawans* paid for the idealism of the Indian Prime Minister. Through this ordeal, they got first hand knowledge of the importance of a balanced foreign policy and the correct choice of advisors. I not only fully used my father-in-law's knowledge of men and times since independence, but I also used him to put some order in my English prose for this manuscript.

I thank Patrice who never forgot to send me articles and clippings on Tibet. I particularly appreciated the interesting articles from *The Modern Review*.

Thanks to Serg and his team for designing the 'prayer-flag' cover of the book and Christine for going through the manuscript and offering to-the-point suggestions. I do not forget Ann, Tency and all my other colleagues and friends who encouraged me in this research.

Mr Narendra Kumar, my editor, needs a special mention. He offered to publish this book from his reputed publishing house without even having seen the manuscript. I am indebted for his confidence. I enjoyed working with Mr. Kumar's sons, Ashok and Ashish. They provided much help.

My gratitude to other members of the team who proof-read the manuscript. Without them this book would have remained in Frenglish, a language quite difficult to read for those educated in Shakespeare's language. Thanks to my sister-in-law Deepti and my old friend Barbara for that. They worked very hard.

I left for the end my 'special' proof reader and wife, Abha. Without her extreme patience — for three years she has put up with books not only all over my study but sometimes in every room of our house — this book had no chance to come out. Abha and my sweet daughter Smiti have not only been very patient but have been the main source of inspiration and encouragement to continue and conclude this research.

To Sri Aurobindo and Mother

My immense gratitude to the Two who 'pulled' me to India some 25 years ago. After pulling me, they 'tied' me here. I often grumble about this 'terrible' country, but what a sweet country too! After all these years, I understand better where the Tibetan Buddhist monks inherited their gentleness and kindness from.

Many in India thought Sri Aurobindo had retired to some nebulous spheres of higher consciousness, but till his last days on this earth he actively followed the world movements. The Editorials of *Mother India* bear witness to his involvement. From his room he saw the great movements which were shaking the earth. He foresaw all the dangers for independent India and in particular the danger of appeasement towards Communist China. He dreamed of a re-united India, a true resurgent Asia, an 'actual' human unity and a new step in the evolution of the human race. When he left his human body in December 1950, India had lost the greatest of her sons without most people in India realising it. The Mother continued his work.

May their vision of a *Life Divine* materialize soon on earth. The Earth needs it. And then perhaps the Big Insects will stop eating the Small Insects.

FOREWORD

When Tibet was free, we took our freedom for granted. We had little sense that it was something we had to prove or even defend, because we were unaware that it was under threat. We simply regarded ourselves as 'the red faced, black haired people of the Land of Snow.' Our physical isolation lulled us into a sense of complacency that left us unprepared for the changes that were to come.

Tibet's long history has been marked by a close and creative interaction with our various neighbours. In former times Tibetans were a war-like nation whose influence spread far and wide. With the advent of Buddhism our military prowess declined, but this change in attitude ultimately spawned rich new relations with India, China and Mongolia that were cultural and religious in nature.

Sadly, we failed to develop sufficient political awareness for the times. Great changes were taking place all around us. To the south India was gaining her independence and to the east China was undergoing civil war and revolution. Meanwhile, Tibet remained much the same. To our cost, we underestimated how these changes would affect us. However, I believe that since then our powerful neighbours have profoundly underestimated how the upheaval that has taken place in Tibet affects them. As a neutral state at the heart of Asia, Tibet has traditionally acted as a buffer between India and China, both now nuclear powers. A buffer that presently no longer exists. As the 'roof of the world' and the source of several great rivers, the Tibetan plateau has also great influence on regional climate, thus environmental changes there have far-reaching effects in East and South Asia. Finally, as a rich repository of living Buddhist culture and tradition, Tibet has a great deal to offer in the quest for inner peace and the encouragement of non-violence and peace in the world at large.

In this book, Claude Arpi, an old friend of Tibet and Tibetans, deals with many of these themes. Taking a long perspective from ancient times to the present he shows how Tibet's interests have always been interdependent with those of her neighbours and vice versa. Consequently, resolution of the current impasse on Tibet will only be settled by dialogue that acknowledges this reality. I have proposed the establishment of Tibet as a Zone of Peace that would address the needs of our neighbours as well as our own. However, such a solution can only be achieved if all the interested parties are prepared to enter into discussions. Until now the Chinese side has resolutely avoided doing so.

Claude Arpi has spent many years of his life in India and has acquired a thorough understanding of the Tibetan issue. While he expresses an admiration for the good spirited resilience of Tibetans that has inspired him in his work, I would like to state my admiration for his own down to earth and practical attitude. He is a man who assesses what needs or can be done and settles down to doing it. This same approach is reflected in this book. I believe readers will find that he casts a much clearer light on the issue of Tibet, which I hope will in turn inspire them to give support to our cause.

July 15, 1999

Contents

Introduction

The year was 1971. That summer I decided to visit Afghanistan during my university holidays. In July, while I was in Kabul I heard some hippies speaking about what they called a 'cool' place called 'Manali.' It was a very 'cool' place in the Indian Himalayas and I was even told that 'cool' Tibetan refugees were living there. Something clicked in my head (or was it in my heart?): "I must go and see these 'cool' guys!" was my immediate resolve.

That day in Kabul, I made up my mind to come to India one day and visit this mysterious place 'Manali.' I did manage to come to India the very next year, and though I could hardly speak English, I decided to make the trip to Manali. I reached Palam Airport early in the morning, jumped into a cab for the Old Delhi Railway Station and boarded the first available train to the North. From Chandigarh I took a bus and on the second day, we reached Kulu from where an old bus took us on the final climb to Manali.

It was on the road between Kulu and Manali that I saw my first Tibetan. This encounter was to change my life.

In India or in Tibet for that matter, everything that happens can be explained by one word — 'karma.' It is a very practical word which explains all that we cannot understand with our little white (or even brown) man's brain. People in Asia believe in the truth behind this word and indeed it is very practical!

It must have been my karma to meet this Tibetan!

During the following weeks I travelled to many places in the Himalayas and I had the occasion to meet many Tibetan refugees who had been rehabilitated by the Indian Government in the hill stations. Most of them were working on the construction and repair of high-altitude strategic roads.

I visited Dharamasala, Dalhousie, Mussoorie, Kathmandu and many other places and the more I met with these peculiar people, the more I became interested in their way of being as well as their history. They had lost everything: their country, their wealth, very often many members of their family and still they could stand on the road and smile.

How could someone educated in a Cartesian country with a modern utilitarian education understand this bizarre phenomenon? We are taught that if one loses everything important and dear in life, one must be sad and grim-faced, there are no two ways about it. In the beginning I thought that the experience of the Chinese invasion and the destruction of their thousand-year old civilization had been too much for them and that something had cracked in their brains.

This might have been true for a few individuals, but a similar experience repeated itself in so many different places, with so many different people....

These guys were indeed cool, as the hippies in Kabul had said.

While in Dharamsala, in the Indian state of Himachal Pradesh, I met their leader, the Dalai Lama and I began to understand something that I had not so far understood: these people had a different set of values than westerners have. They may have lost their material wealth and their country, but they had not lost the deeper human qualities which we call peace of mind or compassion. This was their strength. And their leader was the living example of these qualities.

In seeing this 'simple monk', as he prefers to call himself, I saw that inner strength and the power of compassion are qualities which are practically unknown today in the world. This monk seemed the embodiment of a wisdom which was part of the spiritual and cultural heritage of a nation that had spent most of its time looking 'within', into the heart of man.

Perhaps in the West we spend too much time looking 'outside.' We have been looking to the 'outside' to try to find out how to control the material world and the nature around us, but in the process, we have forgotten the inner qualities and powers of the spirit. Did that Tibetan road worker have the lost key to our number one problem: how to live a contented and happy life?

But one question kept on troubling me: why had this tragedy befallen Tibet? Why had they lost their Himalayan Shangri-La? Was it not a Divine injustice?

The easy answer is of course, "It is karma!" But karma is just a word. What is really behind this word? What terrible sins had the Tibetans committed to invite such so-called karmic retribution?

Why is there such an explosion of interest in Tibet now, at the end of our millennium? The mystery behind the White Clouds which concealed Tibet for centuries is so fascinating for the general public that many are seized by an irresistible urge to discover what was formerly the last 'hidden' kingdom of the Planet.

Had the great Indian master Guru Padmasambhava, who spent many years in Tibet, foreseen this craze when he prophesied:

> When the Iron Bird will fly and horses will gallop on wheels
> Tibetans will be scattered like ants
> All over the World
> Dharma will reach the Land of the Red Man.

The fact that the Roof of the World was a realm dominated by monks and the abode of mystics and yogis living in caves perched on high mountains, adds to the public's interest. As a result, during the last twenty years hundreds of books have been written about Tibet, and the Buddha Dharma has indeed reached the Land of the Red Man.

The question which automatically comes to mind is, why write another book on Tibet?

Obviously if one wants to understand why these people have lost their land, one has first to go through the political history of the Land of Snows. But is that enough?

One discovers soon enough that though Tibet was a politically secluded country, it survived mainly through the contact with its giant neighbours.

The political forces which influenced the Roof of the World during the last two millennia have come largely from two directions: the Southwest (India) and the East (China).

The historical events which led to the flight of the Dalai Lama and the details of his life as an exiled mendicant roaming around the world, begging here and there for a little more peace, love and for a more compassionate world have been relatively well covered. However one immediately observes that little has been written on the regional politics surrounding Tibet, in particular on the political contacts between Tibet and her two giant neighbours. The fact that the political relations between India, Tibet and China have rarely been studied is due primarily to the difficulty of access to primary sources.[1]

After my first experience in Manali, the issue of Tibet and its relation to Asian politics never ceased to haunt me. Why should the nice but weak guys always lose to the bad and tough ones? Why should a very evolved civilization just disappear from the planet? Was it just because Tibet, unlike Kuwait, had no petrol that the world kept quiet? Was it because Tibet refused to use violence that the world community turned away its face when genocide was being committed?

I soon realized that it was no use to study the issue of Tibet without taking into account her relations with her two large neighbours. The key to tension or peace in Asia lies on the Tibetan plateau.

At least on the strategic and ideological levels, the Chinese communists have understood this very well — Tibet is the key to the future of Asia. For their own selfish and expansionist interests, and as a first step in acquiring domination over Asia, the Communist leaders chose to annex Tibet and thereby bring their border into contact with the Indian border.

As soon as they came to power in 1949, the Chinese leaders declared that the "task for the People's Liberation Army for 1950 is to liberate Taiwan, Hainan and Tibet." They asserted that "Tibet is an integral part of Chinese territory" and that the "liberation of Tibet will secure China's western borders." Unfortunately "securing their border" has not been conducive to long term stability and peace in Asia.

An idealistic Indian Prime Minister would understand this too late.

The following chapters are the result of my research into the political relations among these three Asian nations.

I had the good fortune[2] to meet a number of exceptional beings during the course of my interviews with retired Indian and Tibetan officials. I particularly had the good 'karma' to have three long sessions with His Holiness the Dalai Lama.

This has helped me to unravel some of the knotted strings in the Karma of Tibet; though I have to admit that the intricacies of karma

[1]In India these are classified, in China they are closed and in Tibet, they have disappeared.

[2]My good *Lungta*, the 'good wind-horse', the Tibetans would say.

and its circumvolutions are not much clearer to me today than when I met the tall Khampa standing on the Kulu-Manali road, laughing as he slogged to break stones on the road.

I believe that Tibet was a free and independent nation when the Chinese troops invaded Tibet and that Tibet has to become independent again.

It is not only in the interest of the Tibetans to be able to manage their own affairs again, but also in the interest of India, to recover her centuries-old buffer zone. It was such an effective buffer that nobody really knew where the border was before the Simla Convention in 1914. The situation was not much different in 1950. In the forties, the Tibetans themselves were still debating where that border was. As for the Chinese they had hardly put a foot close to the Land of Snows prior to the invasion.

The question is, wouldn't it also be in the interest of China if Tibet was autonomous? Today China is a nation with only one Mantra: 'Money, money, money.' The motto of Deng Xiaoping —'to become rich is glorious'—has perhaps brought more spiritual misery to China than the mad Cultural Revolution of Mao which, even in its madness, was at least driven by some apparent ideals.

Perhaps the day Tibet will be free again, the pragmatic Chinese nation will be able to find a new source of inspiration to rediscover its thousand-year-old civilization. Today the Communist leaders of China are speaking of a 'spiritual civilization' but they only mean it in a materialistic and utopian sense: a perfect classless and stateless Marxist society. How long can an authoritarian state bring contentment to its people? This type of society has already failed everywhere else because nothing can be imposed by force on the human spirit which is searching for higher ideals and for what the French politician and philosopher, André Malraux had in mind when he said that the "twenty-first century will be spiritual, or will not be."

The three civilizations (India, Tibet and China) are extremely old ones and each has, in the course of its history, developed its own characteristics. Each one has also gone through different phases and the current times are certainly one of the most tense and difficult in their more than two thousand year long histories.

The main link which has bound the three nations together and has survived throughout most of the historical period has been Buddhism.

This research which was initially intended to cover the modern period of history has had to go deeper and deeper into the past; so much so that at one point I thought of starting the story millions years ago when the Indian island collided with the Asian plate. Spielberg himself could not have conceived a more dramatic script and eventful beginning.

Without this collision, life could have continued undisturbed on the Indian island for eternity, but it was perhaps neither the destiny nor the Karma of Tibet to remain a sea forever, nor of India to be an island forever. Perhaps the Indian subcontinent had to meet thus the Tethys Sea and create a new range of glorious mountains and the highest plateau in the world. Who knows?

But it would have stretched the history back too far, though there is no doubt that this 'lifting' had incalculable consequences for the history of Asia.

Finally I decided to begin the thread of history at the point where Buddhism was first introduced into Tibet during the period known as the First Propagation of the Buddha Dharma.

It is fascinating to see the changes brought about by this new faith in a people who were one of the most belligerent on earth. The Tibetan Empire which had managed to spread over large parts of China in the West, Persia in the East and most of the Himalayas in the South, was suddenly pacified.

This was the first turning point in the history of Tibet. The powerful empire adopted a religion of love and compassion. As a result it would never recover its past military glory but, on the contrary, it would start another kind of conquest, that of spreading its cultural influence over Central Asia.

From that time, the Tibetan nation directed its energies toward the 'inside' and looked to India, the sacred land of the Buddha, for answers in its thirst for knowledge, spiritual power and creativity. Hundred of monks, lamas and pandits came down from the Himalayan slopes to India to collect the Holy Scriptures or their commentaries. Political life became subservient to and influenced by this inner research. Most of the human and financial resources of the land began to be used to collect scriptures from India, to translate them into Tibetan and protect the new monastic institutions in Tibet.

An event which is usually ignored but which was to have the most serious consequences on the politics of Central Asia is the fact that the Buddhism disappeared from the Indian subcontinent. The source being dry, the interest of the lamas in the land of Buddha quickly disappeared.[3] I shall go into that question.

But the main focus of this study shall be 1950: 'The Fateful Year.' In many ways, it became the turning point.[4]

In 1950, the die of fate was thrown. There are nodal points in history when it is possible for events to go one way or another, — when the tides of time seem poised between the flood and the ebb, when fate awaits our choice to strike its glorious or sombre note, when destiny appears to leave us the choice of our fate. At these points in time, the fruit of a nation's karma matures and it can choose to go forward, or to fall backward.

The year 1950 was certainly one such crucial year for the destinies of India, Tibet and China. The three nations had the choice of going towards peace and collaboration, or tension and confrontation. Each one chose[5] its fate with all the consequences which were to follow.

Decisions can be made with all good intentions—this was probably the case with Nehru who decided to play the card of 'eternal friendship' with China—or with less good reasons in Mao's case.[6] Decisions can be made out of weakness, ignorance or fear, but once a choice is made, events unfold for years and years after.[7] Sri Aurobindo had seen the future when, in early 1950, he wrote:

[3]It remained more of a pilgrimage place for the Tibetans.

[4]Some of my Tibetan informants pointed out that 1949, not 1950, should be considered as the year Tibet was 'liberated' by China. Though it is true that the Chinese troops entered the province of Amdo in October 1949, it was not a massive attack as in the case of Kham province where 40,000 troops had been massed for months in prevision of the invasion. In the case of Amdo, there was no resistance to the Chinese penetration and some Tibetans such as Geshe Sherab Gyatso and Lobsang Tsewang even helped the Chinese to 'liberate' the province. End of 1949 can therefore be considered as the year of the beginning of the 'peaceful liberation' but 1950 is the year of the 'invasion'.

[5]Though it was for Mao, ideology, it was for Nehru idealism and foolishness and for the Tibetans, pure weakness and ignorance of the outside world. (We do not include the Dalai Lama as he was only 15 years old).

[6]For Mao, the 'liberation' of Tibet was certainly a strategic and ideological decision.

[7]Personally too, the year 1950 has a great significance as the one I consider to be my guide, the one who brought me to India in the seventies to permanently settle here, left his physical body. Sri Aurobindo the great Rishi, seer, political and spiritual revolutionary left this world on December 5th.

In Asia a more perilous situation has arisen, standing sharply across the way to any possibility of a continental unity of the peoples of this part of the world, in the emergence of Communist China. This creates a gigantic bloc which could easily englobe the whole of Northern Asia in a combination between two enormous Communist Powers, Russia and China, and would overshadow with a threat of absorption South-Western Asia and Tibet and might be pushed to overrun all up to the whole frontier of India, menacing her security and that of Western Asia with the possibility of an invasion and an over-running and subjection by penetration or even by overwhelming military force to an unwanted ideology, political and social institutions and dominance of this militant mass of Communism whose push might easily prove irresistible.[8]

A few days later Sardar Vallabhbhai Patel passed away: he was the one Indian politician who could perhaps have caused the destiny of India take a different direction. With the loss of Sardar Patel, India lost a man able to act strongly and clear sightedly for the good of India.

With Sri Aurobindo gone, India lost the seer vision that could shed light on her path.

The deeper one delves into the history of this year, the more one concludes that it was, indeed the decisive or 'fateful' year, as I shall call it in the following chapters.

One great pity is that many of the documents of this year as well as those of the three preceding years[9] are still 'classified'.

We can only hope that in a not too distant future, the Indian government will look at its past and decide to open the 'classified' files to historians and researchers.

Analysis of the period of Nehru's governance can only aid in the region's health by encouraging an informed debate and will be a demonstration of the maturity of Indian democracy.

If India wants to seize her future and her destiny, is it not time to look back and draw conclusions from post-1947 politics?

[8]Sri Aurobindo, *The Ideal of Human Unity* (Pondicherry: Sri Aurobindo Ashram, 1972), p. 567.

[9]Most of the pre-1947 archives have been declassified and are now in London.

1

The First Propagation of Buddhism in Tibet

The Light from India

For us, it has always been the Holy Land. It was the birthplace of the founder of the Buddhist culture and the source of wisdom brought to our mountains hundreds of years ago by Indian saints and seers. The religions and societies of Tibet and India have developed in different lines, but Tibet was still a child of Indian civilization.

The Fourteenth Dalai Lama

The Buddha

It is in India, indeed, that more than 2,500 years ago, an event occurred which was to change the face of Asia and the world: a young Prince named Siddartha was born in a small state in the Himalayan foothills.[1]

He was to become the Buddha.

The story of the Buddha interests us because it will be the main link, until the beginning of this century, in the political life of the three nations under study.

Long ago,[2] a young prince was born to King Suddhodana and Queen Maya.

Soon after his birth a Rishi called Ashita noticed a radiance around the palace of Kapilavastu where the Raja[3] and his family

[1]Lumbini, the birthplace of Sakyamuni, is located today in Nepal, a few kilometres away from the Indian border.

[2]Many scholars are now disputing the date which was fixed by Western scholars during the nineteenth century, even according to Tibetan sources the Buddha lived four to five centuries earlier than the accepted date.

[3]Suddhodana was an elected Raja. Small independent republics were flourishing at that time in India.

were staying. The Rishi, who 'knew' about the child, came down from his abode to have a darshan of the little Siddharta and predicted that Siddharta "will become the Saviour of the world, the Buddha".

One day, the young Prince went outside of the palace gates and one after another he saw a sick man, an old man, and a corpse. He then met a sannyasi.[4]

His mind couldn't rest in peace anymore, for he had met the Great Suffering of this world. The life of pleasure and luxury didn't mean anything to him anymore.

"What is the meaning of this life if it is to finish as a corpse?"

To find the answer to his question, the only solution was to leave the palace, his wife and his son Rahul and try to find an answer on the roads of India.

He became a sannyasi and wandered in Northern India, from one hermitage to another, from one master to another. He learned their methods, their Yogas, their practices and sadhanas, but he was still unsatisfied.

Then, all alone with his question, he sat under a peepul tree. He was determined not to move until he attained Enlightenment. For days he was attacked by all sorts of hostile thoughts and even by Mara[5] himself, but one fine morning he attained Enlightenment; his mind was clear, he had got the answer to his question, he had become the Buddha, the Enlightened One, the Perfect One. It was the full moon in the month of Vasya. From that day, his path spread throughout Asia and more recently even in the Western world.

For 45 years, the Buddha walked from one village to another, from one city to the next. He met people of all castes, all ages. In a highly structured society, in which the Brahmin caste had codified most of the customs and the relationships between people, he met everyone, treated everyone with the same respect and taught everyone not according to their rank or caste but according to their understanding and sincerity. He spoke to kings, children, rich merchants or poor peasants, to dacoits and to women.

The life and teachings of the Buddha would have a great influence on the cultural, social and political life of India, Tibet, China and many other Asian nations for centuries.

[4]A mendicant.
[5]Mara is the tempter.

India and Tibet

Tibet indeed is proud of its Indian heritage.

There is no doubt that Tibetan history has often emphasized the importance of Buddhism and India to the development of the culture of Tibet [6] However, the following legend shows that from ancient times, India has been associated with the 'Land of the Gods' in the minds of Tibetan people.

It happened that many centuries before the Buddha Dharma was brought to Tibet, the inhabitants of Yarlung Valley elevated Nyatri Tsenpo as the first king of Tibet. In 127 B.C., legend tells us that he was a sort of God-like Being who descended from the sky using a kind of 'sky-rope'. Nyatri, continues the legend, was originally from India; he was the son of a royal family related to the Buddha's family. Before reaching Tibet, he had been wandering between India and Tibet and finally came down in Yarlung Valley where he met some herdsmen grazing their yaks. The Tibetans believed that he had come from Heaven. They took him on their shoulders and made him the first king of Tibet. This was the beginning of the Yarlung Dynasty of Tibet[7]. The Tibetan royal calendar still dates from that year.

Buddhism was introduced in Tibet in the fifth century (AD) during the reign of Thori Nyatsen, the twenty-eighth King of the Yarlung Dynasty. Once again, the Dharma came from the sky in the form of a casket falling on Yubulakhang, the royal Palace; the casket contained the Mantra of Avalokiteshvara, the Patron and Protector of Tibet. The king was unable to read the scripts, but kept them as a Holy Relic ('the Sacred Scripture') for future generations.

It was during the reign of Songtsen Gonpo[8], the Thirty-third King of the dynasty, that Buddhism became a state affair.

After marrying a Nepalese and a Chinese Princess, the king converted himself to Buddhism. The importance of these marriages needs to be emphasized as they played a vital role in the spread of Buddhism in Tibet. Though Songtsen Gampo had other wives (in particular the daughter of the king of Zhangzhung), it was Bikruti (the Nepalese) and Wengshen (the Chinese) who most influenced the politics and religion of Tibet.

[6]Sometimes even to the detriment of the local pre-Buddhist faith and culture.

[7]In 127 BC.

[8]605-649 AD.

A White Paper published by the Chinese Government in 1992[9] stated that: "By the Tang dynasty (618-907 AD.), the Tibetans and the Hans had, through marriages between royal families and meetings leading to alliance, cemented political and kinship ties of unity and political friendship".

Chinese historians conveniently overlook the Nepalese wedding[10] which is never mentioned in their White Paper or in other publications though the Nepalese princess, married the Tibetan king two years before Princess Wengshen arrived in Tibet and was instrumental in building the Jokhang cathedral and the first Palace on the hill where the Potala is located today in Lhasa[11]. It is one of the many examples that illustrates how modern Chinese historians tend to distort history to suit the Party line.

Would it be correct to say that when King Juan Carlos of Spain married a Greek Princess, Spain became a suzerain of Greece?

China being a patriarchal society, if one followed Chinese logic, the fact that a Tibetan king married a Chinese princess would imply rather that China was becoming a vassal of Tibet. But the two weddings only go to show that during the seventh century, Tibet had cordial relations with both China and the Indian subcontinent.

The double union demonstrates the wisdom of Songtsen Gampo[12] who understood the necessity of a balance between Tibet's neighbours in the East and in the South. In that sense, Brikuti, the Nepalese princess represented not only the culture of the small kingdom of Nepal, but also the faith and the Dharma of the Indian sub-continent.

One also should remember that for a few centuries, Tibet was a strong military power in Central Asia. Though the Chinese Emperor and the Nepalese king were none too keen to 'present' their daughters to the Tibetan king who was considered uneducated and a barbarian, they had no choice but to accept the 'friendly' offer of their powerful neighbour.

---

[9]*China on its Ownership of and Human Rights in Tibet* (Beijing: State Council of the PRC, September, 1992).

[10]As well as the other marriages of Songtsen Gampo.

[11]This Palace was said to be nine storeys high.

[12]Twelve centuries later, the Thirteenth Dalai Lama in his last Testament, was to advise his officials to always keep a balance between the two powerful neighbours.

It is worth mentioning here an interesting episode in the relations among the three nations. It illustrates the power of the Tibetan empire at the time of the Religious Kings.[13] After the pilgrim Hiuen Tsang returned to China in 642 AD, he briefed the Emperor on the state of the Dharma in India and the patronage of the great Indian King Harshavardhana for the Buddhist faith.

To thank King Harsha, the Chinese Emperor decided to send a new mission to India under Wang-hiuen-tse. The mission left China in 646, but by the time it reached India Harshavardhana had already passed away a few months earlier. As the king had no son, one of his Ministers, Arjuna, had ascended to the throne.

Unfortunately, Arjuna was not well disposed towards Buddhism and when the Chinese envoy and his thirty-man escort reached his palace they were slaughtered, with the exception of Wang and one of his ministers who managed to escape to Nepal, from where he sent a message to Songtsen Gampo who decided to immediately dispatch an army of 12,000 Tibetan troops and 7,000 Nepalis. After a short battle in Hirahati in Bihar, Arjuna was deposed and King Kama Rupa of Assam was enthroned. The Emperor of China was said to have been so grateful to Songtsen Gampo for his prompt action that he asked his subjects to build a statue of the Tibetan king on his own tomb.

Some Indian sources dispute this version. However, it does illustrate the warlike capacity of the Tibetan people, their political and military strength and their ability to protect the Dharma when circumstances necessitated it.

"It is difficult to estimate the historical value of this somewhat strange episode, and in any case the truth of the details may be doubted," said Majumdar as there is nothing in the Indian annals to corroborate the Chinese and Tibetan sources.[14] Another interesting point is that the Nepalese and the Chinese Queens of the Tibetan King are said to have played a very active role in dispatching the army to India.

In his Tibet and its History, Richardson categorically states: "Tibet and China, it is clear, were then two powers on an equal

[13]Songtsen Gampo was the first of the Three Religious Kings.

[14]It seems somehow 'logical' that today it is impossible to find any trace of this episode in the Indian annals as most of the Buddhist writings were destroyed by the Muslim invaders if they had not already been destroyed by the brahmanical reformers.

footing. In fact, the Tibetans were regularly the aggressors and, in general, had the upper hand. This was hitherto admitted even by the most hardened Chinese champions of their country's claims on Tibet."[15]

Historically, Songtsen Gampo was the king who forged the Tibetan Empire which at that time extended to the Chinese capital Chang'an (modern Xian) in the East, to the Pamirs and Samarkhand in the West and the Himalayas in the South and was the greatest in Asia. It was the second birth of the Tibetan nation.[16]

During his reign, the capital was moved from Yarlung to Lhasa and a fort was built where the Potala Palace stands today. Perhaps one of the greatest merits of this king was the fact that he sent his Minister Thomi Sambhota to India with sixteen students to study Buddhism and Sanskrit. On their return, they created a new script derived from a Gupta script which is still used today to render the Buddhist scriptures into Tibetan[17]. Translation of the first Buddhist scriptures commenced during his reign.

The Tibetan minister's visit to India marks the beginning of hundreds of visits by Tibetan scholars coming on pilgrimage to the Land of Buddha to discover and bring back to Tibet the teachings of the Buddha in their purity and integrity.

A large number of Indian pandits, tantrics and siddhas attracted by the Roof of the World and its nascent mysticism, would make spirituality the main link between India and Tibet for several centuries to follow.

Numerous texts were translated during the reign of Songtsen Gampo; the king himself took a great interest in the translation work and became a scholar. For the first time, some of the Buddhist precepts were incorporated into the laws of the land.

It was also the beginning of the transformation of a warlike people into a society turned towards inner research and the thirst for knowledge.

[15]Richardson, H.M, *Tibet and its History* (Boulder: Shambala Publications, 1984), p. 30.

[16]Actually it would have been the third birth if one was to count the old kingdom of Zhangzhung and then Nyathri Tsanpo, the first king of Yarlung Dynasty.

[17]Modern studies show that the Zhangzhung kingdom already had a script derived from an old Brahmi script in use in India at the time of the Buddha.

In the process, the Tibetans lost their ability to defend themselves against outside aggressors, particularly their eastern neighbours.

***

> *Tibetans shall be happy in the land of Tibet and Chinese in the land of China*
>
> **From the Treaty signed in 821 between China and Tibet**

Tibet and China

Under the subsequent kings and especially Trisong Detsen (754-797), the Tibetan Empire continued to expand. Its boundaries went so far that at one time the Chinese Emperor had to flee his capital Chang'an (Xian) and a Tibetan nominee was put on the throne.

In year 783 AD, a treaty was concluded which laid down the borders between Tibet and China. An inscription on a pillar at the foot of the Potala Palace in Lhasa recounts these conquests.

It is interesting to note that in the history of the three nations, Tibet and China always had a relation based on force and power, what could be termed a 'political' relationship, while Tibet and India had more of a 'cultural and religious' relationship based on spiritual values.

We shall see that very often during the Yuans and Qing[18] Dynasties, the Lamas of Tibet became the teachers of the Chinese Emperors, but even during these periods, the spiritual relations with China continued to be based on strength and power. This is also true for the first centuries of the Priest-Patron Relationship with the Mongol Khans.

The best proof of this difference in relationship is that India never claimed any part of the Tibetan territory in exchange for providing religious teaching to the Tibetan kings.

In 821, a peace agreement was signed by Tibet and China. The terms of the treaty were engraved on three stone pillars: one was erected in Gungu Meru to demarcate the border between China and Tibet, the second in Lhasa where it still stands,[19] and the third in the Chinese capital of Chang'an.

The Great King of Tibet, the Miraculous Divine Lord, and the Great King of China, the Chinese Ruler Hwang-

[18]The Manchus.
[19]In front of the Jokhang Cathedral.

ti, being in the relationship of nephew and uncle,[20] have conferred together for the alliance of their kingdoms. They have made and ratified a great agreement. Gods and men all know it and bear witness so that it may never be changed; and an account of the agreement has been engraved on this stone pillar to inform future ages and generations.

The Miraculous Divine Lord Thri-tsug De-tsen [Trisung Detsen] and the Chinese King Wits Wu Hsiao-te Hwang-ti, nephew and uncle, seeking in their far-reaching wisdom to prevent all causes of harm to the welfare of their countries now or in the future, have extended their benevolence impartially over all. With the single desire of acting for the peace and benefit of all their subjects they have agreed on the high purpose of ensuring lasting good; and they have made this great treaty in order to fulfil their decision to restore the former ancient friendship and mutual regard and the old relationship of friendly neighbourliness.

Tibet and China shall abide by the frontiers of which they are now in occupation. All to the east is the country of Great China; and all to the west is, without question, the country of Great Tibet....

This solemn agreement has established a great epoch when Tibetans shall be happy in the land of Tibet, and Chinese in the land of China.[21]

The thirty-seventh King, Trisong Detsen sent emissaries to India once again and invited the great Indian teacher Shantarakshita to come to Tibet to teach the Dharma and ordain the first monks.

Richardson in his *History of Tibet* makes an interesting remark: "The religious foundations of Song-tsen Gampo and his immediate successors were quite modest chapels and Buddhist influence

[20]The Tibetan King is supposed to be the nephew while the Chinese Emperor is the uncle.

[21]Richardson informs us that: "The treaty is carved in Tibetan and Chinese on one side of a stone pillar near the Jo-Khang Cathedral of Lhasa. On another side is a historical introduction in Tibetan only; and on the other two sides are bilingual lists of the names of the ministers who witnessed it.

...The frontier appears to have been not far to the west of the Kansu-Shensi border."

probably reached only a small number of the people. The first exponents of the faith were priests from India and China and cannot have had much contact with the mass of the people. Their presence, especially that of the Chinese, might also have had political colour."[22]

But the fact that the king himself adopted the new faith had incalculable effects on the religious, cultural and political future of Tibet.

Soon after his arrival in Tibet, the Indian monk Shantarakshita faced a lot of difficulties due to the strong opposition of the indigenous Bonpo faith. He convinced the king that the only solution was to call the great Tantric Master, Guru Padmasambhava from India to subdue the forces adverse to the new Buddhist faith and overcome the resistance of old Bon practitioners.

There are many accounts of the magical powers of Padmasambhava, but in a very Indian (and Tantric) way, he always tried to convert and use the forces opposing his work instead of destroying them. These forces were later to become the protectors of the new religion.

Here again, we see a difference in attitude between the Chinese and Indian mind. Indian masters always tried to use the capacities and the possibilities of the opposing forces and to convert them to their own truth, while the Chinese first tried to destroy the opposition and later rebuild something more to their liking or their beliefs.

Mao Zedong used this method again and again, particularly during the Cultural Revolution when he spoke of making a clean slate of the old Chinese culture.

But let us come back to Tibet. After performing many rites, 'local deities' in Samye in Central Tibet were subdued[23] and finally the first Buddhist monastery in Tibet was completed in 766.[24] The local deities became the Protectors of the place and Shantarakshita could finally ordain the first Tibetan monks.

Guru Rinpoche, 'the Precious Guru' as the Tibetans reverently call Padmasambhava, is also the author of many famous prophecies. The best known one is about the propagation of the Buddhist teachings in America.[25]

[22]Richardson, op. cit., p. 30.
[23]For a long time, these occult powers destroyed at night the construction work achieved during the day, on the first Tibetan temple.
[24]'Tertons'.
[25]Quoted in the Introduction.

Under Trisong Detsen, Buddhism was established as a state religion and the principle of compassion and non-violence was inculcated into the rather violent and shamanistic population. The king tried to transform the zeal shown by his people in the pursuit of war to a zeal for peace, love and tolerance. As Buddhism penetrated all aspects of life, the once barbarian tribes learned to respect all life forms down to the least insect.

Fishing and hunting were banned and recognized as sins.

This transformation marked the beginning of the weakening of the great Tibetan empire. How to reconcile a great empire with the precepts of non-violence and love for everyone? It seemed an impossibility.

Samye Debate

Before dying, Shantarakshita, the Indian Pandit (known as 'Boddhisattva' to the Tibetans) predicted that a dispute would arise between the two schools of Buddhism that were at that time spreading in Tibet.

The first one — the Chinese school, probably influenced by Taoism — was of the opinion that enlightenment was an instantaneous revelation or realization. It could be obtained only through complete mental and physical inactivity and renunciation. This system of thought had spread throughout China.

The second school taught by the Indian Pandits, known as the 'gradual school' —asserted that enlightenment was a gradual process, not an 'instant' one, requiring long study, practice and analysis and the accumulation of virtues and good deeds. Shantarakshita had brought these teachings with him when he came to Tibet and, having prophesized the dispute, he indicated that one of his Indian disciples, Kamalashila, would come from India to defend the theory of the Indian school.

Over a period of two years (792-794), the famous debate, known in history as the 'Samye Debate' took place in Samye.

Hoshang, a Chinese monk, represented the 'instant school' and Kamalashila who had come from India as prophesied by his guru, defended the Indian view.

At the end of the debate, Kamalashila was declared the winner and the king[26] issued a proclamation naming the Indian Path as the

[26]Trisong Detsen.

orthodox faith for Tibet. The document was written on blue paper with golden letters and distributed throughout the Empire.

From that time on, India became the only source of religious knowledge for Tibet.

This example illustrates the important role that India played in the cultural, spiritual and political life of Tibet in the early period of its history.

While studying the political relations among India, China and Tibet, this aspect of the Tibetan culture and civilisation has to be kept in mind.

Pilgrimage

Another point which throws light on the special relation Tibet had with India is that for centuries India had been the place of pilgrimage par excellence for the Tibetans. In the Tibetan mind India was 'Aryabhumi', the 'Pure Land'. India was the Mecca of the Himalayan Buddhists.[27]

For rich or poor alike, to visit places like Kapilavastu or Lumbini[28] where the Buddha was born, Bodh Gaya, the place where he got enlightenment, or Sarnath where he turned the Wheel of Dharma for the first time in preaching his 'Sermon on the Four Noble Truths', was regarded as the accomplishment of a lifetime.

In his autobiography, the Fourteenth Dalai Lama described his excitement when his first visit to India materialized:

> I was ecstatic. For us Tibetans, India is Aryabhumi, the Land of the Holy. All my life I had longed to make a pilgrimage there: it was the place that I most wanted to visit.[29]

As late as the mid-twentieth century, the great scholar Gedun Choepell spent years collecting information and notes on the Buddhist places of pilgrimage in India, travelling himself as far as Kashmir, Baluchistan[30] and Sri Lanka to try to rediscover some of

[27]It should be noted that Tibet is also for the Hindus a very sacred place due to the presence of the Kailash, the abode of Shiva and the nearby holy Lakes Mansarovar and Rakshas.

[28]Kapilavastu is now located in India nearby what is today the Nepali border.

[29]The Dalai Lama, *Freedom in Exile* (London: Hodder and Stoughton, 1990), p. 123.

[30]To find the birthplace of Padmasambhava and the legendary kingdom of Odyayana.

the places where the Buddha had lived and taught. He even wrote a booklet in Tibetan with a map of the different holy sites which is still in use today.

We should also not forget that the famous (some say infamous) Panchsheel Agreement signed in 1954 by India and China which sealed the fate of Tibet as a nation, dealt mainly with the rights of the Tibetan pilgrims in India and Indian pilgrims in Tibet.

On another occasion the Dalai Lama said: "The relationship between India and Tibet is very unique. For the Tibetans, India is a power land (Aryabhumi). Many higher beings came from that land. For Indians, Tibet is a sacred place. Many Indian have visited the Mansarovar and Mount Kailash. For us here Bodh Gaya is very important."[31]

There is no similar mention in the Tibetan annals about China being a Holy Land.[32]

In fact for the Chinese, Tibet like all the other non-Hans border areas, has always been considered a barbarian province by the Chinese. The Great Wall was built at the cost of hundreds of thousand lives, with the sole purpose of protecting the Chinese against uncivilized barbarians such as the Mongols, the Ugyurs or the Tibetans. Today, the barbarians are more politely called the 'minorities' by the communist regime, but nonetheless they remain second-class citizens in their 'motherland'.

In ninth century Tibet, the old Bon faith was still strong. The Buddhist kings, in spite of a newly found attitude of compassion and even with the help of powerful tantric rituals, could not completely eliminate the Bonpos who were biding their time.

The moment came when Darma, the elder brother of King Ralpachen who had been denied the throne due to his volatile, violent character and his hatred of the Buddhist faith, decided to take revenge on his brother and claim the Tibetan throne.

He planned his coup with some loyal supporters. First Darma decided to get rid of this younger brother and the monk Prime Minister. They were exiled and later assassinated.

[31]The Dalai Lama, *The Spirit of Tibet: Universal Heritage* (New Delhi, Tibetan Parliamentary & Policy Research Centre, 1995), p.79.
[32]Though Wu-Tai-Shan, the Five Peaked Mountain is a sacred pilgrimage for the Tibetans. It is supposed to be the abode of Manjusri. It was visited by the Thirteenth and the Fourteenth Dalai Lamas.

Darma had Ralpachen killed and ascended the throne and with his Council of Ministers lost no time in promulgating new laws to eradicate Buddhism. The temples of Jokhang and Ramoche in Lhasa and Samye in Central Tibet were sealed and the monks had no other choice but to disrobe or face death. They were forced to marry or become huntsmen and carry arms if they wanted to remain alive.

The Indian Pandits who had been invited by Ralpachen to check and revise the translations of the Buddhist scriptures, had to return immediately to India.

From this day, Darma became Lang Darma, or Darma the Bull. The people whispered that he had horns on his forehead as a sign of his devilish character.

It was also said that his tongue was black due to the black Mantras he repeated. The custom has remained in Tibet to show your tongue by way of salutation to demonstrate that you are not an adept of the black faith.

The persecution became so intense that within a few years Buddhism had virtually disappeared from Central Tibet.

In 842, a monk called Lhalung Palgye Dorjee who had been meditating in his hermitage felt that the time had come to stop the negative adharmic actions of the king. He decided to go to Lhasa and kill Darma. For this purpose, he wore a white-lined black cloak and a black hat and he mounted a white horse smeared with charcoal. When he reached Lhasa, he left his horse on the banks of the Kyishu river and proceeded towards the Jokhang where the king was having a meeting with his ministers. He arrived in front of the king, prostrated himself and suddenly pulled out a bow and arrow from beneath his cloak and shot the king in the heart.

Amidst the confusion that followed, he managed to reach the river bank, reverse his cloak and hat, swim his horse across the river and emerged on the opposite bank on a white horse with a white cloak. Thus he escaped the king's troops.

The death of Lang Darma marked the end of the lineage of the kings of Tibet and the beginning of a long period of confusion and decentralization of powers.

The Tibetan state lost its political homogeneity and fragmented into several principalities which fought continuously among themselves.

This did not stop the Tibetan people from focusing their attention on their southern neighbours, India and Nepal.

The period upto the reign King Ralpachen will remain the golden age of Tibetan civilization: it is known in the history of Tibet as the heroic age of the Choe-gye or 'Religious Kings'. Unfortunately, the differences between the original shamanist faith and Buddhism remained latent.

The weakness of the system seems to be that Buddhism had been introduced to Tibet from the top. The kings were the first to be converted and followed later by a class of priests. In the space of two centuries, the Buddha's precepts had had no time to fully percolate down to the ordinary people. It was perhaps this that brought about the quick collapse of the new faith. It does explain, in any case, why there was no open opposition to Lang Darma's destruction of the Buddha Dharma.

However, the new creed remained latent in the spirit of the nation. This allowed it to be revived one century later when the second propagation movement began, bringing about a cultural renaissance in Tibet.

Another point should be made here: the institutionalization of Buddhism has always had as a consequence the weakening of the state. If a king follows in letter and spirit the precepts of the Buddha, he is generally not able to defend his state against attacks from outside or inside. This point will come back again and again in our story.

Hinduism had found an answer to this problem with the theory of the Four *Varnas*, whereby the Dharma expounded by the Brahmanas is defended by the Kshatriyas and sustained by the Vashyas and Shudras.

In Buddhism, the notion of a lay protector exists and Buddha himself was very much dependent on King Bimbisara and his other rich and powerful patrons. But when the patrons themselves become monks (or sannyasis), the state and the Dharma can no longer be defended.

2

The Return of Buddhism to Tibet: the Second Propagation

Tell Atisha how Lang Darma suppressed our religion. Tell how my ancestors were able to reestablish the Buddha Dharma, but still those who know how to practice it properly are rare and the Buddha Dhrama has been sullied by misconduct.

Jangchub Od to Nagtsi Lotsawa

But is it not in consonance with the Buddhist theory of Impermanence that whatever is born must perish one day? History has always witnessed centrifugal forces building great empires around a great personality or a great idea, only to be crushed later by centripetal forces of destruction which erase in no time what was built up with so much vision, pain and effort.

An empire is truly great when the spirit which built it can survive that empire's destruction and reappear under a new and more complete form.

This is what would eventually happen to the Buddhist civilization in Tibet after its systematic eradication by Lang Darma.

By the time King Lang Darma was killed by a Tibetan monk in 842, he had managed to destroy most of the Buddhist institutions in Tibet. An even worse consequence of the persecution initiated by the king was that for the next seventy years, no monk could be ordained.

Lang Darma's assassination in the middle of ninth century marked the end of the Yarlung Dynasty and the collapse of the old monarchical system in Tibet.

The kingdom broke up into many small kingdoms such as Yarlung, Ngari, Purang and Sakya and we had to wait until the advent of the Sakya lineage of rulers in Tibet, in the thirteenth century, to witness a unified control over the country once again.

Though the Tibetan state had lost its political homogeneity and had become fragmented into several principalities fighting each other, this did not stop the Tibetan people led by their local princes or chieftains from focusing their attention on their southern neighbours, India and Nepal.

It is due to the efforts of some of the rulers of the provinces of the erstwhile Tibetan kingdom that a revival of Buddhism became possible on the Roof of the World.

The very fact of being a non-monolithic empire allowed some of the erstwhile pieces to develop a wide variety of ideas through cultural exploration and interchange with India and Nepal that led finally to a deep spiritual renaissance and a cultural unity. During the next couple of centuries Buddha Dharma spread far and wide in the Land of Snows through countless religious and cultural activities.

The spiritual renaissance originated from the Himalayan regions of Spiti and Ladakh in India and Ngari, Tholing and Purang in Tibet; perhaps because they were the closest to India and at the same time had been spared by the Muslim invaders.

Before looking at the movement of this renaissance, known as the Second Propagation, we must have a quick glance at the evolution of Buddhism in India at the end of the first millennium.

Though perhaps the Buddha never wanted to create a new religion, Buddhism as a structured new faith had slowly emerged in India, especially during and after the reign of Asoka. Many great monastic universities such Nalanda, Vikramasila, Bodhgaya or Otanpuri were flourishing in North India. They were patronized by kings or very rich lay patrons and were the main centres of learning and the repositories of the knowledge of that time.

Over the centuries, Buddhism had spread to the territories which are today part of Afghanistan, Pakistan[1], and Central Asia through what is known as the Silk Road.

These centres of higher learning had first risen to prominence when pilgrims from all over Asia began pouring into India to find the source of the wisdom of the Buddha.

Chinese monks[2] kept detailed records of their visits and thanks to the precision of their chronicles, we know the daily life and curriculum of these monasteries at least upto the eighth century.

---

[1]For example, the University of Taxila, near today's Rawalpindi.
[2]Such as Huien Tsang, I Ching or Fu.

Later, in search of the authentic sayings of the Buddha mainly, the Tibetans visited the Buddhist seats of knowledge. Nalanda was the most famous of these great monastic universities and the curriculum covered not only Buddhist scriptures but also linguistics, medicine, debate and science.

At that time, Tantrayana had been incorporated into the teachings of these monastic centres, especially in Vikramasila, the monastery of Atisha. Not only had the Pandits, scholars and abbots studied the Tantras, but many of them had a deep practice of the texts; extensive commentaries on the 'root texts' were also written.

For the purpose of our study, we shall choose two persons who exemplify this renaissance. One is an Indian monk known as Atisha and the other, a Tibetan layman called Marpa. In our view they exemplify the continuous movement of men and ideas across the Himalayas and the manner in which the Buddha Dharma was preserved in its integrity after its decline and disappearance from the subcontinent.

Though opposite in character, upbringing and education, both of them have in their own way contributed much to the renewal of Buddhism in Tibet.

Both have been responsible for many new translations of the original teachings of the Buddha which are still preserve in Tibet. The timely translation of these scriptures helped to preserve them for posterity and benefited many generations of monks.

Less than two centuries later, under the Muslim onslaught and the revivalism of Hinduism, these scriptures disappeared from their land of origin

These translations are reputed to be so precise and accurate that today the texts lost in the original Sanskrit version are retranslated from the Tibetan into Sanskrit[3].

Atisha

Dipankara Srijnana, better known as Atisha, is the first of our examples. He was one of the most famous Indian Pandits of his time. After having studied in all the great Indian universities, he came to Tibet in 1042 to establish many monasteries throughout the country,

[3]For example, at the Central Institute of Higher Tibetan Studies in Sarnath near Varanasi.

restore the lost monastic discipline and eventually found the Kadampa order, which later became the Gelukpa or Yellow sect of Tibetan Buddhism.

The hagiography of Atisha shows him coming into this world in a manner similar to that of the Buddha and the parallels continue throughout his life.

At the age of three, he is said to have been "well-versed in astrology, writing and Sanskrit." During the following years he is supposed to have taken refuge in the Three Jewels[4] and to have observed the novice precepts: namely "studying happily, reciting prayers, seeking out people of noble character, obeying and serving his parents humbly and with sweet words, ... paying respect to holy men.... Looking at the world with heart-felt pity, and helping those who are wretched."[5]

One day, he went with all his retinue to the forest where he met a Brahmin named Zitari "who had the appearance of an Arhat." The Brahmin gave him his first teaching. He explained to him that "the riches possessed by Brahmins and royal persons are like summer flowers that soon decay." Finally he exhorted the prince to abandon his kingdom. The Prince returned to his capital and immediately left for Nalanda where he got a royal reception.

Tibet at the beginning of the second millennium

We have to leave Atisha for a moment to have a look at the situation in Tibet in the first years of the second millennium. The monastic discipline had been declining quickly and the original teachings, especially the tantric teachings, were already lost.

It is only after a first wave of Tibetan students visited India that a new life for the Dharma could flourish once again in the Roof of the World.

Lhalama Yeshe Od, the king of Ngari, one of the principalities in Western Tibet, was to be a great instrument for this revival of Buddhism. He decided to send many young Tibetans to meet saints and scholars in great Indian Viharas like Nalanda or Vikramasila

---

[4]In Buddhist terms, it means taking refuge in the Buddha (the Guide), the Sangha (the Community of the followers of Buddha) and the Dharma (the Teaching).

[5]Lama Thubten Kalsang, *Atisha* (New Delhi: Mahayana Publications, 1974), p. 6.

and to bring back to Tibet the original Buddhist scriptures and translate them into Tibetan. The most famous amongst these adventurers and translators was Rinchen Zangpo.

In those days, the border between Tibet and the Himalayan region was not a fixed border as it has become in the second part of the twentieth century[6]. It was rather an 'undefined' line. For example, the influence of Rinchen Zangpo spread as much in the Tibetan provinces of Ngari or Purang as in Spiti, Lahaul, Kinnaur and Zanskar districts of India.

Although Lhalama Yeshe Od had managed to get many monks ordained, the doctrine of the Tantras was no longer understood and practised by the members of the Sangha. Many pretended to be tantric practitioners, but at the same time refused to follow any of the Vinaya's precepts.

The king, who was very disturbed by this critical situation, decided to send an emissary to India. Gya Tsondru Senge, the emissary, left Tibet with a large quantity of gold and with the task of finding a way to translate as many original texts as he could from Sanskrit into Tibetan. He was also asked to try and locate a Pandit who would be able to subdue the negative forces and bring back the purity of the Dharma to Tibet. He eventually found Atisha who had all the requisite qualities to re-establish the monastic rule in Tibet.

The emissary returned to report his findings to the king of Ngari, who decided to collect more gold and send it to Atisha to convince him to come and teach in Tibet. In order to collect gold, the king decided to visit Turkestan. Unfortunately, the powerful local king of Garlok captured him. His nephew Jangchub Od, hearing of the king's fate, decided to pay a ransom to the Garlok king. He first offered one hundred gold coins, but the king told him that it was not enough. He went back and forth several times, bringing more gold each time, but the king repeatedly refused to release Lhalama Yeshe. Finally, one day Jangchub Od managed to have a private conversation with his uncle who told him that whatever gold he could collect should be used to go to India and to bring back Atisha to Tibet. After all, his life was not so important and he was happy to give it as an offering to the renaissance of the Doctrine in Tibet, he said. His only request to his nephew was that the latter should ask Atisha to pray for him to be reborn as one of his disciples.

---

[6]The Indian 'authorities' became aware of these borders only after the Chinese built a strategic road cutting through Aksai Chin area in the early 50's.

Back in Tibet, Jangchub Od obeyed the last wishes of his uncle
and sent a delegation with a translator to Vikramasila to meet Atisha
and report to him the sacrifice of the old king. For the delegation,
the journey to India was not an easy one, but in spite of all the
obstacles[7], they finally reached the guru.

It was difficult for Atisha to refuse the invitation, especially as
he felt that the old king was himself the manifestation of a
Boddhisattva. He also felt a lot of compassion for the people of Tibet.

He was nevertheless told by a yogini who had some clairvoyance
that if he went to Tibet, he would live to be 72 years, but if he stayed
in India, he would live until the age of 92.

Atisha decided that it was worth cutting his life short if he could
be of benefit to so many sentient beings in the Land of Snows. The
decision was made, he would go.

His departure was not an easy affair as his disciples in India
were not keen to let him go into remote and wild lands. On the pretext
of a pilgrimage to Nepal, he managed to leave his monastery and
after a year's stay in Nepal the party proceeded to Tholing where
the King Jangchub Od was waiting for him.

From that day on, Pandit Atisha was invited to many places in
Tibet. He was requested to teach the precepts of the Buddha, to
consecrate temples, and to ordain and bless new disciples. The great
translator Rinchen Zangpo who himself had built so many
monasteries in Western Tibet, Ladakh and Northern India, requested
the great Teacher to bless his monastery.

Atisha wanted Rinchen Zangpo to accompany him as his
translator, but Rinchen was already old. He showed his white hair
to the Master and requested him instead to bless him for a long
retreat. Atisha agreed and the translator went on a ten-year retreat.
But before being locked up inside his cave Atisha gave him a teaching
called *Lamp on the Path of Enlightenment*. The teaching was supposed
to be easy to understand and practical to follow. It is still used today
by the Tibetan lamas to teach their disciples.

When he had left his monastery in India, Atisha had promised
the Abbot of Vikramasila that he would return to India within three
years. After three years in Tibet, Atisha decided to go to Purang at
the Indian border to fulfil his promise.

Soon after Atisha met his main disciple, Dromtonpa.

[7]And the help of Avalokiteshwara, says the biographer.

Atisha remained for a year at Purang and gave many teachings.

Nagtso Lotsawa, who had brought Atisha to Tibet, was a very worried man for he did not want to cause Atisha to break his pledge. However, he was reassured by Atisha who told him that each time he had tried to cross into India unforeseen obstacles had blocked his return, therefore he was not responsible.

Nothing could now stop the propagation of the Buddha Dharma and Atisha proceeded to Central Tibet where Dromtonpa had arranged for many lamas and lay disciples to meet the guru.

One incident is worth mentioning: once Dromtonpa announced to Atisha that some very high princes were on their way to meet him. In those days, the local princes or leaders acted as Lamas at the same time, there was no separation between the secular and military powers of the chieftains and their religious power. When Atisha saw horsemen with very fancy dresses and decorated horses, he shouted: "Who are these devils?" and hid his face. Dromtonpa explained to the high princes that his master was very strict with the Vinaya rules and could not accept that lamas do not follow the precepts enunciated by the Buddha. The lamas later came back with ordinary dress and were received by Atisha, who accepted them as disciples.

This incident shows the importance attached by Atisha to the monastic rules of conduct. This had been one of the main worries of the old king of Ngari who saw that rules were being neglected day after day and nobody was able to re-establish the original discipline.

He sacrificed his life to see that the Indian Pandit brought back the old discipline still practised in India.

However, in the birthplace of the Buddha, it would soon disappear under the onslaught of Muslim hordes from Central Asia. A new culture based on power and brutality would replace the old compassionate wisdom.

It should also be noted that in the history of Tibet, whenever the strict adherence to the monastic rules stopped, degeneration overtook the Sangha. When monks began to aspire only to political power and wealth, instead of material detachment, Tibet's moral strength vanished and the doors were opened to invaders.

Soon after this incident Atisha met the other hero of our story, Marpa the Translator, when the latter was on his way to India.

This encounter shows how fertile the soil of Tibet was during these few decades, with Indian and Tibetan Pandits, translators and yogis criss-crossing their respective borders in a constant exchange of knowledge and wisdom.

That persons such as Atisha, Marpa or Rinchen Zangpo who have left such a deep imprint on the history of Tibet could have met, is the best sign of the excellence of the Tibetan Renaissance.

He continued to travel for years through Central Tibet with his disciple Dromtonpa who slowly took over the mantle from his old master and began teaching himself.

The way in which the Buddha's Dharma had been spreading since Atisha came to Tibet made him very happy. He once remarked that it was even better than in India.

At the age of 72, as prophesied by the yogini before he left India, he passed away. He had been in Tibet for thirteen years.

The sacrifice of the old king of Ngari had not been in vain, India through one of her great sons had restored the Buddhist precepts to the Land of Snows.

Monks were again monks. Tantric practitioners again understood the deep meaning of the tantric scriptures and above all, the teachings of love and compassion of the gurus of Atisha could be passed on to all — lay people, kings or high lamas.

We could add that India showed her kindness to Tibet when the abbots and monks of the great *viharas* in India allowed one of the most profound among them to leave for the Himalayan mountains to propagate their faith. Perhaps, the wisest amongst them knew that Atisha would not return to the hot plains of the Ganga and that soon their own faith would be replaced by a more blind and less compassionate one.

The political life of Tibet was deeply intermingled with its religious life during this period. It should be noted that the modern concept of 'secularism' which was used by Indian intellectuals influenced by Marxism in the post independence years in India, did not exist in Tibet. Any strong religious or spiritual personality was bound to have an influence on the politics of his times as we will see during the predominance of the lamas of Sakya or later with the Dalai Lamas.

India, like Tibet, had never been 'secular' in this sense. Even from the time of the Buddha when the concept of local democracy had a real and living meaning with elected Rajas working in close collaboration with People's Councils, the power of the spiritual advisor was very great.

Marpa the Translator

The second personage who in our view exemplifies the renaissance of Tibetan culture and spirituality is Marpa Lotsawa or Marpa, the Translator.

Marpa was the Guru of the famous yogi-poet Milarepa, but he was also one of those intrepid translators who sacrificed everything to go to India and meet the greatest yogis of his time (such as Naropa, Jnanagarbha, Kukkuripa, Maitripa, etc.) and to carry back to Tibet over the crest of the Himalayas the Holy Dharma.

We have chosen him as he represents perhaps the most famous of the hundreds of Tibetan lamas or yogis who travelled south, crossed the Himalayas and went down into the hot plains of India in search of the original teachings of the Buddha.

Marpa was a very different character from Atisha. The great Bengali Pandit's life is like a copy of the Buddha's. With his royal lineage, he suddenly discovered the suffering of this world and understood that the only way for him to help others was to live a more meaningful life, closer to the concepts of love and compassion; he then decided to abandon his kingdom and become a monk. Marpa, on the contrary, never abandoned life: he remained a layman who eventually realized the same truths as Atisha.

The other interesting aspect of Marpa's life is that he had as gurus two of the greatest Indian yogis of his time — Tilopa and Naropa. He himself later became the teacher of the great yogi, saint and poet, Milarepa. Today, Marpa is acknowledged as the father figure and founder of the Kagyupa lineage with eminent lamas like Rechungpa, Gampopa, and many others as his other disciples. Ultimately, this lineage was to have a very important role in the political field, especially in the relations between China and Tibet through the different incarnations of the Karmapas.

Marpa was born in 1012, 170 years after the assassination of Lang Darma. Unlike Atisha he was born in a family of rich landowners in South Tibet, in the district of Lhodrak, not far from the Bhutanese border. This was a very rich agricultural region with dense forest and fertile land.

Marpa was a rather aggressive child and his parents thought that the best way to pacify his temper would be to give him a religious education. At the age of 12 he was sent to his first teacher, who named him 'Choeky Lodro' or 'Intellect of Dharma'. Indeed, he had a very brilliant intellect and he soon mastered reading, writing and whatever was taught to him. Unfortunately, his temper was more difficult to control.

According to his biography, his parents taught that the best way to get rid of him was to send him to a monastery, otherwise: "he could cause great harm, killing himself or us, or he could do less harm such as damaging our wealth, fields and home."[8]

His next guru, Drogmi, had visited India and studied Buddhism with Indian scholars or yogis. The idea of travelling to the far-away land of the Buddha must have grown in the mind of young Marpa from the early days.

Drogmi, whose teachings would later be used by the Sakya lamas, was himself a great translator. Many of his translations are still used today in the Tibetan Canon.

It is in the Nyugu Monastery with Drogmi that Marpa learned Sanskrit as well as some colloquial languages of India. According to his biographer, Tsang Nyon Heruka,[9] he must have already been forty years old when he spent three years in Nyugu.

Marpa was a very practical person, though his character was sometimes volatile; he could also be very decisive and when he wanted something, he could become extremely stubborn. When he discovered that there was not enough to satisfy his intellect in Nyugu, he decided to go to the source of knowledge: India. Through his spiritual songs he described his journey on the Tibetan high plateau to the Nepalese border and the hot and humid plains of the Terai.

Always down to earth, Marpa remained three years in Kathmandu, to acclimatize.

Here he met with his destiny[10], he heard of Naropa from two of his future guru's disciples. Naropa was to become Marpa's main guru.

But were not all these difficulties and hurdles on the outer road only a reflection of the trials and purification of the disciple on the inner path?

Marpa himself put many difficulties on the path of his beloved disciple Milarepa, one day asking him to build a tower and the next day to destroy it, only perhaps to teach him not to be attached to the fruits of his actions.

[8]Tsang Nyon Heruka, *The Life of Marpa the Translator* (Boston: Shambala, 1982), p. 6.
[9]'The Mad Yogi of Tsang'.
[10]Or his Karma, depending on how one sees fate.

The history of Naropa is also interesting. He became a scholar and one of the most important abbots of Nalanda and Vikramasila. But his scholarship did not satisfy him and he decided to search for a Guru.

Finally he met Tilopa, a sort of a sadhu who spent his life in meditation and roamed naked around the country. Tilopa had no human guru, but was said to have realized the deeper meaning of all tantric teachings.

Naropa had a tough time and his guru made him go through trial after trial for twelve years. Sometimes he had to risk his life to obey his guru, sometimes he had to do the most outrageous actions especially for someone coming from an orthodox background.

But in the end, his ego was dissolved and in the process he attained the highest degree of spiritual realization.

Tilopa had prophesied that Marpa would come from Tibet and become the main disciple of Naropa and that his lineage would be transmitted through him.

When Marpa arrived at Nalanda, Naropa immediately accepted him as his chief disciple and regent and started giving him all the initiations and empowerment.

After some time, Marpa left his main guru in search of further teachings. Later Marpa returned to Naropa and asked permission to get further teachings from another guru named Maitripa.

At that time, India had quite a few unconventional or 'mad' yogis who behaved in strange ways. They were said to be above normal human conventions. This tradition would develop in Tibet through Marpa who was highly unconventional himself. Milarepa followed this path and a series of 'mad yogis' became notorious including the author of Marpa's biography, Tsang Nyon Heruka.

Maitripa gave two major teachings to Marpa, the first one being related to spontaneous spiritual songs. A yogi goes into a sort of a trance and sings his spiritual experiences in a language understandable to ordinary mortals. This tradition, called *doha* in India, uses a secret language that only initiated people can understand.[11] The most interesting side of the Tibetan tradition of *dohas* was that the teachings could be understood by simple folks.

---

[11]It means that the 'spiritual song' has different levels of meaning — one ordinary meaning for the ordinary followers, and an inner meaning for the initiated ones.

Milarepa, Marpa's first disciple, became the best exponent of these 'spiritual songs' and his *Mila Kumbhum* or *One Hundred Thousands Songs of Mila* became popular with generations of Tibetans from all backgrounds, from the highest lamas to the sinners.

The second teaching that Marpa received from Maitripa was the Mahamudra which was to become the basis of the teachings of the Kargyu school with the Six Yogas of Naropa.

After twelve years of intensive spiritual training and having perfectly mastered many Indian languages, in particular Sanskrit, and having received the most profound teachings available at that time, Marpa decided to return to Tibet.

Before leaving India, a final teaching was given to him and this time not by his guru, but by Nyo, his old companion who had travelled with him for many years. He was jealous of Marpa's realizations and knowledge, and to take revenge on his ex-companion, he threw the books that Marpa had collected over the years into the river Ganga.

It was the ultimate teaching before his departure for Tibet: Marpa realized suddenly how attached he had become to his books and that this attachment was impairing his understanding of the truth behind the words. Suddenly he was awakened and sang a song of compassion for his perverse and unhappy companion.

All this shows that during the eleventh century, Buddhism and in particular Mahayana was flourishing in India. The great monastic institutions as well as individual yogis and tantrics were the repositories of countless teachings, both from the Sutras and the Tantras.

Marpa eventually returned to Lhodrak, got married and took his first disciples. Though living as a layman, his fame started spreading in Tibet. A few years later having collected more gold for a second trip, he returned to India.

It was after his second return that he met his main disciple and poet-yogi, Milarepa. All the famous trials of tower building[12] occurred at that time. Marpa was living the life of an ordinary householder with his wife and children. He was not only farming

[12]Before giving him his first initiation, Marpa asked Milarepa several times to build some towers and each time asked him to demolish them again, saying that they did not conform to his orders.

but also had a small business. Though he had many disciples, for an outsider his character was still rather tough and obstinate. So stubborn was he even then, that after the age of fifty he decided to visit India a third time to meet his guru. He had promised Naropa he would come again to get some final teachings. Family and disciples tried in vain to stop him: he had decided to go and he went.

In India he again met Naropa after many difficulties, 'due to his past karma' says the biographer. Naropa had at that time abandoned all fixed abode and was moving freely without intimating anybody.

Marpa finally got the last instructions from his teachers and returned to Tibet where he divided his time between translating the texts he had brought with him and his family - his disciples who were to firmly establish the root of Buddhism in Tibet.

The lives of Pandit Atisha and Marpa the Translator are mirrors of a society which turned 'within' and gave its energy and wealth for the realization of inner truths and knowledge. The Tibetan Buddhists refer to themselves as 'Nangpas', which literally means 'those who live inside'.

The next couple of centuries followed the trend established by Marpa and Atisha. In the process, the Buddhist teachings could escape the onslaught of the Muslim invaders and were preserved in their integrity beyond the Himalayan barrier.

From this point on, Tibet could find a firm basis to develop its own path. The only weakness of this renaissance movement was that it never took into account the protection of the Dharma and neglected the power necessary to keep intact the teachings of the Buddha against outside forces.

Soon, the same danger that threatened and destroyed Buddhism in India appeared in the Land of Snows. Tibetans lamas were to find an original solution called Choe-yon or Priest-Patron relationship which would work for many centuries and help preserve the spiritual and inner research of the Tibetan teachers.

The words of the Fourteenth Dalai Lama conclude this chapter of Tibetan history:

> However, the frequent visits of scholars and saints between India and Tibet which characterized the early period of Buddhism in Tibet gradually diminished. A number of reasons can be accounted for this development. First of all there was a decline of Buddhism in India. Side by side there was the complete

incorporation of Buddhism into Tibetan thought so that the former dependence was no longer necessary. Tibet had, so to speak achieved independence and was in a position to develop in her own way after the impetus was received from the earlier epoch. Finally, there was the decline in Tibet's military power. From the once powerful empire whose territories had stretched over much of those of her neighbours, the military and political influence of Tibet receded into the remote vastness of the Tibetan plateau. And in the process Tibet lost much of its close geographic ties with its neighbours."[13]

---

[13]Lecture given by the Dalai Lama at the Servants of People Society, New Delhi, 4 August 1966. Reproduced from the *Tibetan Review*, January, 1969.

3

The Decline of Buddhism in India

> *As long as the Bhikkhus meet together in unity, rise in unity, and perform the duties of the Sangha in unity; So long may the Bhikkhus be expected not to decline, but to prosper.*
>
> **The Buddha**

The decline and disappearance of the Buddhist faith from the Indian subcontinent had incalculable repercussions for the politics of Tibet and Central Asia.

Tibet, which had looked south for more than six centuries for the source of its knowledge and strength, had to search for another source and consequently to find new protectors to preserve the Buddha Dharma.

At the same time, the monasteries of Tibet remained the last repositories of the ancient wisdom which had been virtually destroyed and little trace of which was left in its land of origin.

It is interesting to examine the causes of the disappearance of Buddhism from India and to see if any conclusions can be drawn from these events that might explain what happened in Tibet eight centuries later.

In the course of an interview with the Dalai Lama,[1] he mentioned three factors which, according to him, provoked the eradication of Buddhism from the subcontinent: the revival of Hinduism and the conversions undertaken by Shankaracharya; the degeneration of Buddhism which was not kept in its pristine form in the great monasteries; and the loss of princely patronage in Northern India.

---

[1]The Dalai Lama pointed out an excellent article on the subject by Dr. L.M. Joshi, *Reviews on Some Alleged Causes of the Decline of Buddhism in India* (Allahabad: The Journal of the Ganganatha Jha Research Institute, Nov. 1965 - Feb. 1966).

We shall go into the above points in some detail and add one more, the *coup de grace:* the onslaught of the Muslim invaders during the twelfth century.

Historians usually consider the end of the sixth century Gupta period as "the dividing line between the ascendancy and the decadence"[2] of Buddhism.

The Mauryas and Kushanas had been very special patrons for the Buddhist faith, but gradually the Guptas shifted their patronage towards the Brahmanical religion. A restoration of the rites and sacrifices to Brahmanical gods and goddesses occurred during this period and though there was no hostility towards Buddhism, it lost its preponderant place in the state affairs. This is clear from inscriptions during the Gupta period which refer mainly to the Brahmanical cult and very rarely to Buddhism.

Reformers like Shankaracharya revived Hinduism by incorporating some of the new ideas and precepts taught a millennium earlier by the Buddha.

When the Hunas invaded North India in the fifth century, most of the Buddhist monasteries were destroyed. This was a great loss for the Buddhist Dharma because, unlike Hinduism, the strength and vitality of the religion lay mainly in the large monasteries. This has been vividly reported by the Chinese monks, in particular Huien Tsang and I Ching, who travelled in India soon after this period. The fact that the essence of Buddhism was concentrated at a few points such as Nalanda or Vikramasila or Odantapuri made it an easier target for the invaders and looters.

It is certain that these monasteries had amassed immense wealth over the centuries. These *Viharas* attracted donations from devotees and followers and as the monks still followed a strict monastic discipline, these offerings were invested in real estate. The monasteries could own not only huge premises able to accommodate thousands of monks, but also libraries, temples and even villages around the monasteries.

It is said that the caves of Ajanta and Ellora were built by rich merchants who in turn had to borrow money from the monastic authorities.

It has also been said that the Buddhist monasteries were the earliest and most important capitalists in ancient India. Be that as it

[2]R.C. Majumdar, *Ancient India* (New Delhi: Motilal Banarsi Dass, 1994), p. 427.

may, it is certain that they attracted the envy of outsiders and were prime targets for the invaders.

"The monasteries were so to speak the garrisons which maintained the influence of Buddhism in surrounding countries, and as soon as they fell, Buddhism almost vanished from the neighbouring area,"[3] said Majumdar. We should note here the similarity of the situation in Tibet before the Chinese invasion.

The Brahmanical religion was more widespread in the countryside and villages and thereby more difficult to destroy through raids. What happened with the Hunas happened on a much larger and more radical scale during the Muslim invasion of North India at the end of the twelfth century.

The great Chinese pilgrim Hiuen Tsang, who travelled through North India during the reign of Songtsen Gampo, recounted the tale of destruction of thousands of viharas and temples during the Hunas' destructive raids. He saw ruins everywhere, though many monasteries like Nalanda had been rebuilt and were flourishing again. The Chinese monks mentioned the facilities available to the thousands of scholars, such as the most beautiful temples, the large prayer and community halls, the hostels, libraries and observatories.

By the time the Chinese monk Hiuen Tsang (629-645 AD) visited India, the Buddhist faith had begun to flourish again thanks to the patronage of the great king Harshavardhana, but it did not regain the splendour it had achieved during the Mauryas.

From that time the influence of Buddhism shifted to the east with the newly found patronage of the Pala emperors who reigned over Bengal, Bihar and part of today's Uttar Pradesh. The monasteries of Bodh Gaya, Nalanda, Odantapuri and Vikramasila much influenced the spirituality of the Land of Snows and countless Tibetan students, after staying for a few months in Nepal, came down to these viharas through the Himalayas to study the doctrine of the Buddha.

All these were devastated and razed during the raids of the Turkish armies under Ikhtiyar Khalji in the closing years of the twelfth century. As most of the monks were slaughtered, the heart of Buddhism was no more. Today, the remains of Nalanda are testimony to the old splendour and wealth of the Buddhist centres of learning.

[3]Majumdar, op.cit. p. 427.

With the arrival of the barbarian Muslim hordes, the vigour of the monastic life in the hot plains of India was transferred to the desolated caves of the Tibetan high plateau.

The Muslim invasion of northern India at the end of the twelfth century marked the end of the last remnants of Buddhism from the land of its birth, wrote Majumdar.

A Tibetan monk, Dharmasvamin who visited Nalanda in 1235 left us a very sad picture of the plains of Bihar where 1,800 years earlier the Buddha had propagated his message of compassion and non-violence. What he saw in Nalanda was only destruction; he could not recover a single manuscript from what was once one of the richest libraries. Finally, he met an old monk in his nineties who could teach him some Sanskrit. Dharmasvamin studied for some time with the old monk, though once they were warned that the Muslim troops were approaching again and he carried his old master on his shoulders and hid until the raiders had gone.

The image of the old monk on the shoulders of his Tibetan student marks the end of the cultural influence of India over Tibet. The source had gone dry!

As mentioned by the Dalai Lama, apart from the loss of patronage and the Muslim onslaught, the degeneration of the original faith was one of the major factors which brought about the downfall of Buddhism.

Though the Buddhist faith had evolved and the path of Mahayana was prevalent in North India at the beginning of the second millennium, numerous sects had sprung up: many licentious and abhorrent practices had spread and disunity between the different sects, sub-sects and monasteries had weakened the propagation of Dharma. The Buddha had warned in one of his last sermons of the danger of disunity in society and in the Sangha.

Who remembered these prophetic words?

At the end of his life he had summoned all the Bhikkhus in Rajagraha and taught the seven conditions of welfare for the benefit of his disciples.

> (1) As long, O disciples, as the Bhikkhus assemble frequently and hold frequent meetings, (2) as long as the Bhikkhus meet together in unity, rise in unity, and perform the duties of the Sangha in unity; (3) as long as the Bhikkhus shall promulgate nothing that has not been promulgated, abrogate not what has been promulgated,

and act in accordance with the already prescribed rules; (4) as long as the Bhikkhus support, respect, venerate and honour those long-ordained Monks of experience, the fathers and leaders of the Order, and respect their worthy speech; (5) as long as the Bhikkhus fall not under the influence of uprisen attachment that leads to repeated births; (6) as long as the Bhikkhus shall delight in forest retreats; (7) As long as these seven conditions of welfare shall continue to exist amongst the Bhikkhus, as long as the Bhikkhus are well-instructed in these conditions, so long may they be expected not to decline, but to prosper.[4]

Furthermore, the Buddha added that the monks should be devout, modest, conscientious, full of learning, persistently energetic, constantly mindful and full of wisdom. In these conditions, he said Buddhism would not decline, but prosper.

A similar decline would occur in Tibet at the beginning of the twentieth century when intrigues and power struggles between the great monasteries and aristocracy or between the monasteries themselves would be so prevalent that the Thirteenth Dalai Lama would have to issue a strong warning in the form of his Last Testament, but to no avail.

When Brahmanical reformers such as Shankaracharya (788-820 AD) with his great intellectual powers debated with the Buddhist monks whose behaviour was degraded and sometimes depraved, he could easily enforce conversion, the usual penalty for the losers.

The fact remains that during the previous centuries, Buddhism and Hinduism greatly influenced each other. To take an example: Ahimsa, or at any rate a strong insistence on this principle, was a contribution from Buddhism and Hinduism was later influenced by it. High-caste Hindus in most parts of India are still vegetarians today and have a great respect for human life. Sanskrit was adopted as the vehicle for the Buddhist teachings, and the worship of deities was permitted and an element of Bhakti was introduced in the Great Vehicle, while Hinduism began recognizing Buddha as an Avatar of Vishnu on the same level as Krishna or Rama.

[4]Narada Maha Thera, *The Buddha and his Teachings* (Kandy: Buddhist Publication Society, 1980), p. 235.

An interesting aspect of the decline of Buddhism in India is the migration of not only Indian monks and saints to Tibet, but also artists. As Moulik pointed out in his study of Tucci discoveries in Western Tibet: "It is not only the inspiration of Indian art that was responsible for the beautiful frescoes adorning the walls though now in ruin, of Western Tibetan monasteries, but Indian artists themselves migrated into that country and settled there."[5]

Tucci himself said that "The sources of information speak not only of pundits and doctors invited to the court of the kings of Guge or having taken refuge there, in a period which marks the decline of fortune for Buddhism in India, but also of artists, specially from Kashmir who introduced there the Indian traditions.[6]

In another study of Tucci's work in Tibet, Moulik wrote:

> The Mussalman torment which was in its full swing at this time, the hostility of the new sects, the rebirth of the orthodox schools, already gave signs of the decline of Buddhism on the plain of Hindusthan. The monks and saints, the painters and sculptors, from the convents and universities, sacked and menaced by the mussalmans, were gradually drawn into the Himalayan valleys, and were rescued by the magnificent piety of the Kings of Guge. Here on the immense desolation (speaking of today) reigned an unusual fervour of life, cities and temples, monasteries and markets. The artistic genius of India left there its admirable traces which the course of time and carelessness of man are going to obliterate.[7]

To conclude, at the beginning of the twelfth century, Tibet could no longer draw support from its southern neighbour. It had to find a new solution to survive and prosper. This solution will come from the North and the Mongol hordes.

[5]Monindramohan Moulik, *Indian Art in Tibet – Tucci as Explorer and Mystic* (New Delhi: The Modern Review, 1938), p. 491.

[6]Tucci and Ghersi, *Secrets of Tibet* (London, 1935) p. ix.

[7]M. Moulik, *New Light on Indian Civilisation in the Researches of Tucci* (Calcutta: Amrita Bazar Patrika, April 19, 1936).

Indian influence can be seen on the frescoes of Mangnang Temple,
Tibet (c. XI-XIIth century).

4

The Relations with the Mongols and the Yuans

The Genesis of the Choe-yon Relationship

I need a lama to guide me in the right moral direction.
After investigation I found you.
Goden Khan to Sakya Pandita

The history of Tibet took another turn with the rise of the Mongol Empire at the end of the twelfth century. With the Mongol hordes of Genghis Khan overrunning half of Europe and most of Asia, including China, the Mongol Empire was to become one of the vastest the world has ever known of.

It extended from the Pacific in the East, to Europe, Persia and Turkey in the West, Siberia and Russia in the North, and China and Korea in the South.

Before dying, Genghis Khan divided his empire among his four sons. Jochi, the eldest received the territory called Qipchap on the Aral and the Caspian Seas; the second son Chaghatai received territories on the banks of the Onan River, stretching to the southern part of Ili River; the third son Ogedei received the territories on the eastern and western sides of the Altai Range, while the youngest Tolui, got the Great Mongol homeland.

The territory of the Tanguts,[1] who were the closest neighbours of the Tibetans, was annexed in 1226 when Genghis Khan led a punitive expedition against them: they had dared to rebel against the Great Khan.[2] The doors to Tibet were open.

---

[1]One of the numerous Mongol tribes.

[2]It seems that descendants of the Tanguts who fled the armies of Genghis Khan can still be found in Amdo province of Tibet in a place called Minyak.

A solution had to be found by the Tibetan Lamas to defend the integrity of their land and religion against the hordes of Genghis Khan.

The Mongols had not yet heard about the "harmonious blend of religion and politics"! Nor did they know about the Buddhist concept of love and non-violence.

An illustration of their notorious cruelty was seen during one of their campaigns, when the Mongol princes attacked Vladimir[3]. Upset by the resistance of some Russian princes, the Mongols decided to destroy and plunder the city. To keep a tally of how many people were killed, troops were ordered to cut off the ears of the dead, in this way they could find out that 270,000 people had been slaughtered during the attack. The same fate was in stock for Kiev, the Ukrainian capital.

In 1241, the Mongol princes went as far west as Budapest, the Hungarian capital, and then to Austria and Italy; they only returned when they heard about the death of Ogedei, the Great Khan and successor of Genghis Khan. One of Ogedei's five sons, Goden would be the first to invade Tibet.

With a Mongol Khan invading Tibet, a major turn in the history of the Land of Snows was taking shape. It was perhaps the 'good luck' the Tibetans were waiting for.

As we have seen, in the seventh century, Songtsen Gampo, the powerful King of Tibet, had discovered the importance of spiritual values for his own life and for governing his people; similarly, the Mongol Khan, after invading Tibet in the thirteenth century began to look at life from a different perspective and discovered the value of spirituality.

Though Goden knew that the power of the Mongols was supreme and that no one on earth could match this power, his mind felt that religion was also necessary in order to prepare for the next life.

In 1244, he decided to invite one of the leading lamas of Tibet, Sakya Pandita Kunga Gyaltsen, to the Mongolian court to be the imperial preceptor.

Sakya Pandita was summoned to appear at the Khan's court. It was made clear to him that he had little choice but to teach his religion of compassion and non-violence to the Court. The Khan wrote: "Are

[3]Present-day Moscow.

you not afraid of the destruction my huge army can wreak on your people and animals?"

How could the Lama of Sakya have refused especially after Goden had invited him "in the interest of sentient beings and Buddhism."[4]

This letter marks the beginning of the Priest-Patron or *Choe-yon* relationship between the Mongol Khans and the head priests of Sakya in Tibet.

During the following centuries many other prominent lamas of Central Tibet would forge similar types of alliances or relations with other lesser Mongol princes.[5]

The Choe-yon relationship continued to flourish under the next Great Khan, Khubilai, who adopted Buddhism as his empire's state religion. Dogon Choegyal Phagpa, the nephew of Sakya Pandita who had visited the Mongol court with his uncle Sakya Pandita when he was in his teens, became the new preceptor of the court and with the support of the Mongol armies, the highest spiritual and political authority in Tibet.

When the Khan took the initiation from his teacher Choegyal Phagpa, the guru asked his disciple to take three vows. From a Buddhist and historical point of view, the third one was the most important.

At that time, a rite was conducted by the Mongols to control the growth of the Chinese population; a very large number of Chinese were thrown into the Lake Miyou and drowned every year. When he took his initiation, Khubilai Khan made a pledge to renounce this merciless killing of the Chinese and promised his teacher that this sadistic 'rite' would not be performed anymore. In taking this vow, the Khan was demonstrating his eagerness to put the Buddhist precepts into practice.

The teacher was so happy with his new disciple that he spontaneously composed the following verses:

> The colour of the sky is red like blood
> Under the feet is the ocean of corpses
> The forsaking of such a practice is for

[4]*The Mongols and Tibet*, Dharamsala: Department of Information & International Relations, 1996), p. 19.

[5]The powerful Drigung-pa aligned themselves with Mongke, the Tselpas with Khubilai, the Phagdrupas with Heluge and the Taklungpas with Arighbukha.

The fulfilment of Lord Manjushri's wish,
And for the spread of the wholesome Dharma.
It is a dedication to the long-life of the Emperor.[6]

In gratitude, Khubilai Khan offered his Tibetan lama political authority over all Tibet in 1254. He also conferred on him the title of *Ti-shi* or 'Imperial Preceptor'.

In 1261, Khubilai Khan made his Guru the spiritual leader of all Buddhists and proclaimed him as the imperial guru. Choegyal Phagpa was bestowed with many titles such as *'Dharmaraja'* or the more flowery: 'Below the Sky, Above the earth, The Son of the Indian Deity, Emanation of the Buddha, Inventor of the Written Script, Harbinger of Peace, Arya Ti-shi, Master of the Five Sciences.'

It is to be noted that many of these titles such as 'Dharmaraja, Arya, Son of the Indian Deity,' referred to India as the source of the knowledge.

With this distribution of titles, Khubilai Khan had begun an exercise which would later be followed (and often misused) by the Ming and Qing Emperors.

Modern Chinese historians have used these titles conferred by the Mongol Khan as a pretext to justify and perpetuate their control and 'sovereignty' over their weaker neighbour, Tibet. The 'Indian' titles are today shown by the Chinese as proof that the Tibetans were vassals of the Mongols and, therefore, of the Chinese. This type of Chinese argument defies all logic.

To come back to the Khan, a code of precedence was established to regulate the relations with the Tibetan Lamas. This problem of protocol would arise over and over in the relations between the Chinese Emperors and the Dalai Lama. Later we shall see that the Thirteenth Dalai Lama, on a visit to Beijing at the beginning of the century, would insist on receiving the same privileges and reception given to the Fifth Dalai Lama during his visit to Beijing.

The question boils down to: who should have 'protocollary' precedence: the guru (in this case the Lama) or the disciple and protector (the Emperor)?

In the very regulated Chinese court protocol, it was not an easy question to solve. However the following was agreed between Khubilai Khan and Phagpa:

> During meditations, teachings and at small gatherings,
> the lama can sit at the head. During large gatherings,
> consisting of royal families, their bridegrooms, chieftains

[6]*The Mongols and Tibet*, op. cit., p. 14.

and the general populace, Khubilai will sit at the head
to maintain the decorum necessary to rule his subjects.
On matters regarding Tibet, Khubilai will follow the
wishes of Phagpa. Khubilai will not issue orders without
consulting the lama. But with regards to other matters,
Phagpa should not allow himself to be used as a conduit
to Khubilai since his compassionate nature would not
make for strong rule. The lama should not interfere in
these matters.[7]

Having accepted this formula, Khubilai, accompanied by twenty-
five members of his retinue, received the three stages of the Hevajra
Tantra initiation.

These initiations to the Buddhist faith did not stop the Mongols
from continuing their conquests. They had begun to penetrate China
and Indo-China and one after another the local kings or emperors
fell to the superior Mongol force.

After Genghis Khan died in 1227, his son Ogedei continued the
process of integration of the Chinese provinces into the Mongol
Empire. He first conquered Western Xia and in 1234, he exterminated
the Kin regime in alliance with the Southern Song. The following
years the Mongol army concentrated their forces to attack the Songs.
In 1260, after the death of his brother Ogedei, Khubilai Khan declared
himself the Great Khan and in 1271 he became the Emperor of China.
It was the beginning of the Yuan Dynasty (1271-1368). Khubilai Khan
would now be known as Emperor Shizu.

It is strange, that an invader could be made Emperor of China
and recognised as such even by today's communist regime. What is
even stranger is that the entire Mongol Empire became equated with
the Chinese Empire and whatever conquests the Mongol Khan made
became Chinese conquests.

During the following years, the Mongols, now the Yuans
consolidated their new territories and for the first time since the fall
of the Tang dynasty they unified China. The Communist historian
describes it this way: "It helped the development of China in an
unified country of many nationalities."

The Yuans organised the Central Secretariat, the Privy Council
(in charge of military affairs) and the Censorate (responsible for
Government officials). They made the Provinces the highest
administrative units. China was a unified nation for the first time in
four centuries.

---

[7]*The Mongols and Tibet*, op. cit., p. 15.

In Tibet also the Khans were certainly a uniting factor, which helped the Tibetan nation to consolidate around the Sakya hierarchs. This new arrangement brought many developments as well as administrative reforms, such as a new legal system or the opening of a postal service.

As a first stage, the Tibetan monasteries were exempted from taxes by an edict of Khubilai Khan who stated:

> Like the sun, the Buddha Sakyamuni's splendour vanquished the darkness of ignorance and its environs.
> Like a lion, king of the jungle, he vanquished all the demons and non-Buddhists.
> I have a special desire to become the patron of the Buddha Dharma and its monks.
> Therefore, as an offering to Master Phagpa,
> I issue this wholesome Yasa[8] which orders the protection of Tibet's religion and monks.[9]

It has to be noted that this edict of the Great Khan for Tibet was an exception: the taxes and corvées were in force everywhere else in the Mongol empire.

Later through another letter/edict, the lay people were also exempted. In each case, the Khan pointed out that this special favour was due to the religious precepts and initiations received from his guru Phagpa.

In the following centuries, the successive Khans (and later Yuan Emperors) accepted the Lamas of Sakya as their imperial teachers.

The Priest-Patron relationship developed thus: in exchange for their spiritual advice the Lamas were given temporal authority over Tibet while at the same time the country was given protection against outside interference. The principle was similar to the relation between the Sangha and its patron during the Buddha's time: a powerful patron protecting the Sangha and allowing the Dharma to develop and spread. This very unique institution of Central Asia was later to become the corner stone of the relationship between the Dalai Lama and the Manchu Emperors.

The Choe-Yon relationship depended purely on the religious devotion of the patron to the priest and the protection the patron provided to his lama. In some cases the relation continued to exist

---

[8]Proclamation.
[9]From *Bhendey Sheykeyma* quoted by *The Mongols and Tibet*, op. cit., p. 23.

on the basis of guru-disciple alone, even after the political status of the patron had changed. An obvious example of this is the relation between the Mongols and the Tibetans that survived and flourished even after the fall of the Yuan Dynasty and the decline of the Mongol Empire.

However, the most essential element of the relationship was the protection that the patron could provide to his lama and his nation. In many ways it solved the main problem faced by the Buddhist state, which could not survive without the external patronage and support of a strong military power.This relation was so balanced that it did not imply an allegiance of one party to the other. It was an exchange of equals: religious teachings and Buddhist initiations in exchange for military protection. An interesting consequence of this relationship was that while the Mongol emperors were busy spreading their political and administrative influence over Tibet, simultaneously the influence of Tibetan Buddhism was reaching far and wide over Mongolia, China and other territories occupied by the Mongols.

It is also to be noted that not all the Choe-yon relationship acquired a political dimension; in many cases the patron was only expected to provide support to his guru in maintaining his monastery and estates. Several Mongol princes and lesser Tibetan lamas also adopted a Choe-Yon relationship. As we will see in the case of Phagpa, the superiority of the protector was not implicit. How could the disciple become superior to the Guru in any eastern tradition?

The Priest-Patron relationship lasted until 1350 when the Tibetan king Changchub Gyaltsen (1350-1364) replaced the Lamas of Sakya as the most powerful chieftain and leader in Tibet. The new king was mighty enough to dispense with the patronage of the Yuan rulers whose power was declining.

In their White Paper on ownership of Tibet, the Chinese asserted without giving a precise date: "In the mid-thirteenth century Tibet was officially incorporated into the territory of China's Yuan Dynasty."

This is interesting logic. By the same argument Russia and Eastern Europe too should be a province of China, incorporated as they were into the huge Yuan-Mongol empire along with Korea, Vietnam, Burma and Central Asia. The accident of fate that put Khubilai Khan upon the throne of China is not enough to prove that all the other countries which had once been under the yoke of the Mongol Khans were thus a part of China.

China was only one of the provinces of the Mongol empire, while Tibet was an area administered by the Mongols having a special status based on the religious relationship with the Tibetan Lamas. The best proof of this special relation was that the Khan exempted Tibet from paying taxes. In fact, the Yuan Emperor saw himself as a devotee and patron of Tibetan Buddhism.

It needs a good dose of imagination and a strong imperialistic policy to claim ownership on such a flimsy basis.

It is strange that today, the People's Republic is not able to adapt its new political slogans with better suited theories to the end of the twentieth century's logic than that of the imperialist age. Their dream of a stateless socialist society under the guidance of a Han helmsman is hardly feasible, but the Chinese do not like to lose face. To drop an old historical claim is to 'lose face'.

The Priest-Patron relationship continued to be the main feature of Tibet's external relations with the Manchus and Mongolia during the following centuries, until the fall of the Manchus in 1911.

The Chinese have based their claims of 'ownership rights' over Tibet on the relation between the Yuan dynasty of the Mongols and the Tibetan lamas.

> In 1247, Sagya Pandit Gongkar Guamcan, [Sakya Pandita] religious leader of Tibet, met the Mongol prince Gotan at Liangshou (present day Wuwei in Gansu, China) and decided on terms for Tibetan submission to the Mongols, including presentation of a map and census books, payment of tributes, and acceptance of rule of appointed officials. The Tibetan works 'Sagya Genealogy' written in 1629 includes Sagya Pandit's letter to religious and secular leaders in the various part of Tibet saying that they must pledge allegiance to the Mongols... The regime of the Mongol Khanate changed its title to Yuan in 1271, and unified the whole of China in 1279, establishing a central government.'[10]

The letter of the Tibetan lama mentioned above in the White Paper, details and explains the status and position of the Sakya Lama in the Khan's court and the relations which have been established through him with the Khan.

[10]*China on its Ownership of and Human Rights in Tibet*, p. 1.

66   *The Fate of Tibet*

The Great Patron is very happy with me. He said to me:
'You have come here for me, bringing with you such a
young relation in the person of Phagpa. I have invited
you. Others come here out of fear... You should give
teachings with your mind at peace. I will give you
whatever you want. I know what is in your interests.
...The point I wish to convey at this time is that the
Mongol army is unlimited in numerical strength. It
appears as if the whole world is under its sway. Being
mischievous and stubborn, our people might think that
they can get away by escaping.

Sakya Pandita was merely speaking words of wisdom in
addressing his people. He knew the power of the Mongols, he knew
what had happened to the Tanguts in the North and the thousands
of other tribes of the Mongol empire who had tried to rebel against
the authority of the Khans. His advice to his people was not to fight
the Mongols who were too powerful; at the same time the Tibetan
Lamas would use their special position in the court to get the Land
of Snows protected.

He exhorted his people to accept the new relationship:
In the spirit of putting others before self, I have come to
Mongolia to benefit all Tibetans. You must listen to me.
You should not have any misunderstanding regarding
this.
...therefore, if one thinks that one can fight, one's
happiness will be destroyed in the same way a ghost
smothers a sleeping man. I fear such eventuality...I do
not worry for myself. .... Have no concerns how the
Mongols will treat us here. All may keep these words in
mind and stay in peace.[11]

The Priest-Patron relationship had taken shape out of the quiet
influence of the few Buddhist masters on their belligerent Mongol
disciples. Finally, a *modus vivendi*, the Choe-Yon relation emerged
as a model which would help the "harmonious blend of politics and
religion" to prosper.

A more analytical and satisfactory explanation of the Priest-
Patron or Choe-Yon relationship is given by van Praag[12], who studied

[11]Quoted in *The Mongols and Tibet*, op. cit., p. 10.
[12]Michael van Walt van Praag, *The Status of Tibet* (Boulder: Westview Press,
1987), p. 12.

in depth the relations between China and Tibet and the Central Asian states during the last two thousand years:

Two principal constitutive elements make the Choe-Yon: the first is evident from the term itself: Choe-yon is a contraction of:

a. Choe-ne meaning 'the object worthy of religious offering', that is, a deity, Lha, a Boddisattva, an Arhat, and so on, or a Buddhist saint or sage, Jetsun, and:

b. Yon-dak, meaning 'the dispenser of offering' to a religious person or 'object' - that is, a lay person manifesting his piety by making religious offerings to the object of his worship.

Thus, the first element is that the Lama as Choene, the object of worship and offerings, and the respective Khans and Emperors as Yon-dak, the Patron, the worshipper, the giver-of-alms.

The second element is that of protection: the Patron in the Choe-yon relation is bound to protect his Priest and Spiritual Teacher from the enemies of Faith or those of the Teachings. The Lama, in turn sees to the spiritual well being of the Patron and his subjects, and he prays and conducts religious services for their benefit. That such protection did not imply the superiority of the Protector over the Protected (as characterised in European mediaeval relationship) is obvious from the fact that the protected was, above all, the object of the worship. It is evidenced by the fact that the protected was "entitled, as of right, to all assistance, including military services, of His Protector; and that the Protector was obliged, as of duty, to provide these services."

Emergence of the Yellow School

During the fourteenth century, the great reformer Tsong Kapa (1357-1419) founded the Gelukpa Sect which later became prominent and assumed temporal power through its leaders, the Dalai Lamas. The first disciple of Tsong Kapa, Gedun became the first Dalai Lama. This title was given by the Mongol Khans and meant 'Ocean of Wisdom'.[13]

[18]The present Dalai Lama, Tenzin Gyatso, is the Fourteenth.

It is during this time that the great monasteries of Sera, Ganden, Drepung and Tashi Lhunpo were built. The Fifth Dalai Lama, whom the Tibetans called the 'Great Fifth', was the first Dalai Lama to become the political and spiritual head of the Tibetan nation. He united all the Provinces and instituted many reforms; amongst these was the new form of Government known as the 'Ganden Phodang', which lasted until 1959 in Tibet and now exist in exile in India.

The Fifth Dalai Lama also initiated the construction of the Potala on the old Fort of Song-Tsen Gompo.

He established relations with China on an equal footing and visited the Manchu Emperor as the head of a sovereign state.

5

Relations between Tibet and China During the Ming and Early Qing Dynasties

There was no permanent army in Tibet sent by the Qing Court. There were only some forces under the Amban to Tibet, which were stationed in designated barracks.

Wei Jingsheng

The Bestowing of Titles

Most of the Chinese 'evidence' that Tibet has been a part of China since the Yuan Dynasty is based on the bestowing of titles by the Mongols, Mings and Manchus on various Tibetan Lamas. We saw that the process began with the Mongol Khans and their Tibetan teachers, the hierarchs of Sakya. This business continued flourishing during the Ming Dynasty (1368-1644) and Qing[1] Dynasty (1644-1911).

It is difficult for the modern mind to understand the logic behind this practice. The mere fact that the Chinese Emperors, after the Mongol Khans, gave honorific titles to their gurus in Tibet is hardly a legal proof that today Tibet is a part of China.

In 1990, the South African President Nelson Mandela, was awarded the Bharat Ratna[2] by the Indian Government, its highest civilian award; does this mean that South Africa has become an Indian colony?

When Norway's Nobel Committee presents the Nobel Prize to heads of state, does it imply that these heads of state then become vassals of Norway? In which case would Israel and Palestine lose

---

[1]The Manchus.
[2]Meaning 'Precious Jewel of India'.

their sovereignty if Yitzak Shamir and Yasser Arafat jointly received the Nobel Peace Prize?

It would be an overly easy way to annex neighbouring or distant countries.

Are they any reasons for using this old-fashioned methods? Most probably the fact is that China is short of arguments or evidence.

Today China continues to put forward the same line of 'proofs': in a recent White Paper[3], the issuance of titles to Tibetan lamas was again mentioned:

> The Central government of the Ming Dynasty retained most of the titles and ranks of the official positions instituted during the Yuan Dynasty...
>
> ..The third emperor of the Ming Dynasty, Chengzu (reigned 1403-1424) saw the advantage of combined Buddhist religious and political power in Tibet and rivalry between sects occupying different areas. So, he conferred honorific titles on religious leaders in various parts of Tibet such as 'The Prince of Dharma', 'Prince', and 'National Master in Tantrism'. Succession to such princeships needed the approval of the emperor, who would send an envoy to confer the official title on each new prince. Only then could the new prince assume his role.
>
> According to the stipulations of the Ming court, the prince had to despatch his envoy or come in person to the capital to participate in the New Year's Day celebration each year and present his memorial congratulation and tribute.

The White Paper then stipulates all the protocol and details of the presentation ceremony.

It may be noted that the Chinese admitted themselves that there was a 'combined advantage' in bestowing titles and it was the best way to divide the Tibetans on sectarian grounds and eventually rule over the Lamaist State.

One can hope that this mentality will soon change; the opinion of the Chinese dissident Wei Jingsheng, who has a good grasp of Tibetan history, is a ray of light in this direction. Replying to the

---

[3]*China on its 'Ownership...'* op. cit., p. 2.

Beijing White Paper, he commented in his very famous Letter to Deng Xiaoping.[4]

> ... in accordance with agreement and customary practice, the Qing Court and its successor sent troops to Tibet only at the request of Dalai Lama and would return to Sichuan and Qinghai immediately after finishing their tasks as requested by the Dalai Lama. There was no permanent army in Tibet sent by the Qing Court. There were only some forces under the Amban to Tibet, which were stationed in designated barracks.

Wei refers here to the military escorts to the Chinese Amban in Lhasa. During the twentieth century, Britain and India would enjoy similar privileges.

Although during the initial years after Indian independence this would be regarded as a useful privilege by Nehru, it would be abandoned with the rise of the Hindi-Chini-Bhai-Bhai policy.

Wei continues with his interpretation of history:

> [The Dalai Lama] was the supreme spiritual leader of the national religion and enjoyed a popularity even surpassing that of the emperor in three quarters of the Qing territory (Tibet, Xinjiang, Qinghai, Gansu, Sichuan, Yunnan, part of Burma, Inner and Outer Mongolia, provinces in the Northeast and part of Russian Far East). The main reason that the first emperor of the Qing Dynasty made Lamaism the national religion was that "in order to rule the various areas of Mongolia, it is necessary to unite Lamaism." Lamaism became the main force maintaining the unity of China when it had the largest territory in history. The Qing Court, in turn, with its military force and huge amount of financial support, helped Dalai Lama to maintain his supreme position and power as well as sovereignty over much more territory.

It shows an interesting perspective and proves that in the future, leaders with greater insight and knowledge of the political relations

<hr/>

[4]This letter was written by Wei from his prison cell. He was jailed from 1979 to 1998, with only a short break for a few months while Beijing was lobbying to host the Olympics of the Year 2000. This letter is in response to the earlier mentioned White Paper. It is to be noted that Wei wrote to Deng just a few days after the publication of the Paper. It shows that though he was incarcerated in a high security jail, he was still able to get the latest information.

between Tibet and China and the Choe-yon relationship in particular, could help bridge the gap between the Tibetans and the Chinese.

Wei concludes his letter to Deng Xiaoping: "In such a unity, each side became the main condition of the existence of the other side and the word 'tremendous' could hardly describe the benefit each side obtained from this unity. The unity was therefore stable and long-lasting."

Perhaps the most ironic part of the White Paper is the admission it makes that the title the Chinese had given to the Third Dalai Lama is actually an Indian title, 'Vajradhara.'[5]

> ... The central government of the Ming Dynasty showed
> special favour by allowing him to pay tribute. In 1587,
> he was granted the title of Dorjichang or 'Vajradhara
> Dalai Lama'.[6]

Amongst the Tibetans, there were always some takers for the titles, and many Lamas went to Beijing in their individual capacities to collect one title or another as a means of boosting their prestige in Tibet. Apart from the visit of these Lamas who wished to become 'Dharmarajas', there were very few contacts between the Tibetan government and the Chinese court during the Ming Dynasty.

In fact, the Mings were not greatly interested in subjugating Tibet as they were keen to avert a Mongol threat on the issue of Tibet. The main fear of the Emperors was that Tibet might forge an alliance with the Mongol princes, and ultimately pose a danger to the Chinese Dynasty.

The White Paper simplifies the problem: it declares that "the Chinese Ming Dynasty replaced the Yuan Dynasty in China and inherited the right to rule Tibet".

Historical records do not confirm this assertion. As we saw earlier, the relationship between the Mongol princes and the Tibetan leaders was based on the Priest-Patron relationship. The religious part of the relation continued even after the fall of the Yuan dynasty, when the Mings assumed power in China.

It is such historical short cut or distortion which provoked Wei's letter to Deng:

> ... your people have hastily worked out a White Paper
> called Tibet — Its Ownership and Human Rights to
> cover up their incompetence and ignorance which is also

---

[5]In Sanskrit, 'The Immaculate Thunderbolt'.
[6]*China on its 'Ownership...'*, op. cit., p. 3.

your incompetence and ignorance. They are continuing
to use old lies and distortions to deceive you and many
other Chinese people in order to maintain their position
and power. The result will be that at the time when the
majority wake up from their dreams, Tibet will no longer
be part of China.

The fact that the relation between the Yuans and the Tibetan
kings had broken 18 years before the Mings took over power in
China, is not mentioned in the White Paper.

Going by the Chinese logic, the one nation that could claim the
ownership' of Tibet is Outer Mongolia, but even during the
Communist regime, they never asserted such a wild claim.

Another point which the Marxist historians never touch upon is
that the Yuans, the Mongol successors of the Khans, never
administered Tibet directly. The situation of Tibet was similar to
that of some territories occupied by the Mongols, especially in Russia,
which were self-ruled.[7] Maps published in 1914 by the Chinese
government do not show Tibet as a part of the Chinese Empire during
the Yuan Dynasty.

On the other hand, after the fall of the Yuans, the intense religious
ties that Mongol Khans maintained with the Tibetans continued right
up to the advent of the communists and the Stalinist repression. Even
today the Fourteenth Dalai Lama pays regular visits to Mongolia
and is given due respect by the Mongolian authorities and people.[8]

But obviously, the Mings were not keen to see the relation
between the Mongol tribes and the Lamas of Tibet flourish.

To give an example of the 'title game' played by the Mings: when
the Third Dalai Lama, Sonam Gyatso, became the spiritual teacher
of Altan Khan of Mongolia, the Ming emperor stopped giving
rewards and titles to Tibetan Lamas. After this episode, "Lamas
rarely went to China," wrote Ang San Su Khyi[9] in a scholarly paper
she published along with her late husband, the Tibetologist Michael
Harris.

However, it should be noted that the bestowing of titles by the
Mongol Princes was very often a reciprocal arrangement. For

[7]Tashi Tsering in *A Brief Survey of Fourteen Centuries of Sino-Tibetan
Relations* mentioned Galicia, Voynia, Smolensk and Chernigov.
[8]He even visited Mongolia when Mongolia was still a Communist state.
[9]The Nobel Peace Prize Laureate and pro-democracy leader of Burma.

example, the Third Dalai Lama, after having received the title (with a seal) of 'Talei' Lama[10] from Altan Khan, bestowed the title of 'Dharmaraja, Brahma, Lord of the Devas' on the Khan.

In the same way, the Fifth Dalai Lama known as the 'Great Fifth', gave the title of 'Tenzin Choeki Gyatso' ('The Holder of the Dharma, the Dharmaraja') to a Qosot Mongol Prince.

Titles and other rewards were regularly given to foreign princes and dignitaries both by the Mongols and the Chinese Emperors. The Vietnamese, Burmese or Korean rulers were often the beneficiaries of such largesse. But is it anything different from a foreign dignitary visiting India to be conferred an honorary PhD by a University, or Satyajit Ray being given the title of 'Chevalier de la Legion d'Honneur' by the visiting French President?

How do such titles confer 'ownership' of a nation?

The Phagmodru, Rimpung and Tsang Rule

In 1350, while in China the power of the Yuan Dynasty began to decline, the princes of Phagmodru became the major players in Tibet.

Changchub Gyaltsen was the first of these princes who challenged the power of the Sakya hierarchs. In 1358 he marched to Sakya, imprisoned some of the ministers and emerged as the new 'king' of Tibet.

For many Tibetans, his rule was a new golden age in Tibetan history in the sense that for the first time since the religious kings, no foreign 'protector' was required. Shakabpa said:

> He reorganized the administrative divisions of the State. Instead of thirteen myriarchies, he divided the land into numerous districts (Dzong). ... He posted officials and guards at various places along the border with China... The Land was divided equally among the agriculturists, and it was fixed that one-sixth of the crops were to be taken as tax by the administration. New roads and bridges were built... Ferries, consisting of yak-skin boats were put in service.[11]

---

[10]'Tale' was later transcribed as 'Dalai'. It is usually translated by 'Ocean of Wisdom'. This title is still used by the lineage of the ruler of Tibet and Incarnation of Avalokiteshwara.

[11]Shakabpa, Tsepon, W.D., *Tibet: A Political History* (New York: Potala Corporation, 1967) p. 83.

He enforced a 'code of law' similar to the one adopted by the early kings of Tibet with a gradation of 13 kinds of punishment varying according to the gravity of the crime. Enquiry had to be conducted before the sentence was passed.

The Mongol administrative system was systematically replaced by a purely Tibetan one.

Eighteen years after Changchub Gyaltsen had consolidated his rule in Tibet, the Yuan Dynasty collapsed and was replaced by the Ming Dynasty.

The Phagmodru kings ruled Tibet for more than a century, but in 1481, they were replaced by another dynasty: the Rimpung of Tsang.

From about 1565, until the rise to power of the Fifth Dalai Lama in 1642 (two years before the fall of the Ming Dynasty), the kings of Tsang ruled Tibet.

In 1406, the ruling Phagmodru prince, Dakpa Gyaltsen, turned down an imperial invitation to visit China. This decision clearly demonstrates the sovereign authority of Tibetan rulers.

During this period, though the Ming emperors kept some sporadic diplomatic ties with the Tibetan rulers, the Chinese government did not exercise any authority or influence over Tibet.

The Rule of the Dalai Lamas

The advent of the Dalai Lama's lineage and the centralization of power around it was a new factor which brought about a tremendous change in the politics of Central Asia.

During the fourteenth century, the great reformer Tsong Khapa (1357-1419) appeared on the Tibetan stage: he was destined to found a new school of Tibetan Buddhism, the Gelukpa Sect[12] which eventually became prominent, not only in religious matters but also in political affairs. The Gelukpa later assumed political power through their leaders, the Dalai Lamas. Their leadership brought a certain stability to the system of a 'harmonious blend between politics and religion' as the Tibetan system of governance later came to be known. From the time of the Sakya Lamas and their Mongol protectors and patrons, Tibet had lived through a period of great political and social instability, though some progress was made during the reign of the Phagmodrupa and Rimpung kings.

[12]Known as the Yellow Sect.

The main disciple of Tsong Khapa, Gedun Drupa (1391-1474) retrospectively became the First Dalai Lama after the death of Sonam Gyatso, the Third Dalai Lama. He was an erudite monk and the founder of the Tashilhunpo Monastery, the great monastery of Shigatse.

Gedun Gyatso (1476-1542), born like Gedun Drupa in Central Tibet, was recognized as the reincarnation of the Gedun. He also went to Tashilhunpo to study, but later became the abbot of Drepung Monastery. He would retrospectively be known as the Second Dalai Lama. The tradition that the Dalai Lamas live in Drepung was started by Gedun Gyatso and was followed by the next reincarnations, until the Great Fifth Dalai Lama shifted the seat of the Tibetan government to Lhasa.

It is Gedun Gyatso's incarnation, Sonam Gyatso (1543-1588) who became the first Dalai Lama to assume some temporal power in Tibet.

This is the same Sonam Gyatso, who Altan Khan chose as his guru and on whom was bestowed the title 'Talei'.[13] Finishing his studies in Drepung, he achieved great fame as very brilliant scholar and teacher. His eminence reached far and wide; it was only after the third invitation, however, that Sonam Gyatso accepted to go and teach at the Mongolian court. To show his respect, Altan Khan came to receive him at the Tibetan border and accompanied him to his capital.

Sonam Gyatso received protection from the Khan to administer Tibet. He was also given support to build new monasteries in Lithang[14] and Kumbum.[15]

Yonten Gyatso (1589-1616), the Fourth Dalai Lama and the incarnation of Sonam Gyatso, was the first Dalai Lama to be born outside Central Tibet. He was the son of a Mongolian chief. His birth amongst the Mongolian tribes strengthened the religious and cultural links between the two nations. Once he was invited by the Emperor of China to consecrate a temple in Nanjing, but he refused to go to China. This illustrates how little influence the Mings had on Tibetan affairs.

When he came to Tibet to complete his studies, he met Lama Lobsang Chosgyan, a very famous teacher of Tashilhunpo

[13]Now written as 'Dalai'.
[14]In Kham province.
[15]The birth place of Tsong Khapa in Amdo.

monastery, who became one of his main gurus. Lobsang Chosgyan would later become known as the first Panchen Lama.[16]

It was the beginning of a long and close relation between the two Lamas. This relation continued with many ups and downs through successive lives.

During the course of Tibetan history, the Dalai Lama and the Panchen Lama often found themselves in the position of adversaries, but the different incarnations themselves always kept a deep respect for each other. This was not always the case with their respective households and administrations.

The 'political' differences between the Lamas were often created and used either by their respective entourage or by the Chinese and even the British who were interested to divide and rule Tibet.

We should mention here that in 1962, at a time when all outsiders and the media had branded him a Chinese puppet and a traitor, the Panchen Lama ended a religious speech in front of the Jokhang Central cathedral in Lhasa by saying "Long Life to His Holiness the Dalai Lama". It cost him many years of torture and tamzins[17]: a dead ear, a mutilated arm and more than fifteen years of 're-education'.

Fate and men have often placed the student and the teacher in opposing positions, but the reality behind the politics suggests a great closeness and a common vision for Tibet.

In 1644, the Ming Dynasty, a Han Dynasty, was again overthrown by a foreign ruler — the Manchus, who established their own dynasty. This new dynasty lasted until the Chinese Revolution of 1911 led by Dr. Sun Yat Sen. The Manchu rule was known as the Qing Dynasty.

The Great Fifth Dalai Lama

During the rule of Ngawang Gyatso, the Fifth Dalai Lama (1617-1682), Tibet was once again unified under a single Tibetan authority. This Dalai Lama, known as the Great Fifth, was one of the greatest Dalai Lamas. In 1625, his main preceptor, Lama Lobsang Choeki, the Third Panchen Lama, enthroned him.

---

[16]'Panchen' is a mixture of the Sanskrit 'Pandita' and Tibetan 'Chenpo'. It means 'Great Scholar'.

[17]The person undergoing Tamzin or 'public self-criticism' is generally insulted, beaten and sometimes even killed. This was one of the great 'specialities' of the Red Guards during the Cultural Revolution.

In 1638, while he was still very young, he was invited by Gushri Khan, the leader of the Qoshot Mongols to give Buddhist teachings in the court of the Khan. Very pleased with his new Guru, the Mongol Prince bestowed titles on the Dalai Lama who reciprocated by calling the Khan 'the Religious King and Holder of the Buddhist Faith'.

In 1639, five years before the Manchu dynasty overthrew the Mings and conquered China, the Manchu Emperor Tai Tsung invited the Dalai Lama to his capital[18]. The Dalai Lama refused the invitation but sent one of his disciples who was treated with great respect by the Chinese Emperor.

This invitation marked a new beginning in the Priest-Patron relationship between the Qing dynasty and the Dalai Lamas. It continued (with ups and downs) until the early part of the twentieth century when the Thirteenth Dalai Lama visited Beijing and met the Emperor and the Dowager Empress.[19]

It should be noted that at that time, it was not only in the religious interest of the Chinese Emperors, but also in their political interest to open a channel of communication with the Dalai Lamas. To have a strong relation with the Tibetan leaders was the best way to check the Mongol influence in Tibet. The Manchus knew perfectly well the influence and the prestige of the Dalai Lama and the importance given to his advice in the Mongol court.

It is also a fact that historically, with each change of dynasty, China witnessed a period of great turmoil (or 'chaos' for the Chinese), and the border areas were the first to be lost. When the Son of Heaven had his Mandate withdrawn by Heaven, the first 'subjects' to leave the sinking ship were the 'barbarians' located on the periphery of the Empire.

Therefore during this period of chaos, maintaining peace in the border areas was of great importance for the Chinese Emperor. It further justified the several invitations the Manchu Emperor Shun-chih sent to the Dalai Lama to visit him in Beijing.

In 1642, with the support of Gushri Khan, his Mongol patron, the Fifth Dalai Lama became the supreme political and religious ruler of a unified Tibet. His prestige was not restricted to Tibet but went as far as Mongolia, Northern India, China, and many areas of Central

[18]Mukden, today's Shenyang.
[19]Both of whom would unfortunately pass away with a day's interval during the stay of the Thirteenth Dalai Lama in Beijing.

Asia. While maintaining very good relations with his main patron, the Dalai Lama developed a new relation with the Manchu Emperor. A balance had to be kept between the two powerful northern neighbours.

In 1652, the Great Fifth finally decided to go to China.

After long negotiations, both parties agreed upon a complicated protocol for the first meeting between the Emperor and the Lama. The Emperor accepted to come out from Beijing to receive the Dalai Lama. Shakabpa described it thus:

> The Dalai Lama entered the city gate and proceeded through two lines of officials. As soon as the palace came in sight, the Dalai Lama's officials had to dismount from the horses, although the Dalai Lama remained in his palanquin. On entering the palace gate, he stepped out of the palanquin on to a carpet of yellow silk. Halfway to the main door, he was met by Shun-chih Emperor, who just then emerged from his quarters to receive him. The Manchu Emperor clasped the Dalai Lama's hands and they exchanged greetings through an interpreter.[20]

Later they proceeded together to Beijing. The Dalai Lama remained for a couple of months in China before returning to Tibet. While in Beijing, he lived in the Yellow Palace specially built for him by the Emperor. W.W. Rockhill, an American scholar and diplomat in China, wrote about the Fifth Dalai Lama's visit to China:

> The Dalai Lama had been treated with all the ceremony which could have been accorded to any independent sovereign, and nothing can be found in Chinese works to indicate that he was looked upon in any other light; at this period of China's relations with Tibet, the temporal power of the Lama, backed by the arms of Gushri Khan and the devotion of all Mongolia, was not a thing for the Emperor of China to question."[21]

However, the White Paper reiterates the official modern Chinese version of the relations between Tibet and China at the beginning of the Qing dynasty. The Paper states:

[20]Shakabpa, op. cit., p. 115.
[21]Rockhill, W.W, *The Dalai Lamas of Lhasa and Their Relations With Emperors of China, 1644-1908* (London: 1910), p. 37.

In 1653, and 1713, the Qing emperors granted honorific titles to the 5th Dalai Lama and the 5th Bainqen Lama,[22] henceforth officially establishing the titles of the Dalai Lama and Bainqen Lama and their political status in Tibet.

Once again the Chinese use the bestowing of titles on the Tibetan leaders as a proof of their ownership of Tibet. We will not come back to this, except to say that the White Paper conveniently forgets that the Dalai Lama also bestowed a title on the Chinese Emperor.

As for the relation between the Dalai Lama and Panchen Lama, it was following this that the leaders in Beijing began to use the one against the other.

In fact, both Lamas had at that time very cordial relations and when, in 1662, the Panchen Lama Lobsang Chosgyan passed away at the age of 91, the Dalai Lama personally searched for his reincarnation and enthroned him as the Panchen Lama Lobsang Yeshe. In the following years, the Dalai Lama personally supervised the young Panchen Lama's education at the Tashilhunpo.

During the reign of the Great Fifth, the large monasteries of Sera, Ganden, Drepung and Tashilhunpo became more powerful. The Dalai Lama united all the provinces and instituted many reforms; among them was the formation of the 'Ganden Phodang', a new form of Government with the Dalai Lama as its head and a Kashag or Council of Ministers. This system was to last up until 1959 in Tibet.

The Dalai Lama also initiated the construction of the Potala on the old fort of King Songtsen Gompo. The capital was shifted to Lhasa, a civil service was created, a judicial system was introduced as well as a new system of taxation. The most important feature of the government was the merger of religious and temporal governance. We shall later see that this form of government had its own weakness.[23] Often the rulers were too young or not interested in politics, or too weak with regents who were not always suited for the job.[24]

[22]Panchen Lama in Chinese transliteration. Note that the Chinese Government counts the Panchen Lama as the Fifth though he was only the Third.

[23]Particularly during the Regency periods.

[24]Especially during the aborted reigns of the Ninth to the Twelfth Dalai Lamas, who all died very young under suspicious circumstances and were not able to assume their responsibilities.

The Chinese Ambans or Commissioners posted in Lhasa would capitalize on the weakness of the system as well as the intrigues between the different religious sects, the power struggle between the aristocratic families and the rivalries between the big monasteries, to interfere in Tibetan affairs. But we shall look more closely at this later.

In 1679, the Fifth Dalai Lama nominated a very astute and cultivated Regent, Desi Sangyay Gyatso.[25] One of his main tasks was to complete the Dalai Lama's new palace.

Though the Dalai Lama passed away three years later, the Regent kept his death a secret for more than fifteen years! This enabled him to finish the Potala and keep a certain political stability at a time of great upheavals in Tibet and Asia.

The new reincarnation of the Fifth Dalai Lama was discovered by the Regent in a far away place of Southern Tibet. Tsangyang Gyatso, the Sixth Dalai Lama was born in Tawang, which was ceded to India under the 1914 Simla Convention.

The news of the death of the Dalai Lama and the successful discovery of his new reincarnation was one of the best-kept state secrets in human history.

War and Treaty with Ladakh

We should shift our attention now to the western border of Tibet and look at the development on this side of the newly reunited Tibet.

For some time, the King of Ladakh had been harassing the Gelukpa monasteries in Western Tibet. In 1679, the Dalai Lama decided to send Mongol and Tibetan troops under the Tibetan General Gaden Tsewang to deal with the Ladakhis.

The first battles occurred near Purang, but soon the Tibetan commander decided to invade Ladakh and capture King Gelek Namgyal. Being encircled in his fortress of Basgo, the Ladakhi ruler appealed to the Muslim ruler of Kashmir. We should remember that this was the time of Shah Jahan: Kashmir was part of the Moghul Empire, and the Nawab of Kashmir was a nominal suzerain of Ladakh.

With the arrival of the Moghul troops, the Tibeto-Mongol army was first defeated in Bagso and had to withdraw to the vicinity of Panggong Lake. Unfortunately for Gelek Namgyal, the Nawab sent

---

[25]He was rumoured to be the natural son of the Dalai Lama.

him a bill for his support: he had to convert to Islam. Thus he became a Muslim ruler under the name of Akabal Mahmud Khan; he had to build a mosque in Leh and many more clauses were imposed on the poor king who in the end was held hostage by the Nawab.

The situation was getting out of hand for the Ladhakis when the Tibetans entered Ladakh again. Both parties agreed to negotiate a settlement and to use the good offices of the Head Lama of Bhutan who was also the Guru of the Ladakhi king.

A Treaty was finally signed in 1684; the borders between Tibet and Ladakh were demarcated, the regions of Guge, Purang and Rudok were confirmed as part of Tibet, and Ladakh had to pay a tribute every three years to Tibet.

The Peace Treaty with Ladakh was signed at Tingmosgang by Gaden Tsewang on behalf of the Dalai Lama's government. The mediator was the "Drukpa (Bhutanese Lama) Omniscient Lama, named Mee-pham-wang-po"[26] who according to the text of the Treaty "in his former incarnations had always been the patron Lama of the kings of Ladhak".

The most important article of this treaty for our study is the first one: "The boundaries fixed, in the beginning, when king Chide-Nyima Gon gave a kingdom to each of his three sons[27], shall still be maintained."

Apart from the border between Ladakh and Tibet, the Treaty deals with the trade rights of the Ladakhis. To give an example, one of the articles says that "only Ladakhis shall be permitted to enter into Ngarees-khor-sum[28] for wool trade."

A provision was also made for a tribute to the Dalai Lama "A 'Lapchak' shall be sent every third year from Leh to Lhasa with presents."

The Treaty adds:

> The members of the Lapchak Mission shall be provided with provisions, free of cost, during their stay at Lhasa, and for the journey they shall be similarly provided with 200 baggage animals, 25 riding ponies, and 10 servants.
> ...and he sets aside its revenue for the purpose of meeting the expense involved in keeping up the

[26]Mipam Namgyal Wangpo, the Bhutanese Lama
[27]In the tenth century.
[28]Ngari-ko-sum or Western Tibet.

sacrificial lights at Kailas, and the Holy lakes of Manasarwar and Rakas Tal.[29]

Chinese Suzerainty: a Fiction?

The Tibetan system of government might have had many weaknesses, but Chinese control over Tibet was wishful thinking rather than direct and effective control. Even at the beginning of the twentieth century, during the last years of the Qing Dynasty and the first years of the Nationalist regime, the Chinese kept up the same pretension of being the 'suzerain' of Tibet, but every independent observer has contradicted the Chinese claims.

We should nevertheless remember that it cost the successive Chinese regimes nothing to pretend to own Tibet; on the contrary, they knew that their claim could only prove to be an investment in the long run, as indeed it was!

An observation can be made here. Buddhism was propounded partly as a reaction against the prevailing rigidities of Brahmanism which existed at the time of the Buddha. His teachings were in some ways a protest against the extreme codification of Indian society. One major practice to which the Buddha objected was the rigid caste system which defined relations between people as well as their social status. The Brahmins (or Teachers) exercised extreme authority as the traditional repositories and interpreters of the Dharma. The warriors, Kshatriya, held a lesser position as 'protector' (by force when necessary) of this Dharma; they were to allow it to exist and flourish. It is striking and somewhat ironic that the relationship between the Khan (the Protector) and the Dalai Lama (the Teacher) mirrored this ancient social practice.

The balance and health of such an arrangement depended crucially upon the moral fibre and the 'inner' capacity of the leaders of the society – the Brahmins or the Lamas — to be living embodiments of the Dharma.

During periods of degeneration, the status and position of each section of society became even more rigid, each one forgetting its true duties to look after its status. The protagonists became interested in the form more than the true content (and responsibility) of the titles and positions; hence the time was ripe for a reformer to come and bring in a new era, or a new religious teaching.

[29]For full text of Treaty, see van Walt, op. cit., p. 289.

In many ways, the situation in Tibet, Mongolia and China was similar. Originally, the Lamas were the repositories of the Buddha Dharma. This Dharma could survive only because of the strength and armed support of the Patron (the Mongol Khans or the Chinese Emperors). When this relation became too rigid or when the Emperors or their successors stopped believing in the Dharma, the relationship collapsed. This is what happened at the beginning of the twentieth century. But it can be said that the Priest-Patron relationship worked fairly well throughout most of the Qing Dynasty.

6

Troubled Times: the Eighteenth and Nineteenth Century

*If a people abandon military pursuits and make literature
their chief object, they become unable to safeguard their
former position. This should be known.*

**Letter from the Chinese Emperor on a Stone
Pillar in Lhasa**

The end of the seventeenth and the eighteenth Century witnessed
one of the most troubled times in the history of Tibet, comparable to
the couple of centuries after the reign of Lang Darma.

The Regent Desi Sangyay Gyatso knew that he was postponing
trouble when he decided to conceal the death of the Fifth Dalai Lama.
He was only keen to complete the works of his master.

Pholanay Sonam Tobgyal

One of the characters to emerge from the anarchy at the beginning
of the eighteenth century was Pholanay Sonam Tobgyal. He was to
play a considerable role for more than twenty years in the affairs of
Tibet. We shall try to understand these 'troubled times' through the
life of this man.

He first acquired a name as an army commander under Lhazang
Khan, the Qosot Mongol Chief who, after the death of the Fifth Dalai
Lama, killed the Regent Sangyay Gyatso and became the ruler of
Tibet.

After Lhazang Khan had kidnapped Tsangyang Gyatso, the
young Sixth Dalai Lama, the Khan became even more unpopular
with the Tibetans. The anger of the population, the aristocracy and
the big monasteries was exacerbated when he tried to impose a
puppet Dalai Lama[1] of his own choice. Rivalries between different

---

[1]Yeshe Gyatso.

Mongol tribes did nothing to help to stabilize the situation. It is in these difficult circumstances that Pholanay emerged as one of the main figure on the Tibetan scene.

The invasion of the Dzungar Mongols in 1717 saw the end of Lhazang Khan's reign over Tibet, in spite of the spirited defence of Lhasa organized by Pholanay.

The Dzungar commander, Tsering Dhondup, let his troops loose and they massacred, raped and looted Lhasa. Pholanay courageously tried to defend Lhazang Khan, who had taken refuge in the Potala, but he was overpowered by the Mongols. Soon after Pholanay was informed of the death of his master.

Lhagyal Rabten, a Dzungar chieftain, became the new leader of the administration and the old supporters of the Qoshot clan were threatened with death.

Pholanay was arrested and jailed along with many prominent ministers and leaders of the former regime, but through his many contacts with the aristocracy he was freed on the orders of the new regent Tagstepa.

His estate and money which had earlier been confiscated were returned to him, but he refused to join the government because he had not forgiven the Dzungars for killing Lhazang Khan. He decided to retire for some time to his estate.

From there, he worked very hard to organize popular support and recruit an army to overthrow the Dzungar invaders. The Dzungars somehow got wind of his plans, and tried to arrest him again.

In the meantime, it was rumoured that some Manchu troops were riding towards Lhasa. Pholanay figured that this was just the help he needed. However his friends advised him against meeting the Chinese troops. It was indeed a wise political decision, as soon afterwards they were routed by the Dzungar troops.

This did not prevent Pholanay from preparing another uprising against the Mongols and calling the Manchus to the rescue again.

With his ally Kancheney, the Governor of Ngari,[2] Pholanay was now in control of the southern and western provinces of Tibet. He was also in close touch with the Panchen Lama in Tashilhunpo.

A larger Manchu army was advancing towards Lhasa. Pholanay and Kancheney, accompanied by the Panchen Lama, cleverly managed to reach the Tibetan capital before the Manchus.

---

[2]The largest region of Western Tibet.

The Seventh Dalai Lama

At this point, we need to have a look at the life of Seventh Dalai Lama.

His predecessor, Tsangyang Gyatso, the Poet Dalai Lama, had prophesied in his famous poem:

Oh White Crane!
Lend me your wings
I shall not fly far
From Lithang, I shall return

As predicted, the Seventh Dalai Lama was discovered in Lithang in the Province of Kham. Due to the general confusion which prevailed at that time, some Mongol tribes of the Kokoonor region managed to take away the young Dalai Lama to North-Western Tibet where he was warmly received. Later, the Manchus decided to bring him back to the Tibetan capital and enthrone him.

When Pholanay and his troops reached Lhasa, the remaining Dzungar Mongols were driven out by the Manchu troops which were escorting the newly found Dalai Lama to Lhasa.

The great day in Lhasa occurred in October 1720, when the twelve-year-old.Kalsang Gyatso accompanied by the Manchu troops entered Lhasa. But soon after, a new vendetta started, this time against those who had supported the Dzungars.

One of them was Tagtsepa, who had acted as the regent under the Dzungars. Pholanay tried his best to protect this friend who had saved his life when he was in jail, but his appeal was rejected. The ex-Regent as well as some of his ministers were publicly beheaded in front of the people of Lhasa and the Dzungar soldiers were slain on the banks of the Kyichu.

Tsering Dhondup, the Dzungar leader who had been responsible for the 1717 massacre, was able to escape to Dzungaria, but most of his 6,000 troops were massacred by the Manchus and only 500 were said to have survived.

The Dalai Lama was back, but where had the Buddha's compassion gone?

The twelve-year old boy was enthroned as Kalsang Gyatso, the Seventh Dalai Lama (1708-1757). The Manchus installed a committee of seven ministers as the new government which included two Mongolians, two Manchus and three Tibetans.

The Mongol tribes who had accompanied the Dalai Lama to Lhasa withdrew back to the Kokoonor area, while the Manchus kept some troops as a 'peace-keeping' force in Lhasa to avert a return of the Dzungars.

After a year the Committee of Seven was dissolved and the power transferred to five Tibetans, among them Pholanay.

The harmony was not going to last long. During the absence of Pholanay while he visited his estate in Central Tibet, a dispute arose among the other ministers and as a result Sonam Gyalpo, one of the Ministers, was killed.

Though all the parties professed Buddhism as their religion, political murders became a regular affair during the following years. It was the beginning of one of the saddest chapters of Tibetan history and before long Lhasa was witnessing a prolonged civil war.

The intrigues and power struggles did not stop after the execution of the ex-Regent. A new player had joined the field: the father of the Dalai Lama. Many times he tried to manipulate some of the Kalons[3] on sectarian grounds; an ever fertile ground in Tibet.

The Kashag was divided, with some ministers in favour of the Nyingmapa sect fighting for survival against the followers of the Yellow sect, the Gelukpa[4]. Another divisive factor was regionalism. Pholanay and Kancheney were from Western Tibet, while the other Kalons were from Central Tibet. To complicate matters further, as the Kalons were also Governors of the provinces, they had often to be absent from the Tibetan capital. The Dalai Lama's father had a certain advantage as he was the only protagonist permanently residing in Lhasa.

Pholanay played an important and positive role in reducing the sectarian struggle and he even suggested that the Government should help the Nyingmapas to rebuild some of the 500 monasteries destroyed during the Dzungar rule. Though this was not accepted by the other ministers, nor by the Mongol princes who were strongly in favour of the Gelukpas, the Nyingmapas were nevertheless left on their own after Pholanay's intervention.

The death of the Emperor Kangxi was not a good omen for the Tibetans as he had exercised a relatively balanced influence on the political and religious affairs of Tibet. During his reign, not only

[3]Tibetan for Ministers.
[4]The Tibetan Buddhism recognized four main sects: the Nyingmapa, the Sakya-pa, the Kargyu-pa and the Gelukpa.

had he respectfully received the Fifth Dalai Lama in Beijing, but he had always shown great respect for the Choe-yon relationship.

The new Emperor Yongzheng had very little experience and one of his first actions was to pass a decree banning all the Nyingmapa monasteries in Tibet. This was pouring hot oil on a not-yet extinguished fire. The Emperor's decision had one positive consequence: the Kashag was united against it for the first time. In fact very few in Lhasa were happy about the interference of the Manchu Emperor in the religious affairs of Tibet.

Pholanay once more lived up to his reputation of being a fair leader and, even though he was himself a Gelukpa[5], he strongly opposed the imperial decree and was able to convey the Tibetan feelings to the Amban. As a result of his appeal, the decree was not implemented.

However, the situation was deteriorating: the Kashag and people of Lhasa could feel the tension mounting as the friction between the various characters — the Dalai Lama's father, Pholanay, Kancheney and the other Kalons — soured further.

In August 1727, Kancheney was murdered by the other ministers who had invited him to a meeting. The Dalai Lama's father was one of the conspirators. A long series of political murders was to follow, perpetrated mainly against the family members and supporters of Kancheney.

Pholanay was also targeted but he managed to escape and sent a message to the Manchu Emperor informing him of the latest events and requesting him to send a strong army.

In no time, Pholanay managed to unite Tsang and Ngari provinces and to raise a new army to fight the civil war. Even the lamas of Sakya gave their support to Pholanay and a non-co-operation movement was organized: taxes would not be paid to Lhasa until the evil ministers were removed.

Several times the Panchen Lama tried to intervene and stop the blood-bath, but to no avail. In April 1728, a truce was signed between the armies of Lhasa and Pholanay; but it did not last long and the civil war started again. It was only when the army of Pholanay reached Lhasa in July 1728 that it stopped.

The people of Lhasa were pleasantly surprised when Pholanay's troops behaved well and did not loot the city as the previous victors

[5]With a Nyingmapa education.

had always done. Pholanay managed to arrive before the Manchus. From that time on, he became known as Miwang[6] Pholanay.

At the Dalai Lama's request, Pholanay agreed to keep the ministers under house arrest until the arrival of the Manchus.

When the imperial troops arrived and a court of justice was formed, Pholanay asked for clemency for the ministers who had murdered his friend Kancheney. The Manchus decided otherwise. The guilty ministers, their families and some abbots who had supported them were shown Chinese justice: some were strangled, others decapitated, while the ministers themselves were 'sliced' in a death penalty known as 'the death of a thousand cuts'.

The young Dalai Lama and his father were 'invited' to Beijing. They could not refuse and it was a punishment for the father who would have to remain in 'exile' from the Tibetan capital for seven years.

Pholanay started reorganizing the government. One of his first priorities was to immediately trim the Chinese presence from 10,000 troops to 2,000 troops.

The Manchus, who had been called for the second time in ten years to restore back peace in Lhasa, used the opportunity to assert their 'rights' and nominated two Ambans as the Chinese government representatives. Their role was clear: the emperor should be kept informed of all political events in Lhasa and they should, by their presence, influence the policy of the Tibetan government. With a large number of 'peace keeping' troops in the Tibetan capital, the Manchus thought to keep a check on the administration of the Land of the Snows.

Using his diplomatic skills and his contacts with the rulers in Beijing, Pholanay first got permission to raise a Tibetan army and then negotiated the withdrawal of the Chinese troops with the Manchus. He finally succeeded in his plan after giving assurances to the Emperor that one hundred Manchu soldiers were enough to look after the security of the Ambans.

This did not stop the Ambans from continuing their divisive activities. Was it not the best way to keep the Tibetans dependent on them?

From the time he returned to Lhasa until his final years, Kalsang Gyatso, the Seventh Dalai Lama devoted more and more time to

---

[6]'Miwang' is a title meaning 'the leader of the people'.

spiritual matters; eventually he became one of the most scholarly Dalai Lamas.

To keep more time for his religious studies, he devised a new form of government headed by a Council of Ministers or Kashag.[7]

His second achievement was to have built a new Summer Palace a few kilometres outside Lhasa in the Jewel Park.[8] The Phodang (Palace) built by the Seventh Dalai Lama still exists.[9]

With the opening of the Norbulinka Palace, a new ritual began twice a year in Lhasa: every summer the Dalai Lama along with his retinue and all government officials rode in great pomp, from the Potala to the Summer Palace (and back to the Potala in autumn). It was an occasion for the people of Lhasa to have a Darshan of their otherwise reclusive leader. It was also a pretext for rejoicing, singing and endless drinking of chang, the light Tibetan beer.

Symbolically, it was as if the Dalai Lama came down from his Olympus to live at the same level as his subjects for a couple of months. The Great Boddhisattva thus showed his compassion and perhaps took a break from the dark and cold rooms of the Potala as well.

Pholanay the Reformer

Pholanay had the political intelligence to understand that it was time to undertake reforms.

He first helped to improve the religious studies in the monasteries; one of his achievements was a new edition of the Kanjur and Tanjur[10]. He ordered Narthang Monastery, the main printing press in Central Tibet, to engrave these newly edited texts on wooden blocks and print fresh copies.

His rule was one of the most peaceful and progressive of the eighteenth century.

The recovery of peace also brought new opportunities for communication and trade. A postal system was developed with the help of the Manchus; religious persecutions were stopped; law and order was re-established as Pholanay fell with a heavy hand on thieves and robbers. He relaxed the heavy taxation which had made the previous Kashag so unpopular with the people.

[7]Even today, in exile, a similar system of administration is functioning.
[8]'Norbulinka' in Tibetan.
[9]It has become a tourist attraction for foreign and Chinese visitors.
[10]The speeches of the Buddha and their commentaries.

In foreign affairs, Miwang Pholanay obtained the submission of the rulers of Bhutan and Ladakh who began to pay a regular tribute to Lhasa.

The Dalai Lama returned to Lhasa in 1735, but his father was asked to remain in residence some three days' ride from Lhasa.

Two years after the Dalai Lama's return, the Panchen Lama passed away; his reincarnation was smoothly discovered and enthroned.

All in all, the reign of Miwang Pholanay brought peace back to a Tibet devastated by rivalries between the different Mongol tribes, the Manchus and internal and sectarian disputes. At the same time the rule of Pholanay was based on the patronage of the Manchu emperors.

A strange character indeed, in a strange time of instability and change.

We have dealt at length with the times and rule of Pholanay because in many ways it epitomizes the weakness and the strength of the Tibetan system of governance as well as of the Tibetans themselves.

A Divided Society

The sectarian struggle would be a plague on Tibetan history and it is only when stronger leaders like the Fifth, the Thirteenth or the Fourteenth Dalai Lamas emerged on the political stage of Tibet that it would finally be contained.

The other points of fragility were the constant intrigues and the power struggle amongst the aristocracy, which would play a disastrous role again in the first half of the twentieth century.

The instability of the system of a 'harmonious blend between religion and politics' was demonstrated each time a Dalai Lama passed away and before the new recognized Dalai Lama was able to assume power. The twenty crucial years in between were often used by incompetent regents or by foreign powers interested in influencing the Tibetan politics.

Many murmured in Lhasa that the Chinese Ambans found the weakness in the system and several Dalai Lamas[11] died before they reached the age of twenty.

[11]From the Tenth to the Twelfth Dalai Lama:
Luntok Gyatso, Ninth Dalai Lama (1805-1815); Tsultrim Gyatso, Tenth Dalai Lama (1816-1837); Khedup Gyalsto, Eleventh Dalai Lama (1838-1855); Trinley Gyatso, Twelfth Dalai Lama (1856-75).

During the nineteenth century, Tibet had four Dalai Lamas in seventy years (between 1805-1875). Practically it meant that Tibet was without a ruler for twenty years, as the Thirteenth Dalai Lama assumed power only in 1895.

The First Gurkha War

Jampal Gyatso, the Eighth Dalai Lama (1758-1804) lived a relatively long life compared to his successors.

He was a religious person and was not really interested in politics; most of his life was devoted to spiritual search and he preferred to leave administrative matters to his Regents and Cabinet Ministers.

Sensing this weakness, the Gurkhas attacked Tibet in 1788. In Nepal, the Gurkha kings had just succeeded the Mala dynasty whose rulers were Buddhist. The pretext for the attack was a dispute over the currency exchange rate and the use of Nepalese coins in Tibet.

The southern districts of Tibet were invaded and later the Gurkha troops were withdrawn when the Tibetan local commanders promised to pay an annual tribute and signed an agreement confirming the validity of the former boundary. The Nepalese also promised to never invade Tibet again, but Tibet had to pay 300 lingots of silver each year (or 50,000 Rupees) to Nepal.

Tibet agreed to use the Nepalese coins minted by the Nepal Government, and to replace the previous Nepalese currency at the rate of one new coin for one and one-half old coins.

Another clause stipulated that trade between India and Tibet was to be channeled solely through Nepal, while the alternate trade routes to the east and the west were to be closed.

When the Dalai Lama[12] heard about the Treaty and especially the tribute, he opposed the payment of the next installment and thus war started again in 1792. The Nepalese eventually reached Shigatse and the Tashilhunpo Monastery was severely looted and damaged.

During the first attack in 1788, the Manchus had sent only a very small number of troops and refused to be a party in the dispute, but. in 1792, they were called upon by the Tibetans to intervene. Being on their own in 1788 was perhaps the reason why the Tibetans had had no choice but to sign the agreement with the Gurkha government.

[12]And the Amban.

During the second war, the Manchus sent a stronger contingent under a joint Sino-Tibetan command. They fought against the Gurkhas together and followed the invaders back to Kathmandu.

A Treaty was signed between the Gurkhas and the Tibetans in which the Chinese managed to show that both nations were their protectorates.

A message carved on a stone slab below the Potala by the Chinese Emperor wrote:

> Now that the Gurkhas have submitted to me, the Imperial army has been withdrawn, and the completion of this brilliant tenth achievement has been set out in the Letter [on the slab]. Though the fame of this matter was great, it has not been fully manifested. Therefore the proclamation has been inscribed on this monument, that the monument may serve as a memorial for the minds of men.[13]

Here follows a vivid description of the Chinese army expedition against the Gurkhas who were baptized as 'the thieves' by the Emperor.

> During the winter of last year additional soldiers of So-lon[14] and Szechuan came quickly, batch by batch, along the Sinning road, and arrived in the country of the thieves[15] during the fifth month of this year. Immediately on their arrival they retook the country of U and Tsang, and captured the territory of the thieves.[16]

It is to be noted that according to the Tibetans, the estimated strength of the Gurkha army was about 4,000, while the Sino-Tibetan force was about 9,000, of whom more than half were Tibetan soldiers. The text made it clear that the sole aim of the Chinese troops was to push back the invading Gurkhas and once this was achieved, their job was completed and they could return to China.

In his edict, the Emperor warned the Tibetans about the attitude of the British:

[13]Recorded on a stone slab below the Potala. Translation in Bell, Sir Charles, *Tibet Past and Present* (London: 1924), p. 275.

[14]Solon is a district of Gyarong in Kham Province, it shows that some Tibetan troops participated in the operations.

[15]i.e. the Gurkhas

[16]Bell, op. cit., p. 275.

.... Formerly, in the time of King Thang Tha-i Tsung, there was a conference with the Chi-li.[17] As it was shown that (the Gurkhas) were conquered and powerless, he (the Chi-li) said that they would always remain on good terms... It is not fitting to take the Chi-li as an example.[18]

The Emperor also wrote about the image that the Chinese had of the Tibetans: they were weak, according to the Emperor because they spend too much time on 'literature'.

It will be seen that the people of U, abandoning military pursuits, devote themselves solely to literature. Thus they have become like a body bereft of vigour. This is unfitting. If a people abandon military pursuits and make literature their chief object, they become unable to safeguard their former position. This should be known.

The Nepalese had to send a tribute to the Emperor every five years. It is clear that in the eyes of the Manchus, Nepal and Tibet had more or less the same status; the only difference being that the Tibetan status was based on a spiritual relationship between the Emperors and the Dalai Lamas.

In modern times and from a strategic point of view, one aspect of the Choe-yon relation between Tibet and China was what today would be called an 'umbrella' of protection. One comment should be made here: whether in the American intervention in the Gulf or the Chinese intervention in the Nepalese War, a price had to be paid to the protector. The 'protectors' always tend to see their own interests first. Is there ever a free ride?

The Troubled Times: the Nineteenth Century

During the period we have just examined, the working relation between the Tibetan government and the Manchus was very close. But the Manchus soon tried to exploit the weakness of Lhasa's Government and the Dalai Lama's lack of interest in political affairs.

[17]Chi-ling is the Tibetan name for 'foreigners', the Emperor here means the 'British'.

[18]The Emperor means that when the British come to the defence of a weaker nation, they later continue to occupy its territory, whereas the Chinese withdraw once the 'work is completed'. It is a very correct remark, and it is a fact that when the Choe-yon relationship was working with the Manchus, they played their role and withdrew. It is not the case when the same Chinese 'liberated' Tibet in 1950; in spite of Mao's promises, they never withdrew.

In 1793, a 29-Point document called 'Guide-Lines for Administration' was promulgated. Just a year after the Chinese had come to Tibet on the Dalai Lama's request to chase away the invading Gurkha troops, this edict was issued by Emperor Qianlong. It is often cited by the Communist historians as the best proof of the Manchus' control over Tibet.

While the Tibetans regarded the Ambans as ambassadors of the Chinese court in Lhasa, the Chinese saw them more as governors whose role was to administer a colony on behalf of the Emperor. In the 29-Point Regulation, the Ambans were given the same status as the Dalai Lama. This was clearly neither acceptable nor implemented by the Tibetans.

An interesting explanation of the role of the Amban is reported to have been given by Amban Yu Tai to Mortimer Durand, the Foreign Secretary of the Government of India in 1903: "He was only a guest in Lhasa not a master and he could not put aside the real masters, and as such he had no force to speak of."[19]

Rev Huc and Gabet, two Lazarist missionaries who visited Lhasa and wrote extensively about life in the Tibetan capital during the nineteenth century, said about the Ambans: "The Government of Tibet resembles that of the Pope and the position occupied by the Chinese Ambassadors was the same as that of the Austrian Ambassador at Rome."

In fact, most of the time the Chinese Court appointed someone of Manchu or Mongol origin who was likely to be more acceptable to the Tibetans. Sending a Buddhist was often helpful in smoothening out the working relation between the Commissioner and the Kashag.

Another point in the Emperor's letter which was highly objectionable to the Tibetans was that the choice of the reincarnations had to be confirmed by the Qing government: The Regulations says:

> The Qing government holds the power to confirm the reincarnation of all deceased high Living Buddhas of Tibet including the Dalai Lama and the Bainqen Erdeni. When the reincarnate boy has been found, his name will be written on a lot, which shall be put into a golden urn bestowed by the central government. The high commissioners will bring together appropriate high-

---

[19]Sir Percy Sykes, *Sir Mortimer Durand: A Biography* (London: 1926), p.166.

ranking Living Buddhas to determine the authenticity of the reincarnate boy by drawing lots from the golden urn.[20]

The Lhasa Government never implemented this point. When the Eighth Dalai Lama passed away in 1804, the Regent discovered two candidates, one from Kham and the other from Amdo.

After both candidates had appeared in front of the Regent and the Kashag and the necessary tests had been conducted, the candidate from Kham was finally chosen and enthroned as Lungtok Gyatso, the Ninth Dalai Lama.

The Tibetans thus discarded the use of the Golden Urn.

For them, the Regulations were only suggestions made by the Patron to the Priest for a 'Better Government of Tibet' and were advisory in principle. As a proof of this assertion, one can quote a statement made by the imperial envoy and commander of the Manchu army, General Fu K'ang-an, to the Eighth Dalai Lama:

> The Emperor issued detailed instructions to me, the Great General, to discuss all the points, one by one, in great length. This demonstrates the Emperor's concern that Tibetans come to no harm and that their welfare be ensured in perpetuity. There is no doubt that the Dalai Lama, acknowledging his gratitude to the Emperor, will accept these suggestions once all the points are discussed and agreed upon. However, if the Tibetans insist on clinging to their age-old habits, the Emperor will withdraw the Ambans and the garrison after the troops are pulled out. Moreover, if similar incidents occur in the future, the Emperor will have nothing to do with them. The Tibetans may, therefore, decide for themselves as to what is in their favour and what is not or what is heavy and what is light, and make a choice on their own.[21]

It has to be noted here that on all three occasions when Manchu troops marched into Tibet during the eighteenth century, it was at the request of the Tibetan Government or the Tibetan senior leaders

---

[20]This is the same practice that has recently been repeated by the Beijing authorities to justify their choice of the new Panchen Lama.

[21]Ya Han Chang's Biography of the Dalai Lama in *Bhod ki Lo rGyus Rags Rims gYu Yi Phrengba*, Vol. 2 (Lhasa: Tibet Institute of Social Science, 1991), p. 316.

— once to defend Tibet against the Gurkha invasion (1792), and twice to restore civil order after internal troubles (1728 and 1751). Each time, the Choe-yon relationship was invoked. But, as we saw earlier, the continuous fragility of the Tibetan state made it fully dependent on outside support and the bona fide intentions of its 'Protector'.

However the Tibetans were practical people, they did not accept or reject the Emperor's suggestion, they simply adopted some of the twenty-nine points which could be of some benefit for Tibet. The others were just ignored.

The Sixth Panchen Lama Choekyi Nyima told Capt O'Connor: "Where Chinese policy was in accordance with their own views, the Tibetans were ready to accept the Amban's advice; but ... if this advice ran counter in any respect to their national prejudices, the Chinese Emperor himself would be powerless to influence them."[22]

The slow decline of the Manchu dynasty and the absence of Dalai Lamas due to the early demise, rendered the relation less workable. If the protector was not able to protect its sovereignty against outside attacks, the protégé had to suffer or assert its independence or find another protector.

When the protégé himself was not able to fulfil his spiritual part of the deal, the relation was also bound to decline further and eventually disintegrate.

In the latter part of the nineteenth century and the early twentieth century, the Tibetans would manage on their own, in particular when Lhasa fought wars against Dogra invaders (1841-1842), the Gurkhas (1855-1856), and the Younghusband expedition (1903-1904).

The Dogra War

In 1834, a war erupted between the Dogra rulers of Jammu and the King of Ladakh. Maharaja Gulab Singh of Kashmir sent some troops to support the Dogras and in the process the King of Ladakh was deposed by Wazir Zorawar Singh and a Minister called Ngodup was enthroned as the new King and vassal of the Dogras; a yearly tribute had to be paid to Kashmir by the new ruler. But when the new King of Ladakh failed to pay the tribute, the Wazir of Kashmir returned after six years and re-enthroned the old King. Emboldened perhaps by his success in Ladakh, Zorawar thought he could extend his territories to Western Tibet. The pretext came when some disputes arose with the Tibetan traders in Leh.

---

[22]*Diary of Capt. O'Connor*, September 4, 1903.

Traditionally the Tibetans trader visiting Ladakh were provided with free accommodation and transport while staying in Ladakh. These facilities were no longer extended in 1841 and Zorawar Singh decided to enter Tibet and annex a part of Western Tibet.

The Tibetan Generals Dapon Shatra and Dapon Surkhang were sent from Lhasa and they were badly defeated by the troops of Zorawar Singh. Soon after, Tibetan Minister Kalon Pal-lhum was sent from Lhasa with large reinforcements. The fighting lasted for months and in the same way that Napoleon had been trapped by the Russian winter, the Indian troops were stopped by the winter on the Tibetan Plateau. The last battle occurred in Taklakkhar. It lasted for five days during heavy snow fall and the frozen army of Zorawar was decimated, more probably by the bitter climate than the strength of the Tibetan troops. Zorawar Singh himself was caught by a Tibetan soldier and decapitated. More than 3,000 Dogras troops perished in the battle and some 700 others were taken prisoner.

In the 1950s, Prime Minister Jawaharlal Nehru would use this incident as an argument in the Parliament to show that it was impossible for Indian troops to defend Tibet: "About 150 years ago an Indian army had invaded and subdued part of Tibet considered then and ever since as a remarkable military feat in that unfriendly terrain. But the end result was that in the following winter the Indian army froze to death."[23]

The Tibetan troops followed the remaining Ladhaki and Dogra troops fleeing to Ladakh where they stayed for one year, during which time Gulab Singh had ample time to send out reinforcements. As a result, two Tibetan Generals were taken prisoner and brought to Leh where negotiations could start.

Due to a temporary agreement, the Tibetan Generals were allowed to return to Lhasa and it was agreed that neither party would violate the other's territory in future.

The prisoners could decide whether to return to Ladakh or remain in Tibet.

It appears that one third of the Indian troops decided to remain in Tibet and to marry Tibetan girls. They are said to have introduced the cultivation of apricots, apples, grapes and peaches in the southern part of Tibet.

[23]SWJN, Series II, Vol. 15 (1). Interview to I.F. Stone of United Press, New Delhi, 1 November 1950.

In 1842, a final agreement was reached between the two parties and Letters of Agreement were exchanged. Two versions of this Letter exist, one in Tibetan and the other in Ladhaki.

The two main points of the Agreement were that the boundaries of Ladakh and Tibet were confirmed "as fixed since olden times" and that "the Laddakhis shall send the annual tribute to His Holiness the Dalai Lama and his Ministers unfailingly as heretofore and the Shri Maharajah Sahib will not interfere with this arrangement."[24]

It was further stated that: "No restriction shall be laid on the mutual export of commodities e.g., tea, piece goods, etc. and trading shall be allowed according to the old established custom."

Transport and accommodation were to be supplied by the Tibetans visiting Ladakh and vice-versa to the Ladakhis "who come to Tibet with the annual tribute."

The Second Gurkha War

In 1855, two years after the Trade Agreement had been signed between Kashmir and Tibet to "adhere to the same border demarcations that existed previously", the young Eleventh Dalai Lama was enthroned as the political leader of Tibet. Unfortunately, he passed away when he was just eighteen, after having been in power for eleven months only.

The Twelfth Dalai Lama would live only until his twelfth year.

The same year a second Gurkha war broke out. A powerful minister, Jung Bahadur Rana, on the pretext of some trade violation,[25] decided to invade Tibet and occupy the districts of Nyainam, Rongshar, Zongka and Purang.

The Lhasa government immediately sent troops from Central Tibet and Kham, but they were unable to recover the lost territories.

The monks of the three great monasteries around Lhasa volunteered to go on the battlefield, but before they could reach the Tibetan border, the Nepalese had called for negotiations.

A Ten-Point Agreement was signed in March 1856 between Nepal and Tibet. Strangely, the Treaty begins with both States paying homage to the Emperor of China, though the Manchus had not been involved in the dispute and did not even participate in the war.

---

[24]Richardson, op.cit., p. 262.
[25]Charles Bell said that it was because some Nepalese subjects were badly treated by the Tibetans.

> We further agree that both States pay respect as always
> before to the Emperor of China and that the two States
> are to treat each other like brothers, for so long as their
> actions correspond with the spirit of this Treaty.[26]

In the first clause the Tibetans agreed to pay a sum of ten thousand rupees every year to the Gurkha Government.

In the second clause after reiterating their respect to the Emperor of China, the Nepalese promised to provide "all the assistance that may be in its power to the Government of Tibet, if the troops of any other 'Raja' invade that country."

It was an interesting proposal for the Tibetans. Would it be possible to replace the weak Manchu protection by the Gurkha offer?

Unfortunately, when some fifty years later, Tibet was invaded by the Chinese troops of Zhao Erfeng, Nepal would not honour its obligation vis-à-vis Tibet and would not provide the necessary help to repel the Chinese warlord.[27]

In the subsequent clauses, it was agreed that the Tibetan Government would stop collecting taxes from Nepalese nationals; each party would exchange their prisoners of wars; Nepal would restore the territories of Kyirong, Nyainam, Zonka, Purang and Rongshar, occupied during the short war, and would be allowed to open a Mission in Lhasa. The other clauses dealt with the jurisdiction of both states over crimes and extradition of criminals.

As Shakabpa put it: "Thus Tibet regained its lost districts, but Nepal gained annual tribute and extraterritoriality in Tibet." In the long term, it was certainly not bad for Tibet to have another foreign mission in Lhasa.

The End of the Priest-Patron Relationship

To conclude, one can not deny that Tibet was weak and rather divided at the time of the Regulations for Better Governing of Tibet, and whether the Chinese Emperor intended to give an 'order' or an 'advice' makes little difference today. The only shocking fact is that it is quoted today by the Chinese authorities to justify their invasion and occupation of Tibet in 1950.

[26]For text of the Treaty, see P. Uprety, *Nepal-Tibet Relations: 1850-1930*, (Kathmandu: 1980), pp. 213-214.

[27]Though we were told by an informant that sometime in 1950 Nepal offered 500 troops to fight the invading PLA.

The British did the same thing when they forced the Chinese to sign a series of Treaties in the nineteenth century; the policy being that "when your adversary is weak, impose a Treaty (or some Regulations or a Convention) on him, so that even if he becomes strong again, the Treaty will remain."

Though these 'imperialist' treaties were vehemently denounced by the Communists after their take-over of China, they soon learned from their one-time master and continued to impose the same 'unequal' tactics upon a weak Tibet.

The Chinese term the Treaty by which Hong Kong became a part of Great Britain one century ago as 'imperialistic'. In what way is the Chinese position vis-à-vis Tibet different to this very approach than the one British had in Hong Kong?

It cannot be denied that the Manchus exercised some influence in Tibet during the troubled time of the eighteenth and nineteenth centuries, but during this period the Choe-yon relationship worked relatively well. By the mid-nineteenth century the Manchu emperor's role (and the related role of the Amban) had only become a 'constitutional fiction'.

7

The British Imperialist Wave

Contacts between Tibet and British India

> *The Tibetans had come into opposition with the British*
> *Government, and from an exaggerated idea of the*
> *importance of Tibet, and with no conception or*
> *understanding of our ways, they had run against a mighty*
> *power to their hurt and consequent suffering.*
> **Claude White, Political Officer in Sikkim**

In world history, the 31ˢᵗ December, 1600 will remain one of the most
important dates in the evolution of the British Empire. On that day,
two hundred eighteen Knights and merchants of the City of London
formed the East India Company.

Queen Elizabeth I gave her Royal Charter. The objectives were
to take control of the spice trade from the Dutch and to establish a
lasting outpost in the East Indies. The Company eventually
succeeded in establishing a vast colonial empire and securing British
military dominion in the East.

Originally the directors in London had defined straightforward
aims which were purely commercial in nature However, these
objectives soon clashed with the opportunistic vision of the officers
appointed by the Company.

The original aim of the Company was to peacefully and
profitably develop trade with the Asian continent. But to take Clive's
example, his astonishing military achievements had nothing to do
with the original purpose of the Company.[1]

Progressively, the Board of Directors had no choice but to give
up direct control over the officers in the field. So much so that in

---

[1] In fact they met with a chorus of disapproval from London.

1834, the Company, though nominally still a company with
shareholders, was no longer in any way a trading concern, but rather
the military arm of the British Empire and "the authorised ruler of
the vast Indian subcontinent and various other possessions".

Here is how Younghusband described the manner in which
British officers worked for nearly three centuries to expand their
empire:

> ...We who have dealt with Asiatics can appreciate so
> well [the following tactic] taking the opportunity,
> striking while the iron is hot, not letting the chance go
> by, knowing our mind, knowing what we want, and
> acting decisively when the exact occasion arises.[2]

Speaking of George Bogle who was the first British Agent at the
Court of the Panchen Lama to be appointed by Warren Hastings,
Younghusband wrote that Hastings gave his representative an
incredible freedom of action and all the necessary means to realize
his policy:

> I desire you will proceed to Lhasa . . ... The design of
> your mission is to open a mutual and equal
> communication of trade between the inhabitants of
> Bhutan [Tibet] and Bengal, and you will be guided by
> your own judgement in using such means of negotiation
> as may be most likely to effect this purpose.
>
> You will draw on me for your charges, and your drafts
> shall be regularly answered. To these I can fix no
> limitation, but empower you to act according to your
> discretion.[3]

In another passage, Younghusband gives us a description on
how the agents of the Company (or the Empire) were chosen; it helps
us to understand why, when Lord Curzon became the Viceroy, it
was not always easy for London to keep an eye on its local officers.

> These are, of course, ideal methods of conveying
> instructions to an agent, which it is not always possible
> for a high official to give. Lord Curzon would, I know,
> have liked to give similar instructions to me, and, as far
> as providing money, staff, military support, etc., he did.

---

[2]Younghusband, Sir Francis, *India and Tibet*, (London: John Murray, 1910),
p. 11.

[3]Younghusband, op. cit., p. 9.

...great results in many fields, and, what is more, great
men, have been produced by the use of Warren Hastings'
method of selecting the fittest agent, and then leaving
everything in his hands. I do not see that any better
results have been obtained by utilizing human agents
as mere telephones.[4]

This quotation from Younghusband demonstrates the ways and
means the British used to penetrate Tibet; like elsewhere in the
Empire, it was a well-calculated plan using all available means to
reach its objectives. The first, though not always the only, purpose
was trade.

It was Hastings who, as the Representative of the East India
Company at the end of the seventeenth century, first saw the
importance for British trade for securing some sort of friendship with
Tibet.

The Company had started trading side by side with Indian and
Arab merchants in Asia by shipping goods as diverse as cloth from
South India to Sumatra, coffee from Arabia to India. Profits were
used to buy more goods and sell them elsewhere in the Indian
subcontinent. The Company soon opened up trading posts in Madras
and Calcutta and later it was the first to penetrate China, taking tea,
silk, porcelains or cottons back to England on the return voyage.

The Empire was ever expanding.

Regarding Tibet and the Himalayan states, Hastings bided his
time until the right opportunity came to advance his pawn and 'strike
the iron'.

That moment came in 1772, when the Bhutanese attacked Kuch
Behar[5] and took its king prisoner. There was no hesitation in
Hastings' mind. He attacked the Bhutanese and defeated them. At
that point, the opportunity to enter into contact with Tibet emerged.
Younghusband described it thus:

Warren Hastings' policy was then, not to sit still within
his borders, supremely indifferent to what occurred on
the other side, and intent upon respecting not merely
the independence but also the isolation of his
neighbours. It was a forward policy, and combined in a
noteworthy manner alertness and deliberation, rapidity

[4]Younghusband, op. cit., p. 11.
[5]Cooch Behar, in the modern state of West Bengal.

and persistency, assertiveness and receptivity. He
sought to secure his borders by at once striking when
danger threatened, but also by taking infinite pains over
long periods of time to promote ordinary neighbourly
intercourse with those on the other side. Both qualities
are necessary.

It was because Warren Hastings possessed this capacity
for instantly seizing an opportunity, because he could
and would without hesitation or fear use severity where
severity alone would secure enduring harmony, but
would yet persistently and with infinite tact, sagacity,
and real good-heartedness work for humane and
neighbourly relationship with adjoining peoples, that
he must be considered the greatest of all the great
Governors-General of India.[6]

This is the opinion of Younghusband who, one hundred and
thirty years later, was sent by Lord Curzon to strike at the heart of
Tibet and break her splendid isolation from the rest of the world.

For Hastings, the opportunity to enter into contact with Tibet
came in the form of a letter from the Panchen Lama who was the
guru of the ruler of Bhutan. Though recognizing the wrong action
of the Bhutanese king, the Panchen Lama pleaded with Hastings for
clemency.

After the Bhutanese had appealed to him to intercede on their
behalf with the Governor of Bengal, the Panchen Lama wrote to
Hastings — the first letter from a Tibetan Lama to a British officer.

This correspondence between the Panchen Lama and Hastings
would seem to prove that when the Tibetans wanted to, they could
very well break their isolation and have normal contacts with their
neighbours. In fact, as we shall see, the Tashilhunpo was much less
isolated than Lhasa and had more contact with the outside world.
This proximity would be used by British officers in their 'forward
policy' till the middle of the twentieth century. The Chinese Amban
in Lhasa was certainly another factor which contributed to the
isolation of the Tibetan capital, and the presence of many Chinese
monks in the great monasteries around Lhasa tended to increase its
isolation from the South.

[6]Younghusband, op. cit., p. 7.

The British Governor-General had been waiting for an occasion to push his forward policy, and now it had come. Hastings laid the letter of the Panchen Lama before the Board of the Company in Calcutta and informed them that he was proposing a general treaty of amity and commerce between Bengal and Tibet.

After having obtained a passport for a European to proceed to Tibet for the negotiation of the treaty, he put his hopes on Bogle, an employee of the Company. According to Hastings, George Bogle was "well known for his intelligence, assiduity, and exactness in affairs, as well as for the coolness and moderation of temper, which he seems to possess in an eminent degree."

Warren Hastings added that he was "far from being sanguine in his hopes of success, but the present occasion appears too favourable for the attempt to be neglected."

A twenty-eight year old officer, Bogle left the same year for Shigatse to meet the Panchen Lama[7] and negotiate an alliance with Tibet.

Bogle's discussions with the Tashi Lama[8], revolved around a possible alliance between Tibet and British India, "so that the influence of the latter might be used to restrain the Gurkhas of Nepal from attacking Tibet."[9]

The Tashi Lama was quite sympathetic to the arguments of Bogle, but he had to refer the matter to the Regent and the Kashag in Lhasa. They opposed the idea as it would have upset the fragile balance with the Chinese. The Regent immediately said that he needed to get a clearance from Peking which, for obvious reasons, never came.

The entry of a new player in the game was not well received by the old players. The Nepalese were not keen to see an alliance between Tibet and India with their kingdom suddenly sandwiched in between two powerful neighbours. The Gurkha king took the matter to the Tashi Lama, assured him that Tibetans had nothing to fear from the Nepalese[10] and that he would keep a friendly attitude

---

[7]At that time the Panchen Lama was known as the Tashi Lama or Lama of the Tashi Lhunpo, he is usually referred to the Tibetans as the Panchen Rinpoche.

[8]The discussions were in Hindi. The Panchen Lama was quite fluent in the language.

[9]Younghusband, op. cit., p. 19.

[10]Fourteen years later, the Gurkhas would invade Tibet.

towards the Tashilhunpo. He also warned that if Bogle was thinking of war, the Nepalese were well prepared and like Lhasa, Kathmandu wanted to keep the British out of their territory.

The Nepalese King concluded his letter requesting the Tibetan lama "to have no connection with the *Firingies* (English) or Moguls and not to allow them into the country, but to follow the ancient custom (to keep the foreigners out)."[11]

Bogle had many friendly discussions with the Panchen Lama but he finally had to leave the country. He later learned that his appeal,[12] "in the name of the Governor (Hastings), my master, that you will allow merchants to trade with this country and Bengal", to allow the Lhasa government to receive him, had been rejected. However, before he left Shigatse, Bogle met with many traders from Kashmir and Tibet who told him how keen they were to start business with British India.

There is no doubt that it was the influence of the Manchus and their representatives in Lhasa which made Tibet a closed country; this situation was to continue until the middle of the twentieth century. The strong presence of Chinese monks in the monasteries helped to propagate the image of the "firingies" as anti-religious people while the Chinese were co-religionists of the Tibetans.

In this way, the priest-patron relationship made the Tibetans more and more isolated.

The British clearly identified three main obstacles to their Tibetan forward policy and an eventual alliance with the Land of the Dalai Lamas.

The first problem was the antagonism towards the Crown of the Himalayan countries such as Bhutan and Nepal, who felt culturally closer to Tibet[13] than to the British.

The second problem was the presence of the Manchu Emperors (through their Ambans) in Lhasa. We have earlier seen the extreme weakness of the Tibetan system and their total military dependence on the Chinese Patron. When the Patrons were well intentioned, the relations were rather smooth, but when the Emperor's intentions towards Tibet did not follow the spirit of the Choe-Yon relationship, the Tibetans found themselves in a position of definite inferiority, unable to build their own relations with their neighbours.

[11]Younghusband, op. cit., p. 22.
[12]Sent through the Tashi Lama.
[13]Even if it was to invade the latter from time to time.

The third obstacle Bogle identified was the growing influence and presence of Russia in the area. One hundred and thirty years later, the same argument (or pretext?) led Lord Curzon, the Viceroy, to send Colonel Younghusband to Tibet, to establish by military means the 'forward policy' envisioned by Hastings.

However, Governor-General Hastings was not a man to give up his ideas. He immediately planned to send Bogle again to Tibet in 1780, but the death of the Panchen Lama in 1781 and soon after Bogle's own, aborted the new mission.

The next occasion for the British to penetrate Tibet came in 1782 when Samuel Turner visited Shigatse. He described thus the relations between the Tibetans and the Chinese: "The influence of the Chinese overawes the Tibetans in all their proceedings, and produces a timidity and a caution in their conduct more suited to the character of subjects than allies." Younghusband added: "At the same time, they were very jealous of interference by the Chinese, and uneasy of their yoke, though it sat so lightly on them."[14]

This timidity in Tibet's foreign relations — caused by a wish not to hurt the Chinese was one of the factors which led to the invasion of Tibet in 1950.

Captain Turner again proposed an agreement to the Tibetans and although the Tashilhunpo was not against trading with the British, it was refused by the Regent in Lhasa under the Amban's influence. The 'timidity and caution" of the Tibetan leaders had again prevailed.

The problem, as we have seen, was the imbalance in the Priest-patron relationship, especially in the absence of an adult Dalai Lama.

The situation did not improve during the nineteenth century, which saw the birth of five Dalai Lamas; an average of one Dalai Lama every twenty years!

In spite of his promise to the late Panchen Lama,[15] the Raja of Nepal did not keep his words of friendship and in 1788 and again in 1792, he invaded Tibet. We have already seen that the Tibetans had no choice but to call upon the Manchus to help them. Ultimately this resulted in the Manchus claiming suzerainty over both Nepal and Tibet.

---

[14]Younghusband, op. cit., p. 29.
[15]Panchen Tenpai Wangchuk passed away seven years after Bogle's visit.

For a few years the forward policy of the British Empire remained at a standstill. It was only in 1810, that Lord Minto, the Viceroy, sent a new Mission to Tibet led by Manning, a reputed scholar.

The trip was successful in the sense that Manning was the first Britisher to reach Lhasa; he even had several audiences with the Dalai Lama.

A comic situation is narrated by Manning. During his first audience, the 'Grand Lama'[16] wishing to communicate a few sentences to Manning, spoke in Tibetan and through a Chinese interpreter his sentences were translated into 'Chinese Munshi' to another interpreter, who then translated them to Manning in Latin. A complicated affair!

Manning stayed in Lhasa for many months but was finally recalled by the Viceroy. However, he seems to have been so disgusted by the attitude of the British government which had not given him the support he felt it should have, that on his return to India in June 1812, he did not even make an official report about his journey. Manning was to be the last Englishman to enter Lhasa before the troops of Younghusband in 1904.

Again and again, the problem of British field officers being contradicted by London would occur: the Foreign Office did not want to upset the Chinese susceptibilities. It is true that at that time, London had plenty of other problems to deal with in particular, Napoleon in Europe. The extension of the trade with Tibet was indeed not a priority. Indirectly, the British were making their way to Central Asia by subduing the Chinese Empire. The Opium War and the different 'unequal' treaties imposed on China weakened and corrupted China so much that in the early twentieth century, at the time of the Younghusband expedition, the Chinese were not in a position to resist the British advance or to oppose any treaty between the Tibetans and the Viceroy's representatives.

Many other wars and battles kept the British busy during the next fifty years, but in times of peace, they would often have the opportunity to demonstrate their skill in the art of diplomacy.

What could not be done by force could certainly be obtained by less violent means.

However, we should remark here that if the interests of the Chinese and the British were sometimes the same, their means of achieving their goals were radically different.

[16]The Dalai Lama.

In the Chinese tradition, the Emperor of China was the Son of Heaven. His main objective was to keep the Mandate given to him by Heaven to rule the Middle Kingdom and his subjects. The means by which he kept his mandate were not the most important factor. The recent history of China shows that even for a modern emperor such as Mao Zedong, the loss of tens of millions of Chinese lives[17] was not as important as maintaining his mandate over the people.

On the other hand, the main objective of the British was to consolidate and enlarge their trade empire. Leading an empire on which 'the sun never sets', the British crown wanted only to become richer, open new markets, control more strategic positions and eventually bring the Pax Britannia to the world.[18] The British have nevertheless rarely been ready to use the means that the Chinese used. When force or war was not absolutely necessary, London always chose diplomacy. The objective of the Chinese Emperors was domination, while that of the British was trade, and we should remember that it is easier to trade with friends than with enemies.

British India and Nepal

Great Britain started tackling one by one the problems enunciated by Bogle and time was in their favour. They dealt first with Nepal.

In 1814, a British expedition with 34,000 soldiers set out to annex Nepal. But the Gurkhas have always been tough soldiers, and at first a 12,000-strong Gurkha force defeated the British troops. It was only after protracted battles in 1815 and 1816 that the British managed to gain the upper hand.

A Treaty was signed in March 1816 whereby the British could keep a Resident in Kathmandu; Kumaon and Garhwal were ceded to British India and Simla was acquired by the Government of India for their summer capital.

"The north-west frontier of the Company's possession was carried right up to the mountains. A pathway was opened up to the regions of Central Asia."[19]

Nepal was not annexed by the British, who preferred to develop friendly relations and use the support and capacities of the Gurkhas

---

[17]Particularly during the Great Leap Forward and the Cultural Revolution.

[18]As today with United States. "Pax America" is little more than friendly markets.

[19]Roberts, P.E, *History of British India under the Company and the Crown* (London: OUP, 1923).

for their own purposes. These would eventually be very useful —
during the Sepoy Mutiny, the Younghusband Expedition and the
two World Wars.

Ten years later the British made the next move and marched
into Assam. The Company's territory now had a border with Bhutan
and ultimately in 1865, the British attacked Bhutan, which afterwards
became a Protectorate.

Next on the Viceroy's map at Calcutta was the Kingdom of
Sikkim. The annexation of Sikkim or at least control over it by the
British, was of prime strategic importance: Chumbi valley
commanded the entrance to Tibet.

British India and Sikkim

For centuries the major trade route between India and Central Tibet
passed through Natu-la,[20] Yatung in Chumbi Valley and then onto
Gyantse in Tibet. From a military point of view also, the control of
Gangtok and Natu-la was most important. Three steps were usually
taken whenever the empire wanted to expand: first, overtures for
friendship [with Sikkim] while militarily preparing to annex it; then
the offer of a treaty which could be advantageous for the country or
at least for the ruler, encouraging him to remain under the British
wing;[21] and lastly organizing friends among the local chieftains and
officers to make sure that they would serve the interests of the Crown.
Using these principles, a Treaty between Great Britain and Sikkim
was concluded in April 1861.

All the pawns were in place. Nothing would stop the opening of
a trade route between India and Tibet, once the suzerainty of Sikkim
was grabbed from Lhasa by the British crown.

The 'acquisition' of Darjeeling was also a crucial stroke in their
strategy and many English officers could already see the potential
of Darjeeling as a turning point for trade and diplomatic manoeuvres
in the Himalayan region. Similar views were held about
Kalimpong.[22]

The tea industry of Assam, Kumaon and Darjeeling was happy
to find new outlets in Tibet and competed with the Chinese who
supplied brick tea from Sichuan. The English Chamber of Commerce

---

[20]The pass between Sikkim and Tibet.
[21]Today, we would say 'umbrella of protection'.
[22]It became the object of hot debate in the Indian Parliament in 1959.

was not the only one who wanted to penetrate Tibetan territory; many others were interested too. The "loudly expressed wish of various missionary bodies to bring the Gospel to the benighted inhabitants of the roof of the world" added more pressure on London.

The third point of the colonial strategy — to make friends with some selected local chieftains was perfectly executed. Ashley Eden, the Special Commissioner to Sikkim, wrote in a report: "I must place on record the great obligations under which I am to Cheeboo Lama, who supplied a large number of coolies and accompanied me throughout... Without his help, I should have had very great difficulty in dealing with the people of the country. He is universally respected by the Pazcha population and trusted by the Rajah.... He has travelled much in Tibet. He is most influential advisor to the present Raja, and it is mainly through his good councils that the Raja has agreed to throw the country open."[23]

That the Cheeboo Lama was a dubious character was not taken into consideration.

At that time the British had engaged China on the mainland. The Tibetans had no army and were fully dependent on Chinese military support. Calculated or not, it was the correct move by the British at the right time. They had taken one more step towards Tibet.

While the Tibetans were politically and militarily weak, the British managed to 'legally' secure Sikkim from Lhasa, though it was clear that the Tibetans had not surrendered their suzerainty over the small Himalayan kingdom.

There was an increasing uneasiness in Sikkim and Tibet over the British 'Forward Policy', but what could be done? Could Sikkim call Tibet to the rescue? Could Tibet call China? No.

The masters of the moment were the British and they were rather benevolent masters. The Sikkimese had to accept their fate in good spirit and as we have seen, there were already many in Sikkim who were ready to collaborate with the Crown.

In Tibet, it was different. The Government had never dealt with a Western power and the Tibetans knew very little about modern warfare and the latest technologies used by the British army. They knew even less about diplomacy.

---

[23]Dr Taraknath Das, *British Expansion in Tibet : Chapter 1* (The Modern Review, Feb. 1926), p. 143.

In 1886, an incident occurred between the British, now *de facto* if not *de lego* suzerains over Sikkim and the Tibetans.

It started by a (well founded) rumour that the Viceroy, Randolf Churchill was planning to send a commercial mission to Shigatse without the permission of Lhasa. This created a lot of resentment in Tibet and Lhasa decided to send some 200 soldiers to the Sikkimese border to block the way of the proposed mission.

Another incident had irritated the Tibetans. To Lhasa, it came as a warning that their vassal Sikkim was being lost to the British Empire.

The Dalai Lama had sent a mission, led by a Kalon[24], to Bhutan to mediate in an internal matter and after a successful conclusion, the Tibetan minister was returning to Lhasa through the Chumbi Valley. It was customary for the Choegyal[25] of Sikkim to come and meet a Tibetan Minister en route to Lhasa and pay his respects to the Tibetan government representative. The Choegyal who had some estates in the Valley, had always come himself in the past; however, this time he only sent his brother, Trinley Namgyal. This added to the unease of the Tibetans who thought that some external pressure was being brought to bear on the small Himalayan kingdom.

Around the same time yet another irritant emerged: the Tibetans heard in 1876 that the British had signed an Agreement with the Chinese in Chefoo. Though the Government in Lhasa had not been consulted or even informed, one of the clauses concerned Tibet. The British idea was to have the Treaty passed through the back door: as they had not been able to reach Tibet by the South, they would do it through the West. They secured the permission of the Chinese to send a mission to Tibet through the mainland.

Tempers ran so high in Lhasa that the Tsongdu[26], at an emergency meeting, decided to take an oath never to allow the British to enter Tibetan territory. The National Assembly's seal was put on the oath. It also declared that the Chinese Emperor had no power to give passports permitting foreigners to enter Tibetan territory.

[24]Kalon Rampa.

[25]Choegyal is the Tibetan title equivalent to Dharmaraja, the 'Lord of the Religion'. Until 1975, it was the official title of the ruler of Sikkim. The Choegyals have always been related to Tibetan aristocratic families and have owned lands and estates in Tibet.

[26]The National Assembly.

In the meantime, the Kashag was informed that the British were planning to build a guest-house on the border between Sikkim and Tibet, near Jelap-la.

Lhasa resolved to send two Representatives to find out where the border was and to set a check-post to guard it. The border had never been properly demarcated.

Finally, in 1887, a fortified post was built by the Tibetans in Lungthur which according to them, was inside their territory. Unfortunately the British did not agree with the demarcations and demanded their immediate removal.

An ultimatum was sent to the Tibetan commanders to vacate their fortifications before March 15, 1888. At the same time the British sent a formal protest[27] which was forwarded to the Manchus and the Dalai Lama by the Choegyal, Thuthop Namgyal.

Poor Choegyal, it was only the beginning of his problems. Later, he would be put under house arrest and then deposed. He tried to escape to Tibet, but was arrested and jailed. He remained a couple of years in jail and Sir Tashi Namgyal, his son, was born in jail like the Indian God, Krishna; he was destined to become one of the best Choegyals of Sikkim. Thuthop Namgyal was eventually reinstalled as a puppet Maharajah, under an all-powerful Political Officer of the British Government.

Shakabpa wrote about him: "...throughout his life Thuthop Namgyal had avoided intrigues and did his best to deal straightforwardly with both the Tibetan and the British governments. But his opponents had plunged him into difficulties with the British authorities. He was a brave man with strong principles."[28]

Another complication was the situation of the Manchus. Though not in a position to intervene, they told the British that "no marked separation existed formerly between Tibet and Sikkim" and that the Tibetans regarded the kingdom of Sikkim as an extension of their own country. It is probably based on such a principle that, even today, the Chinese have not accepted that Sikkim is a part of the Union of India.

The Kashag replied to the Choegyal that there was no harm in Tibet defending its own borders. But when the British were

---

[27]Against the fortifications which were according to them, on their territory.

[28]Shakabpa, op. cit., p. 202.

determined to advance a pawn, who could stand in front of their military might? This time they were not in a mood to discuss or even negotiate the exact position of the border.

With the pressure mounting, the British positioned more than 2,000 troops of the Sikkim Field Force.[29] The Tibetans sent 900 troops as reinforcement under two generals, Dapon Ngabo and Dapon Surkhang and a Minister, Kalon Lhalu.

Till the last minute the Choegyal tried to mediate, but each party was determined to show the other that they were within their rights. Unfortunately for the Tibetans, their troops were no match for the British, neither in training, equipment nor discipline. The clash which took place at Lungthur was short and the Tibetans were trounced. Those who were not killed on the spot ran away, pursued by the British upto Yatung.

The British version of the dispute is quite different from the Tibetan one and is worth quoting:

> It was in the autumn of 1886 that a party of Tibetans crossed the Jelap La and dug themselves in — walled themselves in.. By so doing they violated the sanctity of Sikkim and challenged our authority as the suzerain power. We referred the matter to the Chinese, and waited patiently for a year for redress, which never came. Then we took action.
>
> This was towards the close of the year 1887. We were precise — almost meticulous — in our language. We said that the evacuation must be effected by the fifteenth day of the following March.
>
> Twice more during the year 1888, in May and in September, did the Tibetans return and twice more they were driven back over the Jelap La.
>
> And then an unexpected thing happened - the stock of British patience was exhausted....[30]

"Forbearance could scarcely go further than this," wrote Younghusband, but "yet it was to be still more strained on many a subsequent occasion."

[29]Formed from the Mountain Artillery, Derbyshire Infantry, the Pioneers, Bengal Infantry, a Gurkha Regiment and the Bengal Sapers and Miners.
[30]Lord Ronaldshay, *Lands of the Thunderbolt* (London: Constable), pp. 113-114.

"Out of forbearance", the British took two years to throw the Tibetans out of what the latter believed was their own territory and the British were so "kind" with the Tibetan "raiders" that they remained only one day in the Chumbi valley in pursuit of the fleeing survivors. Imperial clemency!

But the occasion was not missed, and London used these two years to plan its strategy. The end result of this rather small dispute was a new treaty between the British and the Manchu government regarding Sikkim and Tibet. This would have very serious repercussions on the political relations among India, China and Tibet during the following twenty years.

In the meantime, the British used this pretext to depose Thuthop Namgyal and to enter Gangtok with their army. Sikkimese opponents to the Choegyal were installed as the new puppets in charge of the administration under a British Officer, who henceforth was known as the 'Political Officer'.

The Choegyal kept his dignity and throughout his captivity, refused to address Claude White, the first Political Officer; he even refused to open his mouth if the British officer was in the same room.

The Tibetan and the Sikkimese had understood 'British ways': they knew that it was better to collaborate with a 'mighty power' than to oppose it.

The table was cleared for the next stage, the opening up of Tibet to British trade. The last step the British made was a clever and well-timed move.

They knew perfectly well that Sikkim was at that time a protectorate of Tibet, but they were also aware that Tibet was in too weak a position to defend its rights in Sikkim. At the same time, the Chinese pretended to be overlords of Tibet.

The game was to ask the Chinese to restrain the Tibetans.

It was without doubt the best way to avoid hurting the Chinese feelings while dealing with them and recognizing their overlordship over Tibet. It was also the best way to avoid sending the Manchus into the arms of the Russians. Rumours were rife in Beijing that the Russians were expecting an alliance with China.

The doors were left open for British diplomacy to strike.

This came in the form of a Treaty, signed in 1890 between Great Britain and China, behind the backs of the Tibetans and the Sikkimese.

The "Convention between Great Britain and China relating to Sikkim and Tibet" was signed on March 17, 1890.

The Preamble makes clear that the British and the Chinese "are sincerely desirous to maintain and perpetuate the relations of friendship and good understanding", but it is "desirable to clearly define and permanently settle the boundary between Sikkim and Tibet."

The boundary of Sikkim and Tibet was defined as follows: "the crest of the mountain range separating the waters flowing into the Sikkim Teesta and its affluent, from the waters flowing into the Tibetan Mochu and northwards into other rivers of Tibet." The same principle would be followed twenty-five years later to demarcate the McMahon Line.

The next Article was the most important one for London. China admitted through the Treaty that "the British Government, whose Protectorate over the Sikkim State is hereby recognised, has direct and exclusive control over the internal administration and foreign relations of that State, and except through and with the permission of the British Government neither the Ruler of the State nor any of its officers shall have official relations of any kind, formal or informal, with any other country".

The formal take-over of Sikkim was complete, thanks to a few Tibetans who had crossed over a border pass they believed to be their own.

In Article 3, each party agreed to respect the newly demarcated boundary: "The Government of Great Britain and Ireland and the Government of China engage reciprocally to respect the boundary as defined in Article I, and to prevent acts of aggression from their respective sides of the frontier."

Most of the pending issues were postponed. Questions such as the provision increased facilities for trade in Tibet, pasturage on the Sikkim side of the frontier, or the method by which official communications between the British authorities in India and the authorities in Tibet should be conducted, were held in abeyance. It was decided that within six months negotiations would begin to settle these minor problems. It is to be noted that no Tibetan or Sikkimese representatives were present, took part in or were even informed about the negotiations.

Such were the ways of the mighty colonial powers!

8

From the Russian Threat to the Younghusband Expedition

We regard the so-called suzerainty of China over Tibet as a constitutional fiction.

Lord Curzon, 1903

The element which was to play a major role in the Britain's foreign policy toward Tibet and thereby decide the fate of Tibet as a nation, is what has been called the 'Russian threat'.

One of the origins of this myth — or reality — was an information passed by a Japanese monk called Ekai Kawaguchi to Sarat Chandra Das, the most famous of the Indian Pundits[1], who was spying for the British government.

Pretending like the Pundits to be a Ladhaki, Kawaguchi travelled to Tibet and enrolled himself in the monastery of Sera. He reported that a caravan of 200 camels had arrived in Lhasa from the Northeast. The camels were said to be carrying boxes covered with skins and the drivers refused to answer any questions about their contents. Kawaguchi was told by a Tibetan official that the boxes were a gift of rifles and ammunition from Russia. Even more confusion was brought into the story by the Japanese monk who swore that he had seen 'Made in USA' written on one of the boxes. Later, most of the sources such as Waddell, quoted Kawaguchi as their main source of information in an effort to prove that the Tsarist regime was supplying Lhasa with arms.

We shall have a closer look to see if there is some 'reality' in this myth.

[1]The Indian Pundits were sent by the Government of British India to survey unknown Himalayan areas including Tibet and to gather intelligence reports. Most of the time the British chose natives from the border regions and gave them training near Dehra Dun.

Historians have often compared the moves of the Great Powers in Asia to a chess game, but a truer comparison might be a poker game, as most of the players were adventurers.

Ultimately, it was Lord Curzon and his associate Colonel Younghusband who emerged as the best players, although soon after an initial win,[2] they lost their stake again.[3]

The only perennial losers in all the deals were the Tibetans.

The main moral of the story is that only the rich can play this rich man's game.

One individual played a major role in this game: Agvan Dorjiev. This enigmatic person helped fuel the speculations about a presumed alliance between Russia and Tibet.

Recently, some Russian Foreign Policy Archives have been opened to researchers and we will quote from some notes which have come to light[4] on the presumed role of Dorjiev.

Born in 1854 in the Buryata[5] region of Russia, Dorjiev soon became known as a Buddhist scholar and diplomat. Having shown great capacity in his Buddhist studies, the high lamas of Buryata recommended that he be sent to Mongolia and Tibet to continue his studies. This was a common practice at that time and Kawaguchi said that there were more than 200 monks from Buryata in the Great Monasteries around Lhasa. Travelling on foot, Dorjiev went first to Urga[6] and, at the age of 26, he reached Lhasa where he became very renowned for his extraordinary scholarship and debating skills. He was even noticed by the Thirteenth Dalai Lama who appointed him as one of his debating partners. Thus begun the connection between Tibet and Russia:

Was the link which Dorjiev established with the Tsar a real threat to the British Empire or an imaginary one?

We shall abandon Dorjiev for a moment to try to understand the move initiated by the Buryat monk. We should first realize that the Tibetans had been deeply disturbed by the Convention on Sikkim

---

[2]The entry of the British troops in Lhasa.

[3]They were rebuked by London for signing the Lhasa Convention.

[4]See Nikolai S. Kuleshov, *Russia's Tibet File* (Dharamsala: Library of Tibetan Works and Archives, 1996).

[5]Even today, Buryata is a Republic of the Russian Federation. Most of the population is Buddhist and owe allegiance to the Dalai Lama who has visited the Republic several times.

[6]Today's Ulan Bator in Outer Mongolia.

and Tibet signed in 1890 by the Chinese and the British, for whom it was a breach of the Patron-Priest relationship.

The Tibetans were now aware that the Chinese no longer had the power — especially in the face of Western powers like England, France or Russia — to fulfil their role of protector.

While the chinese wished to reap the advantages of the old relationship at a time of crisis, for example, during the incident on the Sikkimese border, they were not ready or able to defend Tibetan interests.

The Treaty of 1890 along with the fact that the British (and the Chinese) had decided not to inform the Tibetans about its contents, which was of direct concern to them only, was the last straw: for the Tibetans, there was no alternative but to show both parties that their terms were unacceptable.

A note from Dorjiev explained Lhasa's point of view:

The necessity of seeking the patronage of a foreign country was secretly debated at the highest level in Tibet from the moment when the Chinese officials bribed by Englishmen deprived Tibet of the land. I was present at one such meeting and expressed the opinion that Russia should be given preference.[7]

From the Tibetan side, one point was clear; they had lost their protector.

The events which followed should be seen more in terms of the Tibetans seeking to find a new protector than perhaps the Russians trying to expand their empire.

Another factor, which played a role in this complex game was the visit of Prince Henri d'Orleans to Tibet in 1888; he declared that France was ready to have diplomatic relations with Tibet. He even promised the Tibetan Government: "We, the French can save Tibet from the British threat. France and Russia have concluded an alliance and, are now the strongest power in the world."[8]

This corresponded to the time when Lhasa, by force of external pressures, started to become interested in events outside its secluded Shangri-La.

Suddenly many in the Tibetan capital were keen to hear more about these Great Powers who had as much power as the mantras of the lamas.

[7]Kuleshov, op.cit., p. 2, quoting from Russian Foreign Policy Archives.
[8]Kuleshov, op. cit., p. 3.

In this context, it was decided to send a mission to Russia. For the Tibetans, it was a preliminary mission to check the possibility of a shift in their foreign policy.[9] At the same time it was clear that Dorjiev had no power of decision making.

Dorjiev's first journey to Russia

The delegates travelled to St. Petersburg via India, China, Mongolia and Buryata. On reaching St. Petersburg in 1899, Dorjiev had some meetings with important personages at the Tsar's court such as Count Lamsdorff, Count Witte and General Kuropatkin. The general feeling in the Russian Ministry of Foreign Affairs was that Tibet was not a priority. Some Russian officials like Count Lamsdorff suggested that Russia could open a Consulate in Tibet, but the Tibetans themselves were more than reluctant. First of all, the delegation had no power to take such a decision without consulting the Dalai Lama and also Dorjiev knew that the opening of a Mission in Lhasa would have marked the end of the Tibet's closed-door policy. If one country was allowed to have a representation in Lhasa, many other countries would immediately put pressure on the Tibetan government to have the same privilege. "Having allowed the Russians to enter the country, Tibet would have not been able to withstand the influx of other Europeans,"[10] wrote Dorjiev.

In a long letter to the Dalai Lama, he described the people of Russia, the critical position of China and the great future of the 'Russian connection'.

Retrospectively, it is perhaps what would have helped Tibet in the long run; but at that point in time, the Tibetan government was certainly not ready for it.

In fact, it appears that Dorjiev's dream was to have a relationship between Russia and Tibet, which was similar to the one the early Manchus had with the Lamas of Tibet, a sort of Choe-Yon relationship,[11] which would exclude other big powers, particularly the British.

The British crown and specifically the new Viceroy Lord Curzon were not ready to accept this new entrant in Central Asian politics.

---

[9]'Foreign Policy' is a great word, because nothing such as a declared 'foreign policy' existed.

[10]Kuleshov, op. cit., p. 4.

[11]One of the bases of this Choe-yon relationship would have been the patronage given by the Tsar to the Buddhist population of Buryata and Kalmyk.

Percival Landon, the journalist who accompanied Colonel Younghusband to Lhasa in 1904, described the situation:

I do not wish to suggest that Russia in attempting to gain influence in Lhasa, was guilty of anything which reflects the least discredit upon her statesmen. On the other hand, it was farsighted and, from many points of view, an entirely laudable attempt to consolidate the Central Asian Empire which she believes to be her rightful heritage. The only reason the British found it necessary to intervene was that equally justifiable policy which they had themselves deliberately adopted, and their own vastly greater interests in Tibet clashed along the line with those of the Moscovites."[12]

Some rumours that the Chinese were going to sign a Treaty with Russia surrendering their suzerainty of Tibet to Russia, circulated in Lhasa but were immediately denied by the Chinese Foreign Office. What had perhaps lent some credence to the rumours was the continued Russian occupation of Manchuria as well as the refusal of the Tibetans to deal directly with the British.

Percival Landon reported that "Precisely what took place in Russia has not been made public...all that is known is that when he returned to Tibet, (Dorjiev) found himself in the official position of Russian agent in Lhasa."

The British perceptions as expressed by Landon do not seem totally justified because the mission of Dorjiev had nothing secret in it; in fact it was widely reported in the Russian press.

It is true that some reports about the Tibetan delegates' visit were quite extravagant and perhaps helped to fuel rumours; but many papers like the *Novoye Vremya*, wrote a more strategic analysis of the implication of a possible alliance between Russia and Tibet. The Foreign Affairs Ministry's official stand was that it was a religious mission.

The *Journal de Saint Petersbourg* reported the audience with the Tsar in these terms: "On Saturday, the 30th September, His Majesty the Emperor received Aharamba-Agvan Dorjiev who is the first tsanit-hamba[13] to the Dalai Lama of Tibet, in the Palace of Livadia."

And again after the second audience: "On Saturday, June 23, His Majesty the Emperor received Hambo Akhvan Dorjiev and

[12]Percival Landon, *The Opening of Tibet* (London: 1905).
[13]Tsentsab or debating partner.

Kaitthhock Hambo Donir, the Special Envoy [Envoyé Extraordinaire] of the Dalai Lama, at the Grand Palace of Peterhof. After the reception of the envoys they had the honour of being presented to His Majesty the Emperor's Secretary of the Mission, Djantsan Zombon Taitong Puntack, Chief of the Tibet Department.

Sir G. Scott, the British Ambassador to Russia at St. Petersburg inquired about the character of the Tibetan Mission from Count Lamsdorff. He was reassured that though the Tibetan visitors had been described as Envoys Extraordinary of the Dalai Lama, their mission could not be regarded as having *"any political or diplomatic character"*.[14]

Nevertheless, London cabled back to its envoy that "His Majesty's Government could not regard with indifference any proceedings that might have a tendency to alter or disturb the existing status of Tibet."

Soon after the audience Dorjiev left for Tibet, reaching Lhasa in February 1901 via a strange (but at that time usual) route: Peking, Calcutta, Darjeeling, Chumbi Valley, Gyantse and Lhasa.

The return of Dorjiev caused a lot of debate in Lhasa. The Dalai Lama had forwarded the letters of Dorjiev to the Kashag.

Percival Landon explained the prevalent opinion in Lhasa:

> Briefly stated, his arguments were these: you have no strength in the country to resist the invaders, your natural protector and suzerain China, is a broken reed; even at this moment she is entirely under the domination of the British. If you remain any longer trusting to her support, you will find that she throws you as a sop to the Indian government. The English are a rapacious nation and heretical nation; they will not respect your religion....
>
> On the other hand, if you will ask aid of Russia, you will secure the most powerful protector of the world.[15]

Nevertheless some Tibetan ministers thought that France was a good bet as they had been the first to offer their help. Some even thought of the British as an ally.

Dorjiev wrote: "Others consider that it would be wiser to make friends with the English because such neighbours could make a great

[14]British Parliamentary Papers, op. cit., p. 111.
[15]Landon, op. cit., p. 22.

deal of trouble if they became enemies. However, the majority held the view that it would be better to address Russia where Buddhism prospered freely."[16]

The second visit of Dorjiev to Russia

In Lhasa, it was finally decided to send Dorjiev back to Russia with a high-ranking delegation. In March 1901, one month after his return to the Tibetan capital, he left with a delegation for Russia again; this time he travelled by sea to Vladivostok and sailed up the river Amur.

On their way, they saw a Chinese town Aigun where the entire population had been savagely killed and the town itself destroyed. They must have reached the conclusion that a similar fate could befall Tibet if a new protector could not be found.

On their arrival at St. Petersburg, they informed the Tsar that the Russian 'line' had prevailed in Lhasa and they would like to seek his protection.

Though Dorjiev was received with honour, the Russian government was not so comfortable with his visit.

The letter from the Dalai Lama was presented to the Tsar who sent it for translation to the University of St. Petersburg. When it came back the answer was non-committal:

> It was a pleasure to learn of your wish to establish permanent relations between Russia and Tibet, and I have given all possible explanations on this subject to your ambassador.[17]

The Russian Foreign Ministry was as evasive:

> I did not fail to explain in detail, with the assistance of your ambassadors, the means of establishing communications with Tibet, and I hope that the measures taken and the results achieved will fully correspond to your wishes. I do not doubt that, according to your wise and careful wishes, no harm will come to Tibet given Russia's benevolent attitude toward it.[18]

The visit of Dorjiev's delegation nevertheless got a lot of coverage in the local as well as the British press. While the British papers saw the visit as a danger to the interest of the Crown, Russian journalists were more interested by the exotic side of the delegation.

[16]Kuleshov, op. cit., p. 9.
[17]Kuleshov, op. cit., p. 7.
[18]Ibid.

In a colourful article, the Odissi Listok reported that there was a rumour that the Tibetans were a strange people who drank only water. As a result, one of the Tibetan delegates is supposed to have declared, "we were never invited to taste them [vodka and caviar] first because of the language difficulty and then because someone floated an absurd rumour that Tibetans do not drink anything but water."

The Tibetan delegation concluded that it must be the "dirty tricks of the Englishmen"

A note of the Marquis of Landsdowne to Sir G. Scott dated 18 February 1903, explains the reluctance of the Russian government to get entangled in Tibetan affairs. The British Foreign Minister notes:

> During my conversation with the Russian Ambassador today I have referred to the question of Tibet, which we had discussed on the 11th instant. The interest of India in Tibet was I said of a very special character. With the map of Central Asia before me, I pointed out to His Excellency that Lhasa was within a comparatively short distance of the northern frontier of India. It was, on the other hand, considerably over 1,000 miles distant from the Asiatic possessions of Russia, and any sudden display of Russian interest or activity in the regions immediately adjoining the possessions of Great Britain would scarcely fail to have a disturbing effect upon the population or to create the impression that British influence was receeding and that of Russia making rapid advances into regions which had hitherto been regarded as altogether outside of her sphere of influence."[19]

Commercial Agreement between Russia and China

In the meantime the rumours of an agreement between Russia and China on Tibet continued to circulate. Tension was mounting when Claude White, the Political Officer in Sikkim, proceeded towards the Tibetan border.

As a result of the forward policy of the British, an agreement was presumably signed between the Russians and the Chinese in 1902.

[19]Dr Taraknath Das, British Expansion in Tibet (The Modern Review: April 1926) p. 439.

This treaty, known as the "Commercial Agreement between Russia and China" has not been acknowledged by many historians, but it certainly was one of the direct justifications for the events of 1903-04. The main articles run as follows:

Article 1: Tibet being a country situated between Central Asia and Western Siberia, Russia and China are mutually obliged to care for the maintenance of peace in that country. In case trouble should arise in Tibet, China, in order to preserve this district and Russia in order to protect her frontiers, shall despatch thither military forces on mutual notification.

Article 2: In case of a third power's contriving directly or indirectly, troubles in Tibet, Russia and China oblige themselves to concur in taking such measures as may seem advisable for repressing such troubles.

The British were directly targeted in the above Article, and while Article 3 dealt only with religious worship, Article 4 elaborated the future strategic vision for Tibet,

Article 4: Tibet shall be made gradually a country with an independent inner administration. In order to accomplish this task, Russia and China are to be sharers of work. Russia takes upon herself the reorganization of the Tibetan military forces on the European model and obliges herself to carry into effect this reform in good spirit and without incurring blame from the native population. China for her part is to take care of the development of the economic situation in Tibet, and her progress abroad.[20]

Article 4 was obviously the cornerstone of the treaty. The Russians knew fairly well that the Chinese were not in a position to develop Tibet and implant new industries, their reasoning was therefore that the Chinese would have to call the Russians who would find their way into Tibet.

The Imperial Solution

Lord Curzon was in favour of a more radical solution.

The Younghusband expedition was seen by Lord Curzon and the Government of India as the best way to call the Russian bluff. If

[20]Prof. Edwin Maxey, *Tibet, Russia and England on the International Chess Board*, (Boston: The Arena, 1904) p. 28-31.

Russia failed to abide by the Agreement, her prestige would be destroyed in the eyes of the Tibetans and they would have no alternative but to request Britain's help and friendship.

We shall quote some parts of a lengthy report of the Viceroy to the Secretary of State for India. This dispatch dated January 8, 1903 detailed the future British policy for Tibet. First, doubting the usefulness of negotiations, Lord Curzon wrote:

> It does not appear that there is much reason for anticipating a more favourable solution of the Tibetan problem than has attended our previous efforts, unless indeed, we are prepared to assume a minatory tone and to threaten Tibet with further advance if the political and commercial relations between us are allowed any longer to be reduced to a nullity by her policy of obstinate inaction.
>
> The second combination of circumstances that has materially affected the situation is the rumoured conclusion of a secret agreement by which the Russian Government has acquired certain powers of interference in Tibet.[21]

Then Curzon made it clear that the 'addiction' of Lhasa to its policy of isolation was only temporarily 'tolerated' by British India. In those days,[22] the British Empire was one of the Great Powers and smaller nations were only tolerated to exist 'at the will' of these Powers.

> ...The policy of exclusiveness to which the Tibetan Government has during the last century become increasingly addicted has only been tolerated by us, because anomalous and unfriendly as it has been, it carried with it no element of political or military danger.
>
> Curzon was not against having a tripartite conference but it had to be on British terms: it should be held in Lhasa and the Tibetan government should participate as an equal.[23]

Then follow the most famous statement of the Viceroy:

[21]Text of Lord Curzon's letter in Taraknath Das, op. cit p. 438; also in *British Parliamentary Papers on Tibet (1855-1914)*, p. 187.

[22]Is it different now?

[23]The idea will be used again by Sir Henry McMahon in 1913 for the Simla Convention.

In our view, the attempt to come to terms with Tibet through the agency of China has invariably proved, a failure in the past, because of the intervention of this third party between Tibet and ourselves. *We regard the so-called suzerainty of China over Tibet as a constitutional fiction, a political affectation which has been maintained because of its convenience to both parties.*[24]

The only solution was then to open a dialogue, but how to open a dialogue with the recalcitrant Tibetans?

To bring his point home, the Viceroy first made a clear declaration of the interests of an imperial power:

In our view, any country or Government, or Empire has a right to protect its own interests and if those interests are seriously imperiled, as we hold ours to be in Tibet, we hold that the first law of national existence, which is self-preservation, compels us to take such steps as will avert these dangers and place our security upon an assured and impregnable footing.

To conclude, he suggested to London that a 'trade' mission be sent to Tibet under military escort to negotiate a trade agreement.

For Curzon it had become evident that the only way to establish 'amicable relations and communication', was to use force, if necessary. It was the continuation of the Forward Policy of Hastings.

In view of the contingency of opposition, we think that the mission, if decided upon, should be accompanied by an armed escort sufficient to overawe any opposition and resistance to be encountered on the way, to ensure its safety while in Lhasa. The military strength of the Tibetans is beneath contempt, and serious resistance is not to be contemplated.

The report ended with a cautionary note:"... we entertain a sincere alarm that if nothing is done and matters are allowed to slide, we may before long have occasion gravely to regret that action was not taken while it was still relatively free from difficulty."

The iron was hot, it was time to strike.

The above dispatch became the cornerstone of British policy towards Tibet.

[24]Emphasis added by author.

The answer from the Secretary of State for India came on February 27, 1903. Although it was decided to follow a forward policy toward Tibet, London was still very cautious about the plans of Lord Curzon:

> Your Excellency's proposal to send an armed mission to enter Lhasa by force if necessary and establish a Resident, might no doubt, if the issue were simply one between India and Tibet, be justified as a legitimate reply to the action of the Tibetan Government...
>
> But His Majesty's Government cannot regard the question as one concerning India and Tibet alone. The position of China, in its relations to the powers of Europe has been so modified in recent years that it is necessary to take into account these altered conditions in deciding on action affecting what must still be regarded as a province of China.

London was very cautious about the reaction to the larger issues raised by the armed mission to Tibet:

> It is almost certain that were the British Mission to encounter opposition, questions would be raised which would have to be considered not as local ones concerning Tibet and India exclusively but from an international point of view, as involving the status of the Chinese Empire.[25]

London was also of the opinion that the Russians should be requested to make a public statement of their foreign policy regarding Tibet and China and they should be warned of the British Government's "intention to meet any action on their part by more than counter-balancing measures of our own."

However, the Russians remained non-committal over their Tibet policy. In the words of a Russian diplomat: "Although the Russian Government had no designs whatever upon Tibet, they could not remain indifferent to any serious disturbance of the *status quo* in this country. Such a disturbance might render it necessary for them to safeguard their interests in Asia, not that, even in this case, they would desire to interfere in the affairs of Tibet as their policy was not targeted on Tibet in any case."[26]

[25]Taraknath Das, op. cit., p. 439.
[26]Taraknath Das, op. cit., p. 440.

Many like Lord Curzon favoured a forward policy.

To summarise their arguments: firstly the Manchus were weak and their suzerainty was merely a 'constitutional fiction'; secondly nothing was to be allowed to 'threaten' the smooth functioning of the British empire; thirdly the British should use, when necessary the strength of the Nepalese army, fourthly, Tibet needed to be brought under the British ambit to nip the Russian influence in the bud, while no political motive should be 'shown' in taking Tibet under British influence.

Here was the outline of the mission that Younghusband was to take to Tibet the following year.

9

The Iron is Hot

The Younghusband Expedition

For the Tibetan army to challenge the British was like throwing an egg against the rock – the egg could only be smashed.

The Choegyal of Sikkim

Curzon knew that the iron was hot, he had to strike.

If there was one factor that provoked the need for the Viceroy to 'safeguard' the imperial interests of the British Crown, it was the uncompromising attitude of some of the Tibetan leaders.

We shall see during the course of the following events that at the beginning of the century, as happened very often in Tibetan history, two currents of force were prevalent in Lhasa; the progressive and modern led by Kalon Shatra, and the conservative force dominating the Tsongdu. The latter, which was led by the monks of the large monasteries, prevailed in all policy decisions during the first decades of this century.[1]

Curzon was a man in a hurry and he had decided to act.

In June 1903, Colonel Younghusband was dispatched with some troops to Khamba Dzong, inside Tibetan territory. This small British army consisted of five officers and 500 troops. On hearing news of the approaching British army, the Tibetan Government immediately sent two negotiators with the brief to stop the advancing army and to hold talks at a border post called Giagong. A Tibetan-speaking British officer, Captain O'Connor advanced to Giagong to be told by the Tibetan representatives that talks should be held on the spot.

This was refused by the British who continued to advance toward Khamba Dzong arguing that they had permission from the Manchus

---

[1]As a matter of fact, until the Chinese invaded Tibet.

in Beijing to hold negotiations. The Tibetan Representatives tried in vain to block their path.

In the meantime the Tsongdu, alerted by the ominous news from the border, sent an urgent message to their representatives on the border, instructing them not to allow a single British soldier or civilian into Tibetan territory.

But the Tibetan National Assembly was living in the 'white clouds' of the Roof of the World. Wishful thinking, rhetoric and Mantras were not enough to balance the woefully poor preparedness of the Tibetan troops. More was needed to block the decisiveness of the Viceroy and his young Colonel who had decided to force the Tibetans to sit at the negotiating table.

The stubbornness and intransigence of the Tibetan Assembly in refusing any contact with the 'foreigners with yellow eyes' did not help the matters to unfold smoothly.

When more knowledgeable elements, such as Kalon Shatra, tried to make the Kashag aware of the power of the British in the world and the consequences that refusing to deal with them, even to open their letters might have, he was accused of being a spy for the Crown and of having received some bribes from his 'masters' when he was the Resident Representative in Darjeeling.

To be fair to the Tibetans, one should recall their blissful ignorance of the world outside.

At this crucial time, the Tsongdu took over the decision-making power from the Kashag, which was considered to be pro-British; the Great Monasteries were convinced that the British were the enemy of Buddhism and only interested in extending their empire. This may not have been totally untrue.

Once in Khamba Dzong, representatives of the three great monasteries as well as senior Tibetan officers came to meet the British officers. However they immediately got stuck as both parties could not agree on a place where the negotiations could take place. The Chinese Representative in Shigatse also appeared on the stage but he turned back when he was told by the Tibetans and the British that his presence was not necessary.

The British troops were also visited by the Panchen Lama's representative and the Abbots of the Tashilhunpo who unsuccessfully tried to mediate.

Many visitors dropped by, mainly out of mere curiosity.

Younghusband had arrived at Khamba Dzong, but the negotiations remained at a standstill with the Tibetans still refusing to discuss commercial or any other agreements.

Younghusband began to feel that he was being taken for a ride.

When he asked for the Ambans to be witness to the discussions, the Tibetans retorted that the Ambans had nothing to do with commercial matters.

The 'negotiations' on the location of the negotiations went on for a couple of months. The British troops had, in the meantime, started enjoying the countryside: "The British passed their time carrying out impressive military exercises, taking photographs, hiking in the hills, mapping the surrounding countries, botanizing, and geologizing."[2]

Finally after three months the British troops received orders to return to India. The advent of the winter was the main reason for this temporary retreat.

In Lhasa, the power struggle between the conservative forces in the Tsongdu and some of the more liberal (at least better informed) ministers intensified. As a result, four Kalons ended up in jail, accused of supporting the British. One even committed suicide. The Tsongdu was more determined than ever to stop any advance by 'British devils' into Tibet.

Smashing an Egg on the Rock

But Curzon had decided to return. In December 1903, Claude White, the Political Officer in Gangtok sent a letter to the Tibetan Government informing them that Younghusband would be proceeding towards Gyantse to open the negotiations; the Tibetans were requested to send their representatives

The first days of 1904 saw a British expedition led by Col. Francis Younghusband and Claude White with five thousand Sikh and Gurkha soldiers begin their march to Gyantse. They had brought with them rifles, machine guns and artillery.

When the troops reached Tuna, between Phari and Guru, some negotiations started again without much success. The Bhutanese Raja, known as the Tongsa Penlop also tried to mediate at Phari and suggested that talks should start in Gyantse, but he was unable to convince the Lhasa authorities. •

---

[2]Shakabpa, op. cit,. p. 207

The Choegyal of Sikkim, a relative of the Tibetan General[3] who was the military commander in Yarlung valley, advised the latter to negotiate with the British. Dapon Lhading was already aware of the strong reinforcements stationed in Sikkim as support for the troops of Younghusband: "For the Tibetan army to challenge the British was like throwing an egg against the rock — the egg could only be smashed,"[4] wrote the Choegyal. But the Tibetans were not ready to listen.

In the meantime, the Tibetan troops entrenched themselves behind a five-foot wall at Chumik Shinko between Tuna and Guru.

In Asia, one does not start a war before having tea; Younghusband paid a visit to the Tibetan camp at Guru and later received Dapon Lhading at his camp in Tuna; but despite the courtesy calls and offering of scarves, tea and refreshment, the stalemate continued.

The tea parties could have gone on too, but Younghusband was a young man in a hurry; during the course of his final visit to the Tibetan camp, he informed the Tibetan General that he would be advancing towards Gyantse the next day.

An Englishman later wrote: "In 1903 the position of Britain and Tibet, was like that of a big boy at school who is tormented by an impertinent youngster. He bears it for sometime, but at last is compelled to administer chastisement."[5]

There are divergent views on the events which occurred the following day. For Younghusband, it was clear he had to advance:

There was no possible reasoning with such people. They had such overweening confidence in the Lama's powers. How could anyone dare to resist the orders of the Great Lama? Surely lightning would descend from heaven or the earth open up and destroy anyone who had such temerity! I pointed to our troops, now ready deployed for action. I said we have tried for fourteen years inside our frontier to settle matters. I urged that for eight months now I had patiently tried to negotiate, but no

[3]General (Dapon) Lhading.
[4]Shakabpa, op. cit., p. 210.
[5]John Buchan quoted in Patrick French, *Younghusband, the Last Great Imperial Adventurer* (London: Flamingo, 1975), p. 219.

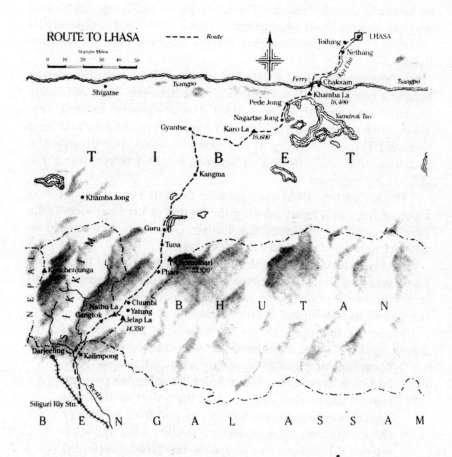

Map showing the route of the Younghusband Expedition in Tibet in 1904.

one with authority came to see me, my letters were
returned, and even messages were refused."[6]

As the British advanced towards the wall, Dapon Lhading and
his junior colleague, Dapon Namseling emerged from behind the
wall and rode a few hundred metres to parley with the British
officers. Younghusband and General Macdonald requested the
Tibetan General to extinguish the fuses of the matchlock guns of
their troops. The Tibetans agreed, rendering their weapons
inoperable for a few minutes. The British surrounded the camp with
their machine guns. At that point of time, the Tibetans were
practically disarmed and Younghusband thought the battle won.
What occurred during the subsequent minutes may remain forever
a question of speculation.

Some reports say that Dapon Lhading started to fire, killing a
sepoy; General Macdonald had no choice but to ask his troops to
fire upon the disarmed Tibetans. However, the Tibetans strongly
denied that they began the firing. How could they have begun to
fire after having extinguished the fuses of their guns?

Dapon Namseling's son later reported:

> Father at that time was a Dapon stationed at Phari. He
> took his army about fifteen miles from Phari to a place
> called Chumi Shengo [Hot Springs]... During the battle
> some of the Tibetans had a gun for which you light the
> fuse and put one bullet [matchlocks] and the rest had
> swords and spears. The British had some guns where
> you could put seven or eight bullets at one time, and
> types of cannon.... All of a sudden the British fired and
> many Tibetan soldiers were killed."[7]

Once started, nothing could stop the massacre. It came to an
end when not a single soul was seen moving on the plain of Guru.

"In a few minutes, the whole affair was over," wrote
Younghusband.

Dapon Lhading was one of the first to be killed but legend[8] has
it that "Lhading-se saw a white horse nearby, and mounting it he
fled eastwards over streams and fields to a mountain. But the British

[6]Younghusband, op. cit., p. 174.

[7]Namseling Paljor Jigme, *The History of a Man's Life and Related Matters*
(Dharamsala: 1988).

[8]Phuntsok Tsering, *The Annals of the All Revealing Mirror* (Lhasa: 1987), p.
398.

opened fire with a cannon, and it was left to mourn the character of heroic Lhading-se"[9] Younghusband however affirmed that the Tibetan General was killed at the beginning of the battle.

One young British Lieutenant commanding the Maxim Gun detachment later wrote: "I got so sick of the slaughter that I ceased fire, though the General's order was to make as big a bag as possible. I hope I shall never have to shoot down men walking away again."[10]

Younghusband was not very proud of his resounding victory: "I have had an absolutely miserable day," he later wrote. "It was a horrible sight, but I feel I did every single thing I could to prevent this, and it was only silliness and ignorance of these Tibetans that caused it." In another letter to his father he admitted that 'it was nothing, but pure butchery. The poor things were penned up in a hollow within a few yards and even feet of our rifles."[11]

That evening when Younghusband tried to understand 'why' this butchery, all the blame fell on the Dalai Lama's obstinacy. Had he not refused all the letters of the Viceroy without even opening them? Had he not obstinately refused to negotiate and discuss with the Crown?

The battle over, something flabbergasted the Tibetans, perhaps even more than the bullets of the 'British devils'. The British officers visited the battlefield, and instead of killing those still alive, the 'devils' ordered British troops to take them to the field hospital. This was an incredible gesture for the Tibetans used to fighting wars on their eastern front with Chinese warlords where no prisoners were taken, leave alone the question of caring for the wounded.

This incident along with the fact that Younghusband paid well for whatever food or fodder he requisitioned on his way to Gyantse, made the Tibetans change their mind about the British; this change of attitude played an important role in future 'negotiations'.

After a few days' stop to care for the wounded, Younghusband decided to proceed to Gyantse. Was he still hoping to find someone to negotiate with?

Not much resistance was offered by the Tibetans and by the end of April, they could set up two camps in Gyantse. It took a few more days and some pieces of artillery to take over the fort and soon the Union Jack was flying on the fort dominating Gyantse.

[9]"Se' is an honorific title sometimes translated by 'Prince.'
[10]Younghusband, op. cit., p 223.
[11]Younghusband, op. cit., p 224.

Younghusband had hoped to meet the Chinese Amban, if not some Tibetan negotiators. However, he received a message from the Amban explaining that the Tibetan government had refused to provide him with transport and he was therefore blocked in Lhasa. Indeed, as Lord Curzon had remarked a few months earlier, the suzerainty of the Manchus was only 'constitutional fiction'.

While in Gyantse, Captain O'Connor was sent to Shigatse where he developed friendly relations with the abbots and lamas of the Tashilhunpo.

It was a tactic which would develop later as a means to try to keep a balance between the two Lamas, or sometimes to divide them in order to rule better over the Land of Snows.

Historically the British always found themselves closer to the Panchen Lama[12] as did the Chinese who often managed, especially during the twentieth century, to manipulate the close attendants of the Lama of Tashilhunpo against the Dalai Lama's government in Lhasa.

Meanwhile, as Younghusband was getting tired of waiting, the morale of the Tibetans was fast declining. As stated by Shakabpa: "It soon became well known in U-Tsang that the British provided medical aid to the Tibetan wounded, who were given cash and presents and then set free... Moreover, the fact the British paid well for firewood, grain, and fodder impressed the local inhabitants."[13]

It was even rumoured amongst the Tibetans that the 'demons' had glasses which could see far away things. Would Younghusband, with his compassion for the suffering Tibetans, become a new Boddhisattva or an addition to the Tibetan pantheon of gods and semi-gods? Younghusband was not interested in his deification, he wanted a treaty with Tibet, and on July 14th he decided to proceed to Lhasa; he realized that he could stay for ever in Gyantse and nothing would happen, except the winter. He had now decided to deal directly with 'The Lama'. Though he had accused the Dalai Lama of responsibility for all the events of the previous months, in particular the massacre of Guru, did he know that the Dalai Lama was on a three-year retreat at that time? It is doubtful.

---

[12]Perhaps due to its geographical proximity to India, perhaps also because the Panchen Lamas were more aware of the outside world and of British India in particular. We should remember that the Panchen Lama spoke Hindi.

[13]Shakabpa, op. cit., p 214.

The last serious Tibetan resistance was organized at Karo-la, the pass between Gyantse and the Turquoise Lake.[14] A large number of Tibetan troops were blocking the way to the pass, but Lt. Colonel Brander and his troops managed to climb to the pass by a mountain path and when the Tibetans found themselves in a position below the British it was too late. More than 300 Tibetans lost their lives in this unequal battle which opened the road to Nagartse and Lhasa for Younghusband.

After a short stop at Nagartse to visit the monastery of Dorje Pagmo, the only female high *tulku*[15] in Tibet and after having enjoyed some boating on the magnificent Turquoise Lake, Younghusband's troops scaled Khampa-la, the last pass just above the Kyushu river in the Lhasa valley, with their artillery and equipment.

At the ferry on the river, they found the Lord Chamberlain waiting for them with a letter from the Dalai Lama urging the British to negotiate on the spot and to refrain from proceeding further to Lhasa. Younghusband's answer was unequivocal: they would negotiate only in the Tibetan capital.

Upon hearing of Younghusband's refusal to negotiate at the bottom of Khampa-la, the Dalai Lama was requested by the Kashag and the Tsongdu to interrupt his retreat and immediately leave Lhasa.

Charles Bell, in the biography of the Thirteenth Dalai Lama, wrote that "...shortly before their [the British] arrival the Dalai Lama fled northward to Mongolia. This was the first time that he had left his own country. He was twenty-eight years old. He left his seal with a priest of especial learning and sanctity."

An old and wise Lama, the Ganden Tri Rinpoche was the formal head of the Yellow Hats sect; he had been appointed as the Regent and given the power to negotiate with the British. He was also given clear instructions by the Dalai Lama in particular to release Kalon Shatra and his colleagues who had dared to advise the government to negotiate with the British at the time of their first incursion on the Tibetan soil. The Dalai Lama's seals were left with the Tri Rinpoche thereby empowering him to sign on his behalf.

The Dalai Lama left for Mongolia on July 30, and four days later the troops of Younghusband marched through the Gate of Lhasa. A

---

[14]Or Yumdrok Yamtso for the Tibetans.
[15]Reincarnated Lama, in this case, a lady Lama.

well-known photo taken at that time shows the troops entering Lhasa through the Stupa, with the Potala in the background .[16]

A comic incident deserves to be mentioned: Younghusband entered the Tibetan capital in 'full-dress uniform' with three hundred men. He described the scene thus: "preceded by a sort of a band from the Gorkhas, we marched right through the city of Lhasa making all the noise we could." The young Colonel felt that the local population was most impressed by the 'Grand Show' and were clapping as the soldiers paraded by. The Tibetan version of the same event is quite different. Kalon Shatra's son wrote: "When the British Officers marched to the Tsuglakhang[17] and other places, the inhabitants of Lhasa were displeased. They shouted and chanted to bring down rain and made clapping gestures to repulse them. In the foreigner's custom these are seen as sign of welcome, so they took off their hats and said thank you."[18]

During the next few days, the man who would later be called 'the last great imperial adventurer' received the Amban, who offered to mediate with the Tibetans. But Younghusband was no fool: he had waited for months for the Amban who 'had no transport'. Now, he decided to deal directly with the Tibetan government.

The Representatives of Nepal and Ladakh also called on Younghusband, who returned the courtesy.

For a few days, the Kashag and the Tsongdu did not dare meet the British devil who had come to destroy their religion. Who would take the first step?

Finally the Regent, a wise and practical man decided to take the plunge and meet Younghusband without further ceremony. Described thus by Shakabpa " Afterwards, the Regent summoned the Kashag and informed its ministers that his meeting with the British had not impaired his well-being in any way. He said Younghusband was a human being like anyone else and was amenable to reason" [19]

The discussions could begin and everyone suddenly lost their shyness. Large quantities of food, fruit and other presents began to pour in for the British officers.

[16]This gate was to be destroyed by the Communist Chinese in the late fifties.

[17]The Central Cathedral in Lhasa.

[18]Shenkhawa, *The Pure Unadulterated Copper of my History* (Dharamsala: 1990), p. 7.

[19]Shakabpa, op. cit., p 216.

Younghusband wrote down the British claims for an agreement.

The main points being discussed were an indemnity for the military expedition, exchange of prisoners, demarcation of the border with Sikkim and opening of trade between India and Tibet.

A Convention, the first one between Tibet and the United Kingdom, was signed on September 7, 1904 in the Great Audience Hall of the Potala by Colonel Younghusband and the Ganden Tri Rinpoche. Senior British officers including the Political Officer Claude White, members of the Kashag and abbots of the three Great Monasteries were present.

It was only much later that the Tibetans realized that this Convention was not such a bad bargain for them. In the seventies, the historian Shakabpa wrote: "It is quite clear that the British were dealing with Tibet as a separate and independent state, particularly since the 1904 convention makes no reference to China or to Chinese authority in Tibet. The Manchu Amban, the Bhutanese representative, and the Nepalese officer merely witnessed the signing of the Convention, but did not sign it themselves."[20]

Can we conclude that the 600 Tibetan soldiers who died at Guru in March 1904 laid down their lives for the independence of Tibet? It would be an exaggeration, but the Younghusband expedition was certainly a blessing in disguise for the Tibetans.

However it is true that if the Tibetans had not been forced to, they would never have signed the Convention. Later the Tibetans acknowledged the importance of this document. In his biography *Freedom in Exile*, the Dalai Lama wrote about the role of the British in Tibet: "As for Britain, thanks to Colonel Younghusband's expedition, there had been a British trade Mission in Tibet for almost half a century."[21]

Indeed London knew about the 'constitutional fiction'.

With the wisdom of ordinary people, a Lhasa street song said:

At first, enemies of your faith they were,
And then, 'outsiders' we labelled them,
But, when in the land their rupees did appear,
They became known as sahibs and gentlemen.

[20]Shakabpa, op. cit., p. 217.

[21]The Dalai Lama added "Even with Indian independence in 1947, the Mission at first continued to be run by the same Englishman, Hugh Richardson. So it was almost impossible to believe that the British Government was now agreeing that China has some claim to authority over Tibet."

We shall elaborate on some of the articles of the Convention and study their implications for the different parties involved in the game.

The Preamble[22] admits that "doubts and difficulties have arisen as to the meaning and validity of the Anglo-Chinese Convention of 1890, and the Trade Regulations of 1893, and as to the liabilities of the Thibetan[23] Government under these Agreements;"

It was more than 'doubts and difficulties' which had arisen as Lhasa had not been taken into confidence by the Chinese and British government before signing a Treaty on its behalf. Until the last moment, the Tibetans had refused to even open the letters and communications from their mighty southern neighbour.

As far as the British were concerned, the Agreement of 1893 had been convenient for them: the annexation of Sikkim was made official. They dealt only with the Chinese, knowing perfectly well of their non-existent power in Tibetan affairs.

They had perfected the tricks of colonial policy.

Then the Lhasa Convention mentioned, in a very British understatement "a disturbance of the relations of friendship and good understanding which have existed between the British Government and the Government of Thibet"

As a matter of fact there was no question of 'relations of friendship' because there were no relations at all between Tibet and the Crown; nevertheless each party was keen *"to restore peace and amicable relations."*

Article 1 stated, the Tibetan Government engages in respecting the Anglo-Chinese Convention of 1890, and the frontier between Sikkim and Tibet.

For the British it was the last step in the process of officialization of the annexation of Sikkim by the British Empire. The main objective of the 1890 Agreement had been the Chinese acceptance of the Sikkim-Tibet border and the authority of the British Crown over Sikkim. The Lhasa Convention of 1904 put the Tibetan seal on British overlordship on Sikkim.

Article 2 said that the Tibetan Government finally "undertakes to open forthwith trade mart." The job started by Warren Hastings had come to fruition after 130 years! Hastings must have smiled in his grave.

[22]Text in Richardson, op. cit., p. 268.
[23]In most documents from the early twentieth century, 'Tibet' is written 'Thibet'.

The chosen trade marts were at Gyantse, Gartok and Yatung in the Chumbi valley.

The Regulations under the Anglo Chinese Agreement of 1893 were confirmed with some amendments. One of these amendments was to keep open the possibility for new trade marts and the assurance by the Tibetan Government that it would not place any restrictions on the existing trade route. It was decided to appoint delegates to discuss the matter further.

The Tibetan Government accepted to keep the same tariff as earlier and maintain the trade route "suited to the needs of the trade." The Convention also provided for the appointment of a Tibetan Trade Agent who would be responsible to receive and forward any letter or communication from the British government to the Tibetan and Chinese authorities. We shall see later the importance of Trade Agents in the politics of the Roof of the World.

Article 6 provoked very strong reactions in many quarters, in particular in London; Younghusband requested the Tibetan Government to pay a sum of 500,000 pounds — equivalent to 75 lakhs[24] of rupees — to the British Government as war indemnity.

The indemnity was supposed to be paid in seventy-five annual installments of one Iakh rupees each, beginning on the 1st January, 1906. When the Convention was ratified at Simla in November of the same year, the amount was reduced to 25 lakh rupees.

Younghusband had also decided to take a security for the indemnity: the British Government would continue to occupy the Chumbi Valley until the indemnity was paid. If Simla and London had accepted this clause, the British would have been authorized to remain in the Chumbi valley until 1979.

The fate of Tibet (and India) would have perhaps been different if Chumbi valley had been part of India during the seventies!

In any case, fortunately[25] for the Tibetans, the period of occupancy of Chumbi Valley was reduced by the Viceroy to three years at the time of ratification.

The Tibetan Government also agreed to "raze all forts and fortifications and remove all armaments which might impede the course of free communication between the British frontier and the towns of Gyantse and Lhasa."

[24]One lakh is equal to 100,000.
[25]Or unfortunately?

Article 9 took note of the Russian threat. The consent of the British Government was necessary if any portion of Tibetan territory was "to be ceded, sold, leased, mortgaged or otherwise given for occupation, to any Foreign Power."

The Tibetan Government agreed that no power should be allowed to intervene in Tibet's internal affairs; no Representatives or Agents of any Foreign Power would be admitted and no "concessions for railways, roads, telegraphs, mining or other rights, could be granted to any Foreign Power."

This was perhaps in reply to the presumed Commercial Agreement of 1902 between China and Russia. It was the beginning of a new phase in political relations between British India and Tibet.

From Younghusband's government there was more suspicion and hostility than rejoicing. London felt that the young Colonel had deliberately disobeyed instructions in signing the Convention, in particular over the question of permanent interference in Tibetan affairs. The European powers had been assured in November 1903 that this was not intended, but in practical terms, the Convention clearly implied long-term involvement. The Government's standing was weak; the British ministers had no wish to be accused by the Opposition of pursuing a 'forward' frontier policy.

> Younghusband was reprimanded for his disobedience. That was palpably unfair. He was a man of honour and initiative; and in the exhilarating atmosphere of a successful expedition in a remote and unknown country he saw the opportunity of securing without difficulty greater advantages for his country than were contained in his instructions.[26]

On his return to India, Younghusband discovered that many did not appreciate that a small commercial and diplomatic mission had turned into a full-fledged military operation. At one point he was even asked to return to Lhasa to renegotiate the Treaty. Eventually, as we have seen, at the time of ratification, the indemnity was slashed from 500,000 Pound Sterling (payable in 75 annual instalments) to 166,000 Pounds (payable in 25 instalments).

In the background of these clashes of will between the Viceroy and Whitehall, was the strong personality of Lord Curzon and the proximity of Younghusband to the Viceroy.

[26]Richardson, op. cit., p. 92.

Such was the Imperial foreign policy; in the following years, the differences of perception between the officer on the spot — either in Lhasa, Gangtok or Simla — and the policy makers in London, would accentuate. Each time the Tibetans would be the losers.

The Younghusband expedition had clarified another point: the Russian presence in Tibet, which had been the pretext of the mission, was non-existent. Where were the hundreds of weapons brought by caravans of camels? During the battle of Guru only three Russian riffles were seized while most of the Tibetan soldiers were equipped only with the old matchlock guns which were totally inefficient compared to the modern weaponry of the British.

Younghusband left India very saddened by all this criticism; however, in England the general public received him as a hero and he was even blessed by a royal audience.

It is difficult to say whether the Younghusband mission was only a colonialist military expedition to subjugate a small (not in size) but peaceful nation, or Mahakala's sword, severing the attachments of the Tibetan Lamas to their nirvanic isolation and bringing the Roof of the World down to earth thereby allowing Tibet for the first time in modern history to put its signature on a Treaty.

On September 23, 1904, the British expedition left Lhasa to return to India. Captain O'Connor remained in Gyantse as the first Trade Agent. He visited the Tashilhunpo in Shigatse again and became friend with the young Panchen Lama. These good relations culminated in a visit by the Tibetan Lama to Calcutta, where he had the opportunity to meet the Prince of Wales and the new Viceroy, Lord Minto.

Shakabpa said that it was the beginning of the "friction between the Tashilhunpo and the Lhasa government." In fact, it had started right from the time of Hastings; but wasn't that the best way for a colonialist state to survive?

We shall conclude, with an anecdote about Younghusband, the British 'imperial adventurer'. The story is about his personal transformation after his Tibetan mission; he was a different man, a new man when he returned to India.

During his stay in Lhasa he had become very fond of the Ganden Tripa. In spite of the political difficulties and their personal backgrounds, they often sat together to discuss religion and philosophy. They developed a very close rapport.

On the last day of his stay, the Tri Rinpoche came to meet Younghusband and presented his new friend a small bronze statue of Buddha. Younghusband was deeply touched when the Holder of the Ganden Throne explained to him: "When we Buddhist look on this figure, we think only of peace and I want you when you look at it to think kindly of Tibet."

The next morning the young Colonel went for a ride; he left the camp with the small statue and when he reached a place far from any human habitation, he dismounted and sat on a rock. Sitting there, looking at the immensity of the landscape, he had a powerful mystic experience. His life was irrevocably changed. From being a great warrior for his empire, he soon became, after his return to London, a crusader of peace and universal brotherhood.

> There came upon me what was far more than elation or exhilaration…I was beside myself with an intensity of joy, such as even the joy of the first love can give only a faint foreshadowing of. And with this indescribable joy came a revelation of the essential goodness of the world. I was convinced past all refutation that men were good at heart, that the evil in them is superficial…in short. that men at heart are divine.[27]

Perhaps the statue of the Tri Rinpoche had had some effect and had given him an 'untellable joy'. At that moment, he felt that "the whole world was ablaze with the same ineffable bliss that was burning" inside him. That is also part of the magic of Tibet.

Historians usually refuse to entertain such stories, but who can say wherein lie the true threads of history? Perhaps this experience marked the end of a chapter in the history of the British Empire. Later on in England, Colonel Younghusband who had since become Sir Francis, became involved in the promotion of World Peace and inter-faith reunion such as the World Congress of Faith. In 1941, he even nominated Sri Aurobindo, the great Indian sage, for the Nobel Prize for literature for his celebrated work, *The Life Divine*.

[27]French, op. cit., p. 252.

10

'Large Insects are Eating Small Insects'

The Difficult Years

> *Large insects are eating and secretly injuring small insects.*
> **The Thirteenth Dalai Lama to the**
> **British Trade Agent**

We have seen that the moment Younghusband reached the bridge at the bottom of Khampa-la, the last step before reaching Lhasa, the young Dalai Lama[1] fled Tibet.

He had no alternative but to escape.

Most of the early foreign scholars, in particular those who wrote about the British expedition, thought that the Dalai Lama made many mistakes by refusing to start negotiations, sending back unopened letters of the British government and fleeing when the expedition was approaching. The fact that most of the historians of this period were British, colours the sequence of events. A scapegoat was easily found in the person of the Dalai Lama.

But things can also be viewed from another angle.

It has to be noted that the Dalai Lama was in the middle of a three-year retreat and this fact was unknown to the British. Like all Dalai Lamas, the Thirteenth had important religious duties vis-à-vis his people and part of his life had to be devoted to religious studies, practice and preaching. This was the disadvantage of a political system based on a 'harmonious blend of religion and politics'.

It is also true that the Dalai Lama was young and inexperienced in international politics. But what could a nation of monks do against the voracious empires which were dividing the world among themselves?

[1] He was only 28 years old.

Younghusband had violated the soil of Tibet and destroyed one after another the hurdles placed on his road by the Tibetan generals. Unfortunately Tibet never received the camel shipment of modern Russian weapons which Kawakuchi, the Japanese monk had announced.

But what might at first sight have appeared as a 'disaster', was perhaps a blessing in disguise. Life on the Roof of the World had not yet been polluted by international politics. Most of the intelligentsia in Lhasa and in the Great Monasteries knew very little about the imperialist designs of the Great Powers. Their main preoccupation was their spiritual progress on their 'graduated path to enlightenment'.

Some forty-five years later, history repeated itself. When news of the Chinese invasion was given to the officials in Lhasa, monks and lay people were picnicking and everyone continued to picnic. No one took an alarmist view of the wireless dispatches from Chamdo.

In 1904 as in 1950, life continued its flow, the chanting of Mantras, meditation and prayers and the petty intrigues which had gone on unperturbed for centuries. What was new?

The British devil was in a hurry, but the Tibetans including the Dalai Lama could hardly understand. What was the hurry?

At this crucial moment, with the British troops two days from Lhasa, the Nechung State Oracle was consulted. His answer was clear: the retreat had to be discontinued and the Dalai Lama had to leave immediately for Mongolia.

In what we could call a pilgrimage of convenience, the Dalai Lama left for Mongolia. His 'official' reason was of course to meet his disciples and give teachings.

The biography called *The String of Wondrous Gems* said:

> The Great Thirteenth realized that there were countless trainees in Mongolia and China in need of his attention. Also, he had a long-standing wish to visit the holy places of the north-east, particularly the birthplace of Lama Tsong Khapa in Amdo and the holy Five-Peaked Mountain in Western China.
> Therefore when the British appeared at the bridge south of Lhasa, he decided that the time had come for him to leave.[2]

[2]Mullin, op. cit., p. 67.

Most probably, another factor played an important role in the sudden decision of the Tibetan leader to leave his country; he was the embodiment of Avalokiteshwara.[3] How could Avalokiteshwara be caught by the devils who did not even believe in religion?

This was the clinching argument; he had to leave.

Candler[4] who was part of the British expedition wrote: "We had been in Lhasa almost three weeks before we could discover where he had fled. To us, at least the flight has deepened that mystery that envelops him, and adds to his dignity and remoteness; to the thousands of mystical dreamers it has preserved the effulgence of his godhead unsoiled by contact with the profane world".

Although, His Majesty's intelligence network was not able to discover the Lama's whereabouts in spite of the "men in Lhasa who would do much to please the new conquerors of Tibet", the local folks on the way to Mongolia knew that their Precious Protector was passing by. The path of his journey was lined with thousands and thousands of nomads who had run from the desert steppes of the Chang Tang[5] to catch a glimpse of their god.

In fact, more often than not, they hardly dared to look at him and their eyes were riveted on their boots. How could they look at Avalokiteshvara himself? Their only hope was that he would look at them, and thus this life as well as their future lives would be blessed by His *Darshan*.

The Dalai Lama made a great effort to stop as many times as possible without endangering his safety; everywhere along the way, he gave short spiritual discourses to his followers.

A grand reception awaited him in Urga:[6] ten thousand Mongols prostrated as he entered the city. At that time, Younghusband and his men were getting ready to leave Tibet. Three months had passed since the Dalai Lama left Lhasa.

He spent the following year meeting thousands of devotees in Mongolia, Buryat, Kalmyk, and Siberia. He gave countless religious discourses, initiations, and empowerment to all. He presided over two Great Prayer Festivals in Urga in 1905 and 1906.

---

[3]The Boddhisattva of Mercy.
[4]Candler, *The Unveiling of Lhasa* (London: 1905), p 235.
[5]The Great Northern Plains.
[6]Today's Ulan Bator.

While in Mongolia he also developed a personal contact wi⁺h the people and, in particular, with their religious leader, the Jetsun Dampa Hutuktu.

He renewed his contacts with the Russian Tsar and St. Petersburg. In Urga, many Russian diplomats called on him, bringing presents and messages from the Tsar. Dorjiev, who had accompanied his master on his escape journey to the North was still around. The British could not have been very happy at this turn of events. It is probably one of the reasons why they felt compelled to sign a Treaty with Russia in 1907, behind Tibet's back.

We shall leave the Dalai Lama for a moment to look at what was happening now in rest of the region which was of deep concern for Tibet.

The Aftermath of Younghusband Mission

The Younghusband expedition was perhaps one of the last great colonial expeditions.[7]

During the decade which followed the emergence of nationalist movements in countries like India or in Africa slowly eroded the foundations of the colonial Powers which collapsed under their own weight around the middle of the century.

However, in 1904, a colonial empire was still very much alive and well with all subjects and vassals being kept under control and the interests of the empire protected at all cost.

Had Curzon not written?

> In our view, any country or Government, or Empire has a right to protect its own interests and if those interests are seriously imperilled, as we hold ours to be in Tibet, we hold that the first law of national existence, which is self-preservation, compels us to take such steps as will avert these dangers and place our security upon an assured and impregnable footing.

While the Qing Emperors had mastered the art of bestowing titles on their 'vassals' to keep them in check, the Kings in London had mastered the art of binding friends and foes alike by treaties.

---

[7]One should count Mao's invasion of Tibet as a colonial military expedition. In fact the twentieth century saw the emergence of a new brand of imperialism, the Marxist variety, its latest avatar being Maoism.

The Convention of 1906

In 1906, the British signed an Adhesion Agreement with China known as "The Convention between Great Britain and China respecting Tibet".[8] It was a balancing act favouring China, in case their help would be required in the future.[9]

The purpose of the Agreement is mentioned in the Preamble. London was "sincerely desirous to maintain and perpetuate the relations of friendship and good understanding which now exist between their respective (Chinese and British) Empires."

The British had to admit that the Tibetans had not been consulted before[10] signing the 1890 Anglo-Chinese Convention. For this reason, the Tibetans had refused "to recognise the validity of or to carry into full effect the provisions of the Anglo-Chinese Convention."

We have seen in the previous chapter that Lord Curzon was of the opinion that Great Britain had no alternative but to sign a separate Treaty with the Tibetans.

In Article I of the 1906 Agreement, the Convention of 1904 was confirmed, subject to some modifications, but what modifications they were!

While the British Government agreed not to annex Tibetan territory as well as not to interfere in the administration of Tibet, the Chinese Government was "not to permit any other foreign state to interfere with Tibet." Hence, the Russian threat was effectively countered.

Article III is more important as it completely changed the meaning and content of the Lhasa Convention of 1904

In Article IX of 1904 Convention, the concessions mentioned in para (d) were denied to 'any Foreign Power': The Government of Thibet engages that, without the previous consent of the British Government (d) No concessions for railways, roads, telegraphs, mining or other rights, shall be granted to any Foreign Power, or the subject of any Foreign Power.

It was clear that for the purpose of the Lhasa Convention, China was a foreign power.

After having pressed for the recognition of Chinese suzerainty over Tibet, the Chinese diplomats managed to get the words 'other

---

[8]*British and Foreign States Papers (1905-06)*, pp. 171-173.
[9]Mainly to oppose the Russian Empire.
[10]And even after.

than China' mentioned, thereby gaining recognition of the special relationship between Tibet and China.

Article III reads:

> The Concessions which are mentioned in Article IX (d)
> of the Convention concluded on September 7th, 1904
> by Great Britain and Tibet are denied to any State or to
> the subject of any state other than China.

One can imagine the difficulty of the negotiations. Why should China give its 'adhesion' to the Convention if it was treated as a foreign country in Tibet?

The British managed to fully preserve their trade interest, in particular the telegraph line which was of vital and strategic importance in order to communicate with their agents.

Article IV accepted that "the provisions of the Anglo-Chinese Convention of 1890 and Regulations of 1893...subject to the terms of the present Convention would remain in full force."

Had seven hundred Tibetans been massacred at Tuna for nothing?

The Tibetans were back to square one. Richardson, the last British head of the Mission in Lhasa admitted:

> The peculiarly privileged position which had accrued
> to the British from the negotiations at Lhasa was
> virtually reversed by the recognition that China was not
> a foreign power for the purpose of that convention and
> had the responsibility for preserving the integrity of
> Tibet. Chinese rights in Tibet were thus recognized to
> an extent to which the Chinese had recently been wholly
> unable to exercise them.[11]

While Younghusband himself had been unable to get the Amban signature on the Treaty when he was in Lhasa, the diplomats in Calcutta and Beijing after 'strenuous and tortuous' negotiations finally convinced China to put its seal on the Convention of 1906.

One has to understand that during all these decades (not to say these centuries), Tibet was a mere pawn in the Great Game between Imperial Powers. They were sharing the world between themselves with little consideration for the weak and poor nations. Hence, the British Government[12] gave more consideration to China than to Tibet or other Himalayan kingdoms.

[11]Richardson, op. cit., p 94.
[12]At least in London.

154

The Fate of Tibet

An array of relationships such as colonies, dominions, vassals, suzerains, etc. helped these Powers to keep control over the 'small insects' — sometimes with bona fide intentions, sometimes only to eat them and use their wealth.

Take India as an example — for millennia India was synonymous with wealth and riches, but by the time the British left in 1947, India was a plundered country, one of the poorest in the world. The big insect had eaten well!

But the most incredible aspect of the 1906 Convention was that the Tibetans neither took part in the negotiations, nor they were even informed of its results!

Richardson had to admit: "British Government has, of course, the right to upset or whittle away the actions of its predecessors; but it seems extraordinarily high-handed or negligent that, after a treaty had been signed directly with the Tibetans, the British Government should have made no attempt to keep them informed of other acts affecting and modifying that treaty."[13]

But that was not all for the poor Tibetans!

The Agreement of 1907 with Russia

In 1907, an understanding between the Russian and the British Empires was reached. The Agreement, called "The Convention between Great Britain and Russia relating to Persia, Afghanistan and Tibet,"[14] was signed at St. Petersburg on August 31st, 1907.

The 'treaty policy' continued; having tackled Tibet in 1904 and China in 1906, London was now neutralizing Russia.

Of course both Empires were "animated by the sincere desire to settle by mutual agreement different questions concerning the interests of their States on the continent of Asia." It was for this purpose that an Agreement "destined to prevent all cause of misunderstanding between Great Britain and Russia" was concluded.

Regarding Tibet, they agreed that the British Government and Russia recognize "the suzerain rights of China in Thibet." It also considered "the fact that Great Britain, by reason of her geographical position, has a special interest in the maintenance of the status quo in the external relations of Thibet."

[13]Richardson, op. cit., p 94.
[14]Bell, op. cit., p. 289-91.

However both parties engaged "to respect the territorial integrity of Thibet and to abstain from all interference in the internal administration."

Article II again gave a prominent role to China: "In conformity with the admitted principle of the suzerainty of China over Thibet, Great Britain and Russia engage not to enter into negotiations with Thibet except through the intermediary of the Chinese Government."

Perhaps it was a policy of convenience for the British Government, but for Calcutta or Simla, it was the end of a possibility to deal directly with the persons concerned.

Acknowledging that the decadent and powerless China was the master of Tibet was the best way to stop the Russians from interfering. Unfortunately, it did not preclude that in the future the *rapport de force* could change.

It is rather surprising that intelligent people like the British could use such short-term artifice in their foreign policy. Perhaps the only explanation is that the British Empire had itself started crumbling. One proof of this was the constant reluctance of London to be seen as a colonial power. When an Imperial Power starts to worry about being seen as an imperial power, is it not the sign of the end of an era?

It is also possible that London's thinking was wholly pragmatic: when the balance of forces would change, treaties would also be changed.

In the Treaty with Russia, special mention was made of the Kalmyk and the Buriat subjects of the Russian Empire whose religious allegiance was with Lhasa. They were given a status similar to that of the Buddhist regions in the Himalayas such as Bhutan or Sikkim which were under the British Crown.

> It is clearly understood that Buddhists, subjects of Great Britain or of Russia, may enter into direct relations on strictly religious matters with the Dalai Lama and the other representatives of Buddhism in Thibet. The Governments of Great Britain and Russia engage, as far as they are concerned, not to allow those relations to infringe the stipulations of the present arrangement.

The treaty was very favourable to the British, for example in Article III: "The British and Russian Governments respectively engage not to send Representatives to Lhasa [on permanent basis]"

For London, it was not a problem because their representative was already posted in Gangtok and could visit Lhasa at any time, he did not need to be officially posted in Lhasa. It was different for the Russians who were so far away.

Similarly in the Article IV: the two Parties engaged "neither to seek nor to obtain, whether for themselves or their subjects, any Concessions for railways, roads, telegraphs, and mines, or other rights in Thibet." The British had already secured the concession for communication from Gyantse to India.

In an annexe to the Convention, Great Britain reaffirmed that the occupation of the Chumbi Valley would cease only after the payment of the indemnity and when the trade marts "have been effectively opened."

But the British diplomats, perhaps anticipating questions from the Russian side, added that "if the occupation of the Chumbi Valley by the British forces has, for any reason, not been terminated at the time anticipated, the British and Russian Governments will enter upon a friendly exchange of views on this subject."

Once again the strangest fact is that although the clause depended on the Tibetan authorities, they were neither consulted nor informed about it.

Such were the ways of the powerful!

The Dalai Lama in China

It is now time to come back to the Dalai Lama. In 1906, he left Mongolia for Amdo and Kham provinces of Tibet. The journey was purely religious in nature. A Christian Missionary, J. Ridley of the China Inland Mission, witnessed his arrival at Kumbum:

> We reached a large camp, which was prepared for him outside the monastery of Kumbum. Here we found hundreds of tents, all pitched in square, with one, a Mongol tent of rich yellow cloth, surrounded by a wall of the same material, where the Dalai Lama was to spend the night. Outside the square were crowds from many different nationalities from different parts of Asia: Mongol princes, with gaily-attired camels, bringing presents from the North; wild-looking Tibetans with matted hair hanging down their backs, riding equally wild-looking ponies, driving unyieldy yaks, thin from travelling, perhaps from Lhasa or unknown regions in

Southern Tibet; Chinese in gorgeous coloured silks; and muleteers with their galled mules.[15]

It really was a blend of religion and politics.

During his stay in Kumbum, the Thirteenth Dalai Lama received a delegation from the Tibetan Government requesting him to come back to Lhasa as the 'yellow-hair' British had left and in any case the Tibetans had found them to be not worse than the Ambans.

But, at the same time, another invitation arrived from Beijing: the Emperor and the Empress Dowager wanted him to visit them in the Chinese capital.

It was not an easy decision, with each party pulling in opposite directions. The British were still suspicious of the Russians, knowing that their 'bête noire' Dorjiev was back in St. Petersburg; it did not augur well for their interests in Tibet.

Did the Dalai Lama know that some negotiations had started between the British and the Chinese to sign a new Treaty behind the back of the Tibetans?

Did he have the premonition that London had condemned Curzon and his Great Adventurer and that Whitehall was ready to give up many of the advantages which accrued to the British as well as the Tibetans from the Lhasa Convention of 1904?

In the meantime the Russians, who were also negotiating with Britain, were not so keen to see the Dalai Lama back in the Tibetan capital. The pilgrimage was very convenient for everyone; the Great Powers would continue to divide up the Roof of the World among themselves while the Tibetan Lama would visit monasteries or give religious discourses.

Another complication cropped up for the Dalai Lama: the Chinese Emperor had just 'deposed' him. Large posters had been pasted on the walls of Lhasa to announce the imperial decision, only to be torn down by the populace.

A question of protocol also added to the confusion: should he go to Beijing, what would his position and status be? The British seemed confused. In Simla, Beijing, St. Petersburg or London, the thought processes of the officers of the Raj and their subsequent line of action, were sometimes diametrically opposed.

On the one hand, if the Dalai Lama were to return to Lhasa, some were of the opinion that it would strengthen the Tibetan

[15]Quoted by Mullin, op. cit., p 70.

position, but nobody knew what to do with the Chinese claim of suzerainty over Tibet, even though the 'fiction' had been blown apart by Younghusband's expedition.

Many knew that Beijing meant intrigue but it was also possible that the Chinese and the Tibetans might forge a new alliance and revive the old priest-patron relationship.

In spite of all the pressures, the Dalai Lama showed his strength of character by deciding that he would go to Beijing and meet the Emperor.

In his Testament[16] written 25 years later, he briefly explained his trip to China:

> When the English marched into Tibet in the Wood
> Dragon year (1905), it would have been convenient and
> easy to adopt a policy of friendship and make efforts to
> please them. But realizing the dangers and implications
> of such a policy in the future, I, in spite of the hazardous
> and difficult journey, went to Peking, the Chinese capital
> via Mongolia. I went to China on the basis of the teacher-
> disciple relationship prevalent since the time of the great
> Fifth Dalai Lama between the two countries.

On his way to Beijing, he stopped for five months on the Five-Peaked Mountain,[17] spending most of that time in meditation and prayer. Was he preparing to confront the Dragon in his own cave? Or was he thinking that once again the Son of Heaven would be converted and he would give back his rightful place as the Preceptor of the Emperor?

Politics could not be completely banned. Among his visitors was the American Ambassador, W.W. Rockhill to whom we owe one of the best descriptions of the Tibetan leader:

> He is a man of undoubted intelligence and ability, of
> quick understanding and of force of character. He is
> broad-minded, possibly as a result of his varied
> experiences during the last few years, and of great
> natural dignity. He seemed deeply impressed with the

---

[16]We have used the translation of K. Dhondup published in K. Dhondup, The *Water-Bird and other Years*, (New Delhi: Rangwang Publishers, 1986), p 143.
[17]Wu-Tai-Shan, the abode of Manjusri.

great responsibilities of his office as supreme Pontiff of his faith, more so, perhaps, than by those resulting from his temporal duties. He is quick tempered and impulsive, but cheerful and kindly. At all times, I found him a most thoughtful host, an agreeable talker and extremely courteous. He speaks rapidly and smoothly, but in a very low voice. He is short in stature, probably about five foot six or seven inches, and of slight build. His complexion is rather darker than that of the Chinese, and of a ruddier brown; his face, which is not very broad, is pitted with small pox, but not deeply. It lights up most pleasantly when he smiles and shows his teeth, which are sound and white.[18]

The Dalai Lama wanted to give the old priest-patron relationship a new and final chance and perhaps he was also curious as to why all his British and Russian 'friends' were so keen not to see him in Beijing.

He finally arrived in Beijing in September 1908, more than four years after he left Lhasa. Had he fallen into a trap?

He was determined to get the same treatment and status as the Fifth Dalai Lama.

But the times had changed and prolonged negotiations began regarding the protocol for the imperial audience. The Chinese officials knew the weakness of the Tibetan military position; they had been defeated by the British troops and even the Lhasa Convention had been nullified by the Agreement ratified in Beijing between Britain and China.

They had decided that the Dalai Lama should kow-tow to the Emperor like any other vassal, and that he would sit on a lower throne than the Emperor's. This was not agreeable to the Dalai Lama.

For Thubten Gyatso, the audience had to follow the same protocol as the one followed by his predecessor. He was the guru of the Emperor, and the Guru could not bend in front of his disciple. "The strong personality in a small body," as Sir Charles Bell later described him, fought well and a diplomatic solution was finally

[18]Rockhill, W.W., *The Dalai Lamas of Lhasa and theirs Relations with the Manchu Emperors* (London: Leyden, 1910).

found.[19] He would meet the Emperor and the Empress separately, making the meeting more informal and dispensing with the rigid court protocol.

A few months later, in October, he was invited to the Palace, where he gave several initiations and officiated at many religious ceremonies.

But Karma struck again, in what was to be the first of a long series of blows which perhaps changed the course of Central Asian history.

On the 21st November the Emperor died. The next day the Empress followed him to the Heavenly Realms. These events marked not only the end of a dynasty, but also the end of an era.

By some strange coincidence the Dalai Lama was present in Beijing at this crucial time. He performed the funeral rites and some believed that he advised the court on the choice of the new Emperor.

One month later, he left for Tibet, reaching Lhasa in December 1909, more than five years after the British troops had crossed the bridge on the Tsangpo river.

But his difficulties were not over.

The Thirteenth Dalai Lama was not ready to bend. More than ever, he was determined to fight to make Tibet an independent state.

Charles Bell later recalled how great was the Dalai Lama's deception that the Choe-yon Relationship was dead and gone; the Chinese Protector was now ready to stab its protégé in the back.

> As he drew nearer to Lhasa the Dalai Lama found that the Government of China had broken their pledges to him not to interfere with his position in Tibet. They were actually attacking the heart of his country. What should he do in such case? His knowledge of the world affairs was almost non-existent.
> Pathetic were the cables which he forwarded to the British Agent at Gyantse for dispatch to "Great Britain and all the Ministers of Europe".[20]

[19]One should not laugh at these protocol complications; at the end of the twentieth century, the same problems are still constantly occurring, for example when the Dalai Lama visited the White House in the nineties, the protocol officers of the American President had to devise a trick whereby the Dalai Lama would be 'unofficially' invited by the Vice-President and the then President would then drop by 'by chance' at the Vice-President's Office. This way, there would be no loss of face for the Chinese and the Americans (?).

[20]Bell, Sir Charles, *Portrait of a Dalai Lama*, (London: Wisdom Publications,1987), p. 93.

He had telegraphed Gyantse stating "Large insects are eating and secretly injuring small insects".

To the Chinese Foreign Office in Beijing he wired his anger at their representatives in Tibet: "We have acted frankly, and now they steal our heart".

In one year, London had handed over to the Chinese and the Russians most of the benefits[21] which had accrued to the Tibetans following the Younghusband expedition.

Fifty years later, a similar policy would be followed by Jawaharlal Nehru who on the pretext of not being an 'imperialist' handed Tibet over to one of the greatest imperialist states ever, the Communist government in Beijing.

Poor Tibetans, history kept repeating itself.

It was the eternal story, "large insects are eating small insects". But the Dalai Lama was a strong character, he was quite determined not to be a weak insect and to act for the best of his country even while dealing with nasty insects.

[21]Except the opening of trade marts.

11

End of the Choe-yon Relationship and the Exile in India

> *My ministers had appealed to me to remain in Lhasa; but had I done so, a situation similar to the Muslim invasion of India might well have taken place, which resulted in many religious institutions being destroyed.*
> **The Thirteenth Dalai Lama on his exile in India**

Butcher Zhao

Now we have to travel back a few years in history to understand the situation in Tibet during the absence of the Dalai Lama.

When the Chinese saw that London was vacillating[1], a new Tibet policy was decided upon and the first action of the Chinese Court was to nominate Zhao Erfeng as the new Army Commander for Tibet.

General Zhao Erfeng, the Chinese warlord and Governor of Sinning, had started his advance inside Tibetan territory soon after Younghusband's departure and begun what the British would call a 'Forward Policy'.

While Zhao was in overall charge of Western China, his brother, Zhao Erxun was responsible for the province of Sichuan. The real mission of the two brothers was clear: to re-integrate Tibet into the Chinese empire.

They began their task by dividing Tibet into different administrative divisions.

The provinces of Amdo and Kham became the administrative provinces of Qinghai[2] and Xikang.

---

[1] By signing the treaties of 1906 and 1907.

[2] Historically Amdo was vaster than the new province of Qinghai. Even today, some parts of Amdo belong to the South of Gansu and the Northwest of Sichuan.

Amdo province was closed in on itself and very few foreigners had been able to visit these remote areas. Kham was relatively more accessible and many missionaries based in Sichuan or Dartsedo,[3] had made regular incursions into the Tibetan province.

The authorities in Lhasa always had difficulty to impose their control on the Khampa population. The sophisticated Lhaseans found the Khampas rather crude, while the Khampas found it hard to respect the officers from Lhasa.

Reading the adventures of George Patterson, a British pastor who lived for a few years with the Pandatsangs, one of the great and powerful families of Kham, is very enlightening. Mutual contempt underlined the relations between the Khampas and Lhasa. In 1950, the same contempt was shown by many of the Khampa chieftains towards Ngabo Ngawang Jigme, the young Governor of Kham.[4] Some people believe that this was one of the factors which helped the Chinese to 'liberate' Tibet smoothly.

Strangely enough, in 1905 when Zhao invaded Kham, Teichman, the British Officer in Sichuan found it a good thing. Kham was finally going to be pacified!

Sensing the weakness of the Tibetan State and London's new policy of appeasing the Chinese and the Russians, 'Butcher' Zhao, as he became known by the Tibetans, advanced into Eastern Tibet.

The French explorer, Jacques Bacot described Zhao differently: "Zhao was a truly terrible man, extraordinarily energetic and hard, he could coldly do things, after reflection, which would surprise us even when we knew that he was a maniac of cruelty."

Meticulously, Zhao began razing monasteries; killing monks and beheading Tibetan officials who were immediately replaced by Chinese officers in his effort to sinicize Kham. Charles Bell wrote: "The memory of Chao Erhfeng's (Zhao Erfeng) ruthless invasion in eastern Tibet, his destruction of the monasteries and killing of monks, has established a memory of bitterness that is still alive in Tibet."[5]

While the Empress in Beijing went on making promises to the Dalai Lama, for the first time the Manchus were departing from their

[3]Or Tachienlu in Chinese, which marked the border between the Tibetan and Chinese areas.

[4]Robert Ford, the Englishman who was responsible for the wireless communications between Chamdo and Lhasa, was himself doubtful of the warrior-like qualities of the Governor.

[5]Bell, *Portrait*, op. cit., p. 398.

role as Protectors of the Land of Snows. What was left of the Choe-yon relationship?

Was that one of the reasons why the Dalai Lama went to Beijing to meet the Emperor and the Empress, in an effort to re-establish the former relationship? Most probably it was.

The skirmishes in Kham at the border of Sichuan were not something new, but they took a turn for the worse with the arrival of Zhao on the scene, coinciding as they did with the decline of imperial power in Beijing.

Traditionally in China, when, at the end of a dynasty, a weak emperor was no longer able to keep his empire together, powerful warlords would emerge on the fringe of the empire to dictate their own laws on behalf of the Emperor.

In 1903, some Tibetans monks in Batang had already revolted against the Manchu troops trying to occupy their monastery, and when the new Deputy Amban travelled through the area and commented on their way of life, he was killed. In reprisal, the Chinese executed more than 300 monks.

In 1905, Zhao visited the same monastery and decided to punish the monks once again; many monks from another monastery in the area who had dared to protest were also executed. In the words of Shakabpa:

> The monks of the neighboring Lithang monastery
> protested against the unfair treatment of the Bah monks,
> who had already been punished. Chao Erh-feng
> summoned the two Tibetan government representatives
> from Lithang and asked them if it was true that the
> Lithang monks were objecting to his methods. When
> the two Tibetans confirmed the report, Chao had them
> executed on the spot...[6]

Tibetans in Chating, another locality in Kham, were very unhappy and just because they had the courage to say so, they also were executed: "When he learned of this, Chao sent his troops to Chating and 1210 monks and laymen were killed." Zhao Erfeng had become 'Butcher' Zhao.

As the Kashag was daily receiving alarming news from Eastern Tibet, it decided to write to the Emperor. It was only after the Amban

⁶Shakabpa, op. cit., p.225.

refused to send the letter to Beijing that they finally understood that it was part of a planned strategy and that the Amban in Lhasa knew about it and was supporting Zhao.

The Tibetan Government had no other option but to send an emissary to Calcutta in order to send the following telegram to Beijing:

> Some of the influential Chinese Ministers in whose hearts the devils dwelt, the Governor-General of Szechuan, and Chao Erh-feng, and the Amban in Tibet, all these having agreed upon an intrigue had played an evil trick like an underground thread.

During all these months the Tibetan government had to be very cautious as the Dalai Lama was still in China and everyone in the Tibetan capital was concerned about his personal well-being.

The Return of the Dalai Lama to Tibet

The Dalai Lama returned to Lhasa in December 1909. The situation was fast deteriorating and although the Tibetan leader managed to reach the Tibetan capital before the Chinese troops did, the Tibetan people were very anxious. When, two months later, the Chinese troops started threatening Lhasa, the Dalai Lama had no choice but to again ask the Nechung Oracle to give him some indications of the path to be followed.

This time Nechung pointed towards the South and India. From there the Dalai Lama could hope to work with the British for Tibet's independence.

Like his successor was to do forty-nine years later, the Tibetan pontiff escaped in the middle of the night to India. Thubten Gyatso was, like Tenzin Gyatso, pursued by Chinese troops. Zhao promised a reward for the head of the Dalai Lama. Everyone in Tibet knew that he got his name 'Butcher' Zhao from his habit of beheading whoever disagreed or stood in his way. The life of the Tibetan leader was indeed seriously threatened at this point.

The history of the defence of Chak-Tsam bridge at the bottom of Khampa-la by a young man of humble origin who was, a few years later, to become the most powerful man in Tibet under the name of Tsarong, is well known. Tsarong with a few of the Dalai Lama's bodyguards managed to defend the bridge for two days and stopped

[7]Quoted by Bell, *Tibet*, op. cit., p. 91.

a large number of well-equipped Chinese troops. Three hundred Chinese soldiers are said to have lost their lives trying to catch up with the Dalai Lama.

Basil Gould, the British Trade Agent in Gyantse, received a wireless message requesting political asylum in India for the Dalai Lama. When the entourage reached Phari, an incident occurred which could have had very grave consequences. The Chinese commander along with twenty-five of his troops met him and asked the Dalai Lama not to proceed to India.

At that point in time, an extraordinary thing happened: the entire population of Chumbi, from Phari to Yatung, came to meet their living god and escorted him as his bodyguards upto the Indian border. The Chinese were 'advised' strongly not to show their faces. Basil Gould who had come from Gyantse also accompanied him.

In Yatung, David McDonald who was to serve as the British Trade Agent between 1905 and1925, officially welcomed him. As the bulk of the Chinese troops were not far away, his earlier plans to negotiate with the Chinese in Gyantse or Yatung in Tibet were abandoned and the Dalai Lama decided to proceed to Kalimpong.

The New Exile

After a week-long reception at Kalimpong, the Dalai Lama left for Darjeeling where he took up permanent residence. He was soon visited by Charles Bell, then Political Officer in Sikkim. A long and enduring friendship started between them; the Dalai Lama was to learn a great deal about the 'modern' world through his new friend.

His life quickly settled to a routine in Darjeeling. He met devotees, gave teachings and initiations and looked after the affairs of the Tibetan State.

> Anyone passing near his house in the morning or evening would hear him chanting his prayers, to the accompaniment of his small hand-drum and bell. And often when he travelled in India he would miss his meals rather than interrupt his meditation. [8]

However, after a few weeks an invitation came from Calcutta. The Viceroy, Lord Minto wanted to meet the Dalai Lama. The Dalai Lama left for Calcutta in March 1910.

[8]Mullin, op. cit., p. 77.

According to Shakabpa, he was received as a head of state and given a seventeen-gun salute (Mullin says twenty-one). He was later escorted in a royal carriage to Hastings House.

The Viceroy held discussions with him, but it was soon obvious to the Dalai Lama that Britain would remain neutral. While providing accommodation and making arrangements for the Dalai Lama's security in India, the British were not ready to antagonize the Chinese or the Russians.

The Chinese were not happy that the Dalai Lama had managed to escape and taken refuge in India. For them, a puppet Dalai Lama that they could control or at least hold as a hostage would have been ideal.[9]

The Dalai Lama nevertheless took the opportunity in his meeting with Lord Minto to clarify his position. One point he made was about the Trade Regulations of 1908 under which the Tibetans could have direct trade relations with the British; he insisted that this at least should be respected. Another of his concerns was the withdrawal of the Chinese troops from Lhasa.

Shakabpa quotes Butler's recollection of the minutes of the meeting with the Viceroy, Lord Minto asked the Dalai Lama the most amazing questions: Did he know the terms of the treaties Great Britain had signed with China and Russia? The Dalai Lama replied that "he was studying them." The minutes of the meeting do not tell us whether the Viceroy was embarrassed to enquire about the Tibetan leader's awareness of the Treaties relating to Tibet which were signed without the knowledge of the Tibetans.

The Dalai Lama nevertheless told the Viceroy that his country did not recognize the Treaties of 1890 and 1906 "in which they had played no part."

The Dalai Lama also informed Lord Minto that he had no communication with Lhasa since his departure and could not envisage going back under the present circumstances. He further explained that he had come with three of his Cabinet Ministers and all his seals, except for the one left with the Regent.

He complained to the Viceroy that all his communications were intercepted since the Chinese had deposed him.

He also took the opportunity to clarify his position vis-à-vis Dorjiev. The Buryat monk was only one of his seven Debate Teachers and his relation with Dorjiev was purely spiritual; in any case, the

[9]They had the same hope for the Fourteenth Incarnation forty years later.

Dalai Lama added, he was back in Russia. We do not know if all this was enough to reassure the British government.

At the end of the meeting, the Dalai Lama reiterated his appeal for help, but the Viceroy very politely replied that he was very happy to "have the opportunity of entertaining His Holiness... he had given instructions that every consideration should be shown to him."

It is doubtful if this was enough for the Dalai Lama who had been expecting the British to stand by the Convention of 1904, but he was slowly learning the hard way about colonial politics. After his contacts with the Mongols in Urga, with the Manchu Court in Beijing and now with the British Crown in Calcutta, he knew that he had no real friends. Here and there he had a lot of devotees and disciples, but all in all, every big nation was basically concerned with preserving its own interests. In the rapidly changing situation, the powerful nations were like the 'big insects' and the smaller ones were there to be eaten.

Was the Dalai Lama himself receiving a teaching on impermanence or the continuous movement of change so dear to the Buddha?

After a few days of sightseeing in Calcutta, he returned to Darjeeling to learn that the situation was fast deteriorating in Lhasa. Some of the ministers had been arrested; the Chinese force had replaced the Tibetan police.

The personal belongings of the Dalai Lama had been confiscated, the treasury of the Government, the Tibetan armoury, the ammunition and mint seized. An ex-Regent who had plotted against the Dalai Lama had even been reinstated and his properties returned.

At the same time a movement of passive resistance had begun in Tibet: instead of paying their taxes to Lhasa, the land owners and rich merchants began sending their revenue directly to Darjeeling. The Chinese felt that they perhaps had been too quick to depose the Dalai Lama. They regretted now not having caught him.

Shamelessly, the Ambans offered the Tibetan leader the restoration of his titles if he returned to Lhasa. The Dalai Lama refused and wrote a long letter to Lo Ti-t'ai, the Amban in Lhasa. In this letter he detailed the sequence of events leading up to his flight to British India. He began the letter saying. "The Tibetan people have never had any evil designs on the Chinese", and then he described his first flight to Mongolia and China, his meeting with the Emperor and the Dowager Empress and their promise to "take care of the welfare of Tibet." On his return to Tibet, he found monasteries destroyed and Chinese troops massing to attack Tibet.

But it was only after infructuous negotiations with the Amban that he concluded that he had no other choice but to go to India.

> Not knowing what would happen if I were captured, I appointed a representative in Lhasa to continue negotiations and I then came to the border of Tibet and India in order to personally conduct negotiations with China.
>
> My ministers had appealed to me to remain in Lhasa; but had I done so, a situation similar to the Muslim invasion of India might well have taken place, which resulted in many religious institutions being destroyed.[10]

His conclusion was clear, the Choe-yon relationship did not exist any more and he could not longer have any confidence in the Chinese:

> I feel there is no further use in my negotiating directly with China. I have lost confidence in China and in finding any solution in consultation with the Chinese.
>
> I have contacted the British, because the 1904 Convention permits us to deal directly with them. The Chinese are responsible for this action of mine.

The Amban had understood too late that the only way to control the Tibetan people was to control their leader. The first step in luring him back to Lhasa was to restore his so-called titles and position and to assure him that everything was fine and peaceful in Tibet. But the Dalai Lama could clearly see through this game.

> You are fully aware of this inexcusable illegal action taken by your troops; yet, you inform me and my ministers that the situation in Tibet is peaceful and that status quo is being maintained. I know that this has been said to persuade me to return and I also know that it is false.

The conclusion was simple, only a tripartite negotiation and agreement could help in finding a durable solution:

> Because of the above, it is not possible for China and Tibet to have the same relationship as before. In order for us to negotiate, a third party is necessary; therefore, we should both request the British government to act as an intermediary. Our future policy will be based on the outcome of discussions between ourselves, the Chinese,

[10]Shakabpa, op. cit., p. 235. Letter from the Dalai Lama to Lo Ti-t'ai.

and the British. Are you able to agree to the participation
of the British in these discussions? If so, please let me
know.

Obviously, the Amban never replied. But the idea of a Tripartite
Convention had been mooted and it would materialize four years
later in Simla.

The Dalai Lama took the opportunity of his self-imposed exile
to visit all the Buddhist holy places in India. He went to Lumbini
where the Buddha was born, to Bodhgaya where he received
enlightenment, to Sarnath where he gave his first sermon and to
Kushinagar where he attained Nirvana. Everywhere he prayed and
meditated. Mullin makes an interesting remark: "His visit and the
re-consecration of these sites was to revive the interest of the many
Himalayan Buddhists in them, giving them a new lease on life."

Mullin adds: "It is interesting to note that the present Dalai Lama
in many ways had continued the work that was then initiated by the
Thirteenth, and that the revival of the Indian Buddhist pilgrimage
places has to a large extent been due to these two incarnations."[11]

In the meantime in Tibet, the Chinese desperately needed public
recognition, so much so, that they tried to pit the Panchen Lama
against the Dalai Lama.

But instead of appeasing the population, this move outraged
the Lhaseans who became particularly furious when the Panchen
Lama moved his residence to the Jokhang and then to the Summer
Palace of the Dalai Lama, the Norbulingka.

During the Butter-Lamp Festival, the Panchen Lama and the
Amban paraded together in the streets of Lhasa in sedan chairs,
visibly trying to copy the Dalai Lama "the Lhasa populace
participated in the ceremony, but only to the extent of dropping
mud and old socks on to the heads of the Panchen Lama and the
Amban".

> The slovenly attired monk
> On the roof of the Jokhang,
> Would have been a thief
> If it were not for the arrival of the Dawn.

'The Dawn' was the name of the Tibetan resistance movement
which mounted pressure against collaboration with the Chinese.
Ultimately the Panchen Lama refused to accept the 'job'. His private
correspondence shows that he still had a lot of respect for the Dalai
Lama.

[11]Mullin, op. cit., pp. 78-79.

In Lhasa, the situation quickly deteriorated and the troops from different regions began to squabble among themselves. The Ambans acted swiftly and had one of the leaders executed. Instead of improving relations, the crisis worsened further.

The situation became really bad for the Chinese soldiers. Apart from the insufficient pay, there were deep divisions between different officers and when the news of the fall of the Manchu dynasty and the revolution of Sun Yat-sen reached Lhasa, many of them deserted and mutinied against the Amban.

The end of the Chinese presence in Tibet came with the news of the death of Zhao Erfeng. After the success of the revolution, he had left Chamdo to take refuge in Sichuan, where he was killed a year later by a revolutionary leader.

Uprisings erupted everywhere in Tibet and the news of the imminent return of the Dalai Lama put fire to the powder. The Dalai Lama himself sent many young officers to organize the resistance and they were successful in defeating the Chinese troops and chasing them out of Tibet.

The return to Free Tibet

In June 1912, the Thirteenth Dalai Lama left Kalimpong for Tibet.

It would take him a few months to reach the capital, but it was the liberated and free capital of a free nation. The Dalai Lama described thus the preceding events in his Last Testament:

> As a result of our past meritorious karma and the numerous prayers and services that were conducted in Tibet, internal strife took place in China. It was no problem, therefore, to completely drive out the Chinese force from Tibet.

After halting a few days in Yatung where the British Trade Agent was staying, he proceeded to Central Tibet. He was escorted by two hundred monks of Sera, Ganden and Drepung Monasteries.

The Dalai Lama did not immediately go to Lhasa. Many Chinese were still staying in the Tibetan capital and though an Agreement had been signed between the Tibetan Cabinet and the Chinese Amban for the repatriation of the Chinese Ambans and their staff and escort via India, some Chinese officials were playing delaying tactics; the expulsion which should have been over in two weeks[12] lasted more than seven months.

[12]According to the Agreement.

The Panchen Lama made an effort to come and receive the Dalai Lama. May be he felt bad; a few months earlier he had been seen to be closely associated with the Chinese Amban. The Lhasa population even thought that he was trying to usurp the Dalai Lama's position.

Once in Tibet, one of the first priorities of the Dalai Lama was to proclaim Tibet's Independence. He had been wandering in Mongolia, China and India with this dream in his mind!

The proclamation was distributed everywhere — to government officials, monks and subjects, all over Tibet. It is dated the eighth day of the first month of the Water-Ox year:[13]

> I am speaking to all classes of Tibetan people.
> ...During the time of Genghis Khan and Altan Khan of the Mongols, the Ming dynasty of the Chinese, and the Qing dynasty of the Manchus, Tibet and China co-operated on the basis of benefactor and priest relationship.

Once again he recalled the sequence of events from the time he went to Beijing, returned to Tibet and fled to British India:

> Having once again achieved for ourselves a period of happiness and peace, I have now allotted to all of you the following duties to be carried out without negligence:
> 1- Peace and happiness in this world can only be maintained by preserving the faith of Buddhism. It is, therefore, essential to preserve all Buddhist institutions in Tibet...
> 2- The various Buddhist sects in Tibet should be kept in a distinct and pure form. Buddhism should be taught, learned, and meditated upon properly. Except for special persons, the administration of monasteries is forbidden to trade, loan money, deal in any kind of livestock, and/or subjugate another's subjects.
> 3- The Tibetan government's civil and military officials, when collecting taxes or dealing with their subject citizens, should carry out their duties with fair and honest judgement so as to benefit the government without hurting the interests of the subject citizens.

Some corporal punishments were banned: the amputation of citizens limbs has been carried out as a form of punishment. Henceforth, such severe punishments are forbidden.

[13]February 1913.

4- Tibet is a country with rich natural resources; but it is
not scientifically advanced like other lands. We are a
small, religious, and independent nation. To keep up
with the rest of the world, we must defend our country..
5- Tibet, although thinly populated, is an extensive
country. Some local officials and landholders are
jealously obstructing other people from developing
vacant lands, even though they are not doing so
themselves. People with such intentions are enemies of
the State and our progress.

From now on, no one is allowed to obstruct anyone else
from cultivating whatever vacant lands are available.

This letter must be posted and proclaimed in every
district of Tibet, and a copy kept in the records of the
offices in every district.

The Dalai Lama from the Potala Palace.[14]

Even today the Tibetans consider this proclamation as the formal
declaration of their independence.

In October 1912, the Government of Tibet sent a letter to the
Viceroy declaring the Tibetan resolve to dissociate entirely from the
Chinese.

The Dalai Lama himself wrote to the Viceroy asking him to send
a British Representative to Lhasa and to help him secure the
withdrawal of all Chinese officials and troops from Tibet; "there
being no hope of continuance of the relationship formerly existing
between Tibet and China."

One of the things, which made the Government of India decide
that the time had come to have a tripartite conference on Tibet, was
this new, assertive role of the Dalai Lama as the political and religious
leader of Tibet.

About one month before the Dalai Lama's proclamation of the
independence of Tibet, a treaty was entered into by Tibet and
Mongolia.

The British certainly knew about the 'declaration of
Independence' proclaimed by the Dalai Lama on his return and the
Treaty signed in Urga with Mongolia. However Charles Bell later
called it the 'alleged treaty'.[15]

---

[14]For text of the Proclamation, see Shakabpa, op. cit., p. 246.
[15]Because the British were not involved.

In *Tibet and its History*, Richardson wrote: "Rumours soon got about that Dorjiev had negotiated a treaty between Mongolia and Tibet. It transpired eventually that although there had been an expression of common policy on account of the strong religious bond between the two countries, there had been nothing which could be described as a binding[16] treaty."

This remark does not explain what constitutes a 'binding' treaty. The large number of treaties related to the status of Tibet signed between 1890 and 1912, can make one doubt the true meaning of a 'binding treaty'.

In fact, the treaties signed during a 'colonial' era are usually binding only on the weak and the colonized parties to the treaty.

In 1913, when Tibet and Mongolia entered into a Treaty, their soil was not occupied by any foreign power and they were two sovereign states merely exercising their fundamental rights to manage their internal and external affairs.

Let us have a look at the Treaty between Tibet and Mongolia signed at Urga in January 1913.

The Preamble said that: "Mongolia and Tibet, having freed themselves from the Manchu dynasty and separated themselves from China, have become independent States, and the two States have always professed one and the same religion, and to the end that their ancient mutual friendships may be strengthened... , have agreed" to sign a Treaty.

In Article 1, the Dalai Lama "approves of and acknowledges the formation of an independent Mongolian State" and the status of the Jetsun Dampa Lama as the sovereign of the land.

In the next Article, the Jetsun Dampa Lama reciprocates and approves the formation of an independent Tibetan State and the proclamation of the Dalai Lama as sovereign of Tibet. This was certainly not binding on the British who preferred to keep the situation vague and thereby all options open.

The Treaty confirmed that both states followed the Buddhist faith and each state promised to protect the other against dangers from without and from within and this for all time.

The following articles dealt with the protection of the citizens of both countries travelling "officially and privately on religious or on State business."

[16]It is not clear how the Treaties signed without the consent or even the knowledge of the Tibetan government, were more 'binding' on Tibet.

Free trade was opened between Tibet and Mongolia with even a special mention of the 'industrial institutions'.

It concluded: "Should it be necessary to supplement the articles of this treaty, the Mongolian and Tibetan Governments shall appoint special Plenipotentiaries, who shall come to an Agreement according to the circumstances then existing."

It was not really correct for Richardson to call it just "an expression of common policy on account of religious bonds."

He also says that the validity of the Agreement was never clearly established.

It is not clear what he means by 'validity'; if he means 'ratified' by London, then in this case, it was certainly not 'valid.' Anyhow, it was clear that for the Government of British India, this Agreement precipitated the urgency of a conference to settle the Tibet issue once and for all.

For the British, war in Europe appeared imminent; they finally had to accept that the Treaties signed with China on Tibet had no relevance, not being implementable in practice. They decided to call all the parties for a tripartite Convention to solve the Tibetan problem and to secure for British India a buffer zone between the British Empire and China and ensure peace and stability in the region.

It was decided that Simla would be the venue of this Conference and Sir Henry McMahon would chair the talks between the Tibetan and the Chinese Representatives.

It was not an easy proposal; for months the Chinese were very reluctant to sit at the negotiating table on an equal footing with the Tibetans.

But diverse factors were putting pressure on the Chinese. They knew that the Dalai Lama was close to the British, especially Charles Bell, after his long stay in Darjeeling. They could fear another Lhasa Convention which perhaps, they would not even be asked to ratify. In Kham, most of the territory which had been taken by Zhao Erfeng had been recovered by the troops sent from Lhasa. The Tibetan army was now better organised and arms and weapons were imported.

After the Dalai Lama's return, the Tibetan army was given three different types of training: one regiment was trained the Japanese way, another by the Russian methods, and a third one by British officers. The result of the experiment was that the Dalai Lama chose the British method and accordingly had begun to have the Tibetan troops trained using this method. This fact worried the Chinese who were also apprehensive of the fact that Mongolia had passed under Russian control.

Would the Tibetans join the British sphere of influence, if they refused to participate in the Conference?

Thus the Chinese felt they had no alternative but to accept the British conditions and to attend the Conference to be held in Simla.

Simla Conference: Sir Henry McMahon is sitting between Lochen Shatra and Ivan Chen. Behind McMahon, stands Charles Bell.

12

The Simla Conference

As it was feared that there might be friction in future unless the boundary between India and Tibet is clearly defined .... I accordingly agree to the boundary as marked in red in the two copies of the maps.
Lochen Shatra to Sir Henri McMahon

The Dalai Lama chose as his representative to the Conference Lonchen Shatra Paljor Dorje, his old and experienced Prime Minister who had dared to suggest negotiations with the Younghusband Mission. His assistant was Trimon, who had prepared detailed documentation on the legal status of Tibet, especially on the eastern border areas. It was in fact one of the great surprises of the conference that the Tibetans had come so well prepared with volumes and volumes of original documents,[1] while the Chinese had no documents to prove their allegations.

The British Plenipotentiary, Sir Henry McMahon[2] was assisted by Charles Bell, the Dalai Lama's old acquaintance from his Darjeeling days.

The brief given to Lonchen Shatra by the Dalai Lama was very clear:

1- Tibet was to manage its own internal affairs;
2- her foreign affairs were to be managed for important matters in consultation with the British;
3- no Chinese Amban or official should be posted in Tibet;
4- Tibetan territory should include all the Tibetan-speaking areas up to Dartsedo in the east and Kokonor in the north-east.

[1] All the documents were to be seen and signed by Sir Henry McMahon, the president of the Conference.
[2] McMahon left his name on the all too famous line demarcating the border between Tibet and India.

The first day of the Conference was spent presenting and verifying the credentials of the plenipotentiaries. The next day each party began to put forward its points. It became clear immediately that the positions of the Tibetan and Chinese delegates were diametrically opposite.

In his presentation, Lonchen Shatra reiterated the points insisted on by the Dalai Lama and asked for recognition of the independence of Tibet. He also wanted the Dalai Lama to be acknowledged as the political and spiritual leader of Tibet. He claimed that the Tibetan territory should include within it all the Tibetan-speaking areas of Kham and Amdo. Lonchen Shatra also requested that the Conference declare the Conventions of 1906 and 1908 invalid, as Tibet had not been a party to them. An indemnity from the Chinese was claimed for the damage and destruction in Lhasa and in Kham following Zhao Erfeng's invasion.

The Chinese stand was very different. Ivan Chen, the Chinese plenipotentiary claimed Tibet as a part of China. He explained that due to the conquest of Genghis Khan, Tibet had become a part of the Chinese Empire. This was further confirmed when the Fifth Dalai Lama accepted some titles from the Chinese Emperor.

Another argument was that the Tibetans had called upon the Manchus for military assistance many times and each time the Emperor had come to provide support. He gave the examples of the Dzunkar and Gorkha invasions.

Regarding Zhao Erfeng, Ivan Chen explained that his government had only acted in accordance with the Treaty of 1908 and his troops were sent to protect the Trade Marts. Another 'proof' advanced by the Chinese Plenipotentiary to show that Tibet was part of China, was that the compensation to be paid under the Convention of 1904 had been paid by China on behalf of the Tibetan Government.

He further claimed that the Amban had the right to have an escort of 2,600 men to control the internal and foreign affairs of Tibet. He requested that a thousand men be stationed in Lhasa and the rest in other places to be decided by the Ambans.

For the Chinese, the status of Tibet had to be restored as per the 1906 Agreement and the border between China and Tibet was to be in Gyamda, some 150 miles east of Lhasa.

The Tibetan delegate managed to counter the Chinese point by point, especially on the problem of demarcation of the territory, by tabling all sorts of revenue documents.

Regarding the payment of compensation for the Younghusband expedition, the Tibetans declared that they had never asked the Chinese to pay the amount of 25 lakhs of rupees to the British and that they were not even aware of the payment.

The British Plenipotentiary was caught between two opposing viewpoints, and on behalf of His Majesty's government, he had to harmonize the two sides.

In the pure British tradition of being 'fair to both parties', he found a way out by dividing Tibet with consequences which can still be felt today.[3] McMahon thought that he could impose on both parties a 'fair deal' which would also have advantages for Great Britain. Tibet would be divided into two parts:

1- 'Outer Tibet' which corresponded roughly to Central and Western Tibet including the sections skirting the Indian frontier, Lhasa, Shigatse, Chamdo; and

2- 'Inner Tibet' including Amdo Province and part of Kham.

The arrangement was as follows: 'Outer Tibet'[4] was to be recognised as autonomous. China would not interfere in the administration of Outer Tibet, nor with the selection of the Dalai Lama. No troops or Ambans would be stationed there. It would not be converted into a Chinese Province. Maps were also prepared showing the boundaries of Inner and Outer Tibet. In the interest of settling the dispute, Lonchen Shatra reluctantly agreed to McMahon's proposal. This was in February 1914.

But then the Chinese delegate started delaying tactics. This gave the opportunity and the time to the Tibetan and the British delegates to discuss their own borders. The object of the talks was the Northeastern areas, between what the British called the North East Frontier Agency[5] and Tibet, from Bhutan upto the trijunction of India, Burma and Tibet.

It should be noted that Sir Henry McMahon and Lonchen Shatra had separate negotiations on this long shared boundary. Contrary to the view prevailing in India today, the Chinese were not invited

[3]It has to be noted that the major stumbling block in the negotiations between the Dalai Lama's administration and the Chinese government was the definition of Tibet's territory. The Chinese only wanted to negotiate for only the Tibet Autonomous Region (TAR), which corresponded roughly to McMahon's 'Outer Tibet'.

[4]What today corresponds more or less to the Tibetan Autonomous Region.

[5]Afterwards, referred as NEFA.

to discuss the question of the border between India and Tibet and their acceptance of the McMahon Line was never sought; nor did they ask anything about the final demarcation.

Exchange of Notes on the Indo-Tibetan Border

Through an exchange of notes between the British and Tibetan Plenipotentiaries, the Indo-Tibet Frontier was fixed in 1914. It is worthwhile to quote these letters that would have important consequences for the future of both nations, especially India which, 48 years later, would fight a war along this Line.

In the first letter dated 24 March 1914, McMahon wrote:

To Lonchen Shatra, Tibetan Plenipotentiary,

In February last you accepted the India-Tibet frontier from the Isu Razi Pass to the Bhutan frontier, as given in the map (two sheets), of which two copies are herewith attached, subject to the confirmation of your government and the following conditions:

(a)   The Tibetan ownership in private estates on the British side of the frontier will not be disturbed.

(b)   The sacred places of Tso Karpo and Tsari Sarpa fall within a day's march of the British side of the frontier, they will be included in Tibetan territory and the frontier modified accordingly.

I understand that your Government has now agreed to this frontier subject to the above two conditions. I shall be glad to learn definitely from you that this is the case. You wished to know whether certain dues now collected by the Tibetan Government at Tsona Jong and in Kongbu and Kham from the Monpas and Lopas for articles sold may still be collected. Mr. Bell has informed you that such details will be settled in a friendly spirit, when you have furnished him the further information, which you have promised.

The final settlement of this India-Tibet frontier will help to prevent causes of future dispute and thus cannot fail to be of great advantage to both Governments.[6]

On March 25, Lonchen Shatra officially replied:

As it was feared that there might be friction in future unless the boundary between India and Tibet is clearly

[6]Shakabpa, op. cit., pp. 256-257.

defined, I submitted the map, which you sent to me in February last, to the Tibetan Government at Lhasa for orders. I have now received orders from Lhasa, and I accordingly agree to the boundary as marked in red in the two copies of the maps signed by you subject to the condition mentioned in your letter, dated 14th March, sent to me through Mr. Bell. I have signed and sealed the two copies of the maps.

Thus the McMahon Line was born in the form of a fat red line on a map showing the Indo-Tibetan boundary in the Eastern sector. The British and the Tibetan delegates signed and sealed the map.

We have to remember that during the negotiations, Tibet and China were more or less at war in Eastern Tibet (Kham) and in spite of a cease fire, the situation was very tense on the border.

The Convention was finally initialled on 27 April 1914.[7]

China pledged not to convert Tibet into a Chinese province, while Great Britain was not to annex any portion of the country.

Hugh Richardson, the last British Representative in Lhasa, summed up the problem: "It was to ensure the reality of Tibetan autonomy but still to leave the Chinese with a position of sufficient dignity."

Convention between Great Britain, China and Tibet

We shall go through some of the Articles of the Simla Convention and study their consequences they had for relations among the three nations.

In Article 2, the contracting parties recognised 'the autonomy of Outer Tibet' and engaged "to respect the territorial integrity of the country, and to abstain from interference in the administration of Outer Tibet (including the selection and installation of the Dalai Lama), which shall remain in the hands of the Tibetan Government at Lhasa."[8]

More importantly for the Tibetans: "The Government of China engages not to convert Tibet into a Chinese province, "while the British Government engaged not to annex Tibet or any part of her [its] territory.

The following Article would have very serious political repercussions when in 1947, the Government of newly independent

[7]See maps on the end pages.
[8]For text of Convention, see Richardson, op. cit. p. 283.

India would take over the mantle from the British. It recognized "the special interest of Great Britain, in virtue of the geographical position of Tibet, in the existence of an effective Tibetan Government, and in the maintenance of peace and order in the neighbourhood of the frontiers of India adjoining States."

This argument would be used in 1950 and again in 1959, 1961 and 1965, when the Tibetan issue came up for discussion in the United Nations. It can also be found repeatedly in the correspondence of the US, British and Indian Governments during 1949-51. Not only did the Government of India step into Britain's shoes in 1947, but it also felt that due to the geographical proximity, the Indian Government naturally had a 'special interest' in Tibet and should give a lead in any policy concerning it. This explains why most of the time during that period, Western governments chose to align themselves with India's position.

In the next Article, the Government of China engaged not to send troops into Outer Tibet, not to station civilian or military officers, nor to establish Chinese colonies on the Roof of the World as well as to withdraw any troops posted in Tibet. The British also agreed not to station military or civil officers in Tibet (except as escorts at the Trade Marts).

However, a high Chinese official was allowed to be posted in Lhasa with a maximum of 300 men. Though he was not called 'Amban', the large escort was intended as a sort of balance to the presence of the British troops stationed at the Marts.

Article 5 had important consequences because the Governments of both China and Tibet agreed that "they will not enter into any negotiations or agreements regarding Tibet with one another, or with any other Power" except with the British Government.

It meant in particular that in 1950, the Government of India which had ratified this treaty with the Tibetan Government could have insisted on having tripartite negotiations, but Nehru felt at that time that the Simla Convention was just an imperialist treaty and should be rejected.[9]

The use of the term 'Foreign Power' to describe China in the 1904 Convention was cancelled. The Tibet Trade Regulations of 1893 and 1908 were also cancelled and the Tibetan Government and the British agreed to negotiate new Trade Regulations for Outer Tibet.

---

[9]Though he believed in the validity of the McMahon Line.

The British Agent in Gyantse was allowed to visit Lhasa with his escort whenever "it has been found impossible to settle" matters from Gyantse. Though the Tibetans had insisted that a British Representative should be posted in Lhasa to counterbalance the presence of the Chinese official, the British were reluctant in view of the Anglo-Russian Convention of 1907. Richardson found the British view "over–scrupulous in view of the Russian advances then taking place in Mongolia."

The borders of Tibet, and the boundary between Outer and Inner Tibet, were drawn on maps attached to the Convention. These thick red and blue lines would later become the object of the 1962 Sino-Indian conflict, though at the time of the Convention the chief preoccupation was the borders between China and Tibet.

The Chinese did not want to accept the new demarcation line between Inner and Outer Tibet and between Inner Tibet and China. After the conquests of Zhao Erfeng, China was not keen to surrender the newly-acquired territories and the Tibetans were more than reluctant to let go of any territories inhabited by Tibetans, especially in areas where Tibetan monasteries were commanding great authority and revenue.

It was the thorniest point of the negotiations and eventually became the pretext for their breakdown. In these areas, the power to select and appoint Lamas and 'high priests of monasteries' and to retain full control of all religious matters remained with Lhasa.

Richardson thus summarized the consequences of the Convention: "In effect, there would have emerged two regions with differing status. Outer Tibet would have been like a self-governing dominion of China, while Inner Tibet would have been the subject of peaceful contention in which the better or more attractive administration could be expected to win."[10]

Although in April Ivan Chen initialled the draft Convention, he received an order from his government not to sign the final Convention. The British were losing their legendary patience: "As it is, the patience of His Majesty's government is exhausted and they have no alternative but to inform the Chinese Government that, unless the Convention is signed before the end of this month, His Majesty's Government will hold themselves free to sign separately with Tibet". Finally, on July 3, 1914, Great Britain and Tibet signed the Simla Convention.

[10]Richardson, op cit., p. 111.

On the withdrawal of the Chinese, a Declaration was signed by the plenipotentiaries of Britain and Tibet declaring that the Convention was to be binding on the Governments of Britain and Tibet and agreeing that so long as the Chinese Government withheld its signature, it would be debarred from the enjoyment of privileges accruing thereunder.

The following para was included: "The powers granted to China under the Convention shall not be recognized by Great Britain and Tibet until and unless the Government of China ratifies the Convention."

Apart from the main Convention, Notes were exchanged, but in view of the Chinese refusal to sign and ratify the Convention, they did not carry much weight. We shall return to these Notes later.

Apart from the diametrically opposed stands of their respective Governments, the delegates seemed to have enjoyed Simla. Bell wrote that even Ivan Chen remained "on terms of personal friendship with us all." He described him as someone with a charming personality. Despite his arguing for his government, he remained 'courteous and honourable'.

A vivid description of Lonchen Shatra is also given by Bell; he "had but seldom left his native land. Yet he showed a knowledge of men and a grasp of political affairs that came as a surprise to many at the Conference. His simple dignity and his charm of manner endeared him to all."[11]

After the Conference, Bell took Shatra and his party for a tour of different places in India and he noticed that the Tibetan Prime Minister greatly enjoyed visiting factories and industrial establishments. When Lonchen Shatra visited the Fort at Delhi he was 'solidly bored', said Bell, but a good zoo always pleased him.

The law of impermanence, however, was knocking at Europe's door. On August 4th 1914, just one month after the signature of the Convention, Great Britain entered the First World War. This perhaps explained the lost patience of Her Majesty's Government and what Richardson called the "disinclination to assume additional responsibilities." London now had to concentrate its efforts on the European front.

Following his stay in India, the Thirteenth Dalai Lama had understood the importance of keeping good contacts in British India,

11Bell, *Tibet:* op. cit., p. 158.

and his friendship with Sir Charles Bell was one of the important factors contributing to the stability of the region.

A few days after the beginning of the War, the Tibetan Prime Minister wrote to Basil Gould, the Political Officer in Sikkim: "Although the Chinese are waging a rigorous war against us in different parts of Kham, Tibet is willing to send one thousand troops to India, to support your Empire, because we realize that the existence of Tibet depends on the continuance of Great Britain's Empire."[12]

The British Political Officer replied that his Government was "deeply touched and grateful to His Holiness" and he assured the Dalai Lama that they "will seek the support of Tibet whenever the need arises". In fact, the troops were kept in readiness until the end of the war.

Conclusion

By not signing the Convention, the Chinese were not only deprived of the benefits of the Convention but also of the Notes exchanged between the signatories. It is in these Notes that the Tibetans made some major compromises, particularly the one that says that 'Tibet forms part of Chinese territory'.

The other benefits that the Chinese lost were the recognition of Chinese suzerainty over Tibet; the right of sending a Representative to Lhasa with 300 troops; the admission that China was not a 'foreign power' for the purpose of the 1904 Convention; and involvement in the selection and appointment of the Dalai Lamas.

The new Anglo-Tibetan Trade Regulations were also signed on the 3rd July 1914. As explained in Article 7 of the main Convention, these were to replace the Regulations of 1893 and 1908 which stood cancelled by this article.

The new Regulations gave tremendous advantages to the British who suddenly became the main and only player in Tibet.

Fights in Kham

The British were now fully involved in World War I and their preoccupations were far removed from the small territorial disputes in central Asia.

We have just seen that by the end of the Conference in Simla, London had managed to fix its Indian border with Tibet, but the

[12]Shakabpa, op. cit., p. 257.

border between China and Tibet remained under dispute. The cease-fire agreed upon during the Convention did not last long.

We should recall that during the Conference, the Dalai Lama had asked that all the culturally and linguistically Tibetan areas, east of the Yangtse upto Dartsedo in the West and Sining in the North-east, be recognized as a part of Tibet. But in September 1914, the Chinese were still in occupation of a lot of these territories.

The Tibetan Kashag decided to remedy this fact and deputed the Kalon Lama[13] called Kalon Chamba Tendar, as the Governor of Eastern Tibet, with the task to take back the territories captured by Zhao Erfeng. Seven Tibetan Generals[14] accompanied the Kalon to Lhodzong where a temporary headquarters was established.

After fierce and prolonged battles, the Tibetans slowly regained their territory. Weakened by the fall of the Manchus and the internal strife which followed the Nationalist revolution, the Chinese retreated and then surrendered.

Finally Chamdo, the Chinese headquarters in Kham, fell to the Tibetans with the active support of the local population.

It was decided to repatriate the captured Chinese troops. The Tibetans considered that it was safer to send them back through India rather than through Sichuan, where the Chinese could easily have been able to regroup.[15]

It was nevertheless not an easy victory for the Tibetans, the death toll was very heavy and three of their best generals lost their lives in battle. In many areas local Khampa troops fought behind the battle lines to free the border areas of the Chinese presence, but due to their poor equipment and the lack of co-ordination between the different chieftains, a large number of these men lost their lives.

In the meantime the Kalon Lama had established the headquarters of the Governor General of Kham in Chamdo. He took the opportunity to reorganize the newly recovered areas, appoint new district officers, and reinforce his troops. After some time, he was once again in a position to send his troops to assist the Khampa leaders of Derge, Markhan, Drayak and Gojo.

[13]The Monk Minister.
[14]Tib. Dapons
[15]Some other Chinese troops settled near the Indian border since they did not have the means, or perhaps the will, to go back to China. Their descendants were still living in Yatung or Kalimpong a few years back.

Tibetans troops eventually reached Yunnan province of China in the South-east and as they were advancing on Dartsedo, their ultimate destination, the Chinese panicked and appealed to the British to mediate.

All this time, the British were much bothered; their main concern was the Tibetan-Indian border.[16] Sir Henry McMahon had not invested much effort in the disputed border between Inner Tibet and China. It was too far away and of too little use for Britain's strategic interests.

It is perhaps only the possibility of a direct treaty between Tibet and China on the eastern border of the Tibet, which woke up the British Representative in China to the reality that the Simla Convention had not really solved the problem of status of Tibet and the demarcation of its border with China.

Teichman, a trouble-shooter working for the Consular Service of the British Government, was sent to sort out the differences between the Tibetans and Chinese and stop the bloody war between the neighbours. Could he find a more permanent truce?

A solution was arrived at in August 1918, and an "Agreement for the Restoration of Peaceful Relations and the Delimitation of a Provisional Frontier Between China And Tibet" was signed by Teichman with Kalon Chamba Tendar and the Chinese General Liu Tsan-ting.

It has to be noted, that once again, as four years earlier in Simla, the tripartite conference was an equal footing; the difference was that the British were merely acting as mediators, their own border not being in question.

However, as clearly stated in the final agreement which was expected to be signed at a later date by the three governments: "This agreement is of a temporary nature and shall only remain in force until such time as the Governments of China, Tibet, and Great Britain shall have arrived at a final and permanent tripartite settlement."

The following articles described mainly the demarcation of the border between China and Tibet. The Yangtse would temporarily be the border between the two countries with the condition that "all the monasteries in the above-mentioned Chinese governed districts,[17] as well as the right of appointing high Lamas and other monastic

---

[16]Which had by now become the McMahon Line.
[17]East of the Yangtse river.

functionaries, and the control of all matters appertaining to the Buddhist religion, shall be in the hands of the Dalai Lama."[18]

The Chinese promised not to interfere in the religious matters in the 'Tibetan' areas. Both parties engaged to check the brigandage, 'evil-doers' and raids across the border. It was further agreed to exchange prisoners "when the Governments of China and Tibet shall have formally accepted this agreement."

Finally the British Consul was chosen to be the final arbitrator in case of disputes: "There shall be no recourse to arms; but both sides agree to refer the matter in dispute to the British Consul for his arbitration". The Chinese and Tibetan authorities promised to help the British Consul to discharge his function and render him all possible assistance in visiting the border posts.

It was to be the last agreement signed by Tibet as an independent nation with the Chinese. The next accord, in 1951, would be the 17-Point Agreement, which witnessed Tibet surrendering its independent status under duress.

"It is clear from the wording of those agreements, and the events which led up to them, that Tibet was a power not to be ignored," wrote Shakabpa.

From the time the Thirteenth Dalai Lama had come back from India and assumed political power till his death in 1933, Tibet remained for all purposes an independent country. Chinese nationals were not even allowed to reside in what the British had called 'Outer Tibet'.

In spite of all the efforts of the new leaders of Chinese Republic to reopen contacts with the Dalai Lama, Tibet remained secluded and did not accept anything from China during the following years.

When the Abbot of the Tibetan monastery of Yungun in Beijing came to Lhasa bringing a letter from Chiang Kai-shek, in which the Chinese President offered all support to the Tibetans if the Dalai Lama would accept to be part of China. Chiang even offered to 'return' the Panchen Lama who was still in China after his flight from Tashi Lhunpo in 1923.

In his reply the Dalai Lama said that he was happy to have cordial relations with China, but he rejected the suggestion that Tibet should be a part of China.

[18]Quoted in van Walt, op. cit., p. 330. Original document from the India Office Record (L/P&S/10/714).

Another letter from Chiang Kai-shek came three years later with a Miss Liu, half Tibetan on her mother's side, but the Tibetan government stubbornly refused to follow up on the Chinese President's proposals

The Southern Border

On the southern side, relations with the British Empire had been cordial but many in Lhasa had began to doubt the power of the British to bring the Chinese back to the negotiating table and get them to sign the Simla Convention.

Were the British only interested in securing their border? Or were they also able to be an effective protector?

It was in this context that London decided to send Charles Bell, McMahon's assistant at the Simla Convention, to Lhasa, to have a frank discussion with the Tibetan leaders. It has to be noted that for once it was London which took the initiative and it was the Viceroys' Office which was shy of extending more help and giving more recognition to Tibet.

One of the considerations might have been that after the Russian Revolution, the Anglo-Russian Agreement had been declared null and void and the danger from that quarter had faded away.

Charles Bell remained in Lhasa for one year and through his many meetings with his friend, the Thirteenth Dalai Lama, he was able to give London a clear picture of the political situation on the Roof of the World. As a result of Bell's visit, the British Government decided to help the Tibetan Government in its development and also to supply a reasonable quantity of arms and ammunitions for its self-defence.

Other projects were also undertaken, such as a telegraph line from Gyantse to Lhasa, a geological survey of Central Tibet, a small hydro-electric plant at Lhasa and the reorganization of the Police.

But the most important aspect for Tibet's security was the training of officers and men by British instructors in Gyantse and in India.

On the diplomatic front, no positive development occurred as "disunity in China, the low prestige of the Central [Chinese] Government and the prevalence of a chauvinistic spirit made progress impossible" wrote Richardson.

On the eastern front, war broke out again in 1931. The pretext was a dispute between the Targye and Beri monasteries of Kham.

The Chinese warlord of Sichuan, Liu Wen-hui, supported Beri unlike Tibetans, especially from areas around Derge who gave their support to the Targye Monastery.

Initially, the Chinese were driven away and when they asked for a cease-fire, the Tibetans refused; so sure were they that this time they would make it to Dartsedo. In the meantime, the Chinese warlord managed to regroup his forces and counter-attacked.

Though the Dalai Lama was keen to reach an agreement through British mediation, it could not be worked out. One of the main reasons for this was that the Nationalist regime in Nanjing did not have much control over their warlords who were functioning *de facto* as small kings, ruling their territories without reference to the central government in Nanking or Beijing.

With the arrival of the new Governor-General of Kham, Kalon Ngabo, and in spite of further reinforcements from Lhasa, the Tibetan troops were pushed back to the other side of the Yangste river.

At one point the local Tibetan chieftains and the Chinese commander signed a cease-fire but when Lhasa heard this, the Tibetan leaders were demoted by the Dalai Lama. Soon after, another front was opened by Ma Pu-Fang, the Muslim warlord of Sining, who began to bring terror to the monasteries of the Amdo region.

A small army was dispatched from Kham but was soon very badly defeated by Ma's troops and the two Rupons (Colonels) were captured along with a large number of troops and their arms and ammunitions. The remaining Tibetan force had no other option but to return to Chamdo. Once again the Tibetans appealed to the British through the Political Officer in Sikkim. But nobody, not even Chiang Kai-shek, could do anything against the warlord who was his own master in what had become Qinghai province.

The Chinese President was, however, very eager to see Tibet and Mongolia 'return to the fold' of the Chinese empire. This was the main reason behind the creation in 1928 of a Mongolian and Tibetan Commission under the Executive Yuan. In the beginning, it was merely to improve the administration of these 'provinces'; however years later, it would be used as a proof that Tibet and Mongolia had always been part of China.

An allegation does not always prove what it alleges, but by constantly alleging, the Chinese believe that allegations can become reality.

We shall see in the next chapter that the Panchen Lama had left Tibet in the early twenties and taken refuge in China. He was fully used by the Nationalist government.

The following remark of the Chinese historian Tieh-Tseng-Li shows how dangerous for the unity and integrity of Tibet was the presence of the Panchen Lama in China:

> ...in 1928, a year after the establishment of the Nationalist Government in Nanjing, the Panchen sent delegates to express his respects to the new regime, and at the same time put forward a request that the Chinese Government assume full charge of affairs in Tibet in order to save it to become a second India."[19]

In 1928, emboldened by the presence of the Tibetan Lama, the Chinese government decided to form the new province of Sikang which included large parts of Kham, and of Qinghai with large parts of Amdo. These were officially declared provinces of China, even though the Chinese government could not immediately assume administrative power due to the rivalries between different warlords of Sichuan and Qinghai areas.

The damage was nevertheless done and the partition eventually became a permanent administrative division of the Tibetan territory in 1965. The Chinese have always been masters at creating divisions which might have no reality today but which could be used tomorrow for the benefit of the Chinese empire.

Although the British position was more clear, as we can see from Lord Curzon's declaration in 1921: "We should regard ourselves at liberty to deal with Tibet, if necessary without referring to China; to enter into closer relation with the Tibetans ...to give the Tibetans any reasonable assistance they might require in the development and protection of the country", the Tibetan issue remained unresolved and the situation on the eastern front was very unstable.

---

[19]Li, Tieh-tseng, *Tibet: Today and Yesterday* (New York: Bookman Associates, 1960), p. 150.

13

The Independent Years

If the Thirteenth's attempt to introduce modern education into Tibet had not met such intense resistance by traditionalists, our history may have taken quite a different turn.

The Fourteenth Dalai Lama

Thubten Gyatso, the Thirteenth Dalai Lama

The personage who played a major role in shaping modern Tibet is Thubten Gyatso, the Thirteenth Dalai Lama. He was in many ways a remarkably liberal and progressive leader. Had his advice and warning been followed, many things would have been different.

A few examples will demonstrate his effort to push his nation on the road to the modern world. On his return from exile in India, he officially declared Tibet's independence. He took the revolutionary initiative of sending a group of young Tibetans to England to study new technologies which could be useful to his country. He recruited and trained an army to defend its borders and maintain Tibet's independence. He reformed the monastic discipline. He saw the great importance for the Roof of the World to have a balance in relations with the Great Powers[1] in its neighbourhood. During the First World War, he offered his support to the Allies. He was even interested to join the League of Nations and took some steps in this direction through his friend, Sir Charles Bell.

Unfortunately for Tibet, he had to struggle against the power of the big monasteries, which were opposed to any opening to the outside world, fearing that their religion would lose its purity. He also had to cope with the intrigues of the aristocracy as well as the imperialist designs of the British and Chinese.

[1]Mainly British India, China, Russia and Mongolia.

In the midst of powerful neighbours and the resistance to progress within Tibet, Thubten Gyatso tried his best to bring Tibet into the twentieth century without losing its own identity.

A Policy of Isolation

The Thirteenth Dalai Lama had tried to break this isolation by sending some Tibetan youth to England; his idea was to have Tibetans regularly studying outside. But the big monasteries were not able to understand his vision and the experiment was stopped. Insularity was certainly the greatest 'mistake' committed by the Government of Tibet in the early part of this century.

But the Tibet of the Thirteenth Dalai Lama had other weaknesses too. Though the 'rule by incarnation' could be seen from many points of view as an ideal system of governance, it had one serious inconvenience. During the interregnum between the death of a Dalai Lama and the attainment of majority by the newly reincarnated Dalai Lama, there was a political vacuum lasting fifteen to twenty years.

The Regents of Tibet have not always been up to the mark and more often than not they were not prepared to look after the affairs of State. The Chinese, through their Ambans or Representatives, made use of this weakness in the system. It was rumoured that the premature deaths of the Ninth and up to the Twelfth Dalai Lamas were not a mere coincidence and the Chinese Ambans certainly took full advantage of their departure.

If one is to analyse the history of modern Tibet and the tragic events of the 1950s, one has to look at the divisions within the Tibetan society. We have just mentioned the intrigues between aristocrats and the negative role of the big monasteries, but we shall go into more detail about the split between the Thirteenth Dalai Lama and the Ninth Panchen Lama, and the dramatic consequences which resulted from their differences.

The antagonism between the Lhasa administration and the chieftains of Kham and Amdo and the confrontation between the leaders of these different provinces worked against the possibility for unity.

After the passing away of the Thirteenth Dalai Lama, disputes and dissension erupted between different factions of the Government and the great monasteries, and the struggle degenerated into a sad dispute between the last two Regents of Tibet, Reting and Taktra.

One of the problems of the old society was that it had difficulty reconciling contradictions. It was not only the Dalai Lama or Tsarong Shape who faced opposition, but also all those who dared to think or act differently. One well-known case is that of the great scholar from Amdo, Gedun Choepell, who was persecuted because he was too far ahead of his time.

The Testament: Night Shall Be Long and Dark

In 1932, one year before he died, the Dalai Lama warned the people of Tibet against certain ills in the Tibetan society.

A few months earlier the Dalai Lama had expressed the wish to withdraw from public life: "I am now of advanced age and it is time I relinquished secular and spiritual duties so that I can start earning merit and concentrate on religious studies, keeping well in mind the future which is what really matters".

After the Government and the people of Tibet had pleaded with him to continue guiding them, he agreed to continue, but he exhorted his people to work hard for the welfare of Tibet, he wrote in his Last Testament:

> Now, when there is peace and happiness, when you have the power, work earnestly and wholeheartedly for the general welfare. Use peaceful methods where peace is due, use force where force is necessary: work and persevere now, that there is no regret later.
>
> In your hands, officials of the Government, holders of the Teachings and my people, lies the future of the country. Without employing wrong and base methods, rise up together and work for the general good of the land...

The Dalai Lama had particularly advised: "Maintain friendly relations with the two great powers, China and India, conscript able soldiers to guard the borders and make them sufficiently strong to ward off those countries with whom we have had border disputes..."

The Dalai Lama had met different people from Mongolia, Russia, England and China. He was fully informed of the world situation; he was aware that the world was changing, he had foreseen the turmoil into which the world would soon be plunged. There was an acceleration in the social evolution, revolutions were erupting everywhere and he knew it. One of his main concerns was to have a strong and self-reliant Tibet and for this a modern and well-trained army was a necessity. It has to be noted that he advised his people to "use force where force is necessary".

Even as a Buddhist teacher, the Dalai Lama never felt that 'strength' or 'self-defence' was against the principles taught by the Buddha. But the big monasteries did not think like he did and most of the problems[2] he faced bore some relation to the recruiting and training of this national army.

At the end of his Testament, he warned his people of the forthcoming 'dark days':

> In my lifetime conditions will be as they are now, peaceful and quiet. But the future holds darkness and misery. I have warned you of these things because of my experience and other important reasons...
>
> The institutions of the Dalai Lama, venerable incarnates and those who protect the Teachings shall be wiped out completely. Monasteries shall be looted, properties shall be confiscated and all living beings shall be destroyed. The memorable rule of the Three Guardian Kings of Tibet, the very institutions of the State and religion shall be banned and forgotten. The properties of the officials shall be confiscated; they shall be slaves of the conquerors and shall roam the land in bondage. All souls shall be immersed in suffering and the night shall be long and dark....

If one looks at history with Tibetan (or Buddhist) eyes, especially at relations among India, China and Tibet, all historical events are consequences of currents, or sometimes undercurrents, which have a much deeper significance.

History is like an iceberg and we are aware only of the most superficial parts; they represent certain 'world movements' that go by the name of 'historical events'.

It is true that in the old Tibetan society, at least at the beginning of this century, Tibetans enjoyed life. Especially the aristocracy had a life of pleasure and enjoyment, what could be called a life of 'silk brocades and picnics'.

It is enough to read the books of the first explorers upto the time of the arrival of the Chinese in the nineteen fifties, to understand that Old Tibet was a very harmonious and protected world living in

---

[2]The dispute with the Panchen Lama; the removal of Tsarong as Commander-in-Chief; the intrigues between his attendants and favourites, etc.

another time and space. The conclusions of the westerners, like Harrer or Ford who were the last to experience the Old Tibet, are similar and unanimous: every one enjoyed life on the Roof of the World.

Certainly there was a lot of difference between the living conditions of the aristocracy (lay and monastic) and the working class. The Dalai Lama and some other leaders were aware of these differences and wanted to reduce them, but everyone including the poor was happy, everyone had enough to eat, life was peaceful and harmonious, in spite of the hardship of daily life. It is perhaps this image of peace and harmony which gave rise to a perception of the mythical world, that caught the imagination of the West.

This incredible harmony was not restricted to the people in the different strata of society; there was also a harmony with nature and even with the gods. Tibet was Shangri-La, paradise on earth, and the fact that Tibet was closed to the outside word helped to contribute to the mystique and magic of the Land of Snows.

This is most probably what the Thirteenth Dalai Lama saw: his people living such a contented life that they forgot to think about the future. They refused to accept that the earth was a sphere[3] and that the world around them was changing at a quick pace. They did not accept the changes brought about by the industrial and democratic revolutions and the anti-colonial movements which were transforming the face of the planet.

The Thirteenth Dalai Lama had also seen the Red wave on the horizon. He had heard about it in Mongolia and Russia and was aware of what was happening there in the name of a new religion founded by a certain Karl Marx.

This religion was more sectarian that any other in the past. For these new high priests[4], all other religions were considered to be poisonous and the new missionaries of the Communist dogma had a clear aim: to spread their credo over the entire world. The new 'religion' had no morals; it could kill thousands or millions of people[5]

[3]The scholar, Gedun Choepell once became angry with his Guru, the famous Geshe Sherab Gyatso who argued with him that the earth was flat. Interestingly, it was Sherab Gyatso who 'invited' the Chinese to enter Amdo province in September 1949.

[4]Such as Stalin or Mao Zedong.

[5]As during the great famine or in the Gulag in Russia or during the Great Leap Forward or the Great Proletarian Cultural Revolution in China.

in the name of the 'People' and do this without re morse. To make things worse, it represented only one class of the people, the proletariat or working class; all other sections of society had to be subdued by force.

In his vision and wisdom, the Thirteenth Dalai Lama prophesied the Red wave invading Asia and steamrolling Tibet. Could Tibet awaken before it was too late? But who wants to wake up from a dream where everything is heavenly and tranquil?

The Thirteenth Dalai Lama passed away in 1933 and returned two years later in a new body; life kept flowing at the same rhythm; nothing could move the Roof of the World until, one day in 1950, on the 15th of August to be exact, the most incredible earthquake[6] shook Tibet.

At the political level, Tibet had no friends left by that time. The British had left India and were only remotely interested in what happened on the Roof of the World; after all, they no longer had any common border with Tibet.

Their successor, the Government of India, was of two minds; some of the more visionary leaders such as Sardar Patel understood the strategic importance of Tibet for the security of India.[7] Ultimately nobody would be able to shake Nehru out of his nebulous dream of a brotherhood with China.

The Dalai Lama vs. the Panchen Lama

At this important juncture of Tibet's history, one of the causes which weakened the Tibetan State was the dispute between the Dalai Lama and the Panchen Lama. The differences between the two Lamas were fully exploited by the Chinese to their own advantage. The British themselves[8] were not innocent in the affair.

Though the dispute between the two religious leaders was never 'personal', the entourage of each of the Lamas used their differences of opinion and interest to assert themselves and further their own personal powers.

[6]This earthquake had a devastating effect not only in Tibet, but also in India, in particular in Assam.

[7]Unfortunately, he would pass away soon after the invasion.

[8]In an article of the Royal Asiatic Society, Alex McKay said that they even engineered a coup to replace the Dalai Lama by someone more malleable. The Tashi Lhunpo was certainly involved.

The split between the Ninth Panchen Lama and the Thirteenth Dalai Lama began over a trivial matter of taxation, although it involved the important issue of national security and the financing of the army.

As we have seen earlier, the Thirteenth Dalai Lama had been exiled twice in the space of a few years. When he came back to Tibet for the second time in 1913, he declared Tibet's independence and decided to give his nation the means to defend itself against future invaders and foreign interference.

We should not forget that between the commencement of the Simla Convention in 1913 until the twenties, Tibet had been waging a constant war with China in Kham Province of Eastern Tibet. This war had cost the Tibetan Government a lot. Even when the British provided arms and ammunition to Lhasa, they had to be paid.

The basic principle of the policy of the Dalai Lama was to provide a modern education to as many young Tibetans as possible and build a strong army for defence purposes[9] based on the British model of military training.

These reforms and the attempts to try to build a new and strong Tibet were not to everyone's taste. From the start the two main 'lobbies' in the old Tibet tried to oppose the changes. Their objections were not only ideological, but primarily with regard to distribution of power and financial accounts.

In introducing a strong army, the Dalai Lama introduced a new force in Tibetan politics. The finances for this new force had to come from somewhere. Like anywhere else in the world, the military lobby was a power to reckon with and when the existing centres of power saw Tsarong[10] building a strong and disciplined force, they began to worry.

Things took a turn for the worse when it became clear that the monasteries would have to pay the bill from the revenue of their estates. Where else could the funds for maintaining and training the new army be found? The aristocrats on their side were disturbed by the system of conscription, which forced their offspring to join the ranks of the army.

[9]After Bell's visit to Lhasa in 1920-21, the British government had agreed to supply small quantities of arms for defence purposes only.
[10]Tsarong was not noble by birth.

The new taxes precipitated matters. The Lhasa Government and the Tashilhunpo Administration of the Panchen Lama held opposite views on Tibet's security requirements.

Another argument used by the monks was that Tibet should be a non-violent nation guided by the Buddhist principles of love and compassion for all other sentient beings, therefore no army was necessary.[11] But could a non-violent state survive, on its own, in the jungle of the 'Great Game'?

The earlier system of the Choe-yon (Priest-Patron) relationship no longer worked in the changed circumstances with the arrival on the scene of first the Nationalists and then the Communists in China. The old relationship had lost its validity. However in the thirties and forties, a strong lobby in the monasteries swung in China's favour and was of the opinion that Tibet's future lay in the East. More often than not the monks were very poorly informed about the developments in Asia and the world and they dreamed that the new 'emperors' in Beijing or Nanjing would follow the same policy as the Manchus had earlier.

The Panchen Lama and his entourage were more than anybody else in favour of an alliance with China. The following years saw the emergence among some young Tibetans of the aspiration for a more secular administration as a means to balance the traditionalist (and often pro-Chinese) attitude of the monasteries. This eventually took different shapes and forms, but the best known amongst these 'reformers' were Kunphela, the Pandatsang brothers, Baba Phuntsok Wangyal, Gedun Choepell and in some ways Lungshar. Each had his own motivation and path, but all of them wanted Tibet to evolve into a modern nation.

Unfortunately the system was not ready to accept any internal changes, the forces of the establishment were still too entrenched and when, in the early fifties, the effects of the reforms started to trickle down, it was already too late; a totalitarian regime had taken over the Land of Snows.

To come back to our story, when the Tibetan Government in Lhasa decided to unilaterally tax the Tashilhunpo for a quarter of the army's expenses, it provided the needed excuse to spark off the

---

[11]Though we shall see later that in the dispute between the two Regents in the forties, the monks were not reluctant to use whatever weapons they had, when they felt the need.

old dispute between Lhasa and the Tashilhunpo. The question of taxation brought many other problems to the surface but the main one was the issue of the administrative autonomy of different provinces and the large estates in Tibet.

The Tashilhunpo administration regarded Lhasa's decision to impose this new taxation as an interference in its internal affairs.

The administrative and taxation system in old Tibet was very complicated. In theory, all the land of Tibet belonged to the Dalai Lama who could distribute land as a favour or reward to people who had served either him or the state well.

Usually, the aristocracy or the important Lamas were the beneficiaries of the Lama's largesse, though it was not always true as we have seen in the case of Tsarong Damdul. But when certain privileges have been extended for a long time, the beneficiaries are not always keen to part with them.

The strength and power of the Lamas was largely dependent on the wealth of their estates or Labrangs. In cases such as Tashilhunpo or Sakya, the estates were so large that they were virtually a state within the State.

The Tashilhunpo administration considered itself a local government and resented being treated as a vassal by Lhasa. This may well have been one of the points, apart from collection of taxes, that the Dalai Lama wanted to make: there was only one Government of Tibet, that of the Ganden Phodang[12] headed by the Kashag with its seat in Lhasa. Internal and taxation policies as well as foreign relations were Lhasa's exclusive domain.

Lhasa first made the demand for extra taxes after the Dalai Lama's return to Tibet in 1912. The Panchen Lama's administration was asked to pay 27,000 Ke[13] of grain for the expenses incurred in chasing the Chinese out of Tibet. The Panchen Lama refused to comply.[14] The argument of Lhasa was that this tax — estimated at a quarter of the overall expenses for the campaign against the Chinese — had a precedent. A similar share had already been paid by the Tashilhunpo during the Gurkha war at the end of the eighteenth century. We have to mention here that in the case of the Gurkha

[12]The Dalai Lama's administration first set up by the Fifth Dalai Lama.
[13]1000 Ke is equivalent to 14 cubic meters.
[14]Though he eventually gave a small portion.

war, the invader came from the South and thus the Tashilhunpo was the principal sufferer, while when the threat came from the East, the Panchen Lama's administration showed less concern.

Relations between Lhasa and Shigatse further deteriorated when in 1917, Lhasa decided to levy a new tax on the Tashilhunpo's estate in Gyantse district: all the 'serfs' had to pay a new *corvée* tax over the usual tax of 100 horses and 300 pack animals. In 1923 a new tax was extended to Tashilhunpo estate itself.

In the meantime the Panchen Lama's administration informed Lhasa that since they could not afford to pay the tax; they would not pay it. But the Lhasa government went on insisting that the taxes had to be paid. After Lhasa had 'verified' through a Commission[15] that the Panchen Lama could easily afford the levies, the affair took a political turn.

Lhasa felt that the Panchen Lama was more interested in asserting his financial and political separateness from Lhasa; this attitude was not acceptable to the Dalai Lama's government.

What made it difficult to find a compromise acceptable to both parties was the fact that the Panchen Lama decided to take the matter to the British Government through the Trade Agent in Gyantse.

The Panchen Lama complained to the British that Lhasa was demanding 650,000 rupees, 10,000 maunds of grain, 2,000 boxes of Chinese tea bricks and that Lhasa had even arrested the Tashilhunpo representatives in Lhasa for defaulting and were refusing to release them until the debt was paid. Mac Donald, the British Trade Agent in Gyantse wrote to the Political Officer in Sikkim on behalf of the Panchen Lama: "His Serenity wishes to know whether the Government of India will mediate between himself and His Holiness the Dalai Lama as he states that his only hope is the assistance of the Government of India."[16]

The fact that the Panchen Lama took the dispute to the British before directly appealing to the Dalai Lama only made the situation worse. As the situation turned sour, the Panchen Lama decided to leave Tibet and after a first abortive attempt to escape, he finally managed to leave for Mongolia. However, before his escape, he made it a point to declare that he had nothing personal against the Dalai

---

[15]Appointed by Lhasa.
[16]Quoted by Goldstein, op. cit., p. 113

Lama: "With regard to the trouble of the Tashilhunpo Government and their subjects, I have submitted representations to His Holiness the Dalai Lama on several occasions, but my requests have not been granted. At the same time His Holiness has always shown me kindness."

He stated that it was certain officers in the entourage of the Dalai Lama, the 'evil-minded person,' had influenced him. He concluded that since he did not want to further embarrass the Dalai Lama, he had taken the decision to leave his seat "for a short period to make it easier for His Holiness the Dalai Lama. I am going to see whether I can secure any one to mediate between us. ...It is quite impossible for me to make the annual contribution to meet the military expenses and I am compelled to proceed to an unknown destination to try to raise funds from the Buddhists [patrons]."[17]

Tibetans troops under Lungshar were sent to try to stop him but Lhasa had reacted too late. Later the Dalai Lama replied to the Panchen Lama that Lungshar had been sent to persuade him to return to his monastery "for the sake of the Buddhist religion and the good government of the country and chiefly for your happiness and prosperity.

The Dalai Lama concluded: "As you and your ministers have left Shigatse and gone to a foreign country, the Tibetan Government will appoint a Zasag Lama (monk administrator) and send him to Tashilhunpo without delay to manage the internal and external affairs for the benefit of all."

The Dalai Lama accordingly appointed an ecclesiastic Prime Minister as the administrator of Tashilhunpo.

In July 1924 the Panchen Lama replied from China once again, telling the Dalai Lama that some evil persons in his entourage had 'an axe to grind' and "have been creating estrangement and inconvenience between us." Apparently one of the complaints of the Panchen Lama was that the entourage of the Dalai Lama had refused him an interview," so as to lay before Your Holiness the real state of affairs as it is in my mind and obtain Your Holiness' true advice as to what is the best thing to be done towards paying this new army expenditure tax".

---

[17]For correspondence between the Dalai Lama and Panchen Lama see Goldstein, op. cit. p. 115 ff. Correspondence available at India Office Record (L/PS/12/4174).

In his reply, the Dalai Lama mentioned that "in order to make permanent the secular and religious rule of Tibet, it was found expedient to assess and collect extra taxes." He also regretted that the two Lamas have not been able to meet due to some individuals in their entourage.

Lungshar played a very active role in blocking their meeting. He had managed to remove Tsarong from his post of Commander-in-Chief and had become the strong man of Tibet. He wanted to impose Lhasa's rule over Tashilhunpo.

After he left Shigatse, the Panchen Lama first went to Mongolia and then reached China in February 1924. Of course the Chinese were delighted to receive him. He was received with full honours by the Emperor and although the Chinese were very much engaged in their own civil war, they felt confident that with the Panchen Lama's card in their hand, they could again have a role to play in Tibetan affairs.

The preceding events marked a watershed in the Dalai Lama's internal affairs and foreign policy. The departure of the Panchen Lama, who was highly revered by the Tibetan people all over the country, was considered a bad omen. He was known to all as a gentle and very erudite Lama. His departure somehow strengthened the conservative forces in Lhasa. Many thought that the British with their 'modern' ideas had influenced the Dalai Lama. Soon after the Dalai Lama's interest in the British protection declined; he perhaps felt that if at this point in time, he was to reinforce Tibet's links with Britain, it would have as an immediate result, the hardening of the Chinese position; therefore no urgency was felt to build a strong army anymore.[18]

The old habit of keeping Tibet closed to the outside world [19] again prevailed. Once more, Tibet had lost a chance to assert itself on the international stage. In the modern period of Tibet's history, the British have often represented the most progressive forces; however, their responsibility for the weakening of the Tibetan state cannot be denied.

After all they had been the first during the Simla Conference to suggest dividing Tibet into two different zones,[20] and when the

---

[18]Especially after the removal of Tsarong.
[19]Or open only to the Chinese side.
[20]Partition of Tibet into Inner and Outer Tibet in Simla, 1914.

Chinese nationalists created the provinces of Sikang and Qinghai, amalgamating more than half of Tibet's territory, the Chinese only borrowed what was a British concept.

The British also had their own commercial and strategic interests in the region and their 'benevolent' help to train and arm a Tibetan regiment was not totally unselfish.

It is also true that they were more concerned with what happened in Tashilhunpo which was relatively close to the Indian border, than with what happened in the remote districts of Kham or Amdo.

After the refusal of the Chinese to ratify the Simla Convention, they could very well have taken a strong stand on the status of Tibet or even declared Tibet an independent state, but for their own political interests they preferred to pursue the politics of ambiguity and vagueness.[21] It has to be noted that as late as 1919, five years after the Simla Convention, Jordan, the British Ambassador in China, was trying to get a Treaty signed between China and His Majesty's Government without the consent or even knowledge of the Tibetans. However, this was accepted neither by Whitehall nor by Delhi.

Nevertheless, all in all, the British and especially some bold officers such as Sir Charles Bell, always encouraged the Dalai Lama and the people of Tibet to stand on their own feet, something which the Chinese Ambans or Beijing never did.

To sum up, we can say that an opportunity for Tibet to assert itself on the international political stage was missed. And new opportunities do not come often.

The Consequences of the Split

The most dramatic aspect of this story was the split between the two religious leaders and the fact that in the following years this was made full use of by the Chinese government to assure its control over Tibet. The story did not end with the passing away of the Thirteenth Dalai Lama and the Ninth Panchen Lama; it continued with their reincarnations and it still continues today with the search for and recognition of the new Eleventh Panchen Lama.

This is the third generation of Panchen Lamas to be used by different regimes in China. Could this be the direct consequence of a petty dispute over taxes? For the Tibetans, it is certainly more the play of greater forces which they believe to be the result of some past actions.

[21]This policy of vagueness will be the hallmark of Nehru's Tibet policy.

Though he had written to the Dalai Lama that he was leaving for a short time, the Ninth Panchen Lama never came back to Tibet, and his reincarnation was eventually found in 1939 in Qinghai province, near Sining.[22] His recognition was more or less imposed by force on Lhasa in May 1951 during negotiations on the 17-Point Agreement.

The deep division between the two highest reincarnations of Tibet was not a good omen for the future and the two Lamas were certainly aware of it, but they could not do much to stop the 'karmic' (or logical depending how one sees it) consequences from reaching their conclusion.

The differences between the two Lamas was symbolic of the division between those who thought that Tibet should assert its independence — build a strong army[23] and have an independent foreign policy — and those who believed in the traditional relationship with China. For the latter, there were two ways to save Tibet; one was for it to use spiritual means to defend itself against outside influence and interference, and the other way was for it to find a Buddhist patron to protect Tibet militarily.

Neither of these took into account the arrival on the Asian stage of a power which believed only in the barrel of a gun and branded religion as a poison. In retrospect, it is a pity that the reforms of the Thirteenth Dalai Lama were blocked by his own people, in particular his own monasteries. He was prevented from building a strong and self-reliant Tibet, with a modern, well-educated and progressive élite that could bring about the necessary changes without destroying the basic Buddhist faith.

Tsarong, Lungshar and Kunphela

The three main favourites of the Thirteenth Dalai Lama were Tsarong Shape, the hero of Chaksam; Kunphela, a monk attending to the Dalai Lama; and Lungshar, a lay official who had accompanied the first (and last) batch of young Tibetans to England for schooling.

Lungshar was supposed to be one of the brightest Tibetans of his time, but was a schemer and some said even an adept of black magic. In the words of Hugh Richardson, he was 'drunk with power.'

---

[22]The present Dalai Lama was born in the same area.
[23]With the help of the British and later India.

Already in England he had behaved so badly that the Tibetan Government had to give the charge of the Tibetan children to Col. Leslie Weir, who would later become the Political Officer in Sikkim.[24]

Until the mid-twenties, Tsarong was the most powerful man in Tibet after the Dalai Lama. Though born into a poor family, he became the Dalai Lama's favourite when, in 1910, he saved the Lama's life. The Dalai Lama was on his way to India and Chinese troops were attempting to capture him when Tsarong with a few hundred of the Dalai Lama's bodyguards stopped the Chinese near the Chaksam Bridge on the Tsangpo River,[25] one day's journey from Lhasa. Tsarong delayed the Chinese long enough to allow the Dalai Lama to take refuge in Chumbi Valley and later India.

When the Tibetan leader came back to Tibet two years afterwards, he remembered the services of Tsarong and gave him the name of a noble family and an estate. Due to his proximity to the Dalai Lama, Tsarong became the strong man of Tibet; he was nominated the senior most Minister and the Commander-in-Chief of the Army.

In the mid-twenties, through constant scheming, Lungshar managed to have Tsarong demoted and sent to India on one more pilgrimage of 'convenience'. By the time Tsarong returned from India, Lungshar had become the new master of Tibet.

The pro-British foreign policy of Tibet began to tilt towards China, especially after the flight of the Panchen Lama to China.

Lungshar used his post as the leader of the National Assembly to influence the Dalai Lama and the monks. He even managed to convince the big monasteries against the great danger of 'modernization'.[26] The direction of opening up Tibet to the outside world and the preparation of an armed force was more or less abandoned.

---

[24]Some historians believe that the rumours that he behaved badly while in Great Britain had been planted by the British intelligence agencies because Lungshar was much too interested in reform movements such as "women's liberation" among others which had begun to take root in Great Britain and which were considered a danger to the stability of the Empire. Some even said that Lungshar had been sent by the Dalai Lama to study political reforms which could be applied inside Tibet.

[25]The Tsangpo river will become the Brahmaputra once in India.

[26]In fact 'Britishisation" of the Tibetan Culture.

The third player in the game, Kunphela was the personal attendant of the Dalai Lama. In the last years before the Tibetan leader's death in 1933, Kunphela rose to become the chief favourite and the most powerful person in the Roof of the World.

The struggle of these three men represented in many ways the changes occurring in Tibet and the entry of Tibet into the modern world. Their struggle focused around the control of the army.

While Tsarong was perhaps the only one with a vision of the strategic interests of Tibet in the Great Game and the importance of the army for the future of Tibet, Lungshar saw it more a personal tool in pursuit of his personal aim of controlling Tibet. He always resented Tsarong's being at the head of a strong army and worked very hard to convince the Dalai Lama of the danger of Tsarong's becoming too powerful.

In the mid-twenties Lungshar, who was also holding the Revenue portfolio, became Commander-in-Chief in place of Tsarong. It was at this time that Lungshar reached his zenith. Then Kunphela entered on the stage. Like Tsarong, he was from a poor peasant family but had been chosen by the Dalai Lama to be his personal attendant. He was intelligent but not well educated. The two new and powerful leaders could only clash.

Slowly Lungshar began to lose his influence over the affairs of the government; his arrogance and unscrupulous behaviour attracted a lot of enemies.

Kunphela was nominated as the new Commander-in-Chief and Lungshar was partially demoted. Around that time, Kunphela had created a sensation by driving around Lhasa in the Dalai Lama's Austin car. But Lungshar bided his time.

Although Kunphela was the new strong man of Lhasa, he tried to remain just and do his duty to the best of his abilities. He was at times authoritarian and once he is said to have dismissed a minister and several officials for the inefficient handling of a construction work. For many years he had no official government job, but derived his authority from the fact that he was the *Kuchar*, the person always in presence of the Dalai Lama.

Margaret Willamson, the wife of the British Political Officer, described him in this way:

> Kunphe-la was a tall, good-looking young man of twenty-eight. Next to the Dalai Lama himself , he was

undoubtedly the most powerful person in Tibet at the
time. He held no official rank but constantly attended
His Holiness, who in fact treated him like a son. Of high
intelligence, he was the sort of man whose undoubted
talents would inevitably bring him to the fore
anywhere.[27]

A few years before his death, the Dalai Lama had appointed
Kunphela as head of the Drapchi Office which comprised the coin
and currency mints and the munitions factory. He was also
responsible for the Drongdra Regiment. This crack regiment,
composed of members from the 'better families',[28] was very modern,
well-equipped and efficient. According to Willamson, Drapchi had
"an air of energy and efficiency which is rare in Tibet".

The problem for Kunphela who had no official rank was that he
made many enemies in the aristocracy, especially among the
ministers who resented the fact that his power was not due to his
blood, but to his proximity to the Dalai Lama. His regiment was
also feared by many in Lhasa.

Willamson is said to have remarked that Kunphela had "many
enemies and will be in a very difficult position after the death of the
Dalai Lama."

Kunphela remained in power until the death of the Dalai Lama
in December 1933. The first few days after his death, Kunphela was
for many, the favourite for the post of Regent and his name was so
proposed. But the monasteries decided to choose otherwise and a
young Lama the Reting Rinpoche was chosen from among the high-
incarnated Lamas.

Soon after, Lungshar and the National Assembly accused
Kunphela of having kept secret the Dalai Lama's disease and of
precipitating his death by administering some wrong medicine in
connivance with the Nechung State Oracle and the Private Physician
of the Dalai Lama. The great schemer Lungshar managed to incite
the monks in the monasteries to ask: "How could the Dalai Lama
have died so suddenly?"

Many witnesses were brought to the Assembly and finally
Kunphela himself had to appear. He explained that the Dalai Lama

[27]Willamson, Margaret P., *Memoirs of a Political Officer's Wife* (London:
Wisdom Publication, 1987), p. 100.
[28]As its Tibetan name indicates.

had stated in his 'last Testament' a year earlier that he had not many years to live and as he was often subject to colds, he had not worried.

But Lungshar knew the weakness of Kunphela and engineered a mutiny of the Drongdra Regiment. It was not difficult as the troops were raised from the 'better families' who did not appreciate an enforced recruitment.[29]

When the soldiers began marching towards Lhasa to present their petition to the Kashag, Lungshar announced that the Assembly was threatened by the manipulations of Kunphela and asked the monks of Sera to come and defend the arsenal and the mint. The Kashag took stock of the situation and posted some troops of the bodyguards at Drapchi. The 'mutineers' of the Drongdra Regiment were disarmed and were later forbidden to re-join their barracks. The tool in the hand of Kunphela was no more.

The next day in the Assembly when the hearings began again, the supporters of Lungshar launched a blistering attack against the Dalai Lama's favourite and he was accused of murdering the Dalai Lama.

He was arrested and discussions started about the punishment to be inflicted on him and his supporters such as the Pandatsang brothers. A few days later, most of the assembly cooled down and admitted that the Dalai Lama had not been murdered. However, Kunphela was accused of having kept the condition of the Dalai Lama a secret. He and his relatives were banished and all their properties confiscated. He left for exile to Kongpo in south Tibet.

Many officials felt sorry for Kunphela who had always been the Dalai Lama's favourite and had served him well. His energy and efficiency were well remembered. Once more, the forces of progress had been suppressed and the conservative forces had won. Lungshar was the new master of Tibet. But not for long!

Lungshar committed his first blunder soon after he took over from Tsarong as Commander-in-chief of the army. One Tibetan named Gyalpo who was married to a Nepalese girl had illegally opened a liquor shop in Lhasa. When an arrest warrant was issued against him by the Magistrate of Lhasa, he took refuge in the

[29]Though the rich families would often send some of their servants to serve on their behalf. From a military point of view, a crack regiment cannot be formed by forced conscription.

Nepalese legacy where he was given refuge by the Nepalese Resident. Lungshar decided to send the police inside the legacy to arrest Gyalpo. This was in contravention of the Treaty of 1856 with Nepal and it nearly triggered a war between the two countries. Eventually the British managed to mediate and the affair was settled. Lungshar, however lost his prestige as well as his post in the army, although he continued to be a Finance Secretary.[30]

The fall of Lungshar came soon after he succeeded in eliminating Kunphela. After dismantling the regiment of Kunphela, Lungshar gathered some young officials and officers and established an organization called the 'Happy Union'.

The official aim of the organization was to bring social reform in government circles. However a few officers in the inner circle around Lungshar knew that the real purpose had far-reaching consequences: Lungshar was planning to introduce a secular government in Tibet. One of the conspirators, Rimshi Kashopa, reported the plans to Kalon Trimon, a Cabinet minister who brought it to the notice of the Regent, who in turn ordered the immediate arrest of Lungshar.

The residence of Lungshar was raided, incriminating documents establishing the facts were found. It was also proved that he had planned to assassinate Kalon Trimon. The sentence was very severe: Lungshar was deprived of his eyesight and condemned to life imprisonment. It was the end of Lungshar; but the infighting had made Tibet the real loser.

Khampa vs. Lhasa

The Pandatsangs belonged to one of the great Khampa families engaged in trading. They had come into prominence at the beginning of the reign of the Thirteenth Dalai Lama when they became major trading partners with the Tibetan government. This started when one of the brothers, Nyima, helped the Dalai Lama to come back to Tibet after his exile in India and protected him day and night with his personal army.

The wool business developed tremendously in the following years and Nyima established a network spreading from Kalimpong to China with its headquarters in Lhasa. The Pandatsangs like many other trading families of Kham (such as the Andruktshangs), formed a new bourgeoisie who had travelled a lot in Asia and often

[30]One of the four Tsipons.

assimilated the new concepts of the West.[31] They were keen to introduce these ideas in Tibet where the most conservative elements — the clergy and the aristocracy — kept a firm hold on the society.

One of the Pandatsang brothers, Yarphel who looked after the family interests in Lhasa, was suspected by the National Assembly of supporting Kunphela. Though the communications network was not very developed, rumours travelled fast in Tibet. After hearing of the events in Lhasa, another brother, Tobgye decided to act; he believed that the Lhasa government would soon arrest not only Yarphel in Lhasa but the rest of the family in Kham.

The Khampas were not ready to be 'bullied' by Lhasa and after having checked through a divination that 'his brother was in danger', Tobgye decided to declare a sort of self-rule or autonomy for Kham. They took over the city of Markhan and attacked the arsenal at night, capturing some mountain guns and at least 500 rifles. However, the Khampa troops were defeated and in the end disbanded.

When the news of revolt in Markhan reached Lhasa, the Kashag immediately decided to seal the properties of the Pandatsangs in the Tibetan capital and to arrest Yarphel. At the same time, the Kashag wrote to the British government requesting them to freeze the assets of the family in Kalimpong.

But before the British could act, the case was solved in Lhasa. Pabongka Rinpoche, a very famous Lama, accepted to personally plead their case with the Kashag and the National Assembly. He explained that Yarphel had no knowledge of his brothers actions in Kham and he could not be made a scapegoat for them. He further told the Cabinet of Ministers and specially Trimon Shape, the senior most minister that if the Kashag decided to seal the Pandatsang business, it was Tibet which would suffer the most since they had a monopoly on the wool market, even vis-à-vis the United States. Business was business, even in old Tibet!

The Kashag understood this argument well and the matter was settled. The British were informed of the revised decision. Some street-songs of course said that the money of rich Khampas had bribed Trimon Shape.

[31]In fact not only those of the West, but also those introduced during the freedom struggle in India and the Revolution in China. For the Tibetans, the *plaque tournante* of these new ideas was Kalimpong.

Though the matter was closed, this incident showed again the deep divisions in the Tibetan society at the time of the Dalai Lama's death.

The words of one Lama whom the author interviewed resound again: "The Dalai Lama had no other choice but to leave his terrestrial body at that time due to negative actions accumulated by the Tibetans."

The deep resentment of the Khampas against the Lhasa government which had crystallized in the Markhan revolt, would reappear a few years later when the Chinese forces invaded Tibet. Not only the Pandatsangs but most of the Khampas as well felt that they were treated by the Lhaseans as barbarians who knew only how to fight. For the aristocrats of Lhasa posted in Kham it was often an occasion to get rich quick.

The contempt shown by the Lhaseans towards the Khampas was reciprocal and has been well described by George Patterson and Robert Ford. In 1924, F.M. Bailey, the Political Officer in Sikkim, even noted that at some places in Eastern Tibet, people preferred the Chinese rule to the transport *corvée* imposed by Lhasa.

In conclusion, it is a great pity that Tibet did not take advantage of its years of independence to introduce necessary reforms to join the concert of nations and to prepare itself to fight the battle against the Communists invaders as one.

14

Before the Avalanche

No one in Lhasa or elsewhere foresaw the speed with which the avalanche was about to descend.

Hugh Richardson

In the years following the death of the Thirteenth Dalai Lama, most of the energies of the Tibetan nation were turned towards finding the new of incarnation of their leader and enthroning him as the Fourteenth Dalai Lama.

The political life of the Roof of the World practically came to a halt, with the exception of the Chinese who took the occasion of a condolence Mission in 1934 to return to Tibet and leave a Representative posted in Lhasa.

However a few issues remained unsolved: mainly the border problems with China and to a lesser extent with British India.

Tawang

We shall say a few words about the latter and mention the British position in the forties regarding the North East Frontier Agency[1] and the McMahon Line and briefly how certain officials saw the situation on the ground.

We have seen that during the Simla Conference in 1914, Lochen Shatra and Sir Henry McMahon had separate talks about the Indo-Tibetan border in the Northeast. An agreement was reached in April 1914 and letters and maps were exchanged.

The Tibetans accepted to cede the area north of the Sela Pass inhabited by the Monpas to British India. This area surrounds the Tawang monastery and includes a few nearby valleys. The

[1]Known as NEFA.

compromise was accepted by the Tibetans after the British
Plenipotentiary promised to pressure the Chinese government to
approve the demarcation of the border between Tibet and China.
But as we saw earlier, the Chinese government eventually refused
to ratify the Simla Convention.

The position of the British government was made clear in a note
from Anthony Eden to Dr. T. V. Soong in August 1943.

The note says:

> *Since the Chinese Revolution of 1911, when Chinese forces
> were withdrawn from Tibet, Tibet has enjoyed de facto
> independence.*[2] She has ever since regarded herself as in
> practice completely autonomous and has opposed
> Chinese attempts to reassert control.
>
> Since 1911, repeated attempts have been made to bring
> about an accord between China and Tibet. It seemed
> likely that agreement could be found on the basis that
> Tibet should be autonomous under the nominal
> suzerainty of China, and this was the basis of the draft
> tripartite (Chinese-Tibetan-British) convention of 1914
> which was initialled by the Chinese representative but
> was not ratified by the Chinese Government. The rock
> on which the convention and subsequent attempts to
> reach an understanding were wrecked was not the
> question of autonomy (which was expressly admitted
> by China) but was the question of the boundary between
> China and Tibet, since the Chinese Government claimed
> sovereignty over areas which the Tibetan Government
> claimed belonged exclusively to their autonomous
> jurisdiction.
>
> The boundary question, however, remained insuperable
> and, since the delay in reaching agreement was
> hampering the development of more normal relations
> between India and Tibet, eventually in 1921 the Secretary
> of State for Foreign Affairs (Lord Curzon) informed the
> then Chinese Minister (Dr. Wellington Koo) that the
> British Government did not feel justified in withholding
> any longer their recognition of the status of Tibet as an

---

[2]Emphasis added by the author.

autonomous State under the suzerainty of China, and intended dealing on this basis with Tibet in the future. This is the principle which had since guided the attitude of the British.[3]

On the ground, the Tibetans continued to consider the Tawang area as part of the Tibetan territory and the Dzongpöns[4] of Tsona had not stopped levying the taxes, sometimes as far south as Senge Dzong and Dirang Dzong, after 1914.

The British administration of Assam was faced with a difficult situation. These areas were so remote[5] and without proper roads or even tracks, that the administration found them very difficult to penetrate. It was also clearly not a priority for the British to assert their rights accrued from the Simla Convention.

Gould Visit to Lhasa

Finally in 1944, London decided to send Sir Basil Gould, the Political Officer in Sikkim, to Lhasa to discuss with the Tibetan Government some 'adjustments' on the McMahon Line. "We must hold Tibetans to their treaty engagements while being prepared, if so advised, to consider slight adjustments of frontiers in favour of Tibet in the neighbourhood of Tawang. His Majesty's Government are not prepared to forego their treaty rights with Tibet."[6]

While the diplomatic parleys were on, the administration of Assam was slowly trying to penetrate inside what is today the state of Arunachal Pradesh. The first 'penetration' of the British Administration in Walong (Lohit) and Siang sectors began around that time.

During the negotiations that followed in Lhasa, the Tibetans were ready to agree to the validity of the Simla maps and in particular to the McMahon Line, but wanted to postpone the process, for a new factor had appeared on the Tibetan stage.

Shen Tsung-lien, a Chinese Buddhist, had just been appointed as the Representative of the Chiang Kai-shek government in Lhasa.

[3]Quoted in Goldstein, op. cit., p. 401. Letter from Anthony Eden to Chinese Minister Soong dated 5 August 1943, (FO371/93001).
[4]District Magistrates.
[5]At least from the Indian side.
[6]Quoted in Goldstein, op. cit., p. 412. Memorandum from the British Foreign Office to the British Embassy in China (FO371/46123)

The Tibetans felt that it offered a chance to settle the old border dispute with the Chinese.[7]

The Sino-Tibetan border was a priority for the Kashag. They felt that, if they raked up the Tawang issue at this time with the Tsongdu (National Assembly), the issue might be exploited by the Chinese and used to their advantage during the talks.[8] Gould saw the point of the Tibetan Foreign Office and accepted to take up the matter with his government.

In November 1944, he wrote to New Delhi asking if it would be possible to "postpone action on the McMahon areas for a short time. Kashag anticipated that the Chinese-Tibet issue would come to a head soon."[9] In fact, he pleaded the Tibetan cause.

In an *aide-mémoire* dated 4 December given to the Kashag, Gould suggested that "my government would be willing to alter the frontier so as to run from Sela, not to the north of Tawang but to the south of Tawang."

This was conditional to the recognition of the Simla Convention and the rest of the McMahon Line: "My Government have no design on Tibetan territory. But my Government do intend to maintain their rights; and they are glad to observe that the Tibetan Government do not dispute these rights."[10]

Gould further accepted that the British would not object to voluntary contributions for monasteries being collected even south of Sela, though the British Government would prefer to make a lump sum contribution. He thought that if the Tibetans accepted this clause, it would make a big difference for the British in terms of occupancy of the territory; it was no longer a question of a tax paid by the local population to its government but a voluntary contribution to a religious institution.

In compensation, the Tibetan Government was asked to refrain from exercising any authority south of Sela where the posts established by the British would remain.

---

[7]Soon after the war, the Generalissimo declared that: "he was even ready to accord them independence, if they fulfil the "economic requirement".

[8]In the fifties all the claims of Communist Chinese over the NEFA areas are based on the Tibetan claims and the revenue collection from Tsona and Tawang monasteries in these areas (Dirang Dzong, Senge Dzong, Tawang).

[9]Telegram No. 364 from Gould to External Affairs Department, New Delhi dated 4 November 1944, (FO371/41589).

[10]Aide-mémoire from Gould to Tibetan Foreign Bureau dated 4 December 1944, (FO371/46121).

However, due to some other factors, in particular the refusal of the British Government to actively support Tibetan autonomy and help Tibet participate in a post-war Conference, no agreement could be reached. At the same time, London did not want to upset China which had been an ally during the War.

The Tibetans themselves were busy with petty internal problems and could not concentrate all their energy on 'foreign' matters.

The progress of the British administration continued during the first months of 1945. In April, the Tibetans wrote a strong protest to the Government of India through the British Mission in Lhasa:

> If the officers and troops stationed in Kalaktang and Walung are not withdrawn immediately, it will look something like a big insect eating a smaller one and thereby the bad name of the Government of India will spread out like wind.[11]

Hopkinson who succeeded Gould as a Political Officer went to Lhasa the following year, to try once more to sort out the McMahon Line issue.

In a meeting with Surkhang Shape, the Tibetan minister asked the Political Officer 'with a knowing air', "whether our Government had fulfilled all the eleven articles of the 1914 Agreement." Hopkinson added that his tone implied that "we had not".[12]

A more interesting point raised by Surkhang was that "British policy has changed. The British are now giving Indians liberty. What benefit will it be to the 'English Government' to take portion of Tibetan territory?"

The main question boiled down to why the British who had not done anything for thirty years, suddenly as they were getting ready to leave India, engaged in a forward policy towards these remote areas?

London was aware of the dilemma.

In the Foreign Office in London, the opinion of many officials was not very different from the Tibetan position. Sir R. Campbell wrote in 1945:

[11]Letter from the Tibetan Foreign Affairs Bureau to the Government of India dated 27 April 1945, forwarded by the Mission in Lhasa to the PO in Sikkim and later to Delhi, (FO371/46122).

[12]Surkhang refers to the fact that Lochen Shatra had 'ceded' Tawang as a compensation for the acceptance by the Chinese of the Sino-Tibetan border. As the Simla Convention was never ratified by the Chinese government, the Tibetans were perhaps not feeling bound by the 'cession' of Tawang.

There are the makings of a complicated dispute in which we might find it difficult to explain why we were undertaking an occupation policy at this time to enforce a line which was drawn some thirty years ago and which is so obscure that it was discovered in 1935 that neither the Political Officer in Sikkim nor the Government of Assam were even aware of its existence.[13]

In the meantime, the Tibetans continued to exercise their control north of Sela and the British kept their outposts in the South.

The British administration carried on the same policy and a year later, a senior British official from the Assam government, Mills, had a meeting with the Tibetan authorities of Tsona and Tawang. After the meeting Mills came to a similar conclusion as that of Gould: a compromise had to be found. First of all, Sela Pass was the natural geographical border between India and Tibet. He estimated that if the British administration had to take over upto the McMahon Line, the cost of the operation for the British exchequer would go up four times.[14] It also discovered that the Monpas were much closer ethnically and culturally to the Tibetans than to the other tribes of Assam.

However, Mills introduced a house tax system for the population south of Sela. This new tax was relatively well received and insured the effective control of the Government over all the tribes south of Sela. The above events were to have considerable consequences for Sino-Indian relations.

It is a pity that this matter could not be settled amicably between the Tibetan and the British Governments before the British left India, for a war might have been avoided in the process.

The only conclusion we can draw is that at the time of independence and for a few years afterwards, the McMahon Line although in theory agreed by both concerned parties[15] was in practice a very vague notion.

[13]We should note an earlier reference in which the present Dalai Lama, during the course of an interview was laughing at his own government for not knowing about the details of Simla Convention. According to Camphell, the situation was not very different in the British administration.

[14]For example, an Assistant Political Officer for Tawang would have to be appointed, roads built, etc..

[15]The Tibetans and the Indians.

Zhou Enlai in his voluminous correspondence with Nehru on the subject fully utilized this contentious issue to his advantage.

In 1959 he made it clear to Nehru that the McMahon Line "has never been recognized by past Chinese governments, or by the Government of the People's Republic of China, yet (the latter) ... has strictly abided by its statement of absolutely not allowing its armed personnel to cross this line in waiting for a friendly settlement of the boundary question."

Zhou cleverly added: "China has not even stepped into this vast area which, not long ago, was still under the jurisdiction of the local government of the Tibet region of China."[16]

This summarizes the difficulty of the Government of India's position vis-à-vis these areas: on the one hand Nehru considered the 1914 Simla Convention as a remnant of British imperialism, while at the same time he swore by the McMahon Line (a direct result of the Convention) as the Indo-Tibetan border. The British, for their part, bargained for a line that they could not, even after thirty 30 years, physically control but over whose 'rights' they were also not ready to compromise.

The Chinese take the cake, as per Zhou's admission that "China has not even stepped into this vast area", but when they invaded Tibet, by that mere fact they became the 'owners' of Tawang area.

The Congratulation Mission

Towards the end of 1945, the Lhasa Government thought it would be good for Tibet to send a Mission to visit Tibet's neighbours, India and China. Had not the Thirteenth Dalai Lama insisted on the importance of a balance between the two great neighbours?

It was also an occasion to get a feeling for the political situation after World War II.

A delegation was nominated and, as always in Tibet, it was under the joint leadership of a lay person and a monk official. Zasag Kheme (Sonam Wangdu) and Zasag Thupten Samphel were the first officials to leave for India and meet the Viceroy since the Thirteenth Dalai Lama's escape in 1910. They were to convey to the British

---

[16]Ministry of External Affairs, Notes, Memoranda and Letters Exchanged and Agreements signed by the Governments of India and China, known as White Papers (New Delhi: Publications Division, 1954-61), Vol. III, page 47. Letter from Zhou Enlai to Nehru dated 16 November 1959.

government 'congratulations' from the Tibetan Government on their victory in the Second World War.

The strategy would remain the same in coming years: a balance had to be kept between the two great neighbours; they were therefore to proceed afterwards to Nanjing to meet Chiang Kai-shek.

Two years later, the Trade Delegation under Shakabpa would follow the same route, visiting first India and then China. In performing this balancing act, the Kashag thought that it would eventually prove to the world that Tibet was an independent country sandwiched between two Asian giants.

Another reason to break the policy of isolation at that point in time was the pressure from the Nationalist Government of Chiang Kai-shek, who wanted the Tibetans to attend the Chinese National Assembly.

In August 1945, Chiang Kai-shek in a speech had promised "a high degree of autonomy" and even hinted at the possibility of Tibet being granted independence from China. He said:

> As regards political status of Tibet, Sixth National Kuomintang Congress decided to grant it a very high degree of autonomy to aid its political advancement and to improve living conditions of the Tibetans. I solemnly declare that if the Tibetans should at this time express wish for self-government our government would, in conformity with our sincere traditions, accord it a very high degree of autonomy. If in the future they fulfil economic requirements for independence, the nation's government will as in the case of Outer Mongolia help them attain that status.[17]

Though the Tibetans felt that for all purposes they were already independent, it would be good for them if that status were to be recognized by the British and the Chinese Governments. We should remember here that in spite of the British and Tibetan efforts, the Chinese had never ratified the Simla Convention.

Lhasa did not want the delegation to fall into a trap while in China; they knew too well that the Chinese could try to make them a party to some unwanted decisions of the Chinese National Assembly with regard to the Tibetan affairs. For these reasons, the visit to India assumed even more importance.

[17]Quoted by Melvyn Goldstein, op. cit., p. 536. Copy of Telegram from British Embassy in Chungking to the Foreign Office in London.

They arrived in India in January 1946 and stayed first in Calcutta for a few days before proceeding to Delhi.[18] In Delhi, the Mission met the Viceroy, Lord Wavell and presented him a letter from the Regent and some presents from the Tibetan Government. The delegation stayed three weeks in Delhi during which time they met the American Ambassador and delivered some gifts from the Dalai Lama for President Truman. They also met the Chinese Ambassador who invited them for dinner.

After visiting Delhi, the delegation went on a pilgrimage around India before returning to Calcutta from where they were to fly to China. While they were travelling around India visiting many Buddhist sites, an incident occurred which showed the difficult 'diplomatic' situation of the Tibetans.

A few British officials were very keen to keep some measure of control over the Tibetan delegation and fearing a trap in Nanjing, they tried to delay their departure from India. It was even suggested that they should travel by sea, so that they would reach after the session of the Chinese National Assembly had concluded.

Hopkinson, the Political Officer in Sikkim, tried to delay their trip to China fearing that once in China, the Tibetans would deal directly with the Chinese government without referring to His Majesty's Government. The resourceful British officers found a trick to keep them for a few more months in India: the Tibetan delegates coming down from the Roof of the World to the hot cities of Central Indian plains, contracted a sort of prickly heat. Hopkinson immediately had them examined by a British doctor who told them that they had a highly contagious disease and that they should return immediately to a hill station (in Gangtok) and remain in quarantine until the healing process was over.

Unfortunately for the British, the Tibetans did not accept the diagnosis and decided nevertheless to proceed to China. This incident demonstrates that each of the parties involved in the triangular game did not want the other two parties to interact bilaterally and were highly suspicious of any visit, whatever its purpose, to the other's territory.

[18]A young fifteen-year old boy Rinchen Sadutshang who had been educated in India and who could speak some English, joined the team as one of the translators. He would later become a member of the team headed by Ngabo Jigme to Beijing in 1951. After the 1959 exile, he worked in the Private Office of the Dalai Lama. We owe most of our information to him.

The delegates were joined by Gyalo Dhondup and P.T. Takhla who spoke perfect Chinese. They were the brother and brother-in-law of the Dalai Lama respectively. Lhasa thought that they would prove useful in the negotiations with Chiang Kai-shek.

In the meantime, the Tibetan National Assembly in Lhasa decided to send a long letter addressed to President Chiang Kai-shek. Following is a resume of the long nine-point missive which explained in detail the Tibetan Government's position vis-à-vis China:

1- Tibet and China have a centuries-old relationship. It has been described as a Choe-yon relationship; it is the relation between a Priest and his Patron who is supposed to protect the Priest. The Dalai Lama is the temporal and religious leader of Tibet.

2- Tibet is the fountainhead of the precious teachings of Buddha. China should help in preserving this source. Tibet is an independent nation and it will keep on maintaining, developing and protecting this 'dual' system (political and religious).

3- Tibet consists of Tibet and Greater Tibet (including the province of Amdo and Kham). The Dalai Lama is the leader of all these territories.

4- The peace and security of the borders rests on the stable and unstained relations between China and Tibet. But on the same point, the Tibetans claimed many parts of 'greater Tibet' which had been annexed during the past centuries by various Chinese warlords.

5- Tibet is a fully independent state managing its own religious, foreign, domestic and military affairs under the Dalai Lama and neither the Chinese nor any other government should interfere in this management.

6- All the residents of Tibet, native and foreign, should respect the law of the land, even the Chinese representative should not create tension or disputes within Tibet. Here the Tibetans also brought in the issue of the Chinese Mission in Lhasa, saying that if the Tibetan Government were to allow a Chinese Mission in Lhasa, they could not refuse the same facilities to other countries. They therefore suggested that diplomatic relations with China should be conducted through wireless via the Tibetan Mission in

Nanjing. Other missions in Tachienlu and Beijing could also be opened to facilitate the contacts.

7- The Chinese government should recognize all Tibetan passports when Tibetan nationals travel to China.

8- Chinese traders and others who want to visit Tibet should apply to the Tibetan Government for entry visas and the Tibetan nationals wanting to go to China will apply through the Chinese Government.

9- There are many great nations in the world, many have achieved wealth and might, but only one nation has dedicated itself to the well-being of the whole of humanity, and that is Tibet. The note added that if the Chinese were to return the territories taken away from Tibet, it would have a world-wide effect: "...the nations of the world may not suffer disasters, war, famine and so on.... As you know this will have great bearing on the stability of China's political system." A more concrete consequence was that "...it will render unnecessary the need for both China and Tibet to station large security forces along their respective borders."

The point about the stability of the political system of China has proved less obviously prophetic, at least in the short term – given the 'stability' of Communist China.

Was it right to send such a strongly worded letter to Chiang Kai-shek before entering into any formal negotiations?

But Tibetans, as we shall see again later, knew little about diplomacy. The letter was sent directly to Nanjing through a Tibetan official. It is not clear whether the British knew about the letter, but we can assume that even if Richardson did not know of all the details, the main points were certainly known to him. Lhasa was too small a village for something to happen without everyone (and especially British intelligence) knowing it.

Article V of the Simla Convention had expressly stated that: "The Governments of Tibet and China engage that they will not enter into any negotiations or agreements regarding Tibet with one another, or with any other Power, excepting such negotiation and agreements between Great Britain and Tibet."

It was probably clear to the British government that the Tibetans were trying to negotiate a new agreement with the Chinese behind their back. But due to the 'drafting skills' of the Tibetan National Assembly, the negotiations were still-born.

The Tibetans thought that Chiang Kai-shek would give an immediate and favourable answer to their letter so that they could return to their snowy homeland as they had been instructed to do.

Unfortunately for the poor Tibetans, the Chinese were mainly interested in showing that the Tibetans were part of the 'five-race family'. Their primary objective was clear: the delegates should attend the National Assembly as the Representatives of Tibet.

A cat and mouse game began that was to last for a few months, long enough for the Tibetan delegates to still be around at the time of the Assembly session in November 1946.

They were invited to come and discuss the contents of their letter with the members of the Chinese Assembly and they knew that the Assembly had the supreme power to decide the policies of the Chinese government. They could not escape; the trap had worked. They decided to participate as 'observers' in the deliberations.

Many reasons have been given for the delegation's delay in completing its official duty which was only to congratulate the Chinese for the victory over the Japanese forces. First Chiang Kai-shek refused to reply to the Tibetan Assembly's letter or even to acknowledge it. Another reason which delayed the delegates was that the gifts brought for the government officials and in particular for the President were sent by sea and they had to wait for their arrival before they could officially meet Chiang Kai-shek and his government. In the meantime, they were taken for tours around China.

A strange incident which lowered the morale of the Tibetans was the unexpected demise of the wife of Kheme Zasag, the lay leader of the delegation. One evening she suddenly felt unwell and went to bed with a severe headache. Her temperature rose higher and higher.[19] Hearing about it later in the evening, Chiang Kai-shek sent his personal physician. She was even visited by the American General Marshall, who was in Nanjing at that time. He also sent his personal doctor. Finally she passed away in the early hours of the next morning.

[19]Our informant told us that: "at one point it was so high that there were no marks any more on the thermometer."

The Tibetans believed that it was a natural death, but it was a rude shock for Kheme Zasag and he took a long time to recover from the loss of his wife, especially in a foreign environment.

The Chinese were certainly not unhappy at the delay provoked by the sudden death of the leader's wife. It was in fact a blessing for the Nationalist government because, 'official' delegates from the Tibetan government would attend for the first time the National Assembly. Usually the Chinese had to resort to subterfuge by inviting sympathizers from different parts of Tibet and baptizing them delegates from one province or another.

Among the official Tibetan delegates, it is also probable that many were not averse to attending the Assembly and lobbying in front of the Chinese deputies for their case based on the Kashag's nine-point letter. It was even rumoured that the good treatment that the Tibetans delegates had received helped certain delegates to soften their stand and feel quite happy to participate in the deliberations.

'Chinese hospitality' was a very old tradition, which had often helped to 'soften' the attitude of those who were the beneficiaries of such a welcome reception.

Under similar circumstances, some years later many foreigners, including some Indian diplomats, would fall under the charm of the tough Communist liberation fighters.

The Assembly session finally began and day after day, the credulous Tibetans lived in the hope and belief that the topic of the Tibeto-Chinese border dispute would be taken up.

In the meantime, while discussing the new Constitution of China one day, the Tibetans noticed that the Article 4 said, "all the people of the countries whose delegates are present in this Assembly are subjects of the Kuomintang government."

They suddenly woke up, but it was too late. They cabled Lhasa in their secret code and soon received a wire from the Kashag asking them to repudiate Article No 4 and, if this was not acceptable to the Chinese, to withdraw from the Assembly.

Before walking out of the Assembly, they were directed to state their points clearly, namely that they had come only on a Goodwill Mission and their only aim in attending the Assembly was to discuss the nine-point letter from the Tibetan Government to the Generalissimo. They were also instructed by Lhasa to make a point in the Assembly that the other Tibetans attending the Assembly were not official representatives.

"It was a political game. I later realized (I was at that time so young, I did not know what was going on) some Tibetans also had come, the Chinese had called them from Amdo, some from Kham," said Sadutshang.[20]

It had become clear to most of the Tibetan delegates that the Kuomintang considered Tibet as a part of China and that they would not give away their snow-covered 'province' so easily.

A few years later the Communists used exactly the same technique in inviting representatives of 'minorities' to attend the National Assembly or other functions, in Beijing. They were offered pompous titles and the Communist sympathizers[21] were made the 'official' representatives.

The Asian Relations Conference

On January 30, 1946, Jawaharlal Nehru wrote to Mahatma Gandhi:

>...You know that there is going to be an Inter-Asian Relations Conference in the last week of March in Delhi. This Conference has assumed an unusual importance and it is going to be very representative indeed. Almost every country of Asia from the west to the east and south, including the Arab countries, Tibet, Mongolia and the countries of South-East Asia as well as the Asian Republics of the Soviet Union, will be represented by leading men. That is going to be a unique event in history. Because of this, various European and American Governments are taking an interest in this and are even rather apprehensive because they fear the development of an Asian bloc.[22]

Nehru wanted Gandhi to participate in the function. He later accepted.

At the end of 1946, a rumour circulated in Lhasa that a delegation of the Tibetan Government would be invited to India to attend the Conference. Finally, Hugh Richardson, the British Representative in Lhasa, handed over the official invitation from the Indian Council of World Affairs to the Tibetan Government. He advised the Tibetan Foreign Office that it would be a good opportunity for them to show Asia and the world that Tibet was *de facto* an independent country.

[20]Interview, December 1997.
[21]Like Geshe Sherab Gyatso or Baba Phuntsok Wangyal.
[22]SWJN, Series II, Vol. 1, p. 111.

When the news was confirmed, Teiji Tsewang Rigzing Sampho and Khenchung Lobsang Wangyal, the nominated leaders of the delegation began their preparations for the long journey to represent Tibet for the first time at an international Conference.

At that time they thought that the main topic of the Conference would be the border delimitation. In any case, they wanted to be ready for any eventuality and be able to present their own position.

They collected seven boxes of original documents relating to the Indo-Tibetan borders, including the original Simla Convention documents. They thought that they could eventually claim back some parts of the NEFA and perhaps also Darjeeling, Kalimpong and some areas in Ladakh.

Soon after the Tibetan New Year, sometime in early March 1947, the delegation including two other members (the son of Teiji Sampho, Tenzin Dhondup), two Geshes[23] and two interpreters departed from Lhasa carrying presents for all the Indian leaders in their luggage.[24]

They journeyed first to Dromo in the Chumbi Valley, where they were joined by a messenger of the Kashag bringing a Tibetan flag that they were requested to hoist during the Conference. They then proceeded to Gangtok and Calcutta.

In Calcutta for the first time they heard about the Chinese protest against their representation at the Conference. The Chinese had objected saying that they would represent Tibet and that it was not necessary to have a separate delegation of Tibetans. Very disturbed, the delegation sent their servants ahead to Delhi to check if the Chinese had succeeded to have their invitation cancelled and if their accommodation was still being kept. On receiving an assurance from the Indian Government that they were still very much invited to the Conference as a separate delegation, they proceeded to Delhi.

They probably did not know that their presence had been discussed at the highest level of the Government, with K.P.S. Menon writing to Sarojini Naidu about the Chinese delegation wanting the Tibetan representatives to be listed as Chinese representatives. Nehru himself replied to Menon a few days before the beginning of the Conference:

[23]Doctors in Buddhist philosophy.
[24]We owe some of this information to a report written by Sampho, the leader of the delegation. This paper was published in the Tibetan Review, New Delhi, June 1987, p. 19ff.

Unable to understand Chinese attitude to Asian
Conference when Conference Organisers have fully
explained the position which is in no way injurious to
Chinese interests. Non-official cultural conference
cannot be expected to consider political niceties. We are
unable to say whom Tibetans represent till they come.[25]

Once in Delhi the delegation called on the Prime Minister
designate who immediately told them that the Conference was not
a political conference and that they should not present any papers
on the border dispute. The delegates nevertheless explained in detail
"the independent status of Tibet for thousands of years, its political
and religious development since King Songtsen Gompo and the
spiritual and temporal rule of the Dalai Lamas."

The Tibetan leaders assured Nehru that they would not be the
first to raise the border issue but that they would "not remain a silent
spectator if the Chinese did".

Later, they called on Sarojini Naidu, Sardar Patel and Gandhi
who told them privately that a brochure on the proceedings of the
Conference would be published and that it was the best way for the
Tibetan delegates to demonstrate their independence. This brochure
would be distributed all over the world. Gandhi also told them that
"though he was not wise and well educated, he had the experience
of an old man, therefore he would welcome their questions."

One of these questions was about the closing of Tibet to
foreigners. Gandhi replied that they "should allow people from
outside to visit Tibet and at the same time send Tibetans abroad to
see the world." He further told them that just as the Tibetans follow
Buddhism, many people around the world follow different religions
"which teach the same thing for the good of humanity."

When they left they promised to send him an English or Hindi
translation of some teachings of Lord Buddha but as one of the
delegates said later, "unfortunately, we were not able to fulfil his
wish as within a few months he was assassinated."

The plenary session of the Conference was held in Purana Qila.
The leaders of each of the thirty-two delegations were sitting on the
dais behind a plate with the name of the country and the flag of the
country. Tibet had its own flag with the snow-covered mountains

and the two snow lions representing the dual po⹁ ⹁ers of the Dalai Lama.[26] There was a huge map of Asia behind the delegates on which Tibet was shown as a separate country.

The nationalist Chinese delegation strongly objected to the presence of the Tibetans and the display of the map. They said that they were the only ones authorized to represent 'The Tibet's part of China.' Some say that the organizers accepted to remove the map in order to avoid a show down, though Tenzin Dhondup Sampho, the son of the Tibetan leader, said this was not the case.

Nehru in his welcome speech said that he was welcoming the delegates and representatives from "distant Asian countries and from our neighbours, Afghanistan, Tibet, Nepal, Bhutan, Burma and Ceylon to whom we look especially for co-operation and close and friendly intercourse."

Teiji Sampho said in his opening speech that "our Tibetan Government received an invitation to join the Asian Relations Conference. We are a country which administers its subjects on the basis of religious aspirations. And specially Tibet had friendly relations with India from ancient times...."

After the inaugural session, the participants were divided into small groups to discuss various subjects. It appears that it was during these sessions that the Chinese delegates tried to prove that Tibet was only a part of China and hence they were the true representatives.

One incident is worth mentioning here. One day, the Chinese Ambassador in India invited the Tibetan delegation for a dinner and during the course of the evening, he tried to bribe them.

He told them first that the Chinese Government was looking after the Tibetan interests; the Nationalist Government had already taken up the problem of some lost Tibetan territories in Mon[27] and the case of the Indo-Tibetan border in NEFA area with the Americans, the British and the new Indian leaders.

In fact, it was true that the Chinese had already taken up the matter of Mon with the British Government. The Ambassador told the Tibetan delegation: "We Chinese feel that it is better that you let us talk and handle this border issue. It will be more effective and more influential if we talk about it."

[26]The political and spiritual powers.
[27]Tawang district of Arunachal Pradesh.

Later on, during the dinner, the Chinese delegates told the Tibetans that the Chinese Government had sent Rs 10,000 (a huge sum in 1946) for each of the leaders and Rs 5,000 for each of the other members of the delegation. This money was supposedly for the expenses during the Conference. They were told that they could collect their money in a day or two.

The Tibetans politely refused saying that their Government had already provided for the expenses and that they had more than enough money. They also thanked the Chinese delegates for showing their concern for the 'lost Tibetan territory in Mon'.

They made clear to the Chinese that they had been told that the Conference would not discuss the border issue, but if the matter came up for discussion they would certainly argue their case themselves as they had come prepared for that. The major problem of the undefined borders between China and Tibet was not touched that evening. But the story was not finished.

A couple of days later, a Chinese official came to meet the Tibetan delegates at their residence and told them that they had received a message from Chiang Kai-shek saying that he absolutely wanted the Tibetans to take the money.

Again, Sampho had to politely refuse, but the Chinese official could not accept this refusal and most probably fearing for his own head if he returned to the Embassy without having handed over the money, he requested Sampho to send a personal telegram to Chiang informing him that he was refusing the money. It was done and perhaps the official's head was saved.

Before leaving, Sampho had one last meeting with Nehru to thank him, saying that the Asian Relations Conference had a very great significance for Tibet. The Indian leader is said to have retorted that it 'was their biggest gift to Tibet'.

Although the Tibetans considered it a political and diplomatic victory for their cause, it is not clear even today what the exact purpose of the Conference was. It was most probably only an occasion for the newly liberated nations of Asia to meet together and see how they could "expand their relationship beyond London." It was most certainly a way for Jawaharlal Nehru to show that he was soon to be the new leader of a free Asia.

An official document published during the Conference states that one of the purposes of the Conference was to see: "How to terminate foreign dominion, direct or indirect, and to achieve freedom to direct their affairs in accordance with the will of the people concerned."

Nehru gave one of his idealistic speeches: "Peace can only come when nations are free and also when human beings everywhere have freedom and security and opportunity. Peace and freedom, therefore, have to be considered both in their political and economic aspects."

The main interest for us in the Asian Relations Conference is that early in 1947, all the Indian leaders and the interim Government of India recognized Tibet as a separate and independent nation. A few months earlier, Nehru had responded to a telegram of congratulations from the Tibetan Government on the occasion of the formation of the Interim Government by saying: "My colleagues and I are most grateful for your kind message. We look forward with confidence to the continuance and strengthening of the close and cordial relations which have existed between our two countries since ancient times."

Indeed Tibet was still free and living in peace in its splendid isolation, but not for long!

And when the delegation returned to Kalimpong they were given the disturbing news from Lhasa that Tibet was close to a civil war due to the power struggle between the previous Regent Reting Rinpoche and the present one, Taktra Rinpoche.

They were requested to remain in Kalimpong for some time to help confiscate some of the properties of the former Regent Reting.

It was indeed a bad omen that inside Tibet, the religious leaders were struggling for power when outside Tibet there was a possibility for Tibet to be recognized as an independent state.

15

India Becomes Independent

The Government of India would be glad to have an assurance that it is the intention of the Government of Tibet to continue relations on the existing basis.

Letter from the Indian Government to the Tibetan Government (July 1947)

The First Prime Minister of India

An event that was to affect the future of both independent India and Asia, was the selection of the future Prime Minister of India.

In early 1946, the Indian National Congress had to elect a new President. It was an accepted fact that the leader who was elected Congress President would eventually become the first Prime Minister of independent India. In the meantime he would be designated as the Vice President of the Viceroy's Executive Council.[1]

Though Maulana Azad, the outgoing president was keen to be re-elected, many felt that his chances were minimal. Jawaharlal Nehru, a close friend of Azad, was very keen to be elected himself. On April 24, nine days before the final date for the nominations, when Gandhi heard about Azad's wish, he sent him a letter saying: "When one or two Working Committee members asked me, I said that it would not be right for the same President to continue.... If you are of the same opinion, it may be proper for you to issue a statement and say that you have no intention to become President again... In today's circumstances I would if asked, prefer Jawaharlal. I have many reasons for this, why go into them?"

Right from the start Gandhi indicated his preferences and so Azad was out of the race. But it is important to analyse the reasons

---

[1]The quotes in this part are found in Rajmohan Gandhi. ed., *Patel: a Life* (Ahmedabad: Vallabhbhai Patel Memorial Society, 1991).

for Gandhi favouring Nehru. Perhaps first and foremost was Jawaharlal Nehru's British education.

Almost a year later Gandhi declared that: "Jawaharlal cannot be replaced today whilst the charge is being taken from the British. He, a Harrow boy, a Cambridge graduate, and a barrister is wanted to carry on the negotiations with the Englishmen."

The argument should have been reversed, and it ought to have been argued that someone with deeper roots in Indian culture would be more suitable to negotiate with the British, but it is not our intention to go into these details here.

Another point was that Gandhi knew and even said that Sardar Patel would accept to work as Nehru's deputy while the reverse might not have been possible. He also said that Nehru was better known abroad and was more likely to help India play a role in international affairs.

It is certain that Gandhi thought it would be easier to influence Nehru than Sardar Patel. In a letter to the King, the Viceroy, Lord Wavell, acknowledged that Sardar Vallabhbhai Patel was "the recognized 'tough' of the Congress Working Committee and by far the most forcible character amongst them... He is probably the only one capable of standing up to Gandhi."

For all these reasons, Gandhi was determined to have Jawaharlal Nehru elected as the new president of the Congress.

Three candidates remained in the race: Acharya Kripalani, Jawaharlal Nehru and Sardar Patel. The Working Committee of the Indian National Congress and the Pradesh Committees[2] were asked to choose between the three.

Sardar Patel was easily the most popular in the Congress, especially in the States. Everyone knew his efficiency and the fact that he also had the required toughness in tackling difficult problems. He had 12 out of 19 Pradesh Committees nominate him.

An incident, which could have changed the history of India, occurred on 29 April, on the last day for nominations, when it was discovered that nobody had proposed Nehru's name. Kripalani 'in deference to Gandhi's wishes' circulated a nomination paper in the name of Nehru that day and it was signed by many during the course of a Working Committee meeting.

Once Nehru became one of the official candidates, Kripalani withdrew his nomination and requested Patel to follow suit. He

[2]State Committees.

prepared a statement for the purpose. Patel is said to have passed on the statement to Gandhi who, in spite of his strong preferences wanted to remain fair. He told Nehru: "No Pradesh Committee has put forward your name, only the Working Committee has." Nehru remained silent. After Gandhi received confirmation that Nehru would not take the No. 2 slot in a ministry headed by Patel, he returned the statement (prepared by Kripalani) to Patel, who had no option but to obey his leader and sign the withdrawal of his candidature "so that Nehru could be elected unopposed."

Patel signed out of respect for his political mentor. It was the first of a long series of unanimous 'elections' in the Indian National Congress.

In the following months and years, Patel remained fair in his actions; even though he may have felt deeply hurt, he did not say a word or show it.

History should grant him his greatness. He may not have agreed with the way the election was conducted but had the straightforwardness to put the interests of the state before his own sentiments and aspirations.

Nehru had also been given a chance to withdraw, but he did not do it, Patel did.

That is the difference between the two leaders. India would pay dearly. Though history can not be rewritten, there is no doubt that the future would have been different for the new nation if the Sardar had emerged as the new President of the Congress.

Nehru took over from Azad in early July at an All India Congress meeting and on July 22, he received a letter from the Viceroy inviting him to lead the Interim Government.

Dr. Rajendra Prasad later said that: "Gandhi has once again sacrificed his trusted lieutenant for the sake of the glamorous Nehru."

We have looked at length at the so-called election of the First Prime Minister of India because in the subsequent years, Nehru and Patel were to have diametrically opposed views of India's security threats and the Tibetan issue, particularly on the relations that India should have with her yet-to-be neighbour, Communist China. At that time Tibet was still an independent nation and India and China were not yet neighbours.

Tibet was still a large buffer zone between the two giants.

15 August 1947: India is Independent

The Congratulation Mission showed that the Tibetans were novices at the diplomatic game. Things had begun to move too fast for them. For centuries they had lived a peaceful religious life on the Roof of the World. There were very few foreigners in Tibet who had managed to trespass into Shangri-La in modern times.

It was only the more adventurous characters, some with good intentions and some not, who managed to sneak into the mythic Kingdom. Those who made it were amply rewarded with instant celebrity, as for instance the French explorer, Alexandra David-Neel.

Irrespective of trespassers or world events, life in Lhasa went on as usual. All over the world people were talking about Revolution, Independence or the end of Imperialism, but these notions meant very little in Tibet. These words were only understood by the few who had gone to Darjeeling or Kalimpong to study English,[3] or to Chungking or Nanking to learn Chinese.[4]

For most Tibetans and especially for the monks in the Great Monasteries around Lhasa, 'independence' only meant that they could go on practising their religion as they had done for centuries. Perhaps in this domain they felt in a way closer to China, because China was for them a Buddhist nation. They knew that for generations the relationship between Tibet and China was called 'Choe-Yon', the relation of a priest with its patron.

It was in this the way that the autonomy of Tibet had been protected for centuries.

Only a handful of senior officials who had engaged in negotiations and in drafting the treaties with the British in the early part of the twentieth century (especially at the Simla Convention) knew the importance of this new world concept of independence.

How many in Tibet even amongst the Shapes[5] or members of the National Assembly knew the details of the Simla Convention? Had an opinion poll been conducted in Tibet in 1947 and the Tibetans asked to say if 'Tawang' belonged to India or Tibet. 'Tibet' would have received 100% votes.

[3]Mainly the offspring of the aristocratic and business families of Lhasa or Kham.
[4]Like Baba Phuntsok Wangyal or Rabga Pandatsang.
[5]The Four Cabinet Ministers.

The Thirteenth Dalai Lama who was certainly a great visionary leader had seen that it was necessary for the Tibetans to open their eyes to the outside world and this is the reason why he began sending young children to be educated in England.

In 1920 he also tried to approach the League of Nations[6] to see if Tibet could become a member state, which would have given international recognition to the de facto independence which Tibet then enjoyed. Only a handful of his countrymen could understand his reasoning at that time, and the great monasteries and many aristocratic families who were more interested in their personal privileges did not support him in his approach. Fear of losing their privileges led them not to accept, much less undertake, the necessary reforms.

It can only be said that it was a missed opportunity. Could the fate[7] of Tibet have been different? One fact is certain — it would not have been so easy for China to 'liberate' Tibet.

Whatever may have been the happily harmonious situation in Tibet during the late forties, the world around it was changing fast.

The Tibetans had made their first foray with some success as we have seen, with the Congratulation Mission to India and China before the British, their supposed protector, left India. What was to happen with the successors to the British?

The Tibetans had learned to deal with officers of the British Raj; many of whom had been truly sympathetic to their cause and religion. Officers like Sir Charles Bell, for example, advised the Thirteenth Dalai Lama and made him aware of the way to deal with the Western world.

The Tibetans were quite alarmed when they first heard of the departure of the British from India. Would the new Indian Government be willing to play the same role as the British had played? And supposing that they accepted to play this role, would they have the strength to do so effectively?

Every nation knew that the British had enough muscle to implement their policy decisions. When they had a treaty with

---

[6]Through Sir Charles Bell, see Tsering Shakya, *Tibet and the League of Nations* (Dharamsala: Tibet Journal, Vol. 10, No. 3), p. 48-56.
[7]Or Karma for the Tibetans.

another nation, they had the capacity to implement its clauses. Would newly independent India have the courage and the means to do the same? Richardson, who was to continue as the head of the Indian Mission in Lhasa wrote:

> In 1947 the speed with which the British Government was divesting itself of its responsibilities in India caused the Tibetans to wonder whether they were about to be deprived of the diplomatic support they had hitherto enjoyed in their difficulties with China without anything being provided to take its place.
>
> ...It was left to the British Mission in Lhasa, with little official guidance, to reassure the Tibetans as far as possible.[8]

Viceroy Mountbatten was a man in a hurry and his thoughts were only concentrated on how to get rid of the 'jewel' of the British Empire as fast as possible, regardless of the loss in human life and the harm to the Indian subcontinent. The Land of Snows was not on his agenda.

At the time of India's independence, Tibet was considered a more or less independent state by the British government. The new Indian Government followed, for some time, the same policy. The only restriction was a token suzerainty by the Chinese, conditioned by their acceptance of the complete autonomy of Tibet.

The first communication of the Government of independent India to the Foreign Office of the Tibetan Government was to request the latter to ratify the Simla Convention. By itself this formal request from the Government of India to the Foreign Office of Tibet was the best proof of Tibet's independent status in 1947.

> The Government of India would be glad to have an assurance that it is the intention of the Government of Tibet to continue relations on the existing basis until new arrangements are reached on matters that either party may wish to take up. This is the procedure adopted by all other countries with which India has inherited treaty relations from His Majesty's Government.[9]

[8]Richardson, op. cit., p. 173.
[9]*Notes, Memoranda......*, op. cit., Vol. 2, 1959, p. 39.

Richardson diplomatically said that the Tibetan Government acknowledged the message but did not make any immediate reply.[10]

We do not know if it was the Nationalist Government who, during the Asian Relations Conference, had put in the Tibetans' minds that the territories they lost from the British in 1914 at the Simla Conference should be regained, but when the Tibetans refused to ratify the Simla Convention until these territories were returned, they made the newly independent Indian Government suspicious of the Tibetan intention and this, at a time when Tibet needed all its potential friends.

This was in fact one of the most preposterous actions of the Tibetan Government and even now after fifty years, the only excuse one can think of is that the Tibetan Kashag and National Assembly were very inexperienced in dealing with foreign policy matters. It was not without reason that Jawaharlal Nehru and other officials were very displeased with the Tibetans.

When during an interview with the Dalai Lama we asked him if the Kashag had not committed a great mistake in refusing to immediately ratify the Simla Convention and bargained instead for the return of Darjeeling, Kalimpong, Tawang, etc. to Tibet, he replied:

> Yes, it is my strong feeling. At that time the Tibetan Government should have send a strong delegation to celebrate the Independence of India. Of course that was a big mistake.
>
> About Kalimpong, Darjeeling, I do not know. But about Mon [Tawang] in NEFA area, I remember that around 1948-49, at that time I had no responsibility. I heard and noticed that a special Tibetan National Assembly took place and a British mission came to see the Kashag in the Potala. I remember some of the people of the British Mission who came (I think Richardson was one of them). Along with them, there were some people dressed in Sikkimese dress. From my window in Potala, I noticed that and I was told that the Tibetan National Assembly was taking place, the session was going on because some troops of the Indian Army were entering through

[10]The Tibetans were claming the 'lost' territories of Darjeeling, Kalimpong, Arunachal Pradesh and certain parts of Ladakh before ratifying any treaty. The Chinese will use this Tibetan claim to claim all these areas in turn as part of the People's Republic. The conflict of 1962 was born out of these claims.

Tawang area. The Tibetan government wanted to protest. It was an indication that at that time because Tawang and these areas were in possession of the Tibetans, they wanted to hold on to these areas, although in 1914 at the Simla Convention the border was already demarcated and the [Convention] was signed. But perhaps most of the Tibetans did not know about Simla (the Dalai Lama is laughing). On the spot when some Indian officials came [in Tawang], the Tibetan officials said: 'This is our land' (*laughing*)
They did not know that the Government had already decided in 1914. Finally I do not know what they [the National Assembly] decided.
Such a wonderful Government! (*laughing and laughing*).[11]

Had the Tibetan Government ratified the Simla Convention on August 15, 1947, India and Tibet would have been bound by a formal Treaty.

It is difficult to say today whether it would have made a difference, but it is certain that the only wise course for the Tibetan Government would have been to reply immediately[12] through the Indian Representative in Lhasa asserting its faith in the Simla Convention and accepting the Indian Government as the successor to the British.

India would automatically have assumed the legal rights and obligations of the British. But was Nehru willing to assume the 'imperial' mantle of the British? It is another question.

On August 15, the British Mission at Dekyi Lingka in one of the Kundeling estates in Lhasa became officially the Indian Mission. Hugh Richardson, a faithful friend of the Tibetans was nominated the first Indian Head of Mission.

Nehru later said: "...in the early days after independence and partition, our hands were full and we had to face very difficult situations in our country. We ignored Tibet. Not being able to find a suitable person to act as our representative in Lhasa, we allowed for some time the existing British representative in Lhasa."[13]

[11]Interview with the Dalai Lama, March 1997.
[12]In July-August 1947.
[13]Foreign Affairs Record, April 1959, IV, p. 120.

The fact that India accepted for three years to be represented by an Englishman in Lhasa shows an interesting side of the Indian character which is totally opposite to that of the Chinese. Whatever might have been the political and practical compulsions for India, to accept yesterday's enemy as today's representative demonstrated a level of tolerance which is unthinkable in China.

In Lhasa, "the transition was almost imperceptible. The existing staff was retained in its entirety and the only obvious change was the change of flag. After about a year the British Civil Surgeon was replaced by an Indian doctor; and an Indian officer joined the British officer in charge of the Mission for training," wrote Richardson.[14]

In Tibet the change might have been minimal, but the Tibetans discovered soon enough that tremendous changes were shaking Asia, and the ancient Tibet of brocade and picnics was about to disappear.

Tibet Arms Itself

Tibet started to feel these changes and many in Lhasa believed it was time for Tibet to empower itself against its eastern neighbour.

When the British Mission changed over to the Indian Mission, the Kashag requested military help from India. Some weapons were eventually supplied, comprising 144 Bren guns with 360,000 rounds of ammunition, 168 Sten guns with more than 200,000 rounds of ammunitions, 1,206 .303 rifles with 250,000 of rounds of ammunition and 42 Varey pistols with 630 rounds.

The Government of India however refused to sell the mortars and anti-aircraft guns which Tibet had requested.

The following year, Tibet's Army Chief met the Indian Representative in Lhasa and requested him again for continuous supply of arms and ammunition from the Indian Government. The supplies were on a payment basis and the Tibetans had agreed to pay Rs. 100,000 as an instalment on the first consignment.

During the same year, the Tibetans took steps to create a regiment of 1,000 soldiers. The recruits were to be found from among unemployed youth and even beggars. This idea had soon to be abandoned, but it showed that the main problem in raising a decent army in Tibet was the problem of recruitment.

Elsewhere in the world, one joined the army out of patriotism or idealism or on account of an ideology as for example, the young Chinese peasants following Zhu De, or Peng Dehuai or Mao. But Tibet being a Buddhist nation, joining the army was not considered

---

[14]Richardson, op. cit., p. 173.

to be something glorious. It was considered more patriotic to join a monastery and learn how to perform elaborate rituals, which helped to propitiate the gods who would protect the motherland against external aggression.

This did not mean that monks themselves were reluctant to use weapons when they found it necessary for their own purposes. For example, in 1947 during the upheavals following the arrest of the ex-Regent Reting Rinpoche, the monks of Sera Je College fought a pitched battle with the government troops.[15]

Other recruits, especially officers, were raised from among young aristocrats. This was considered as a sort of a tax or corvée owed to the government, though some could escape by paying someone else to take their place. All this contributed to the fact that the Tibetan army was not a very professional army in the real sense.

Having dropped the idea of raising a new one, the Drongdra Magmi,[16] the old regiment of Kunphela, was revived. The troops however were always short of ammunition and training with live ammunition was not possible due to the need to conserve the available stocks of ammunition.

A welcome change in the Tibetan administration greatly benefited the preparedness of the Tibetan army, it was the creation of specific portfolios for the Shapes.[17]

While Kalon Lama Rampa, assisted by Lukhangwa[18] and one of the Drungyigchenmo[19] was responsible for external affairs, Surkhang Shape was put in charge of the military expenses and supplies. He was assisted by Tsipon Ngabo Ngawang Jigme.[20]

[15]One informant in fact told us that one of the complaints that the Government of India had received was that some of the weapons sent by the Government of India to be used by the Tibetan Army had found their way into the monasteries. We have not been able to confirm this information, though another informant told us that it could not have happened on a large scale.

[16]Translated as 'Better Family Regiment'.

[17]The Cabinet Ministers.

[18]A few years later, he would become the Prime Minister and who would try to resist the Communists taking over the Tibetan administration.

[19]The four Drungnyigchenmos or monk officials were in charge of the Ecclesiastic Office which supervised all religious and monastic affairs in Tibet and at the same time had a say in all secular and political affairs of the Land of Snows.

[20]A couple of years later, Ngabo entered Tibetan history by signing "under duress" the 17 Point Agreement with the Communist government in Beijing. He is still alive and living in Beijing.

Ragashag Shape and Tsipon Namseling were put in charge of the defence and recruitment. It was the first time that Kalons were given distinct portfolios with the entire responsibility for their respective Departments. Under the new arrangement, they could take important decisions in case of urgent matters without referring than to the National Assembly Even in Tibet things had started to change!

Heinrich Harrer, the Austrian explorer who lived for seven years, in Tibet recalled: "The flat pasture around Lhasa were transformed into training grounds for the troops. New regiments were formed and the National Assembly decided to call on the richer classes to furnish and equip another thousand men. It was left to them to enlist in person or to find substitutes.... There was a great deal of patriotic enthusiasm."[21]

Not only had the army to be trained, paid and fed, but supplies had to be organized in case of war. Without a motorable road it was no easy thing.

Another example of the change of attitude was the permission given by the National Assembly to open the border between India and Tibet to motor traffic. They even went a step further; they accepted the idea of an air link between Lhasa and India. A British company, the General Electric Co. was given a contract to built a small hydropower station to supply electricity to Lhasa. The Company was the first to be permitted to land in Lhasa. The permission was given under the Regent's seal.

It should be noted that it was an important strategic decision to open Tibet to air traffic. Due to the high altitude of Lhasa and the rarefied atmosphere, the flying and more importantly the landing of planes posed many problems which required much experience on the air force's side.

The fact that the landing strip needed to be much longer in higher altitudes and the airplane engine more powerful, was an interesting challenge for the Indian Government. The permission given to General Electric also had important strategic consequences in the event of military intervention in the Himalayan region, though for India defending Tibet was more a question of political decision.

[21]Heinrich Harrer, *Seven Years in Tibet* (London: Penguin Books, 1983), p. 235.

But in 1949, Tibet was still recognized as a more or less independent country. If it were not so, would the Government of India have continued to supply arms and ammunition directly to the Tibetan Government without informing the Chinese? In fact, all the dealings between the Indian officials and the Kashag were kept very secret from the Chinese.

During these critical times, building an army was for the Tibetan Government only one aspect of the preparations. Though they understood the importance of mobilizing military means to defend their country, they also thought to focus on strengthening the spiritual forces of the nation.

For this purpose, religion, by all standards the most powerful element in the life of the Roof of the World, had to be invoked. New ordinances were issued and new officials employed to implement this policy. The officials were given plenty of money and a free hand to organize the campaign. All the monks in Tibet were ordered to attend public services at which the Kangyur[22] was to be read aloud. New prayer flags and prayer wheels were set up everywhere. Rare and powerful amulets were brought out of old chests. Offerings were doubled and on all mountains incense fires burned while the wind, turning the prayer-wheels, carried supplications to the protecting deities in all the corners of heaven.

Harrer summarized the preparations by saying: The people believed "with rocklike faith that the power of religion would suffice to protect their independence."[23]

The Trade Mission

It is perhaps from Tsarong Zasag, one of the leading aristocrats from Lhasa and a former favourite of the Thirteenth Dalai Lama, that the idea of a Trade Mission to different countries first emanated. Tsarong was always seen as 'pro-western' and one of the few persons in old Tibet who felt that Tibet should not remain closed in upon itself (or open only to China). The delegation to the Asian Relations Conference on its return from Delhi had reported to the Kashag on the talks they had had there with Indian and foreign leaders and in particular, on the advice given by Gandhi.

---

[22]The Buddhist Canon.
[23]Henrich Harrer, op cit., p. 239.

The Fate of Tibet

The next occasion to venture out of Tibet came from the mint in Drapchi near Lhasa.[24] Tsarong and one of the Finance Secretaries, Shakabpa[25] who were responsible for printing paper currency for the Tibetan Government, felt that there should be a back-up for the printed currency and for that purpose, gold had to be purchased abroad.

> In 1947 there was very little of either grain reserve or gold. Tsarong was worried about this situation, since we were continuing to print new currency. He used always to say that the paper money had to have some backing... He used to talk about a foreign country where all the people suddenly came and asked to change the paper money in silver and gold and the government had nothing, so the Finance minister had to commit suicide.[26]

In October of 1947, only three months after India had become independent, the Kashag decided to send a delegation to India, the United Kingdom, the US and China. The young Tsepon Shakabpa headed the delegation which was comprised of three other members, one of them being Yarphel Pandatsang, who was from one of the richest trading families of Kham and the brother of Tobgye, and who was behind the revolt in Kham in the thirties.

Shakabpa cites three reasons for sending the Mission abroad:

1- Tibet's non-Asian exports, chiefly wool, followed by musk, fur and yak-tails, were usually sold by way of India. All trade business was negotiated through India, which paid Tibet in rupees. The object of the Trade Delegation was to seek the relaxation of the Indian control on Tibetan exports and to request payment in dollars or pound sterling instead of rupees.

2- The Delegation was to purchase gold bullion for the backing of Tibetan currency.

3- As the world was not properly informed of Tibet's political status, and since what it did know was chiefly from

[24]Tsarong Zasag had at that time responsibility for the mint.

[25]Tsepon Shakabpa later became the chief negotiator with the Indian Government and after 1959, served the Dalai Lama's administration-in-exile in diverse capacities, in particular as Representative of the Dalai Lama in Delhi. He became the first Tibetan historian to write a modern history of Tibet.

[26]Goldstein, op. cit. p., 570.

Chinese sources, it was necessary for Tibet to open formal relations with other nations of the world. To demonstrate Tibet's independent and sovereign status, Tibetan passports were issued to the members of the delegation for travel abroad.[27]

The Tibetan delegation was to travel with a passport printed on beautiful handmade paper. In political terms it was perhaps the most significant outcome to be achieved by the delegation.

Although it appears at the end of the list, it is clear that the third point was the most important and pressing one for the Kashag.

On their previous expedition, the Tibetans had discovered that the foreigners, even though non-Buddhist, were perhaps not so bad. Was it not in the economic and diplomatic interests of Tibet to establish contacts with other countries in Asia and the world?

The fact that one of the Pandatsang brothers was included in the Delegation was a mean of giving a voice to the Kham Province of eastern Tibet while at the same time, representing the interests of big business in Tibet.

Later, some observers said that the inclusion of Pandatsang was only a pretext to conduct some 'personal' business under government cover, but this has never been proved. Shakabpa was one of the first Tibetans to have a sense of history[28] and he was without doubt primarily interested in establishing the political status of Tibet as an independent state.

Tsarong, who was a clever official, had for decades dealt with government officials and specially with the Tsongdu[29] and the big monasteries. He knew that the resistance to such a mission would most probably come from the conservative abbots, who would apprehend the danger of 'pollution' of their religion if further contacts were established with foreign countries.

But Tsarong Zasag also knew that the abbots, who were the administrators of the largest estates and the biggest 'tax collectors' in Tibet, could understand 'money talk.' He told them: "What money the monasteries and monks have from doing religious services, etc. just now is merely paper. In case something happens and you or the

[27]Shakabpa, op. cit. p., 295.
[28]At least in the modern way. Gedun Choepell, the scholar rebel of Amdo should also be mentioned.
[29]The Tibetan National Assembly.

monks bring this to us to exchange for valuable objects such as gold or silver then I have nothing to give you."[30]

The argument was strong enough for the Assembly and the representatives of the monasteries to immediately give the green signal to the Kashag to send Shakabpa and his colleagues into the 'wild world'.

They left via the Chumbi Valley and reached Kalimpong in November 1947 and were in Delhi a month later. As they had for the Asian Conference, they brought letters and presents for all the leaders whom they were scheduled to meet.

The first people they called on were the Viceroy, Lord Mountbatten and the Indian Prime Minister. They then began the commercial negotiations and for the purpose met with K.P.S. Menon, the first Indian Foreign Secretary and Harishwar Dayal, an officer from the Ministry of Foreign Affairs who was soon to be posted in Gangtok as the Political Officer in charge for Tibetans affairs.

The Tibetans immediately asked for $ 2,000,000 from the Government of India. Their point was that Tibet was a land-locked country and that her only access to the outside foreign trade was through India. They had to use the port of Calcutta exclusively. When Tibet exported goods, the payment was sent to Lhasa in Indian rupees since India refused to consider that the goods were only in transit. But when Tibet had to import other items from other countries, it had to pay in US dollars.

Shakabpa later explained the situation to the US attaché in Nanjing thus: "We demanded [in Delhi] that, in as much as we are using the port of Calcutta as transport centre only and in as much as the Tibetan products from Tibet are only in transit to other countries through India, they must not withhold the US dollars which the Tibetans earned from export of Tibetan products and that Tibet should be free to import American goods with these dollars."[31]

While in Delhi they met Gandhi at Birla House. Tney offered him a ceremonial scarf, a Khatag.[32]. When Gandhi discovered that the material for the scarf was imported, he expressed shock that such

[30]Goldstein, op. cit., p. 571.

[31]USFR 193.0031, Tibet 12-2448. Letter from Shakabpa dated 28 February 1948.

[32]A ceremonial scarf made of silk used to welcome a guest or present to a host; a symbol of pure heart and a wish for a long life.

a symbolic object for the Tibetans was in fact not locally manufactured.

Shakabpa could not explain this point to the Mahatma, but recalled later that they were "deeply moved by the straightforward advice of the Mahatma."

One interesting historical point to note is that no breakthrough could be achieved in the negotiations because Jawaharlal Nehru was quite upset that the Tibetan Government had refused to accept the Government of India as the successor of the British government. The letter from the Government of India sent to Lhasa had not been answered for months by the Kashag who wanted the Indian Government to return first all of Tibet's 'lost territories'.

When the Trade Mission of Shakabpa came first to Delhi in January 1948, the Government of India and the Prime Minister gave them to understand that the immediate need was for "Tibetan and Indian relations to be put on some official basis."[33] The Indian government refused to talk about the trade matters unless the Tibetans recognized that the Indian government was "the legal inheritor of the treaties, rights and obligations of British India."

As the Trade Mission did not have the mandate to discuss political matters with Delhi, they decided to inform Lhasa about the stalemate. Since no decision was forthcoming from Lhasa, Shakabpa had no alternative but to continue on their journey to China.

It is strange that Shakabpa does not mention this problem in his *Political History*, most probably because being an astute politician, he could perfectly understand the odd (not to say foolish) Tibetan position, but he could not do much, apart from sending telegrams to Lhasa to explain the situation to his conservative government.

B.N. Mullik, the Director of the Indian Intelligence Bureau, summed up Nehru's feeling when he wrote "this ill-advised claim [to lost Tibetan territories], made by the Tibetan Government resulted in the temporary loss of a certain amount of Indian sympathy for Tibet."[34]

It would take another six months[35] for Lhasa to announce that Tibet had accepted India as the successor of British India. In the meantime a lot of harm had been done.

[33]Goldstein, op. cit., p. 574.
[34]Mullik, *My years with Nehru-The Chinese Betrayal* (Delhi: Allied Publishers, 1971) p. 54.
[35]On June 11, 1948.

Richardson, who was the head of the Indian Mission in Lhasa,
wrote about the Indian rights inherited from the Simla Convention:

> ...it appeared at that time [in 1947] that the rights were
> of value to the Indian Government to the same extent as
> they had been to its predecessor and that the Indian
> Government was anxious to secure Tibetan consent to
> the transfer of the whole of the British heritage.[36]

A few years later, Nehru would refuse the same rights and term
them as 'imperialist' rights inherited from a colonial empire.

But in 1947 Lhasa was living in another world.

The Delegation ultimately remained in India for a couple of
months before being directed by the Kashag to proceed to their next
stop: Nanjing.

The Trade Mission in China

Arriving in China at the end of January 1948, they were informed
that Gandhi had just been assassinated. "Members of the Delegation
deeply regretted the shocking news," said Shakabpa.

To enter China, they had to abandon their Tibetan passports as
there was no question of the Nationalist government recognizing
the Handmade Tibetan passports. Though they had tried before
leaving Delhi, they had not even been able to get US and British
visas. They had been told to first proceed to Nanjing and apply from
there.

While in China, the first presidential elections were in 'full swing'
and the Tibetan delegation was invited to attend the National
Assembly as the official representatives of the Tibetan province; a
new constitution had to be adopted and their presence was very
important, they were told. The clever Shakabpa told the Chinese
that they were only a 'Trade Mission' and they were not entitled to
assume any political role.

During their stay they had the opportunity to meet Chiang Kai-
shek. After his re-election as a President of the Republic of China
they met him again; this time they had received instructions from
Lhasa to congratulate him on behalf of the Tibetan Government.

But the Chinese were not so happy with this 'Trade Mission'
travelling around the world with Tibetan passports. After having
been refused entry into China with their Tibetan passports, the

[36]Richardson, op. cit., p. 176.

delegates were told by the Chinese that it was not proper for them to visit the US and UK. The Nationalist Government explained that such visit would create complications with foreign countries, especially with regard to the matter of passports.

When Shakabpa politely refused to use the Chinese passports, they were 'offered' US $ 50,000 for their 'expenses', which he again politely refused. The Kashag had provided them sufficient funds for their expenses abroad, he explained.

One interesting point to note is mentioned in the report of the meeting between the US ambassador to China and Shakabpa in February 1948:

> The displeasure of the Tibetans at any suggestion of the
> Chinese or Indian sovereignty over their territory was
> quite evident in the discussions which they had with
> the Embassy officers. The Tibetans seemed to resent both
> the physical, geographical and economic domination of
> Tibet by India and the attempted political domination
> of the area by China.[37]

It was not easy for the Tibetans to travel. First they had travelled to India on a Tibetan passport, and then they had gone to China on a separate Chinese passport. Then they needed entry visas from the US and British embassies in China to visit these countries. The problem was further complicated when they discovered that to be able they needed an exit visa from China before they could get their entry visas to the US. Both visas had to be recorded on the same passport; but Shakabpa was firm in his decision to continue his trip only with a Tibetan travel document. He had understood the importance of these pieces of paper for the future status of Tibet. What could be done?

They finally decided to leave via Hong Kong with their Chinese passport and when they informed the Chinese that they were returning to India they were granted exit visas. Once in Hong Kong, they clandestinely got a British entry visa stamped on their Tibetan passports. The British knew about their plans but decided to keep them secret. The Chinese later complained to the US government on how they had been deceived by the Tibetans who, on the pretext of trade negotiations, had been allowed to enter the States.

---

[37]Goldstein, op. cit., p. 580.

Was the whole exercise a diplomatic success for Shakabpa and his Tibetan colleagues? Once more, it was not (and would not be for years) a very clear situation. On one side, they managed to avoid attending the National Assembly, having learned a lesson from their colleagues of the Goodwill Mission of 1946. They also succeeded for the first time to use Tibetan passports which were duly stamped with visas from the two most powerful nations of the world, but at the same time they had to use Chinese passports while in China,

Shakabpa had certainly become wiser after the Chinese experience and this is probably the reason why in the following years he would not show any interest in going to China for negotiations.[38] He knew how difficult it was to avoid compromises and bad deals during a trip to the Chinese capital.

He would also explain the Tibetan position to John Stuart, the American Ambassador in Nanjing as well as to his British and Indian counterparts.[39]

The Chinese realized too late that they had lost face: a Tibetan delegation was proceeding to the West without their consent. Their so-called control over Tibet which had in fact been a myth since 1912, was revealed.

The Return to India

The Trade Mission returned to India in January 1949 after some successes during its trip to the US and the UK where they met the American Secretary of State and the British Prime Minister, but they also discovered the limits of their 'independence.' It was clear that the British government preferred to remain vague about the status of Tibet, in order not to antagonize the Chinese.

Great Britain no longer had a common border with Tibet, but in her Hong Kong colony, there was still one with China!

However, the visit of Shakabpa and his colleagues to the US provoked a discussion in the State Department regarding the status of Tibet. Henderson, the American Ambassador to India, was of the opinion that in the event of a Communist take-over of China, the United States should be ready to recognize the independent status of Tibet. The State Department agreed with this policy: "If Tibet possesses the stamina to withstand Communist infiltration — and

---

[38]He stayed in Delhi for a few months in 1950.
[39]The famous K.M. Pannikar.

the embassy in Delhi seems to feel that it does — it would be to our interest to treat Tibet as independent rather than to continue to regard it as a part of a China which has gone Communist."[40]

When Shakabpa reached Delhi, many things had changed in India. Though by now the Tibetan Government had accepted that the Government of India was the successor to the British India, Nehru was beginning to look with admiration at the new regime in China which was rapidly taking over from the Nationalists. While Nehru advocated the rights of the people of Indonesia and the African countries, his position vis-à-vis Tibet (and especially China) was not firm anymore.

The problem of Kashmir had not yet been resolved and Nehru had realized that the United Nations Organization had its limitations and was not able to solve an international conflict in a fair way. The UN Commission's truce proposals had not helped in Kashmir.

Economically, the situation was not very easy for India with the migration of people from East to West Bengal, mounting labour unrest and uncontrolled inflation. It was against this background that Shakabpa returned to Delhi for talks with the Indian Prime Minister.[41]

He first "made a request for the grant of two million dollars to Tibet for the purchase of gold" to back up the Tibetan currency. According to the minutes of that meeting, Nehru "pointed out that India was herself suffering from a severe shortage of dollars" but he promised that "the Government of India would do their best to meet essential Tibetan requirements." When Shakabpa explained that gold was essential for lowering the prices of commodities in Tibet, an unconvinced Prime Minister replied that "rise in prices was due rather to shortage of goods than to inadequate gold backing for currency".

The next question raised by Shakabpa was about free transit facilities through India for Tibetan exports and imports. The Prime Minister remained very vague saying that the matter had been "referred to the Ministries of Finance and Commerce for detailed

[40]USFR, 693.0031, Tibet/1-849. Memorandum on US policy towards Tibet by the Far Eastern Affairs Department of the State Department to the Chinese Affairs Division dated 12 April 1949.

[41]SWJN, Series II, Vol. 9, p. 471. Record of Nehru's talks with the Tibetan trade mission led by Tsepon Shakabpa at New Delhi on 8 January 1949 as reported in the minutes.

consideration and that the considered views of the Government of India were expected to be communicated to the Trade Mission." Shakabpa was assured that the question "would receive very careful consideration from his Government."

When Shakabpa explained that "Tibetans were a poor people and that the Tibetan Government was very anxious to improve their economic condition," Nehru made two broad suggestions for the achievement of that object:

> He told the Mission that, in view of lack of technical personnel and capital and of modern means of transport and communication in Tibet, it was difficult for large-scale industries to be established. It was, therefore, advisable for a country like Tibet to plan her economic development in accordance with the suggestions made by Mahatma Gandhi for India. Tibet should undertake the establishment of cottage and small-scale industries.

The Prime Minister proposed to send some experts from the All-India Village Industries for three months in the summer to advise the Tibetan Government.

Nehru also "suggested a careful survey of the mineral resources of Tibet. He said that even though it was difficult for India to spare trained geologists he would try to make the services of two or three such people available to the Tibetan Government for a few months in order to undertake a preliminary survey of the mineral resources of Tibet."

These experts would report directly to the Tibetan Government.

The minutes concluded by saying that "The Prime Minister assured the Trade Mission that his Government entertained the most cordial feelings of friendship for Tibet, her Government and people and that it would be his constant endeavour to foster the relations of friendship existing between the two peoples."

This appears to demonstrate that in the first months of 1949, Nehru still believed that Tibet was a separate entity with a separate government and that the Indian and Tibetan people had distinct relations.

One of the worries of the Indian government was that if gold was purchased by the Tibetan Government, it could be smuggled back into India. Finally, in March 1949 India agreed to release $ 250,000 in currency for the purchase of machinery and other essential items, but not gold. But the stubborn Shakabpa refused the deal.

His patience paid off two months later, when the Government of India modified its previous order and agreed to the purchase of gold by the Tibetan government. Accordingly, gold was purchased in the US, dispatched to Calcutta and then sent on mules to Tibet.

Expulsion of the Chinese from Tibet

On July 8, 1949, Chen, the acting head of the Chinese mission in Lhasa, was called by the Kashag and informed that he and his staff as well as all Chinese working in schools and hospitals had to leave Tibet. The pretext was that the Chinese Mission no longer had any relations with the Nationalist Government and was not accredited with the new government. In fact, the Tibetan Government was afraid that some (if not all) members of the Chinese mission in Lhasa would switch over to the new Communist regime in Beijing 'for bread and butter', as Richardson put it. The Chinese were swiftly expelled by the Tibetan Government and their bank accounts were frozen in India on the request of the Tibetan Government.

The move had been prepared for more than a year by Tsipon Namseling who had made a detailed list of Chinese agents in Lhasa. The remarkable feature was that secret had not leaked out of the Kashag Office during all that time. It was a record of sorts for a small village like Lhasa.

The Indian Mission was later informed about the *fait accompli*. "It was a complete surprise for the Indian Mission" Richardson commented later.

However the Chinese were expelled with courtesy and a band accompanied them until they were outside of Lhasa.

The cable that Nehru sent to the Political Officer in Sikkim demonstrates the position of the Government of India vis-à-vis Tibet in 1949 and makes interesting reading:

2. We are concerned over the Tibetan Government's decision to turn out all Chinese officials in Lhasa. These officials were appointed by the National Government of China. Their wholesale expulsion will naturally be regarded as an anti-Chinese rather than anti-Communist move. And the Government of India, by letting them into India without any travel papers in contravention of all passport regulations, will be regarded as privy to this move.

3. We can however understand the desire of the Tibetan Government to get rid of persons suspected of subversive

tendencies and officials sympathizing with them. From the Tibetan Government's own point of view it would seem better for Tibetans to expel these suspects rather than all Chinese officials in Lhasa.[42]

Nehru was ready to help to a certain extent when he informed the Political Officer in Sikkim that "there are many difficulties in the way of the Government of India receiving and looking after these suspects. Nevertheless, in view of our friendly relations with the Tibetan Government, we are considering the possibility of giving them passage. We would be gravely embarrassed if they stayed in India."

He concluded by suggesting:

... that unless you or Richardson have any further comments the position of the Government of India should be tactfully explained to the Tibetan Government. The Tibetan Government are the best judges of their own interests but to us it would seem unwise on their part to take any steps which in effect mean the forced discontinuance of the Chinese Mission in Lhasa. The objects of the Tibetan Government will be served by expelling the suspects and officials associated with them. If any of the Chinese, left behind, indulge in objectionable activities they can also be similarly dealt with. Such gradual and considered action will appear justified in the eyes of the world, but not the precipitate action now contemplated.

It is clear that a few months before the Fateful Year, the Government of India, "in view of [its] friendly relations with the Tibetan Government", was ready to help Lhasa with its security concerns. Not only Delhi treated Tibet as an independent entity, but the Government of India accepted that they were the best judge of their problems.

---

[42]SWJN, Series II, Vol. 12, p. 411. Cable to Harishwar Dayal, Political Officer in Sikkim dated 26 July 1949.

16

China Becomes Red

The Communists Take over China

> *Some people have ridiculed us as the advocates of*
> *omnipotence of war. Yes, we are: we are the advocates of*
> *the omnipotence of the revolutionary war, which is not*
> *bad at all, but good and is Marxist.*
>
> Mao Zedong

Before entering into the events of 1950, 'the Fateful Year', and the
upheavals that followed that changed the map of Asia, it is interesting
to look at the players, their motivations, their characters and the
cards in their hands.

The end of the forties saw the entry of a new player in the Great
Game of Free Asia: Red China. To set the tone for the year to come,
a commentator in the *World Culture of Shanghai* wrote in September
1949:

> The India of Nehru attained dominion status only two
> years ago, and it is not even formally independent in
> the fullest sense of the word. But Nehru, riding behind
> the imperialists whose stooge he is, actually considers
> himself as the leader of the Asian peoples. Into his slavish
> and bourgeois reactionary character has now been
> instilled the beastly ambition for aggression, and he
> thinks that his role as a hireling of imperialism makes
> him an imperialist himself. He has announced that
> Bhutan is an Indian protectorate, and now proceeds to
> declare that 'Tibet has never acknowledged China's
> suzerainty in order to carry out his plot to create an
> incident in Tibet'.
> Under the long standing influence of British
> imperialism, the bourgeoisie of India, of whom Nehru

is the representative, have learned the ways of imperialists and are harbouring intentions against Tibet and Sikkim as well as Bhutan. Furthermore Nehru, to carry favour with his masters, the Anglo-American imperialists, is placing himself at their disposal, and shamelessly holds himself as the pillar of the anti-Communist movement in Asia.[1]

He concludes that: "Nehru has already been made the substitute of Chiang Kai-shek by the imperialists."

The above article summarized in communist terms some of the beliefs and convictions of the Chinese Communist leaders. First, Nehru wanted to be the leader of Asia[2]. Second, the Chinese goal was to bring Communism to Asia and, at a later stage, to the whole world in accordance with the Marxist theory of spreading the Revolution. The 'struggle' was between capitalism and socialism, and the Chinese leaders were convinced that in the attainment of their goal, Nehru was an obstacle. Third, it was clear that Tibet was strategically and ideologically a very important base in Mao's attempt to achieve an ideal socialist world.

On October 1, 1949 the Chinese Communists proclaimed the new People's Republic of China. Under the chairmanship of Mao Zedong and with Zhou Enlai as the first Prime Minister and Foreign Affairs Minister of the new Republic, the Communists had taken over the most populous country in the world.

"The Chinese people have stood up, long live the Chinese Communist Party," Mao told the million Chinese assembled on the Tiananmen Square, on October 1, 1949.

Dr Li, his future doctor who had just come back after completing his studies abroad, later wrote: "I was so full of joy my heart nearly burst out of my throat, and tears welled up in my eyes. I was so proud of China, so full of hope, so happy that the exploitation

[1]Quoted by P.C. Chakravarti, *India-China Relations*, (Calcutta: Firma KL Mukhopadhyay, 1961), pp. 161-162.

[2]This assertion was certainly not entirely false, but there was also nothing wrong in India trying to lead Asia. Nehru's actions in the following years would show that he in fact did everything to play this role.

The first example was the organization of the Asian Relations Conference in March 1947.

and suffering, the aggression from foreigners, would be gone forever."[3]

In the months following the take-over, the new regime never missed an opportunity to tell the world through Radio Beijing and the Chinese Press that they were going to be the liberators of Asia. Mao Zedong himself, in a message to the Indian Communist, Party stated in October 1949: "I firmly believe that relying on the brave Communist Party of India and the unity and the struggle of all Indian patriots, India will certainly not remain long under the yoke of imperialism and its collaborators. Like free China, free India will one day emerge in the socialist and People's Democratic family; that day will end the imperialist reactionary era in the history of mankind."[4]

After the 1962 war many Indian leaders spoke of the 'Chinese Betrayal', but we shall see in the following pages that in fact the Chinese Communists never 'betrayed' anything: right from the moment they came to power[5] they announced clearly their goals and objectives and they were always determined to take all necessary actions, including bluff, appeasement, blatant lies and, if necessary, the barrel of the gun, to achieve their objectives.

In the fifties, Zhou Enlai played the game of 'Hindi-Chini Bhai-Bhai'[6] perfectly with India. It was part of the gamble: the Chinese Government had to prepare its military actions (in particular, to build the necessary infrastructure in Tibet) to materialize their declared mission.

Regarding Tibet, there is no doubt that the Government of India knew about the Chinese plans because as early as August 1950, while the Tibetan delegation was waiting for the newly appointed Chinese Ambassador in New Delhi to start negotiating the fate of Tibet, Zhou Enlai told Panikkar[7] that the liberation of Tibet was a 'sacred duty'.

Though he promized that the Chinese would "secure their ends by negotiations and not by military action,"[8] troops were massed in Sichuan on the other side of the Yangtse river.

[3]Dr Zhisui Li, *The Private Life of Chairman Mao* (London: Arrow Books, 1996), p. 15.

[4]*The Communist* (Bombay: January 1950).

[5]We could even say from the time of the 'Long March'.

[6]'The Indians and Chinese are brothers'.

[7]Panikkar had *"expressed the hope that the Chinese would follow a policy of peace in regard to Tibet."*

[8]K.M. Pannikar, *In Two Chinas* (London: George Allen & Unwin, 1955), p. 105.

On one side of the chessboard was the Indian Prime Minister, Jawaharlal Nehru, who was an idealist, not to say a dreamer or a romantic and for him the means more than the goal to be achieved were of supreme importance. Zhou and Mao viewed the world differently: only their goal was important and the ways and means of reaching their final destination was not relevant. Two opposite world views were confronting each other!

Unfortunately for India, one of the few pragmatic leaders, Sardar Patel, would soon pass away. Nehru, alone on the Indian political stage, was unable (or unwilling) to grasp the Chinese mind.

His advisor, Panikkar, the so-called 'Asian' expert was a mere loud speaker for the Chinese regime. He was too enamoured of the new regime in Beijing and his own idea of the 'resurgence of Asia', to be able to clearly analyse the developing situation. Frank Moraes wrote: "Watching Panikkar, I could not help feeling that his sense of history had overwhelmed him. He saw himself projected into the drama of a great revolution, and his excitement had infected him."[9]

There was nobody better than Pannikar to carry the Chinese propaganda to the Indian leadership during the following years.

To come back to the Communist Chinese motivations, we should listen to what Mao declared after the 1962 attack on the Indian garrison in NEFA and the subsequent withdrawal without apparent reason. The Chairman's comments say a lot about the Chinese mentality:

> People may ask if there is contradiction to abandon a territory gained by heroic battle. Does it mean that the heroic fighters shed their blood in vain and to no purpose? This is to put the wrong question. Does one eat to no purpose simply because he relieves himself later? Does one sleep in vain because one wakes up and goes about? I do not think the questions should be asked thus; rather one should keep on eating and sleeping or fighting. These are illusions born out of subjectivism and formalism and do not exist in real life.[10]

It was clear that illusions and subjectivism and formalism did not interest Mao, for he dealt only with 'real life'. For him and his comrades, the only thing which mattered was their final goal.

[9]Frank Moraes, *Report on Mao's China* (New York: Mac Millan, 1953), p. 18.
[10]Quoted in Chakravarti, op. cit.

This was discovered too late by the Indian leaders. Many years later, the Intelligence Chief, B.N. Mullik, a Nehru loyalist wrote: "However, in everything that Mao Zedong does there is a purpose and a method, and, whilst keeping the main aim always before him, he often makes compromises in the details to prepare conditions for the next step forward."[11]

It is a pity that the Director of Intelligence Bureau did not understand this earlier.

A very practical example demonstrates the difference of attitude and mentality between the Indians and the Chinese on the question of maps.

When they took over China, the Communists had maps ready showing large parts of Korea, Indochina, Inner Mongolia, Burma, Malaysia, Eastern Turkestan, India, Tibet, Nepal, Sikkim and Bhutan as part of China.

Nehru himself admitted in the Indian Parliament: "China in the past had added vast territories to her empire and her maps still showed that she included portions or the whole of many present-day independent countries to be within that empire."

While China was engulfing half of Asia in its maps, in March 1950 the Government of India published a 'White Paper on States.'

It was an authoritative document which has been cited in the Supreme Court of India. In an annexe to this Paper was a map of India showing the boundary of the entire western sector of the Tibeto-Indian border as 'UNDEFINED.' In the 'middle sector' of the boundary, up to the trijunction of the Nepali-Indo-Tibetan border, the map was still marked as 'UNDEFINED.' However, on the same map, the McMahon Line (between NEFA and Tibet) was clearly defined.

This map, published by the Ministry of States two months after the Indian Constitution was promulgated, had been drawn by the Survey of India. It was only after Nehru's visit to China in 1954 that a new map was printed by the Survey of India with the western and central Indo-Tibetan boundary clearly defined. At that time the Chinese were working at full steam on the Tibet-Sinkiang Highway through Indian territory (Aksai Chin).

[11]B.N. Mullik, op. cit.

For India, it was already too late and she was in any case swimming in the euphoria of the Five Principles[12] of Indo-Chinese 'friendship'.

Zhou Enlai later cleverly used these maps (of 1950) in a *Letter to the leaders of Asian and African countries on the Sino-Indian Boundary Question* in November 1962 to show how India was an expansionist country.

Still today the Chinese do not recognize Sikkim as a part of India and disregard India's strategic interests and special bonds with Nepal and Bhutan.

More farcical, Gegong Apang, the former Chief Minister of Arunachal Pradesh, was recently refused a visa to visit China on the grounds that as a resident of Arunachal, he was a Chinese national. Amusing Chinese logic!

Communist China basically remained an expansionist empire and for India, with her idealistic and 'friendly' foreign policy doctrines, it was practically impossible to oppose her giant neighbour. What can happen when one player is bluffing with good cards, while the other one is shying away with no cards?

In fact if one studies the history of India, one sees that India never had expansionist tendencies while China — whatever the colour of the regime in Beijing — always had very strong imperialist tendencies.

The famous historian Dr. R.C. Majumdar sheds light on the traditional Chinese way of thinking and acting:

> There is, however, one aspect of Chinese culture that is little known outside the circle of professional historians. It is the aggressive imperialism that characterized the politics of China throughout the course of her history, at least during the part which is well known to us. Thanks to the systematic recording of historical facts by Chinese themselves, an almost unique achievement in oriental countries.... we are in position to follow the imperial and aggressive policy of China from the third century BC to the present day, a period of more than twenty-two hundred years - ... It is characteristic of China that if a region once acknowledged her nominal suzerainty even for a short period, she should regard it

12'Panch Sheel' in Hindi.

as a part of her empire for ever and would automatically revive her claim over it even after a thousand years whenever there was a chance of enforcing it.[13]

To take an example on the Indo-Tibetan border, once in 1943, the Tibetan Government claimed Walong, a small estate in NEFA, as theirs. Though the matter was later settled through discussions between Hopkinson, the Political Officer in Sikkim and the Tibetan Foreign Office in Lhasa[14], one of the first places attacked by the PLA in the late fifties was Walong. It had become a Chinese territory just because it had once been claimed by the Tibetan Government.

Unfortunately, the new leaders of independent India were not able to see through the game. For India, the spirit of attachment to her territory and the need for expansion has never existed traditionally. To quote Sri Aurobindo, the great sage and nationalist leader, in *The Foundation of Indian Culture*:

At no time does India seem to have been moved towards an aggressive military and political expansion beyond her own borders, no epic of world dominion, no great tale of far-borne invasion or expanding colonial empire has ever been written in the tale of Indian achievement. The sole great endeavour of expansion, of conquest, of invasion she attempted was the expansion of her culture, the invasion and conquest of the eastern world by the Buddhistic idea and the penetration of her spirituality, art and thought-forces. And this was an invasion of peace and not of war, for to spread a spiritual civilisation by force and physical conquest, the vaunt or the excuse of modern imperialism, would have been uncongenial to the ancient cast of her mind and temperament and the idea underlying her Dharma.

Another point that should not be forgotten is that the new regime in Beijing, besides being the inheritor of the traditional Chinese expansionism, was also the inheritor of the imperial regime. Mao was the new 'Son of Heaven.' If we add to this tradition the revolutionary zeal of the Marxists, the strength of the combination doubles.

---

[13]R.C. Majumdar, *The Organiser* (New Delhi: Special Dewali Issue, 1965).
[14]It was decided that though it remained British territory, taxes could be collected by Lhasa.

Indeed, it was a most formidable mix: the strong superiority complex of the ethnic Chinese and Marxist ideology. As we have seen above, it was not only Tibet, Taiwan and Hainan that had to be 'liberated' but also India and ultimately the whole world.

Traditionally, the Emperor of China was the 'Son of Heaven.' His mandate to rule came directly from Heaven and he had to rule 'all under Heaven.' He therefore held the dual function of priest and king: the spiritual and temporal power. The administration of the Emperor was not man-made, it had a cosmic dimension.

One interesting characteristic of this tradition was that the people had a role to play in it because, "Heaven sees as the people see; Heaven hears as the people hear", which in practical terms meant that the Emperor's mandate was conditional. If the Emperor did not rule to the satisfaction of the people, if calamities, earthquakes, floods and revolutions occurred, it was the sign that Heaven had been betrayed and therefore the Dynasty had to change.[15]

Mao inherited the mantle of the traditional Emperors in becoming the Chairman of the People's Republic and the head of the People's Liberation Army.

During the following years, Mao would always follow the same pattern of returning to the People whenever things got out of hand or when internal or external pressure mounted. Two examples are the Great Leap Forward and the Great Proletarian Cultural Revolution, during which he appealed to the masses to renew his mandate to rule.

Another inheritance from traditional China was the contempt of the mainland Chinese (the Hans) for their 'vassals' of 'Outer China.' For the Chinese, China is the centre of the world: the term for 'non-Chinese' is 'barbarian.' One should remember that the Great Wall of China was built for the purpose of separating Chinese from 'non-Chinese'.

All those who have visited Tibet since the Chinese occupation have been struck by the contempt shown by the Chinese towards the Tibetans. This remark is also valid for Inner Mongolia, Turkestan and all regions 'occupied' by other Chinese 'minorities.'

A very complex tributary system was used by the central power to control all the provinces. Basically the barbarians from outside

---

[15]It is what happened in China a few months before Mao (and Zhou Enlai) passed away.

China proper had to pay a tribute to the Chinese Emperor on a regular basis and in return, the Emperor bestowed titles and other advantages on his vassals.

Depending on the strength of the empire at different periods of history, the tributary system was implemented or was not. Whenever the Chinese empire was strong it was easy to demand tributes and gifts from the nearest vassals or Inner Tributaries and to insist on the performance of kow-tow in front of the Emperor. In the case of refusal there was always the possibility of sending imperial armies to the vassals. But for the Outer Tributaries the 'vassalage' was more nominal and often depended on the vassal's acceptance of the Emperor's overlordship.

For Tibet, as we have already seen, the relation was on another level and it was defined as a Patron-Priest and not a Suzerain-Vassal relationship. It flourished mainly during non-Han dynasties such as the Manchus or the Yuans.

Marxist Ideology

One of the main themes of socialist ideology as expounded by Karl Marx in *The Capital* is that the workers of the world constitute 'one community.' The problem of the exploitation of the proletarian class is the same the world over, therefore the 'workers of the world should unite'.

This confirms that in the mind of the Chinese leaders, 'revolution' was never limited to the mainland but had to be spread to all the so-called 'barbarians' in Outer China (Tibetans, Mongols, Turks, Manchurians, etc.) and then to the whole of Asia and finally the rest of the world. Mao's letter to the Indian Communists quoted earlier was clear on this point: India also had to be 'liberated'.

The second feature of Marx's theory is that there must be a 'class struggle.' History has only progressed through fights, struggles, conflicts between the capitalist and the socialist forces. "Revolution is not a tea party", Mao had warned.

While Nehru or the Dalai Lama, both adepts in the philosophy of non-violence, were ready to accept many compromises to avoid struggle or conflict, the Chinese did not find anything wrong in war and struggle. Mao went so far as to tell Khrushchev that the Russians could kill half of the Chinese population, the other half would remain and would produce children again. The Russian atom bomb was therefore a mere 'paper tiger'.

Mao noted in *Problems of War and Strategy*: "Some people have ridiculed us as the advocates of omnipotence of war. Yes, we are: we are the advocates of the omnipotence of the revolutionary war, which is not bad at all, but good and is Marxist."

Based on the materialist conception of history, Marx explained further that the driving forces of history were the material relations between classes.

It is certain that a theocratic regime like that of Tibet or a democracy like that in India did not fit into the framework of an ideal society as defined by Mao.

Another gap between China and India as well as Tibet was created by the mentality of their leaders. Nehru, Pannikar and their followers were philosophers, 'dreamers', and idealists, but for Mao or Deng only action and if necessary violent action could bring about the changes they were aiming at. "The philosophers have so far only interpreted the world, the point is to change it," said Mao.

At the end of the Revolution, after a phase of dictatorship of the proletariat, Marx envisages a 'stateless, classless society.' The first phase to reach this stateless society was for Mao to engulf as many countries as possible in the Chinese Empire.

We shall see in subsequent chapters that some politicians like Sardar Patel, Acharya Kripalani and Dr. Lohia also had a clear idea of what was happening, and saw the danger for the security of India; unfortunately it was not true of the Indian Prime Minister.

Mao Zedong repeatedly made his aim clear: "There are two winds in the world, the east wind and the west wind. There is a saying in China: 'If the east wind does not prevail over the west wind, then the east wind will prevail over the east wind'. I think the characteristic of the current situation is that the east wind prevails over the west wind; that is, the strength of socialism exceeds the strength of imperialism."[16]

Though these words were pronounced in 1957, for the Great Helmsman "it was clear that for China there was no question to let the west wind prevail, it was the 'sacred duty' of the Chinese to look which side the wind blows."[17]

'Sacred duty' to liberate Tibet, to make the East wind prevail!

[16]Mao Zedong, *Problems of War and Strategy* (Peking: Foreign Language Press, 1954), p. 18.
[17]Barnett Doak, *Communist China and Asia* (New York: Harper, 1961) p. 106.

From the above, it is clear that for Mao, the final goal was of supreme importance. War, struggle, death were only a part of life, like eating or sleeping. It could not by any means be a sin as it was for Nehru or for the Dalai Lama.

General Li Chi-Min went to a similar extreme when he wrote: "Modern Revisionists have exaggerated the consequences of nuclear war, the results will not be the annihilation of mankind. Over the debris of a dead imperialism, the victorious people would create very swiftly a civilization thousand time higher than the capitalist system and a truly beautiful future for themselves."[18]

Though many times Mao Zedong said that "power comes from the barrel of the gun", in fact he was not too attached to the barrel of the gun; his main interest was the atom bomb. Most of his conflicts with the USSR in the fifties centred around the possession of the bomb. And where better than Tibet to locate sites for testing and storing nuclear missiles?[19]

The Chinese people have exemplified two characteristics during their five-thousand year history: one is their attachment to the land, including what they perceive as their land, and the second is their obsession with power, their thirst to dominate other peoples, other nations. A third one can be added: the Chinese do not like to lose face. These characteristics explain most of the actions of the Chinese leadership from 1949 until today.

On one side of the Himalayas, the Indian leaders 'dreamed.' To quote K.M. Pannikar upon assuming charge as the first Indian Ambassador in Beijing in early 1950: "The People's Republic of China and the Republic of India, representing the oldest communities in the world, are now in a position to cooperate effectively for mutual advantage and for the welfare of their people. The two sister republics of Asia, which between them contain over a third of the world's population, can through their co-operation become a great and invincible force."[20]

Pannikar was thus defining the policy the Government of India would follow blindly for years, even decades: 'friendship at any cost'

---

[18]*The Statesman*, Calcutta, 25 June, 1960.

[19]It was in the fifties that the 'Ninth Academy', China's main nuclear research centre, was built on the Tibetan High Plateau.

[20]Broadcast from Beijing Radio in English on May 21, 1950.

with China, even at the cost of risking her own security; surrendering her buffer zone and losing large parts of her territory.[21]

Even then Mao was planning the invasion of India.

A Planned Strategy

The first plan for 'liberating' the people of Asia was made in the mid-twenties by Stalin who, on the occasion of the opening of the University of Orient in May 1925, spoke about the socialist revolution being the motor of the national liberation movements: "You have to win your own independence", he said. The bourgeois moderate parties had to be isolated and the leaders of the working classes and the peasants had to unite their force under the banner of independent communist parties. He also stressed the importance for Communists to ally themselves with leaders of national liberation movements and the working class in industrialized countries.

In February 1948, an Asian Communist Congress was held in Calcutta which would have very serious repercussions for the Asian Communist movement.

Under cover of a South-East Asian Youth Conference, this Congress decided upon a change in orientation of the revolutionary policy. The Asian Communist parties resolved to play a preponderant role in the struggle and to "initiate and lead violent insurrections and civil wars in the South and South-East countries."

This Conference was followed by a Second Congress of the Communist Party of India. A newly elected Central Committee condemned the Draft Constitution of India and Ranadive, the General Secretary, felt that the time was ripe for the final solution. A programme of insurrectionary activities for installing a revolutionary government was adopted.

While in West Bengal the Communist Party was banned, V.K. Krishna Menon, the Indian High Commissioner in London was receiving a delegation of the British Communist Party who had come to plead for the release of their Indian comrades.

Nehru wrote apologetically to Menon: "The West Bengal Government banned the Communist Party without informing us".

In November 1949, a meeting of the World Trade Union Association was held in Beijing. Moscow accepted that the New

[21]We should not forget that India is the only country in Asia which has since her independence, lost large parts of her territory, with the exception of Tibet, which lost her entire independence.

China would take the lead and conduct the 'liberation' of all the people of Asia. With Soviet help, a detailed plan was prepared by a Liaison Bureau located in Beijing. A co-ordination Bureau was created in Beijing; it would become the nodal centre for national independence movements of Asian countries.The objectives were clear: to create revolutionary cells and with the help of working classes bring about the liberation of the entire South and South-East Asia through guerrilla warfare that would later spread to cities. The case of Vietnam was given as an example. The insurrections, which occurred in many places in Asia — Burma, Malaysia, Indonesia, Philippines — during the following year, were the result of this Conference.

The history of Mao's China is a tale of well-planned and well-executed moves. All the events from 1949 onwards have been unfolded in a perfectly calculated sequence: the invasion of Tibet in 1950; after a very vague protest by the Indian Government and the adjournment of the Tibetan Appeal to the UN (at India's instance), the 1951 Sino-Tibetan 'Agreement' (forced on the Tibetans under duress); then the 1954 'Panchshila' Policy (neutralizing India under the Hindi-Chini.Bhai-Bhai bluff); the first incursions on Indian soil at the end of the fifties; the crushing of the Tibetan uprising in 1959, and finally the 'teaching of a lesson' to India in October 1962.

Mao was a great strategist and he never forgot what his final goal was; it will be therefore wrong for Nehru and his advisors to later talk about 'surprise' and 'betrayal.'

The Indian leaders had only fooled themselves by believing in the Hindi-Chini Bhai-Bhai doctrine, while the Chinese aims were always clear, loud and publicly announced. Nowhere these plans were hinting to a friendship with India.

The 'liberation' of Tibet was the first step to 'liberate' other peoples of South Asia. The Vietnamese Revolution organised by Ho Chi Minh was another step.

In October 1951, after the 'liberation of Tibet, the Chinese intervention in Korea and the successes of Ho Chi Minh in Vietnam, Zhou Enlai presented a report on Foreign Affairs. He said:

> Under the influence of the success of the Chinese
> Revolution, the consciousness of the Asiatic people has
> grown to an unprecedented level, the liberation
> movements are growing day after day. The unity of all
> the people of Asia will create a powerful force without

rival in Extreme-Orient, and it will push forward the great wheel of history in the sense of the movement for the independence and liberation of the people of Asia.[22]

No doubt the term 'liberation' was meant in the sense that the Tibetans had begun to bitterly experience. In this grand plan, India was only a 'target' for a similar export of a 'People's' revolution.

Strategic Location

It is stated by Ginsburg in his study on Communist China and Tibet that "he who holds Tibet dominates the Himalayan piedmont; he who dominates the Himalayan piedmont, threatens the Indian subcontinent; and he who threatens the Indian subcontinent may well have all the South-east Asia within his reach, and all of Asia."[23]

Mao the strategist knew it very well, so did the British who had always managed to manoeuvre to keep Tibet as an 'autonomous' buffer zone between their Indian colony and the Chinese and Russian empires. The Government of India, upon inheriting the past Treaties of the British, should have worn the British mantle with its advantages for Indian security and its sense of responsibility vis-à-vis Tibet; unfortunately for fear of looking like a neo-colonialist state, they failed to do this without giving any thought to the consequences which would follow.

The strategic position of Tibet became even more visible when China joined the restricted circle of the nuclear nations.

Is there a more ideal place than the Tibetan high plateau to position intercontinental ballistic missiles with nuclear warheads pointed towards India and Soviet Union?

Other Factors

Some other factors have to be taken into account to fully understand subsequent events. Apart from Marxist ideology, another point was the leadership of Asia.

The Chinese believed that traditionally they were the leaders in Asia. The fact that Nehru also aspired to lead Asia, antagonized the Chinese against him.

The Asian Relations Conference in March 1947 in Delhi and a second Conference on Indonesia in 1949, saw Nehru take the initiative for the leadership of Asia.

[22]Raoul Salan, *Indochine Rouge* —.*Le Message d'Ho Chi Minh* (Paris: Presse de la Cité, 1975), p. 50.

[23]Gingsburg & Mathos, *Communist China and Tibet* (The Hague: Martinul Nijhoff, 1964).

The Chinese were not long to reply:

In his assumption of the role of the vanguard in the international gamble against people of Asia, Nehru has committed a series of malicious intrigues, all following the victorious march of the liberation movement of the Chinese people. As early as the days prior to India's independence, Nehru had called the Pan-Asian Conference....Early in 1949, Nehru called another Asian Conference in New Delhi, outwardly with the motive of mediating in the Indonesian dispute, but actually for undertaking a preliminary discussion of South-east Asian alliance. On February 28, 1949, Nehru nominally to mediate in the Burmese civil war, called a conference of the British dominions, the real purpose of which was to discuss the strengthening of measures for the Anti-Communist alliance in South-east Asia.... and so up to the recent act of Nehru in serving as the hireling of Anglo-American imperialism in the attempt to invade Tibet.[24]

There is no doubt that most of the positions taken by Nehru and his subsequent actions were dictated by his ambition to lead Asia and the 'non-aligned' nations. He built up the image of a modern-thinking leader with his frequent visits abroad. His offers of mediation in many conflicts such as Korea helped to promote this image.

Many newly independent nations, especially in Asia, started looking towards India as their advisor, guide and protector.[25]

This role was not acceptable to the Chinese leaders.

The 'coup' of Tibetan 'liberation' was a master-stroke. It demonstrated to the world who the real leader of Asia was, while showing that India was incapable of defending a smaller country, and thus Nehru was only a 'paper tiger'.

[24]Quoted in Girilal Jain, *Panchsheela and After* (Bombay: Asia Publishing House, 1960), Chapter 1.

[25]For Tibet, this image of Nehru and India in the third world had a reverse effect, as most of the nations were ready to align with India, but when India refused to assume her responsibilities vis-à-vis Tibet and bent backward for the sake of Chinese friendship, these nations understood that India could not be the leader it pretended to be. Why did India have one standard for Indonesia and another for Tibet?

Ideologically the 'liberation' of Tibet meant that the Marxist theory could spread to another 'feudal' country; it was a real 'liberation' in Marxist terms.

Furthermore China was re-establishing her *de facto* suzerainty over Tibet, which had been lost many decades ago. It was the first step towards the South, the opening of the gateway to India and to other countries that China was claiming as her own — Nepal, Bhutan, Sikkim, etc. It should not be forgotten that Mao had termed Tibet the palm of the hand and the five fingers were Ladakh, Sikkim, Nepal, Bhutan and NEFA.

Accusing someone else of a crime that you intend to commit is also very typical of the Chinese mentality and tactics. Attack being the best form of defence, a few months before the 'liberation' the Chinese propaganda was speaking of "the recent act of Nehru in serving as the hireling of Anglo-American imperialism attempt to invade Tibet."[26]

The Government of India followed a strange policy of appeasement. The more virulent the attack or insult, the harder they tried to appease the Chinese and become their friends. The Hindi-Chini Bhai-Bhai slogan was the outcome of this movement: each time China made a step forward, India bent over backward to appease Chinese susceptibilities.

Another strange stand of the Government of India were Nehru's double standards; he backed the defence of Indonesia and Algeria and, in similar circumstances, refused to do anything for the Tibetan case when his own borders were threatened.

Another fact which explains the motivation of the Communists leaders in invading Tibet was the *lebensraum* needed by the fast-increasing Chinese population. A few figures will explain the problem. The policy of the Chinese Government to send settlers into the 'Provinces' or 'Autonomous Regions' started very early.

By 1987, 75 million Han Chinese had settled in Manchuria. In Eastern Turkestan (Xinjiang), 7 million Hans settled in an area where only 200,000 Hans had lived in 1949. In Inner Mongolia, the settlers have outnumbered the Mongols (8.5 million for 2 million), while in

---

[26]In 1950, there were only six foreigners in Tibet: Harrer and Aufschneiter, two Austrian prisoners of war who had escaped from a camp in India and who were involved in civil works in Lhasa, two British radio operators, Reginald Fox and Robert Ford; George Patterson, a priest who was living in Kham; and Nedbailoff, a White Russian in Lhasa.

Tibet the Han population today is estimated at 7 million to which the 500,000 troops of the Liberation Army should be added, making the Tibetans a minority in their own country.

In an article[27] entitled *A Vast Sea of Chinese Settlers Threatened Tibet*, the Dalai Lama wrote:

> The area where I was born, the Kokonor region of north-eastern Tibet, now already has a population of 2.5 million Chinese and only 700,000 Tibetans, according to recent Chinese newspaper reports. The Chinese claim to be giving special care and attention to the so-called Tibet Autonomous Region, which comprises only the western and central parts of Tibet, but they are sending large numbers of young Chinese colonists into eastern and north-eastern parts of our country.

We should also point out that the Communist Party in China has "grown up as an army and not a civilian organization like any other communist party." Mao's strength was in the People's Liberation Army, "military virtues and military men have been elevated to a position of new prestige in the Chinese Society, and the population of the country has been fully mobilized to support the military establishment."

After the revolution China had the largest army in the world and it was in Mao's interest to keep this army busy.[28]

'Liberation' tasks had to be given to the army and Tibet was an ideal job. Strategically, the next steps in the Marxist Revolution could be prepared and ideologically, Mao and his colleagues were liberating a feudal 'province' poisoned by its belief in the 'opium' of religion and under the servitude of 'a clique of lamas'.

It can be said that India despite her good intentions, her non-violent and non-aligned policy, had not been able to prepare the country with the necessary strength to convert her ideals into a possible concrete reality. We shall see the consequences of this policy during the Fateful Year.

---

[27] *The New York Times*, August 1985.

[28] Though it is true that they were busy at the same time on the Korean front.

17

Don't Rock the Boat

The Months before the Fateful Year

> *The emphasis [of the Tibet policy] was on not 'rocking the boat'.*
>
> **Advice from a British diplomat to his American counterpart**

Having gone through some of the Chinese motivations, it is also interesting to look at the position of the other players, mainly India and the Western powers, at the time Mao was declaring the new People's Republic of China from Tiananmen Square.

The year 1949 saw all the players exercising great caution. Nobody knew how to react to the Communist regime in Beijing, the new entrant in the game.

In one of his letters to the Premiers[1] of the Indian provinces, Nehru wrote:

> In any event, what is likely to happen is a consolidation of the Communist regime in about two-thirds of China and the advance of the Communist forces towards the South. Within a few months they should occupy the whole of China. It is possible that a splinter government might be formed in Canton, to oppose the Communists. But this is hardly likely to achieve anything. We may take it therefore that the whole of China will be under the control of the Chinese Communists within a few months.[2]

On another occasion he told to the Foreign Secretary:[3]

> In view of developments in China, we should keep in

---

[1]Later known as Chief Ministers.
[2]SWJN, Series II, Vol. 10, p. 303. Letter to the Premiers dated 1 April 1949.
[3]SWJN, Series II, Vol. 11, p. 389. Note to the Foreign Secretary, 5 June 1949.

close touch with their reactions in Tibet, and we shall think of the policy we should pursue there in case anything happens. The first thing to do is to get fairly full reports from Kashgar as to what is happening there.[4]

A few days later, he however clarified the Government of India's stand on China. In reply to a telegram from Pannikar who was still the Indian Ambassador in Nanking, he made it clear that India would not ally with the US. This would be one of the policy decisions with regard to China:

...the American Ambassador is reported to have said that the Indian Government had promised to cooperate with the U.S.A., in China. We have of course done no such thing. Our Ambassador might be informed that we do not proposed to align ourselves with anybody in regard to China.[5]

On the pretext of being 'non-aligned' or 'neutral', Nehru would systematically refuse to 'work' with Western governments. The practical result, at least for the Tibetan issue, was that this neutrality very often became synonymous with an alignment with the Chinese position.

Another interesting point to note is that India had accepted Tibet as one of her friendly neighbour in 1949. It is apparent from the following quotations. On March 1949, in a speech on Indian foreign policy, the Indian Prime Minister declared:

The nearby countries always have a special interest in one another and India must, inevitably, think in terms of its relations with the countries bordering her by land and sea. What are these countries? If you start from the left, Pakistan; I would also include Afghanistan, although it does not touch India's borders; Tibet, China, Nepal, Burma, Malaya, Indonesia and Ceylon. In regard to Pakistan, the position has been a very peculiar one owing to the way Pakistan was formed and India was divided.[6]

Later he added: "our relations with them [our neighbours] are quite friendly. Take for instance, Afghanistan is exceedingly friendly

[4]Ibid.
[5]Ibid.
[6]SWJN, Series 2, Vol. 10, p. 464. Speech at the Indian Council of World Affairs on 22 March 1949.

and our relations with Tibet, Nepal and all these countries roundabout are also very friendly. In fact, I think I am justified in saying that there is no country in this wide world today with which our relations may be said to be inimical or hostile."

On July 20, 1949, after a visit to Ladakh, he wrote in another letter to the Premiers of the Provinces: "Ladakh is a little known area and deserves notice for a variety of reasons. It is, as you know a frontier area and on an airfield near Leh there was a signpost pointing out directions to Tibet, China, the Soviet Union and other surrounding countries."[7]

It is clear from the above statements as well as others by the Indian Prime Minister that Tibet was a separate entity from China.

In 1949 Nehru was not overly worried about the situation developing in China. In a letter to John Matthai dated September 10, he wrote:

> Recent developments in China and Tibet indicate that Chinese Communists are likely to invade Tibet sometime or other. This will not be very soon. But it may well take place within a year. The Government structure of Tibet is feeble. A Lama hierarchy controls the whole country, the majority of whose population is very poor. Any effective attempt by the Chinese Communists can hardly be resisted, more especially as the greater part of the population is likely to remain passive and some may even help the Communists. On the other side at Sinkiang, Soviet influence is already strong.
>
> The result of all this is that we may have the Chinese or Tibetan Communists right up on our Assam, Bhutan and Sikkim border. That fact by itself does not frighten me.[8]

Three important points have to be noted here; they would remain the corner-stone of the Indian Government's policy on Tibet. Firstly, Nehru had accepted that Tibet would be invaded; secondly, for Nehru and his advisors Tibet was a rather primitive country and social reforms were long overdue. We shall see that Nehru was not completely adverse to a small dose of socialism to wake up the 'lama hierarchy' to the social realities of the twentieth century.

[7]SWJN, Series II, Vol. 12, p. 297. Letters to Premiers of Provinces.
[8]SWJN, Series II, Vol. 13, p. 260. Letter to John Matthai.

The third point is that Nehru 'was not frightened' at the idea of having a new neighbour on his northern border. It would be a major point of difference with Sardar Patel, the Deputy Prime Minister.

Tibet Isolated

In reading through the correspondence between the US and British embassies in India and their respective governments, one point is obvious: even in 1949, the Western powers had very little information about what was going on inside Tibet. India was perhaps slightly better informed about the prevailing conditions due to the regular reports of the Indian Agent in Lhasa, but in general, intelligence agencies had practically no knowledge of the political forces at play within the theocratic Tibetan society.

Tibet was still a very mysterious land.

In 1949, in order to remedy this situation, the British Foreign Office and the American State Department wanted to send covert missions to Tibet to get first-hand information. Their main problem was that they "were discouraged by GOI which at present has a practical monopoly on Tibet's foreign relations," as Henderson, the American Ambassador to India put it in a cable to Dean Acheson, the US Secretary of State.

Ultimately the proposed visit had to be postponed until 'after the winter' and finally abandoned in 1950 due to the changed situation in China and the communist threat over Tibet. But the fact remained that in 1949 India had 'a practical monopoly' of Tibetan foreign relations and communications.

An event which would have grave political consequences for the future was a letter sent by the Kashag to the Chairman of the People's Republic of China on November 2, 1949.

Similar to the earlier letter sent to the Government of India demanding the return of the 'lost territories' of Kalimpong, Darjeeling, Tawang and others, the letter from the Tibetan Government to Mao Zedong[9] was couched in tough language.

> Tibet has from the earliest times up to now, been an
> Independent Country whose Political administration
> had never been taken over by any Foreign Country; and

[9]To Mr. Mautsetung (sic), Chairman of the Chinese Communist Govt, Peiping.

Tibet also defended her own territories from Foreign invasions and always remained a religious nation.

In view of the fact that Chinghai and Sinkiang etc are being situated on the borders of Tibet, we would like to have an assurance that no Chinese troops would cross the Tibetan frontier from the Sino-Tibetan border, or any such Military action. Therefore please issue strict orders to those Civil and Military Officers stationed on the Sino-Tibetan border in accordance with the above request, and kindly have an early reply so that we can be assured. As regards those Tibetan territories annexed as part of Chinese territories some years back, the Government of Tibet would desire to open negotiations after the settlement of the Chinese Civil War.[10]

Many friends of the Tibetans including Richardson and Harishwar Dayal[11] tried to dissuade the Kashag from dispatching this letter which would certainly be seen as a provocation by Mao. But the Tibetan Cabinet stuck to its decision and sent the letter.

Soon after, the Tibetan Government also wrote to the US Secretary of State that if Mao would ignore the Tibetan letter and take an aggressive attitude in sending troops to Tibet, "then the Tibetan Government will be obliged to defend her own country by all possible means. Therefore the Tibetan Government would earnestly desire to request every possible help from your Government."

Though the Kashag requested the American Government to "consider extensive aid in regards [to] civil and military requirements", no specification was given to the Secretary of State who was just asked to "send a favourable reply at the earliest possible opportunity."

Richardson, the Indian Agent in Lhasa had also informed his Government as well as the British that the Tibetan Government had decided to appeal to India, the US and UK for military help.

We have to note here that Richardson who was working for the Government of India sent copies of his weekly and monthly reports

[10]Quoted by Melvyn Goldstein, op. cit. p. 624 from the British Foreign Office Records files (FO371/76317).
[11]The Indian Political Officer in Sikkim who was, at that time, on a mission to Lhasa.

to the British Government also. In a sense, it has been a grace for historians as these papers are today available for public scrutiny in the India Office Library and Records in London, while in New Delhi they would probably have remained 'classified' for another couple more decades.[12]

It appears that when Pannikar returned from Nanking, he informed his government that Tibet "was wide open from [the] east and any efforts [to] help Tibet would merely involve India in conflict with Chinese Communists."

Several times, the British High Commission reminded the Government of India that India was "the heir of British policy of preserving integrity of Tibet." The British even proposed to "furnish GOI arms and equipment for [the] latter to give to Tibet." The British Government was ready to give a "guarantee of support in case of complications with Chinese Communists."[13]

The American Government was certainly interested in such a proposal. But the Government of India's position was too vague to be of any help for the Tibetans. When on November 16th, the Indian Prime Minister was asked in a press conference about the position of Tibet in relation to India, he declared:

> About the position of Tibet, I may say that for the last 40 years or so, that is to say, during the regime of the British in India, a certain autonomy of Tibet was recognised by the then Government of India and there were direct relations between Tibet and India.
>
> As regards China's position in Tibet, a vague kind of suzerainty was recognised. All these things were never clearly defined as to what the position was, matters remained vague and they have remained vague in that way. We have a representative in Lhasa. We trade with them directly but in a vague sense we have accepted the fact of China's suzerainty. How far it goes, one does not know.[14]

[12]Though it may have not been 'diplomatically' correct for Richardson to pass his correspondence to his previous employer.

[13]USFR, Telegram 893.00/11-2149 from The Chargé in India (D'onavan) to the Secretary of State, New Delhi, November 21,1949.

[14]SWJN, Series II, Vol. 14, p. 191.

The word 'vague' was used five times in a few sentences. How to better define the position of Nehru's Government vis-à-vis Tibet at the end of 1949?[15]

Later, in a discussion with an American Embassy official, Bajpai said that Nehru's remarks "were purposely vague, as final policy had not as yet been evolved." However he added that "if the Communist Government of China endeavoured to take over Tibet, [the] situation would be very difficult. The Government of India wanted as much as possible to keep the status quo: they "recognized Chinese suzerainty over Tibet but that same time Tibet had always exercized a certain independence in its dealings,"[16] with the Indian Government.

Unfortunately this 'vagueness' prevailed right upto the fatal day in 1962.

However, Sardar Patel was not in favour of vagueness, and in June he wrote to Nehru:

> We have to strengthen our position in Sikkim as well as in Tibet. The farther we keep away the Communist forces, the better. Tibet has long been detached from China. I anticipate that as soon as the Communists have established themselves in the rest of China, they will try to destroy its autonomous existence. You have to consider carefully your policy towards Tibet in such a circumstance and prepare from now for that eventuality."[17]

One point was clear: the Government of India was not ready to get involved in a full-fledged military operation in Tibet.

However, in the summer of 1949, the Chief of Army Staff sent a young intelligence officer to survey the eventual routes that could

[15]And unfortunately at the end of 1950's.

[16]USFR, Telegram 893.00/11-2149 from The Chargé in India (Donovan) to the Secretary of State, New Delhi, November 21, 1949.

[17]The comment of Patel about Tibet had come after a letter from Attlee to Nehru about the danger for Hong Kong of the Communist victory. Patel had written to Nehru: "as regards Attlee's letter to you, if I may suggest, you might send the draft reply to me before dispatching it to London. It is possible I may be able to offer some useful suggestions." But Nehru did not think so and replied: "The reply to Attlee about Hong Kong has already been sent... Meanwhile, the Communists in China are behaving very correctly towards the foreigners and even business is continuing to some extent."

be used to bring troops and ammunition in the event of a 'political' decision to defend Tibet.

The fact that this covert mission took place and this with the knowledge of K.P.S. Menon, the Foreign Secretary, is proof that in the summer of 1949, the Government of India was still keeping all its options open. In the words of this officer who later became one of the most decorated Generals of the Indian army:

> My mission was very simple. It was to see the routes in these areas. In the army, we are always prepared for eventualities. The Army does not decide to go anywhere, but should we be asked to go anywhere, we must know where the routes are. In fact the army does not make any recommendation at all [that we should go for war or not].[18]

He made his recommendations, nothing was impossible, after all Younghusband had done it 45 years earlier under much more compelling conditions, but it was a 'political' choice.

A few months later, the American *Chargé d'Affaires* was told by San Jevi, an Indian intelligence official that at an "interdepartmental meeting held to discuss Tibet it was decided [that the] most GOI could do was send moderate supply [of] small arms plus a few officers to instruct Tibetans how to use them." India was not ready to "become involved in any military adventures in Tibet."[19] It was understandable and in conformity with the logic of Nehru's philosophy of non-violence.

Though the Governments of the US and UK agreed with the Government of India on many strategic considerations regarding an attack on Tibet, the main concern of the Western powers was the tendency on the part of Government of India to "throw up its hands and say nothing could be done and retire to its own frontiers." The Western diplomats felt that there was "too much of a tendency in that direction" on India's part.[20]

We shall later see that many Indian politicians shared this perception.

[18]Personal Interview.
[19]USFR, Telegram 893.00/11-2149 from The Chargé in India (Donovan) to the Secretary of State, New Delhi, November 21, 1949.
[20]USFR, Telegram 893.00 Tibet/11- 2249 from The Chargé in India (Donovan) to the Secretary of State New Delhi, November 22, 1949.

At the end of 1949 the opinion among Western diplomats in Delhi and in particular Ralph Stevenson, the British High Commissioner, was that Mao would not "for some considerable time wish to face cost and difficulty of mounting expedition into Tibet, where no great material advantage was to be derived".[21]

Western analysts believed that the Communists would leave Tibet 'alone' for a long time and that the only threat Tibet might face in the near future was the communist infiltration which would eventually weaken Tibet from within.

However, everyone in Delhi was conscious of the danger of the Tibetan Kashag provoking the new Chinese Government through the kind of letter it had sent to Mao demanding the return of its border territories.[22]

The Tibetan Government had little experience in diplomacy. What further complicated the situation was that the big monasteries could not understand that Tibet was not in a position to twist anyone's arm or to make demands for 'lost' territories either from India (in 1947) or from China.

Through all available channels, the Tibetan Government was advised not to 'rock the boat.' For this reason, the proposed British and American Mission in Tibet was cancelled.

On November 3, the Kashag sent another message to the American Secretary of State, asking it this time to support Tibet's admission to the UN:

> As Tibet being an independent state, we have no dangers from other foreign countries but in view of the spread of communism and their successes in China, there is now an imminent danger of Communist aggression towards Tibet.
>
> As all the world knows that Tibet and Communist China cannot have any common sympathy by reasons of religion and principles of life which are just the opposite, therefore in order to defend our country against impending threat of communist and also to preserve our future independence and freedom, we consider it most

[21]USFR, Telegram 893.00 Tibet/11-2349 from The Chargé in India (Donovan) to the Secretary of State, New Delhi, November 23, 1949.

[22]As well as the one sent to the Government of India two years earlier demanding the lost territory.

essential for Tibet to secure admission of her
membership in the United Nations General Assembly.[23]

A similar appeal was sent to the Indian and British Governments.
However, nobody was keen to support such a demand. The main
argument of the Indian Government was that in the Security Council,
the Soviet Union would use its veto and it would therefore be a
waste of time and energy for everyone concerned. Further it would
unnecessarily infuriate the Chinese.

The British Foreign Office in New Delhi also expressed the
opinion that the USSR would veto the Tibetan application to the
UN. They suggested that "the Kashag be explained of the position
of the Western Governments through Indian resident in Lhasa."

An interesting point has to be noted here: London sent a similar
message to Karachi "for information [of the] Pakistan Government
and to obtain its views."

We do not know if the Pakistani Government ever replied to
this communication but it shows that London considered both Delhi
and Karachi as the inheritors of the British colonial legacy. Pakistan
could thus have been one of the inheritors of the Simla Convention.
We should remember that Pakistan had occupied a part of Kashmir
which shared very close historical links[24] as well as a border with
Tibet. In the early sixties, Pakistan eventually 'ceded' some of these
areas to China.

In the meantime, Acheson wanted to put pressure on India to
take a stronger stand. In a cable to Henderson, he stated: "Dept
suggests you may find opportunity use Commie threat Tibet to
emphasize GOI dangers to India itself arising from Commie China
and unrealism semi-detached attitude India respecting
developments in China."

Many in the Indian Government were not at all concerned by
the communist threat. In their view the new regime in Beijing was
far superior to the old Nationalist regime and a dose of communism
was considered by many, such as Pannikar, as a blessing for Tibet.

Tibet had no friends.

The fate of this peaceful religious nation was not the concern of
any great powers. A paper from the British Foreign Office clearly

[23]Reproduced in USFR, Telegram 501.AA/12-349 from the Tibetan Cabinet
Ministers to the Secretary of State, Gyantse, December 3,1949.
[24]Balistan

stated that: "while British still interested in Tibet maintaining its autonomy, Tibetan problem is almost exclusively of concern to India."[25]

When finally the matter of Tibet's admission in the UN was discussed between K.P.S. Menon and the US Ambassador, Menon was categorical: "...admission [of] Tibet [is] hopeless, [A] UN debate would unduly agitate Tibetan question and might provoke earlier action by Chinese Communists."

In the same dispatch, it appears that there were differing views among the senior Indian diplomats; the cable of Henderson said: "In absence Bajpai, British fear negative viewpoint set forth [in Embassy Telegram] will prevail."[26]

By that time, it was quite clear that, left alone, Nehru would tilt in favour of a more 'negative' approach to the Tibetan issue. One remark from Henderson gives quite a clear picture of the situation. India had the monopoly over not only the foreign policy of Tibet, but also its communications. In a cable to Acheson, he wrote: 'we have to recall that, in last analysis, we can communicate with Tibet now only via India, and similarly that Tibet can only communicate with non-Communist world via India."[27]

The strategic and political importance of India vis-à-vis Tibet was emphasised again and again by the Western powers and when the Tibetan issue came up for hearing at the UN in November 1950, it was once again the Indian position which would prevail. Except for Pakistan and Burma, no other country had any border with Tibet.

The fact that in early December the Government of India had already decided to recognise the new regime in Beijing was certainly not a fact that found favoured with the Tibetans.

The Harishwar Dayal Mission

Harishwar Dayal, the Political Officer in Sikkim visited Tibet for two months in September-October 1949. He returned to Delhi early in December. During his stay in the Tibetan capital he had a wide range of discussions with the Tibetan Kashag.

[25]USFR, Telegram 893.00 Tibet/12-1249 from the Chargé in the United Kingdom (Holmes) to the Secretary of State London, December 12, 1949.
[26]USFR, Telegram 501.AA/12-1449 from the Ambassador in India (Henderson) to the Secretary of State New Delhi, December 14,1949.
[27]USFR, Telegram 893.00 Tibet/12-1549 from the Ambassador in India (Henderson) to the Secretary of State New Delhi, December 15,1949.

During his first meeting with Surkhang Shape and Luishar Thupten Tharpa, the talks centred mainly on the supply of arms and ammunition to the Tibetan Army and the revival of the 'Better Family' Regiment.[28]

Dayal argued that he saw the provision of training to Tibetan troops as the main role for the Indian government.

The Kashag requested Dayal to supply 20 two-inch mortars, 20 three-inch mortars, 10,000 two-inch mortar bombs, 10,000 three-inch mortar bombs, 2,000,000 rounds of .303 rifle ammunition and 1,000,000 rounds of Sten gun ammunition.

Eventually an agreement was reached and the entire supply was delivered during the next couple of months. Only the request for anti-aircraft guns was turned down.

It was also agreed to train a detachment of twelve Tibetan soldiers in the use of Bren and Sten guns in Gyantse.

A few months earlier, an Indian Colonel had already visited Tibet and discussed this matter with Depon Kunsangtse, a Tibetan General. It was accepted in principle that India would train some Tibetan troops in Gyantse.

As mentioned earlier, while in Lhasa, Dayal tried to dissuade the Kashag from dispatching its letter to Mao and rocking the boat once more, but his effort was in vain.

In the second official meeting in November the discussions centred on the decision of Tibetan Government to increase recruitments to their army. They wanted to build a force of 100,000 against the then strength of 13,000. Richardson was of the opinion that 50,000 soldiers would be enough to defend the borders. The problem, was who would equip this force?

By now the Kashag had understood that the Indian Government was the key; they requested some assurance from the Government of India.

The Tibetans realized that even if the Americans or the British wanted to help, they could not do so without the active support and collaboration of the Government of India.

Dayal seemed mainly interested in the protection of the Indian trading posts at Gyantse and Yatung. We have to note here that at the end of the forties the Indian Government was still attached to its extraterritorial rights in Tibet. They clearly saw the advantages and

[28]Drongdra Regiment

were not ready to surrender them under the pretext that they were 'imperialist rights.'

When Dayal came back to Delhi, he was impatiently awaited. He reported to his government but also informed the British High Commission of the situation in Lhasa and his talks with the Tibetan Government.

Dayal brought also interesting news from his discussions with Richardson in Lhasa.

Contrary to the analysis by the Western powers, the Indian Agent in Lhasa believed that the Chinese Communists would "likely move into Tibet next summer [1950]." In his opinion, it would not be very difficult and would take less than three months for the Chinese Liberation Army to travel from Tachienlu (Dartsedo) at the Sino-Tibetan border to Lhasa.[29] His opinion wasn't taken seriously by the Western powers who thought that it was Richardson's personal view and only reflect the prevailing opinion in Lhasa where threatening broadcasts from Beijing radio had created much alarm. British intelligence regarded his "view with considerable reserve." Retrospectively, it appears more like wishful thinking on the part of the British Government as information had started pouring in from Hong Kong also about war preparations in Western China.

Richardson had also forewarned about the infiltration of Communists agents into Bhutan, Nepal and India. He told Dayal that it was relatively simple for the Chinese to use this method.

The Americans also hoped for the best: in a cable to the Secretary of State, Henderson echoed London's position: "Despite Richardson's views re timing Communist invasion, British here apparently feel difficulty of terrain, problem of adjustment to extreme high altitudes and constant winds, difficulty of feeding troops, lack of material or accessibility resources to exploit, preoccupation Communists with internal problems all combine render dispatch of Chinese military expedition unlikely in near future and to make alternative infiltration and gradual conquest from within more attractive."[30]

---

[29]In fact, he was quite right. It would take three months after the signature of the 17-Point Agreement between Tibet and China for the Chinese troops to reach Lhasa. They entered the Tibetan capital in September 1951. Richardson did not count the break during the winter when the Chinese consolidated their 'liberation' of Kham.

[30]Telegram 893.00 Tibet/12-1649:from the Ambassador in India (Henderson) to the Secretary of State, New Delhi, December 16,1949.

One interesting point to note is that at the end of 1949, the British believed that Tibet was an independent nation though they were not ready to recognize it for fear of rocking the boat. This was confirmed by a cable from Henderson to Acheson[31] that said, "during the conversation Mr. Graves showed me a Hansard report of December 14, 1949, in which was published a letter from Mr. Eden to Dr. T.V. Soong[32] under date of August 5, 1943 and an accompanying memorandum setting forth the British position with respect to Tibet. Mr. Graves stated that it was his view that this still represented the British position in regard to Tibet."[33]

An officer of the Ministry of External Affairs told the American Ambassador in Delhi that for India, "no purpose would be served in raising question of political status of Tibet at this time. Ministry feels that making issue of Tibetan question at present might precipitate Communist decision invade pursuant their declared intention liberating country."[34]

The American Ambassador rightly doubted that the Indian Government would bargain for the recognition of Beijing regime against the guarantee of respect for Tibetan autonomy.[35] Though the Indian officer said that his government had not yet decided about the application of Tibet in the UN, it is quite certain that it was out of question; Nehru's priority was the sponsorship of Communist China's entry in the UN and the Security Council.

Here also Patel did not agree with Nehru. He wrote to the Prime Minister on December 6: "It seems your intention is to recognize China soon after the UN session ends, even if it means that others are not ready by then or prepared to do so. My own feeling is that we do not stand to gain anything by giving a lead."

Nehru immediately replied: "Our advisors[36] are of opinion that it would be definitely harmful to recognize... after the

[31]The Chinese Foreign Minister in visit to London in 1943.
[32]See text pp. 214-215.
[33]Telegram 893.00 Tibet/12-2149. Memorandum of conversation with the Director of the Office of Chinese Affairs (Sprouse) [Washington] December 21, 1949.
[34]Telegram 893.00 Tibet/12-3049 from the Ambassador in India (Henderson) to the Secretary of State, New Delhi, December 30,1949.
[35]In fact the Note was written one day before the Indian recognition of new Beijing regime (31 December 1949).
[36]Most probably K.M. Pannikar and V.K. Krishna Menon.

Commonwealth have done so. It would mean that we have no policy
of our own, but follow the dictates of other countries."

It was also clear for Henderson after a talk with the Ministry of
External Affairs officials; he knew that Delhi would press for the
recognition of Tibetan autonomy during future 'diplomatic
negotiations'.

His opinion was that Pannikar would not "wish allow question
further Tibet disturb cordial relationship he hopes establish between
Indian Government and Chinese Communists." He was quite right.
Pannikar would start to tilt even more towards the 'East' after
assuming his post in Beijing in mid-1950.

The Government of India thought that after recognizing the
Chinese Communist Government, they could 'initiate diplomatic
talks ' with the Chinese regarding the status of Tibet. New Delhi
was "strongly in favour of continuance Tibetan autonomy to same
extent as has been case in past."

On November 16, 1949, Jawaharlal Nehru had said in a press
conference that "India has always recognized the suzerainty of the
Chinese Government over Tibet but Tibet is considered as an
autonomous unit and India's dealings with Tibet are on that basis."[37]

Nehru's Government was also quite clear about the military help
for Tibet. They had "received number requests for arms and
ammunition from Tibetan Government, [they] had complied with
some of these requests, and will send more in future. It cannot,
however, render active military assistance in form of dispatch troops
to Lhasa."[38]

This is confirmed by B.N. Mullik, the IB Director who recorded
in his book *My Years with Nehru — China's Betrayal* the following
account of a meeting with K.P.S. Menon, Pannikar and General
Cariappa, the Indian Chief of the Army Staff:

> On the question of India sending troops to stop the
> Chinese, Pannikar explained that legally India's action
> was indefensible. However, when the question was put
> to General Cariappa, he quite categorically said that he
> could not spare any troops or could spare no more than

[37]SWJN, Series II, Vol. 14, p. 191.
[38]Discussion with Jha, Joint Secretary, MEA, Government of India in USFR,
Telegram from The Ambassador in India (Henderson) to the Secretary of State,
New Delhi, December 30, 1949- 1p.m..

a battalion for Tibet, so-hard-pressed was he with his commitments on the Pakistan front and with the internal troubles raised both by communal and Communist forces.

He was also clear that this battalion could not go much further than Yatung or at the most might be able to place a company to Gyantse. Moreover, he explained that the Indian army was not equipped and trained to operate at such heights and would be at a serious disadvantage against the Chinese army which had much better training and experience in fighting in the extreme cold plateau and were even better armed, having acquired all the arms which the USA had poured into China to bolster the KMT army. What Carriapa said at that time was indeed very discouraging and disappointing because I had also favoured military intervention in Tibet to save it from China.[39]

As the end of 1949 neared, certain conclusions could be drawn.

First, India recognized Tibet more or less as an independent country. The Political Officer in Sikkim was dealing directly with the Tibetan Foreign Bureau in Lhasa and not through Beijing for all political and diplomatic matters related to Tibet.

Another proof of Tibet's status in the early years after India's Independence was that New Delhi was supplying arms and ammunition directly to Lhasa. Though these arms were meant for defence purpose, they were for all practical purposes to be used against a Chinese attack. However, the Government of India was not ready to get involved in a full-fledged war on the Tibetan High Plateau.

Another factor which would play an important role in the following months was the over-importance that Nehru wanted to give India in world affairs.

The following quote makes interesting reading:

Whatever problem in Asia you may take up, somehow or other India comes into the picture. Whether you think in terms of China or the Middle East or South East Asia, India immediately comes into the picture. It is so situated that because of past history, traditions, etc., in regard to

[39]Mullik, op. cit., p. 80.

any major problem of a country or a group of countries of Asia, India has to be considered. Whether it is a problem of defence or trade or Industry or other economic policy, India cannot be ignored.[40]

We shall see that these words would boomerang when India abandoned a weak Tibet to its fate; it would then become clear for other 'non-aligned' nations that India was not in a position to play the role she pretended to play in world affairs.

Richardson, the 'British' Head of the Indian Mission with Tsarong Shape and the Nepalese Representative in Tibet.

18

1950: The Year of the Iron-Tiger

The Beginning of the Fateful Year

> *It was like an artillery barrage – which is what we assumed*
> *to be the cause of both the tremors and the noise: a test of*
> *some sort being carried out by the Tibetan army...Some*
> *people reported seeing a strange red glow in the skies in*
> *the direction from which the noise came...*
> **The Dalai Lama on the ominous earthquake**
> **shaking Tibet on August 15, 1950**

For centuries Tibet had remained isolated. The nation's energies and time were consecrated to achieving spiritual goals, its defence was neglected and until the beginning of the twentieth century, nobody, except the Thirteenth Dalai Lama, had been much bothered by international developments.

In a way, formal recognition or boundary delimitation had been forced on the Tibetans by Younghusband's invasion and later by Sir Henry McMahon at the Simla Conference. At the end of the forties, Tibet had begun to wake up at the sight of the dark clouds gathering around the Land of Snows: an atheist "east wind" was threatening to blow over the sacred Shangri-La.

The first signs that mythical Tibet was soon to vanish forever were beginning to appear. Of these, the earthquake was the most striking.

The Thirteenth Dalai Lama knew about the danger and had recognized the real face of the Communists; in 1932, in his last Testament, he warned his people:

Precautions should be taken at a time when the forces
of degeneration are most prevalent and when
Communism is on the spread. Remember the fate that

befell the Mongolian nation when Communists overran the country and where the Head Lama's reincarnation was forbidden, where property was totally confiscated and where monasteries and religion were completely wiped out. These things have happened, are happening and will happen in the land of harmonious blend of Religion and Politics.[1]

Nobody listened!

Unfortunately 1950, the Iron-Tiger year was to be a fateful year for Tibet. For India too, the repercussions of this year's events would be incalculable.

It began on New Year's day! Or rather on New Year's eve, when the Government of India decided to hurry through the recognition of the Communist regime in Beijing.

The first consequence was a warning note heard the next morning in the broadcast of the New China News Agency. It proclaimed "the task for the People's Liberation Army (PLA) for 1950 are to liberate Taiwan, Hainan and Tibet... Tibet is an integral part of China. Tibet has fallen under the influence of the imperialists."

The Communist regime was taking the initiative. During the following months China would never miss a chance to assert again and again that Tibet was part of China's territory.

On January 22, an interesting conversation took place in Moscow between Mao Zedong and Joseph Stalin:

> Mao Zedong: I would like to note that the air regiment that you sent to China was very helpful. Let me thank you Comrade Stalin, for the help, and ask you to allow it to stay a little longer so it could help transport provisions to Liu Bocheng's troops, currently preparing for an attack on Tibet.
>
> Joseph Stalin; It's good that you are preparing the attack. The Tibetans need to be subdued. As for the air regiment, we shall talk this over with the military personnel and give you an answer.[2]

During the first months of 1950, the only thing which was not known to the Chinese was the degree of resistance of the Tibetans:

---

[1]Tibet.

[2]See *Cold War International History Project Bulletin:* (Winter 95/96) reproduced in Grunfeld, Tibetan Review, Delhi, April 1996, p. 20.

would the Second Army of One-eyed Liu[3] march triumphantly into Tibet as the liberators, or would Tibet have to be liberated by force?

By the end of 1949, the Red Army had already entered certain areas of Eastern Tibet, mainly in Amdo Province, but though the 'liberation' of Tibet had started, the invasion had not yet taken place. The Chinese knew that the real test would be the 'occupation' of Kham.

This was what was at stake in the negotiations between the Chinese Ambassador and Shakabpa, the Tibetan representative in Delhi. Had the negotiations succeeded, the PLA would have come to Tibet 'invited'. Shakabpa knew it and it explained why for many months, though the Chinese had given him an ultimatum to 'conclude' the negotiations by September, he was not keen to proceed to Beijing. For the Chinese, if Tibet accepted to be a part of China, there would be no problem since China would only be entering its own territory.

We should not forget that Mao's favourite 'teacher' was Sun Tzu who said: "To fight and conquer in all your battles is not supreme excellence; supreme excellence consists in breaking the enemy's resistance without fighting."

By September, the negotiations had failed to bring the desired result for the Chinese and strategically Deng had to attack Tibet before the winter; after that, it would have been impossible for the young PLA to advance into the Roof of the World.

Role of Deng Xiaoping

We should mention here the role played by China's 'last Emperor', Deng Xiaoping in preparing the 'liberation' of Tibet.

Before he passed away a couple of years ago, Deng Xiaoping had been considered, in India and abroad, and especially in the United States, as a reformer, the father of the 'four modernizations', the leader who brought economic prosperity to the Chinese masses. But there is another side to Deng Xiaoping.

At the time when Mao was entering Beijing in 1949, Deng was posted as the Political Commissioner for the Western Region in Sichuan. As such he was responsible for the Second Field Army with his old companion, Liu Bocheng, the 'one eyed' veteran General. He had been a leading advocate of an early start to 'democratic reforms'

[3]Liu Bocheng.

in the Tibetan areas of Kham and Amdo, which had been incorporated in Qinghai and Sichuan provinces.

Liu Bocheng and Deng Xiaoping had long been comrades. During the war against the Japanese both were leaders of the 128th Division, the elite formation of the PLA. It was to become the Second Army during the struggle against Chiang's troops. The partnership between the two had always been very successful especially during the One Thousand Li Campaign when they diverted the Nationalist forces to allow Mao to defeat some other Kuomintang units.

Deng must have known his Tibetan enemies very well: their spies in the great monasteries of Tibet must have reported on the divisions within Tibet between the most progressive strata of the society which had traditionally been pro-Western and the more conservative monks in the monasteries who were against the modernization of the Tibetan army.

Deng also knew that Tibet's southern neighbour, India, was led by a pacifist Prime Minister who would do anything to avoid war or tension.

Pannikar had most probably managed to convince his contacts in the Chinese government that all 'white men' were imperialists and that it was time for the Asian nations to reject the hostile imperialist forces.

He must have assured Zhou Enlai that India was against the war and the use of force. Deng like Mao had no problem in using force.

After the green light to attack Tibet was given to Deng from Moscow by Mao on Jan. 2, 1950, all the responsibility for the preparations was left to Deng.

On Jan 10, 1950, Mao is said to have sent another telegram to the Second Field Army "ordering that the preparation of the liberation should be accelerated, and agreeing with Deng Xiaoping's proposal that the liberation of Tibet should be started simultaneously from all directions — from Sichuan in the east, from Yunnan in the south, from Qinghai in the north and from Xinjiang in the west."[4]

It would take eight months for the 18th Corps of the Second Field Army to get ready to march through Kham and defeat the ill-equipped and poorly motivated Tibetan army.

[4]Quoted from Lodi Gyari, *A Personal Legacy Left Untouched - Reflections on Deng Xiaoping's Role in Tibet*, World Tibet News, Canada, 19 February-1997.

A blend of forceful diplomacy and display of strategic tactics, a better knowledge of the enemy were chiefly responsible for the advance of the PLA in Tibet.[5]

The way the Tibetans themselves surrendered and quickly signed 'under duress' the 17-Point Agreement must have surprised even the Chinese. Nothing could stop the Chinese troops reaching the Indian border and consolidating their newly acquired territory.

The plans of Mao Zedong for 1950 had been made clear: China had to liberate 'Taiwan, Tibet and Hainan'. But while the Number One target was definitely Taiwan, he also knew that the other two would not cause too many problems.

During the course of interviews, we have very often asked informants as to why India did not help Tibet; the main reason given was that "we cannot take on two enemies at the same time, we cannot open two fronts at the same time and India was already busy with Kashmir, so there was no possibility to fight another battle on the Roof of the World."

It is certainly here a question of national temperament, but Mao had no problem with taking on three enemies at the same time and even a fourth in June, Korea.

We shall see later how Mao was reluctantly dragged into the Korean war; he had not planned to get involved and eventually it forced him to abandon his target Number One, Taiwan. The course of the history of China would change in the process.

The Last Warning

On the evening of August 15, a terrible earthquake shook Tibet. "This was no ordinary earthquake; it felt like the end of the world,"[6] writes Robert Ford, the British Radio operator working in Chamdo (Kham). "Mountains and valleys exchanged places in an instant, hundreds of villages were swallowed up, the Brahmaputra River was completely rerouted and for hours afterwards, the sky over the south-eastern Tibet glowed with an infernal red light, diffused with the pungent scent of sulphur."[7]

---

[5]Deng and Liu would be congratulated by Mao a few months later when they came to Beijing to celebrate the first anniversary of the Communist Republic (October 1, 1951). Indeed the 'liberation' had been unexpectedly smooth and without real problems.

[6]Ford, op. cit., p. 94.

[7]John Avedon, *In Exile from the Land of Snows* (London: Wisdom Publications, 1985), p. 40.

294   *The Fate of Tibet*

Suddenly, everyone in Tibet understood that the time had come.

The Last Testament came back to the mind of all, but it was too late, the die had been cast long ago. Now Tibet would have no choice but to go through the ordeal with only one hope — that it would not be too painful and long.

The Negotiations that Never Were

Negotiations between the Tibetans and the Chinese were to begin in spring 1950 at the initiative of Gyalo Dhondup, the second brother of the Dalai Lama who had married a Chinese girl whose father was a member of the Mongolian and Tibetan Commission in the Nationalist Government. After the Communists had taken over China, the same Office was given responsibility for the 'minorities', in particular those from Tibet and Mongolia.

Both parties were keen to negotiate, but for different reason; Tibet wanted to settle its border with China and as indicated in the Kashag's letter to Mao regain its 'lost' territories and China wanted to 'liberate' Tibet as smoothly as possible.

The Chinese suggested Hong Kong as the venue for the negotiations as it was 'close to China' and 'neutral' for the Tibetans.

The first hurdle came when the British refused a visa to the Tibetan delegation to enter Hong Kong. The official objection from London stated that it might not be advisable for His Majesty's Government to issue diplomatic visas to the delegates because Tibet was not an 'independent' country but 'only autonomous.'

This view was not unanimously shared in the Foreign Office and some officers thought it only fair to provide a visa to the delegates, even an ordinary visa on their Tibetan Passport as had been done in 1948 for the Trade Mission.

Other officers had another valid argument: if visas were not granted to Shakabpa and his colleagues, the negotiations could not take place at all. It was in the interest of everyone (including the British) that the negotiations succeed and the Tibetans attain a greater autonomy.

The debate on these two major questions went on for some time among the British officials in London. Should the British Government help the Tibetans to negotiate a settlement with Communist China? If so, then should they grant a diplomatic or an ordinary visa to them, and this on a Tibetan travel document or on some other document?

The matter was further complicated when K.P.S. Menon, India's Foreign Secretary thought that no good would be achieved by the contact between the Tibetan and the Chinese delegates in Hong Kong and the best alternative for the delegates was to postpone their journey.

From the British archives it appears that "the Government of India will clearly be happy if we refuse the necessary visas. On the other hand they do not seem anxious to take any action or give any advice themselves in the matter."[8]

It is not clear why K.P.S. Menon and the Government of India were not keen on the negotiations. Most probably the Indian Foreign Secretary was not happy to see negotiations happen so close to China. The other issue was that the negotiations would have a great impact on India's security and India certainly wanted to be consulted.

Further, we should remember that Tibet and Independent India had ratified the Simla Convention and both parties were bound by this treaty. It was perhaps a hot potato[9] for Nehru and K.P.S. Menon, but nevertheless Article V[10] must have been in their mind.

India had stepped into the Britain's shoes and the Article remained valid.

It is a great pity that one has to refer to the British and American Archives to try to reconstruct what happened in India fifty years ago. The day the Indian Archives are opened up for researchers, this point like so many other unclear details will hopefully be clarified.

Finally, the Government of India informally told the Tibetans that they would not mind if the negotiations took place in Delhi. But the Tibetans were still keen to proceed to Hong Kong and Shakabpa went ahead with his preparations. In the meantime, the Governor of Singapore took a strong stand: he categorically refused to give a transit visa to Shakabpa. In the situation, everyone had his own axe to grind and one can only feel sorry for the poor Tibetans. The fate

[8]Quoted in Goldstein, op. cit., p. 648. Telegram from UK High Commissioner to London dated 8 March 1950 (FO371/84468).

[9]In a sense that the Convention had, for Nehru 'imperialist' connotations, having been signed in Simla between British India and Tibet.

[10]Article V said: "The Governments of China and Tibet engage that they will not enter into any negotiations or agreements regarding Tibet with one another, or with any other Power, excepting such negotiations and agreements between Great Britain and Tibet."

of their nation, their thousand-year old culture was tossed around at the whim of officials in London, New Delhi, Hong Kong and Singapore.

The general motto seemed to have been "remain vague as far as possible." It was probably easier for the world community (and even for an idealist Indian Prime Minister) to let the weak Tibetan nation be devoured by the Chinese Dragon than to stick its neck out for a weak and non-violent people. Do not the big insects always eat the small ones?

It was clear that Tibet was no longer a matter of prime importance for London, but for India, the stake was larger. Nehru's government had inherited the British treaties, the British duties and the British borders, mainly the McMahon Line and the 'undefined' border in Ladakh. Should not India have made sure that her security would not suffer in the bargain?

A very ordinary problem, a simple visa, had been brought to a high political level. With the prevailing situation, everyone began giving his opinion: one British officer even commented in a file that Shakabpa[11] "was a slippery customer and obviously out to make the best deal he can with Peking."[12]

As if it was not the role of an envoy to make the best possible deal for his country!

But Shakabpa was a stubborn man, he decided to approach things from another angle: he applied to the Government of West Bengal for a visa to Hong Kong. To his surprise perhaps, West Bengal granted him a 'gratis official courtesy' visa.

Unfortunately for the Tibetans, this 'oversight' of the West Bengal Government was unacceptable to the British. When it was so discovered, the British High Commissioner took up the matter with the Government of India which in turn tried to cancel the visa.

Shakabpa who had already booked his tickets to Hong Kong objected. The drama did not end there: Shakabpa referred the matter to Lhasa.

The Tibetan Foreign Office in Lhasa took the opportunity to clarify the aims of the mission. They wanted to find an arrangement

---

[11]He was presumably referring to the fact that Shakabpa had to use two passports when he visited China with the Trade Mission in 1948.

[12]Quoted in Goldstein, op. cit., p. 648. Telegram from Hong Kong Governor to London dated 8 March, 1950 (FO371/84468).

with the Chinese Government for the continuation of Tibet's present independent status.

It was also stated that from Hong Kong the Mission had been ordered to get in touch with the Chinese Government. In case the Chinese Government summoned them to China, they had to immediately report to Lhasa for further orders. The cable concluded that the Tibetan Government hoped that "facilities for entry into Hong Kong will be arranged."

It was becoming clear that the Indian Government would feel more secure with the outcome of the talks if the negotiations were to be conducted in Delhi with the newly appointed Chinese ambassador.

We can well understand the position of the Government of India. K.P.S. Menon who had been posted in Chungking and Nanjing knew fairly well the 'trap' into which the Tibetan delegates had fallen in 1946 during the Goodwill Mission in Nanjing. Menon had enough knowledge of the Chinese way of functioning to guess that if the Tibetans were to go to Hong Kong, the Chinese would certainly find ways to pull them to the mainland where they would be at a great diplomatic disadvantage. It would ultimately mean a treaty or an agreement to which India would not be a party and might have serious strategic implications, considering the length of the border between India and Tibet.

The position of the British was relatively clear: they had left India and now it was India's business to deal with the Tibetans.

However, the Tibetans found this quite unfair considering that for the past forty years or so they had relied on the British Government to be their spokesmen. Tibet's contacts with other world governments were through the British; as Shakabpa put it in a telegram to the Deputy High Commissioner in Calcutta, "we sincerely hope that the good and friendly relations existing between our Governments for so many years will be considered."[13]

In the meantime, New Delhi changed its mind. Now they thought it would better if the Tibetans were not stopped from going to Hong Kong on 'technical grounds'.

The new theory was that if prevented from going to Hong Kong, the Tibetans would be pushed into the arms of the Chinese and if they were really sincere about negotiating in Hong Kong they should

[13]Quoted in Goldstein, op. cit., p. 648. Letter from Shakabpa dated 24 May, 1950 (FO371/84468).

be given the possibility to do so. It would help the Tibetans to save face if they had full diplomatic visas valid for a limited period of time.

A more interesting point is mentioned in the note: "Government of India further point out that in these circumstances it would be tactless to refuse to accept Tibetan passports particularly as an addition to 1948 precedent."[14]

They also quoted "grant of visas on Tibetan passport to four Tibetans in 1914[15] and to Mr. Phela Se on recommendation of Sir Charles Bell about 1920."[16]

In 1950, the Government of India still accepted Tibetan passports for Tibetans travelling officially to India. This procedure was also known and accepted by the British Government.

Shakabpa finally booked the tickets to Hong Kong for June 4th.

The drama was to continue right up to the end. On June 4th, two members of the delegation managed to check in with their luggage, but after boarding, they were requested to disembark. The next day Shakabpa flew to Delhi where he met with K.P.S. Menon. He also met Sir Archibald Nye, the British High Commissioner, who made it clear that the British Government was in favour of the negotiations being conducted in India for the following reasons:

1- The imminent arrival of the new Chinese representative to India.
2- The poor state of British relations with the Chinese People's Government
3- The good relations between India and China making Delhi a more suitable place
4- The fact that Peking evidently did not wish to deal with Tibetan Mission on equal terms.

The problem for the Tibetans was that they were receiving information from eastern Tibet that the People's Liberation Army was close to the Upper Yangtse which was the traditional border between the jurisdiction of the Lhasa Government and Sichuan Province of China.

[14]Quoted in Goldstein, op. cit., p. 648. Letter from UK High Commissioner in Delhi to London dated 1 June 1950 (FO371/84468).
[15]The four Tibetan students who went to England.
[16]Phela Se (or Phalese) had been sent by the Thirteenth Dalai Lama to London to meet his friend Sir Charles Bell and study the possibility for Tibet to enter the League of Nations.

It appears that the Chinese government was ready to offer the Tibetans full autonomy within the People's Republic[17] but Lhasa was certainly not prepared to accept that proposal.

It was only the pressing situation in Tibet which had caused Shakabpa to accept the risk of going to Hong Kong. Personally, he certainly preferred to negotiate in Delhi on more solid ground.

Nonetheless, he remained particularly firm on the issue of the passport. His point was that if the Tibetans were denied the use of their Tibetan passports, they would be in a weaker position right from the start of the negotiations. The Chinese knew perfectly well that these passports had been used in the past and if, this time, they were denied, it would be conclusive proof that the British Government had changed its position towards Tibet and an acceptance of their contention that Tibet was not a separate entity. The talks would thereby be spoiled before they even began. In either case, the Tibetans had no chance of getting a fair deal.

As negotiations for the negotiations went on, Shakabpa referred the matter to Lhasa, Nye did the same to London and everyone once again gave their opinion. The Tibetans had arrived in India on March 6 and it was now mid-June: the monsoon was about to break in Delhi but no concrete breakthrough was in sight for the Tibetan delegates. At the same time the news from Kham and Amdo was worse than ever.

Many in the Foreign Office preferred to maintain the status quo which meant keeping the status of Tibet as vague as possible, just as the Indians had done since India took over from the British.

Vagueness and ambivalence provided both Delhi and London the opportunity to keep all their options open.

On June 17, a message from the Kashag finally arrived to say that Lhasa had agreed that the negotiations could be held in Delhi. Finally Shakabpa could go back to his base in Kalimpong to wait and see if the Chinese would agree to conducting the negotiations through their newly appointed ambassador to India.

Before leaving Delhi, Shakabpa once again had a long talk with the British High Commissioner and some American officials.

---

[17]It is what was 'forced' on the Tibetans one year later through the 17-Point Agreement. Unfortunately for the Tibetans, the clause relating to the Tibetan autonomy and the role of the Dalai Lama was never respected by Beijing afterwards.

During an informal talk with Nye, Shakabpa asked the High
Commissioner his private opinion of the consequences of the failure
of the talks with the Chinese. Nye told him that he could foresee
four possibilities:

1- China might invade Tibet to impose its regime.
2- The Chinese might try to subvert Tibet through infiltration
   and by encouraging disaffection.
3- They could try to induce Tibet to agree to their terms by
   diplomatic means using threats and promises.
4- If diplomatic efforts failed, they might also leave Tibet
   alone.

We shall see that the Chinese later implemented Points 1 and 3.
They first invaded Tibet and later imposed an agreement on a weak
Tibetan delegation.

Shakabpa then came to his main question to Nye: if China
attacked and militarily invaded Tibet, would the British Government
help?

The reply from Nye (though not officially on behalf of his
government) was NO and he repeated there was NO prospect for
the United Kingdom's military help in such a circumstance.

The same question was asked of Henderson, the American
ambassador in Delhi, who also replied in the negative. To be fair, he
could not encourage the Tibetans to believe that the US Government
would consider it feasible to offer aid. Nevertheless he added that
the US had in some cases accepted to provide help to countries which
were threatened by Communists. It was also conveniently called a
private and personal talk.

The matter was later formally discussed between the US and
British Government. The conclusions were that it was not an easy
task to help the Tibetans as the terrain was not favourable and that
in any case it was up to the Indian Government to decide since the
arms or equipment would have to be brought in through India. The
British made it clear once more that their interest in Tibet arose from
its proximity to India and that interests were now vested with the
Indian Government.

One should note the different standards applied to the Eastern
front, in Korea, where America and its Allies were ready to go into a
full-fledged war to defend South Korea. On the Western front,
nobody was ready to do anything for Tibet, not even issue a visa.

Tibet was left alone. Pannikar had just arrived in Beijing and he would soon send dispatch after dispatch to New Delhi to prove that friendship at any cost was the only way to fight the 'last traces of imperialism in Asia'.

For Pannikar[18] the loss of Tibet was worth the price of liberating Asia from 'Western dominance'. But for the Tibetans, was yellow dominance better than white?

It was the beginning of the non-aligned policy of the Government of India, a policy which amounted to India opposing whatever came from America or the West and very often supporting whatever came from Moscow or Beijing.

Many voices protested in India, but they were sacrificed on the altar of a chimerical new friendship with China. All critics were silenced until the fateful day in October 1962, when the folly of the Krishna Menons and Pannikars appeared for the first time to the public eye in India. By that time the inexperienced, gentle, non-violent Snow-lion had been devoured by the Dragon.

However, at the end of June 1950 everything was still not lost for the Tibetans; they still had friends in India and abroad. Many Indian politicians including Sardar Patel, Acharya Kripalani, Dr. Rammanohar Lohia and even some diplomats in the Ministry of External Affairs certainly saw clearly the importance for India of trying to save the inoffensive Tibet.

Shakabpa remained in India during the following months and waited for the situation to change. The new Chinese Ambassador was announced in Delhi and he thought he could have preliminary discussions with him.

In September Shakabpa came to Delhi to meet the Indian Prime Minister who enquired about the progress of the talks. Nehru seemed unaware that the talks were supposed to have been held in Hong Kong. The minutes of the meeting said:

> The Prime Minister enquired why they should be reluctant to go to Peking now when they were willing to go there three or four months ago. Mr. Shakabpa explained that they had instructions then to go to Hong Kong only and not to Peking. The Chinese had agreed to send a representative to Hong Kong to talk to them,

[18]And Nehru.

with the understanding that all important questions would be referred by him to Peking.[19]

It is strange that Nehru did not know that the talks were fixed in Hong Kong and not in Peking. One can safely conclude that there were differences of opinion in the Indian Foreign office and the Prime Minister was not informed of all the details of the 'negotiations' prior to their commencement.

> The Prime Minister told them that although India was perfectly agreeable to Delhi being the venue, it was not for him to suggest this to the Chinese. As the parties to the proposed talks, it was for China and Tibet to settle where the talks should be held.

Later Nehru explained why he thought the British had refused to grant visas for talks in Hong Kong: "...this was because they did not like to give the impression that they were taking part in the talks." For the Indian Prime Minister India was clearly not ready to 'give the impression' that India was interested. Shakabpa pointed out the precedent of the Simla Convention in 1914 when the British had invited the Tibetans and the Chinese for a Tripartite Conference and asked "why this could not be arranged now?" Nehru only repeated that "it was not possible for India to urge Peking to hold the talks in Delhi. This would mean that India had a dominant position over China and Tibet."

One point is sure: the Chinese did not want the negotiations to take place in India.

The minutes of the same meeting mention:

> Mr. Shakabpa stated that his Government had written to the Chinese Government suggesting Delhi as the venue. This letter had been returned from Hong Kong, probably by the post office. Similarly, a telegram containing the same suggestion had failed to reach Peking.

Using an old Tibetan technique, the Chinese refused to open the letters and sent them back unopened.

Did the Indian, British or American diplomats know about the talk between Stalin and Mao? Probably not! Mao Zedong and his Political Commissioner in Sichuan had long since decided to invade

---

[19]SWJN, Series II, Vol. 15, p. 434. Conversation with the Tibetan delegation, 8 September, 1950.

the Land of Snows; the detailed plans for the final 'liberation' of Tibet were ready. When the Chinese Ambassador took his post in Delhi in September, the time was ripe for the fatal blow. Winter was coming, there was no more time to waste.

All this time, the Western and Indian diplomats had only been playing the game of the Chinese Government. The fate of Tibet was already sealed. What had been announced on January 1ˢᵗ had to be accomplished!

An interesting information is given by Warren Smith in his *Tibetan Nation*: a Scottish missionary, Beatty working in eastern Tibet affirmed that he was told by a PLA officer that "large numbers of yak, wild and domestic animals would be needed to feed the PLA troops [in Tibet]. The PLA officers and men talked of going on to India once Tibet was in their hands."[20]

It was certainly Mao's plan, but he had to start from the beginning and soon, "the task of marching into Tibet to liberate the Tibetan people, to complete the important mission of unifying the motherland, to prevent imperialism from encroaching on even one inch of our sovereign territory and to protect and build the frontiers of Motherland"[21] would be achieved.

[20]Smith, Warren W., *Tibetan Nation* (New Delhi: HarperCollins, 1997), p. 273 quoted from *Invasion of Tibet by Chinese's Liberation Army*, US National Archives, (793B.00/8-2150).

[21]Xinhua Communiqué, November 1, 1950, Peking.

19

From All Sides

Tibet Invaded

You are afraid we shall be cut off in Chamdo? Do not worry, Phodo, the gods are on our sides.
Ngabo Ngawang Jigme to Robert 'Phodo' Ford

The Korean War

It is not possible to understand the happenings of the Iron-Tiger year - the Fateful Year without having a closer look at another event of 1950.

On June 25, 1950 North Korea crossed the 38th parallel and began invading the South. Soon after the Western nations got involved under the auspices of the UN. We shall see the serious consequences of the Korean crisis on the Tibetan issue. While the international community reacted strongly to the Korean attack they virtually turned a blind eye to Tibet's predicament.

The attitude of the Government of India towards the Tibetan issue would largely be dictated by the role that Nehru wanted to play in the Korean affair. For the Western powers, their involvement in the Korean peninsula appeared to stop them from taking bolder initiatives in favour of Tibet. These limitations became very apparent at the time of the Appeal of the Tibetan Government to the United Nations in November 1950. It is absolutely clear from the American archives that the main strategic interest of President Truman and Dean Acheson, his Secretary of State, was the fate of Korea and Formosa.

As we saw earlier, the People's Republic had announced that the two main fronts to be opened in 1950 were Taiwan and Tibet (and the island of Hainan), in that order. Korea was never mentioned.

At the beginning of the summer, everything was more and less ready on the Tibetan front. In Delhi, everybody was awaiting the

Chinese Ambassador. The Tibetan negotiators were busy running around for visas to Hong Kong while being assured by the Government of India that Communist China was serious about a negotiated settlement with the Lhasa government.

In India, the 'liberation' of Tibet and its incorporation into the 'Motherland' were often taken as nothing more than socialist slogans. In any case, Nehru and his colleagues were not averse to the injection of a small dose of socialism into the Roof of the World.[1]

From their base in Sichuan, Mao's faithful and efficient lieutenant, Deng Xiaoping and his military colleague Liu Bocheng were preparing for the onslaught on Tibet. They had been sending Tibetan emissaries such as the Gethak Lama to Chamdo to pacify the Tibetans and put their suspicions to rest.

The aristocracy and the monks were busy with their picnics and their normal life. There was a widespread belief that in the end the truth would prevail.[2] The predictions of the Thirteenth Dalai Lama were long since forgotten.

If worse came to worse, it was thought that the Government could order the big monasteries in Lhasa or Chamdo to perform extra prayers, to secure the help of the Gods to protect the Land of Snows and its culture.

On the other side of the Yangtse, Deng knew that he had to attack before the winter. It is quite certain that the date had been fixed and the so-called negotiations in Delhi or Hong Kong were only delaying tactics.

It is also clear from the memoirs of Takser Rinpoche, the elder brother of the Dalai Lama who was the Abbot of the Kumbum monastery in Amdo province in 1949-1950. He was told in the spring of 1950, by the Political Commissioner in Sining, that it was not only Kumbum and the adjacent areas which were going to be 'liberated' but the whole of Tibet.[3]

In the meantime the elite Chinese troops were preparing for a landing in Taiwan.

[1]The same policy of introducing social and democratic reforms was pushed by Nehru's government in Nepal and Sikkim.
[2]We can suppose that India also believed in its national motto: 'Satyamev Jayate' meaning 'The Truth alone shall prevail'.
[3]Thubten Jigme Norbu, *Tibet, ma Patrie* (Paris: Albin Michel, 1963), p. 231.

According to Krushchev's Memoirs, it is Kim Il-Sung who first had the idea of the Korean war and discussed it with Stalin sometimes in 1949.

He thought that like the Chinese people, who had been thrilled to be 'liberated' from the Nationalist 'tyrant' Chiang, their South Korean brothers were eagerly waiting for the North Korean troops to cross the 38th Parallel and free them from the imperialist dictatorship.

Although it might have been discussed between Stalin and Mao at the end 1949 or at the beginning of 1950,[4] it now appears that the Chinese knew nothing specific about the attack until it occurred. Mao learnt about it only through the *Reference News*, the uncensored Chinese translation of all the dispatches from news agencies around the world.[5] It is now quite certain that Big Brother had kept his younger Chinese 'brother' in the dark.

Stalin's calculations were simple; he knew from the declarations of Truman and Acheson that the US government had banned military support to Chiang Kai-Shek and that eventually the Communist regime would be recognized. Furthermore, in early 1950 Acheson had declared in San Francisco that both Korea and Formosa were beyond the US defence perimeter.

For a few months, Mao kept his decision to enter the war pending. His objectives were still those he defined on January 1: Taiwan, Hainan and Tibet.

In September, at a meeting of senior Army Commanders in Beijing, Zhou, Liu Shaoqi and Mao discussed the reorganization of the army, but Korea was not discussed. During this meeting, Marshall Peng Dehuai gave a report of the strength of the PLA and stated that Tibet was not a problem, but for Taiwan, the training and equipment would have to be improved if there were to be a chance of success.

In Beijing everybody hesitated, Mao knew that the United States had the atomic bomb and that they could easily attack defenceless Chinese cities. He also was aware that the Liberation Army was used to getting its food from a sympathetic local population and the bulk

[4]During the month that Mao stayed in Moscow waiting for Stalin to agree to meet him and eventually sign a treaty of eternal friendship between China and USSR.

[5]The *Reference News* are circulated among very senior Party members in Zhongnanhai, the residential enclave of Party senior leaders..

of its arms and ammunition came from defeated enemies. Would it be as easy to take weapons from the Americans? And what about food in a foreign land where the troops did not even know the language?

In September all this weighted on Mao's mind, but there was yet another factor. Could he accept that the imperialist 'paper tigers' might come to his doorstep, at a time when his only dream was of liberating Asia from all the imperialist forces? Could he accept a defeat of the East wind?

By now, he knew that he had fallen into a trap set up by Stalin, who had planned the strategy at a minimal cost for the Soviets.[6]

At 1 a.m. on October 1,[7] to celebrate the first anniversary of the new Republic, Zhou Enlai called his 'neutral' friend K.M. Pannikar to request him to inform the United States that if the US forces continued to advance towards the border marked by the Yalu river, China would have no other choice but to intervene.

Truman thought it was a trick or just propaganda from the Chinese. The response of MacArthur was to demand the immediate surrender of the North Korean troops. The Americans knew that China was not prepared and did not have the troops and equipment necessary to come to Kim's defence.

From the beginning, Stalin had nothing to lose, even the equipment provided to the North Koreans was not very important and soon it would be Mao who would be entangled in the Korean mess. A weak China was advantageous for the Soviets. Stalin was determined to remain the Big Brother.

Dr Li, the Private Physician to Mao, reported in his book: "History had taught him [Mao] to befriend distant states and be wary of those that are near, and he continued to distrust Soviet expansionism."[8]

A meeting was held that same October day in Beijing to decide the future course of action and whether China should entertain the

[6]Some of the information contained in this Chapter comes from Salisbury, Harrison, *The New Emperors, China in the Era of Mao and Deng* (Boston; Little Brown & co., 1992).

[7]Since the Long March most of the Chinese leaders suffered from insomnia and as they used to work all night long and only go to sleep after a heavy dose of sleeping pills. The quantity of pills swallowed by Mao was phenomenal.

[8]Li, op. cit., p. 118.

request from Kim. China had no armoured corps, no air force worth
a name. In spite of these odds, Mao decided that China would go to
the defence of North Korea. The pride of the Chinese nation was at
stake and China never liked to lose face.

On October 7th, 1950, Order No. 1 in the name of the Central
Military Committee was issued naming Marshal Dehuai as the
Commander-in-Chief of the operations.

We have gone at length into Communist China's entry into the
Korean war, because it must be the first and only time in the annals
of military history that a country opened two fronts at two opposite
ends of its 'empire', on the same day, with what could appear to be
two totally unrelated motives.

Simultaneously, on that same October 7th, 1950, the Second Field
Army led by Deng Xiaoping and One-eyed Liu crossed the Upper
Yangtse and entered Tibet to 'liberate' the Land of Snows. Mao was
so sure of his strength that he decided (probably on the assurance of
Deng Xiaoping) that a second front could be simultaneously opened.

It is said that one of Deng's qualities was that he knew everything
about his enemies, and he certainly knew that Tibet was weak and
divided. He knew that India would not interfere: Zhou must have
told him that the Indian Prime Minister Nehru was a pacifist and
nothing would happen from that side. Zhou had received indirect
(and perhaps direct) assurances from Pannikar that India would not
intervene.[9]

We know the subsequent history, Mao sent millions of soldiers
to Korea to defend the socialist ideology, and millions died, including
his own son, Mao Anlong.

On the western front Peng[10] was right — Tibet could not offer
any resistance. It was only a question of getting the seal[11] of a pliable
Ngabo on an Agreement. This was done in May 1951.

---

[9]We shall see that a week earlier, Pannikar had consciously changed the
word 'suzerainty' to 'sovereignty' to define the status of Tibet vis-à-vis China.

[10]The Dalai Lama once told us that Peng was 'his favourite Chinese'. The
old Marshall (and Defence Minister) was certainly one of the most courageous
and honest leaders to emerge after the Long March. He was eventually 'sacked'
by Mao for opposing the Great Leap Forward and trying to save tens of
millions of Chinese from a certain death during the man-made famine of 1958-
61.

[11]The Dalai Lama said that it was a forged one.

The consequences of the Korean war would be incalculable for Asia. We can cite some of them. The Korean crisis kept Nehru busy and blind to everything else. His dream of playing a role on the international stage had found the ideal opportunity.

He would be the mediator between the Western and the Socialist world. In the process, he was ready to sacrifice the security of his country's border. Zhou managed to keep the Indian diplomacy busy for several years and most of the time allayed their doubts on the strategic importance of Tibet. While South Block 'slept' through the early fifties, Beijing clandestinely built military roads in Tibet. By the mid-fifties, at the peak of the Hindi-Chini Bhai-Bhai campaign, the main roads to the Indian border[12] and Sinkiang had been completed.

Another consequence of the Korean war was that Mao had to drop his plans to invade Taiwan. This was a great 'coup' for Stalin who had been striving to weaken China. A strong and united China would have challenged his leadership of the Communist world. The thorn that was Formosa was destined to remain in the foot of the Beijing regime for the next fifty years.

But the map of Asia had changed, Tibet became an occupied nation and India acquired a new neighbour, China, a vastly different kettle of fish than the peace loving Tibet.

Nepal

Instead of studying history books, one might as well seek answers in the stars. What was going on, on this 7th day of October in that Fateful Year?

Peng Dehuai was taking over the Chinese Army on the Korean front and leading the Chinese Dragon into one of its most devastating wars. Thousand of miles to the west, Deng Xiaoping was invading a small peaceful country living in its Buddhist paradise and further South, revolution was brewing in another Himalayan kingdom, Nepal. King Tribhuvan and his family had to seek asylum in the Indian Embassy in Kathmandu.

Nepal had been administered for the past two hundred years by the Rana family who were known as Maharajas and were holding the post of Prime Minister of Nepal. The Kings belonged to another family[13] and were merely figureheads.

---

[12]To Sikkim via Chumbi Valley and NEFA via Tsona.
[13]The Shahs.

But lately, King Tribhuvan had been trying to introduce popular reforms which had been resisted by the more traditional Maharaja Mohan Shamsher, a Rana.

A week before the ominous day tensions had grown worse between the King and his Prime Minister. The King had asked the Indian Embassy in Kathmandu if he and his family could be given protection as he feared for his life. The Rana Prime Minister resented more and more the reforms, seeing them as a personal attack on his rule and as an interference by his 'democratic' Big Brother, India.

Nehru said: "Efforts were made by the Prime Minister to get the King to abdicate, but the latter refused to do so."

At this point in time, C.P.N. Singh, the Indian ambassador to Nepal, convinced the Indian Prime Minister that the King should be given shelter and protection. The Nepali Prime Minister's son went to the embassy in an attempt to pressurise the King to abdicate, but Tribhuvan, sure of the Ambassador's support, reiterated that it was out of question.

The same day the Rana Prime Minister decided to crown one of the King's grandsons (even through Tribhuvan had not abdicated) and make him the new king of Nepal. In the midst of this Himalayan high drama, Delhi decided to act firmly and refused to acknowledge the new King. It stood firmly by King Tribhuvan.

Was the coup in Kathmandu linked with the attack on Chamdo or the crossing of the 38th parallel in Korea? It is difficult to say, but though there are no apparent links, it is certain that the infiltration of Communist forces into the Himalayas had begun, just as Richardson had predicted a few months earlier. One thing is certain, the Indian Ambassador to Nepal had a strength and strategic vision that Pannikar did not have.

Vietnam

In Vietnam the situation was clearer; the Communists had begun an armed struggle to overthrow the French 'imperialist' forces.

A French General who served for many years in Vietnam later wrote:

> "[General] Giap then thought that the time had come for the general counter-attack – the third and last phase of his war plans. The Communist Chinese were at the border; the promised material help could soon become a reality".[14]

<hr />

[14]Salan, op. cit., p. 29.

In the first days of October, at the time Liu Bocheng's men were crossing the Upper Yangtse to 'liberate' Tibet, Giap with 25,000 men attacked the French troops who were trying to vacate the border posts with China. It was too late for them. Within 8 days, the French troops had been decimated

"The wind was blowing toward abandoning (Indo-China) in spite of the strength of our battalions in the Delta," wrote General Salan.

It is only with the arrival of the very charismatic General De Lattre de Tassigny that the French would be able to stop the Communist advance at least till the Dien Bien Phu debacle.

The resolutions of the Youth Congress in Calcutta a year earlier had been put into action: the national movements of liberation were advancing hand in hand with the Communist progression in Asia.

China Invades Tibet: 'The Gods are on Our Side!'

The rumours of an impeding attack had started trickling in from August.

Pannikar knew it, he knew that the Chinese had already entered in the Chinese-controlled areas of Kham (Sikang). In a communication to the Chinese Foreign Office on 2 October he informed the Chinese that the Tibetan Delegation would be leaving India shortly to Peking and had expressed the hope that further military action would, therefore, not be necessary. "It will help the peaceful settlement of the Tibetan question if the Chinese troops which might have entered territory under the jurisdiction of the Lhasa authorities could restrict themselves to western Sikang."[15]

In Chamdo, Robert Ford, the British radio operator employed by Lhasa had arrived in December 1949. He had already spent some months in Lhasa with another Englishman, Reginald Fox, who operated a radio set for the Tibetan Government.

Ford, 'Phodo Kusho' as the Tibetans called him, had brought with him brand new radio sets that he found nicely packed in crates when he first arrived in Lhasa. During World War II, when the Burma road was closed, the Lhasa government had authorized two Americans to proceed with a reconnaissance mission seeking possible supply routes between China and India. To thank the Tibetan Government, the President of the United States had sent three radio

[15]SWJN, Series II, Vol. 15 (2), p. 332.

sets which were still packed in their crates in 1948. Many officials in Tibet were not keen to have foreigners operate these sets, but as no Tibetans had yet been trained to use them, they remained packed up in crates.

From Chamdo, Ford soon established a daily link with Lhasa. He was also able to monitor the world news from Beijing and Delhi.

From the remote capital of Kham Province, on new year's day 1950, Ford heard an ominous communiqué broadcast by the People's Republic of China: "The task for the People's Liberation Army for 1950 is to liberate Taiwan, Hainan and Tibet."

Soon after his arrival in Chamdo, one of Ford's first tasks was the training of some young Indians of Tibetan stock who would be able to operate the radio sets. The idea was to send them to the Sino-Tibetan border to monitor the movements of the Chinese troops. This border which had been 'shifting' during the past decades and even centuries, was now situated some one hundred miles east of Chamdo and followed the course of the Upper Yangtse.

It is difficult to ascertain the true number of Tibetan troops stationed on the 200 mile long border along the banks of the Yangtse[16], Goldstein speaks of about 3,500 soldiers,[17] but Ford estimated their strength to be much less.

Whatever might have been the number of Tibetan soldiers, they were no match for the Second Field Army led by the Political Commissioner in Sichuan. On the other side of the great river more than 40,000 much better equipped troops waited to 'liberate' Tibet.

One of the major problems faced by the Tibetans was the lack of unity between the local chieftains and the Lhasa government. It was not a new problem but a heavy toll would be paid for the antagonism between Lhasa and the Khampas at this crucial point in the history of Tibet.

The Chinese Liberation Army was also much better trained and disciplined than the Tibetans. They had received very clear instructions. A Proclamation stating the *Three General Rules and the Eight Things to Keep in Mind* had been issued. The General Rules were: "You must obey orders, You cannot take even one needle from the masses, you must turn over to the government things acquired from the enemy."

[16]Tibetan 'Drichu'.

[17]He is quoting Chinese sources, sometimes more reliable for this type of information.

The Eight Things to Keep in Mind included advice such as: "You must speak gently, you must buy and sell honestly, you must return the things you borrow, you must not tease or bother females, you may not abuse prisoners of war."[18]

On October 11 at 11 p.m., Ford had just finished speaking to his mother in England on the radio and was preparing to go to bed, when he heard a faint tinkle of bells coming from the east. "As bells grew louder I heard another sound, the clip-clop of horse's hoofs." Ford added, "...it passed my house on the way into the town. I saw the rider's fur hat and the silhouette of the barrel of his riffle sticking up above his shoulder."[19] Ford immediately recognized an Army messenger riding towards the Residency where Ngabo Ngawang Jigme, the new Governor of Kham was staying.

The next morning Ford was awakened by his servant who announced: "Phodo Kusho, the Chinese are coming! They've crossed the river at Gangto Druga and killed all the troops."

Gangto Druga was on the main trade route between Kangting and Chamdo. A Tibetan garrison was posted there.

Five days had already passed since the Chinese began the 'liberation', but for reasons known only to himself, Ngabo Shape[20] had refused to spare a radio set for the border post to monitor the advance of the Chinese troops.

Ford tried many times to convince Ngabo to send a wireless set to Riwoche in August-September, but the Governor was not interested in listening to Ford, a very junior official in the Tibetan Government. From Ford's side, he had to keep the etiquette in addressing the Governor and present his suggestions as politely as possible:

"Your Excellency, the spare portable radio is ready to go out at the shortest notice", Ford told Ngabo, indirectly suggesting that a radio should be sent to the border.

"Good, Please keep the batteries charged," replied Ngabo.[21]

"They are always fully charged. Either or both of the Indian operators are also in constant readiness to go out," hinted again Ford.

---

[18]Quoted from Goldstein, op. cit., p. 644.

[19]Ford, op. cit., p. 108.

[20]Ngabo as Governor of Kham had a Cabinet Minister rank and was referred to as Ngabo Shape.

[21]Ford, op. cit., p. 110.

"Very good, we may need to send the station at any time," answered Ngabo.

That day Ford did not want to leave the Residency without getting a clear answer about Riwoche: "Would you like me to send the radio to Riwoche now, Phodo?" the Governor finally asked. "Yes, Your Excellency," said Ford.

"You are afraid we shall be cut off in Chamdo?" asked the Governor. But Ngabo thought the army reinforcements had made the defence of Riwoche very strong. "Do not worry, Phodo, the gods are on our side." [22]

This discussion summarized the Tibetan world view. Unfortunately for them, the world had changed and the consequences would soon be tragic for old Tibet.

The main border post at Gamto Druga had been overrun by the Chinese who used the same strategy as in Korea. Wave after wave of soldiers soon overpowered the Tibetan defenders, who fought well but were finally massacred.

In the meantime another Chinese regiment crossed the Yangtse above Dengo and advanced rapidly towards Dartsedo, marching day and night.

In the South, the 157th PLA Regiment crossed the Yangtse and attacked the Tibetan troops near Markhan. When they reached Markhan, the local Tibetan Commander, Derge Se, surrounded by the Chinese troops, surrendered his force of 400 men.

Poor Ford! He had planned to use the southern route to escape. Now this route was also cut off. The net was slowly closing on Ford and on Tibet.

The northern front lost ground day by day and the headquarters of the central zone was soon lost to the waves of young Chinese soldiers. They caught the fleeing Tibetans at night in a place called Kyuhung where the Tibetans were decimated. The road to Chamdo was open. Lhasa was finally informed on October 12 that the Yangtse had been crossed.

At the same time, the opera season was in full swing in Lhasa. The aristocracy and the Government were busy. For the Tibetan officials opera and picnic were sacred!

In Chamdo no one panicked, though the number of prayers was increased. More and more lay people joined the monks and began

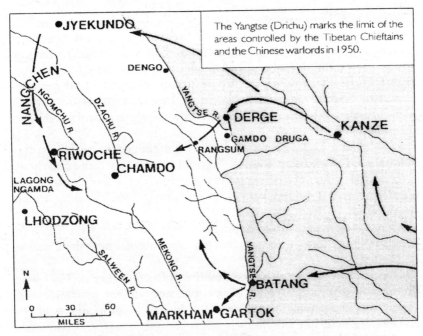

The Yangtse (Drichu) marks the limit of the areas controlled by the Tibetan Chieftains and the Chinese warlords in 1950.

Map showing the routes of the Chinese invasion of Tibet in 1950.

circumambulating around the monastery, the incense smoke went higher and higher in the sky, the gods had to be propitiated. Ford said that the monks believed that "only the gods could give Tibet victory — which was unanswerable — and they were doing their bit by praying. They would pray twice as hard, or rather twice as often, and that would be of more use than taking up arms." [23]

"The gods are on our side," was the most often repeated mantra in the town.

The greatest excitement in Chamdo was the latest divination that Shiwala Rinpoche, the head lama of the local monastery, had just performed. It was on all tongues, the great news had spread like wildfire: "Shiwala Rinpoche says that the Chinese will not come." Everywhere there was a sigh of relief. The Gods had won!

The Britisher in Ford commented that Shiwala Rinpoche's statement was perhaps good for morale "but it seemed to me that something more Churchilian was needed."[24]

[23]Ford, op. cit., p. 112.
[24]Ford, op. cit., p. 113.

The Dalai Lama recalled: "Towards evening, during one of the performances, I caught sight of a messenger running in my direction. On reaching my enclosure, he was immediately shown in to Tathag Rinpoche, the Regent...I realized at once that something was wrong. Under normal circumstances government matters would have to wait until the following week. Naturally, I was almost besides myself with curiosity. What could this mean? Something dreadful must have happened."[25]

The young Dalai Lama said that he managed to peep into the Regent's lodge and spy on him. "I could see his face quite clearly as he read the letter. He became very grave. After a few minutes, he went out and I heard him give orders for the Kashag to be summoned."

The Dalai Lama discovered later that the letter was Ngabo's telegram informing the Regent that the first outposts near the Yangtse had fallen.

One of the problems as seen by the political leader of Tibet was that Tibetans were peace-loving people, non-violent by choice and to join the army was "considered the lowest form of life: soldiers were being held like butchers."

In the circumstances and keeping in mind the deep division between the Tibetans from Lhasa and the Khampas, what could have been done? Perhaps as the Tibetans themselves explain, the Karma of Tibet had 'ripened' and nothing or nobody could stop it.

The Dalai Lama remembers that "the Chinese suffered greatly from difficulties of supply on the one hand and the harsh climate on the other. Many died of starvation; others must have certainly have succumbed of altitude sickness."[26]

But Deng Xiaoping, Liu Bocheng and their men were used to hardship and bitterness. They had gone through worse when the Nationalists were trying to catch up with them during the Long March. It was without doubt easier for the People's Liberation Army to fight ill-equipped Tibetans than the sophisticated weapons of McArthur's troops in Korea on the eastern front.

In the meantime, Ford was trying to catch the latest world news on his wireless, but there was nothing about Tibet. One of the greatest dramas of the twentieth century was unfolding without anyone knowing it. When the world heard of it, it was already too late.

[25]The Dalai Lama, op. cit., p. 55.
[26]The Dalai Lama, op. cit., p. 56.

Over, the next few days, many Tibetan officials came to Ford's radio station to try to hear the reaction of Lhasa, thinking that the Kashag would immediately appeal to the world community for help. They expected Lhasa to respond quickly before it was too late. But nothing! Nobody could understand what was going on!

One day Ford went to Ngabo to show him the news summary and he was reassured by the Governor not to worry. The Tsongdu and the Kashag were deliberating and once a decision was taken, it would be announced.

"Radio Lhasa had no more to say the next day, or the day after that."

Finally about 10 days after the Chinese had crossed the Upper Yangtse, Ford heard an announcement from Delhi: Shakabpa and the Tibetan delegation were denying any attack on Tibet.

"Wonderful government!" the Dalai Lama once told us with reference to some other subject and he laughed and laughed.

They were simply not living in this world. But their world was disappearing, without them or the world realizing it.

On 26 October, a news report from Calcutta stated:

Tsepon Shakabpa, leader of seven-man delegation to Peking told PTI today that this delegation was proceeding to Peking irrespective of the reported Chinese Communists invasion of Tibet. He had received final instructions from Lhasa to conduct negotiations in Peking on future Sino-Tibetan relations only last Sunday, he said. The Delegation had not discussed the future of Tibet with the Chinese Ambassador in New Delhi during their stay there. They had only informal talks. A member of the delegation said that they were more interested in religion than in foreign affairs. He thought Tibet was of no significant strategic importance from military point of view.[27]

"Wonderful government!" To send a delegation more interested in religion than in foreign affairs to discuss with Mao the future of their nation!

On 27 October, *The Hindu* in Madras published the following piece:

The Tibetan Delegation which left New Delhi this morning en route to Peking remained unperturbed over

[27]*The Hindu*, Madras, 27 October, 1950.

the reported entry of the Chinese troops into Eastern Tibet and the leader of the delegation pointed out that the area in question was always disputed territory, both China and Tibet claiming it as part of their territory. New Delhi is generally inclined to believe the reported movement of troops may be related to some border incidents but not to any general invasion by Chinese troops. The fact that the Tibetan delegation left New Delhi for Peking for formal negotiations and settlement of the future status of Tibet at the suggestion of the Chinese Government is cited in support of the view entertained by New Delhi.

Nineteen days after the Chinese invaded Tibet, its negotiating delegation was not informed (or pretended to be not informed) of the development and they were innocently proceeding to Beijing. The previous day the Indian Prime Minister had given one of the speeches he loved to deliver that could electrify the masses: it was reported by *The Hindu*:

Pandit Nehru said that while vast millions of people all over the world were 'hankering and hindering after peace' feverish preparations for war were also going on in many parts of the world and this is a serious contradiction which had to be solved. 'The only way to bring peace', the Prime Minister thought was 'for the people of the world and the different countries to cast away fear from their hearts and minds and think and do the right thing'.[28]

Poor Tibetans, they thought they were doing the right thing in calling upon the gods for help and in completing the Opera Festival. One thing is for sure — there was no fear in Lhasa and Chamdo.

In the meantime, things were getting hotter on the eastern front, it was reported in *The Hindu* on 26 October that there were "300,000 Chinese Red on border with North Korea and Manchuria", while the Government of India "has not yet received an official report of the invasion of Tibet by Chinese troops, a spokesman of the Government of India said here today."

Strangely enough Lhasa was keeping quiet. In the words of Robert Ford:

[28]*The Hindu*, Madras: 27 October, 1950.

While Fox was away there was no news in English, but
I continued to relay the news in Tibetan and in Chinese...
Not a word was said about the invasion.

"I don't understand," I said when it was over. "The
Chinese have attacked Tibet. Tibet wants help. Peking
is silent for obvious reasons. What on earth can Lhasa
gain by pretending the war does not exist?" No one
answered.

When Ford decided to take the news summary personally to
Ngabo, the only thing the governor could say was: "I will tell you
confidentially, Phodo [Ford], that the National Assembly is meeting
in Lhasa now."[29] "The National Assembly was evidently having a
long session", added Ford.

The analysis of Ford may be correct when he said:

I could only think it was a matter of habit. The Lhasa
Government was so used to the policy of saying nothing
that might offend or provoke the Chinese that it kept it
on after provocation had become irrelevant. It was still
trying to avert a war that had already broken out.[30]

On October 19, Robert Ford was arrested and charged with
having killed the Gethak Lama and spying for the imperialists. He
spent five years in Chinese jails.

It was only on October 25 that the Chinese themselves announced
to the world that Tibet was 'liberated.' A brief communiqué of the
New China News Agency (Xinhua) said: "People's army units have
been ordered to advance into Tibet to free three million Tibetans."

On November 10, Xinhua News Agency said that Mao and Zhu
De were "deeply concerned about the prolonged oppression of the
Tibetan people by the British and American imperialism."
Accordingly, they had decided to "move into Tibet to help the
Tibetan people to shake off the oppression for ever."[31]

[29]Ford, op. cit., p. 115.
[30]Ibid.
[31]Ling Nai-Min, *Tibetan Sourcebook* (Hong Kong: Union Research Institute,
1964).

20

India's and the World Reaction

> It is ...not necessary to repeat that [the Government of
> India's] interest is solely in a peaceful settlement of the
> issue.
>
> **Note from the Government of India**

It is rather strange that on October 12, a day after Chamdo was informed of the Chinese entry into Tibet, *The Statesman* in Calcutta published a detailed report from its Darjeeling correspondent about the Chinese invasion. It was denied in New Delhi because no confirmation had been received from Pannikar and the report was termed by the Government as "a hotch potch story based probably on caravan stories".

Even stranger, a few days later, Shakabpa, also denied the news of the invasion in Delhi. Ford said: "But for the Tibetan delegation to deny that there has been Chinese aggression several days after the news of the invasion had reached Lhasa, could only mean either that the delegation had not been informed or that it had been told to keep quiet."

The British radio operator added: "The action of the Lhasa Government would have been easier to understand if it had intended to offer only a token resistance to the Chinese and then sue for peace, but it was not doing anything of the kind. The resistance was real, and Tibet's subsequent appeal to the United Nations showed that there was never any question of surrender. I could only think it was a matter of habit."[1]

After two weeks, some rumours of the attack had begun spreading, mainly in Kalimpong and Beijing. Pannikar decided to act.

[1]Ford, op. cit., p. 115.

On October 21, he sent a Memorandum to the Ministry of Foreign Affairs of China:

"It is ...not necessary to repeat that [the Government of India's] interest is solely in a peaceful settlement of the issue. ...It has, however been reported that some military action has taken place or is about to take place, which may affect the peaceful outcome of these negotiations."[2]

Then the note started lecturing the Chinese, basically saying: "if you do not behave well, how can we defend your case in the UN!" India was losing its centuries-old buffer zone which preserved the Himalayas as a zone of peace, but Pannikar's only concern was about China's application to the UN.

In a cable[3] to Panikkar[4] on October 22, Nehru clearly showed that he knew about the advance of the PLA in Kham:

Our information from Lhasa is that Chinese forces are still advancing and Riwoche, Dzokangdzong, Markhan and Chamdo have fallen. Also that Lhodzong is expected to fall soon. Unless it is clear that these forces are halted and there is no imminent danger of invasion of Tibet, there is little chance of Tibetan delegation proceeding to Peking. We have been pressing them to go but cannot continue doing so in view of military movements threatening invasion.

I confess I am completely unable to understand urgency behind Chinese desire to 'liberate' [Tibet].

Nehru added: "Anglo-Americans, no doubt, dislike idea of China spreading out right up to Indian frontier but they are not in a position to do anything about it."

[2]Memorandum of the Government of the Republic of India on the question of Tibet, delivered by the Indian Ambassador on 21 October, 1950 to the Chinese Foreign Ministry in Peking.
The Notes exchanged between the Government of India and China are available in Chanakya Sen's *Tibet Disappears*.
[3]SWJN, Series II, Vol. 15 (1), p. 437. Cable from Jawaharlal Nehru to Panikkar dated October 22.
[4]Panikkar reported a discussion with the Chinese Vice Foreign Minister Chang who reiterated his Government's resolve to 'liberate' Tibet. He added that they were still waiting for the Tibetan delegation to arrive, though some interested party was 'opposing and obstructing' a negotiated settlement. It was a lie: the PLA had already crossed the Yangtse two weeks earlier. Panikkar was fooled by his interlocutor.

Should it not have been rather India which 'disliked' having someone 'right up to' her border?

Nehru rightly concluded that the Tibetans "are afraid of China dictating terms which will amount to complete surrender of autonomy which Tibet has enjoyed during last four decades. ...They have no knowledge how to deal with other countries." He confirmed that the Tsongdu "which is summoned on occasions of national emergency," has been in session in Lhasa since 19th October.

In his Indian Note to the Chinese Government, it is pathetic to observe that the Indian Ambassador to China could not or would not see even a hint of the strategic implications[5] for the security of his own country.

We shall see that the invasion of Tibet was to have the most serious repercussions for the next fifty years of India's history:

> The Government of India would desire to point out that a military action at the present time against Tibet will give those countries in the world which are unfriendly to China a handle for anti-Chinese propaganda at a crucial juncture in international affairs. The Central People's Government must be aware that opinion in the United Nations has been steadily veering round to the admission of China into the organisation before the close of the present session.
>
> The Government of India felt that military action on the eve of a decision by the General Assembly will have serious consequences and will give powerful support to those who are opposed to the admission of the People's Government to the United Nations and the Security Council.
>
> At the present time when the international situation is so delicate, any more that is likely to be interpreted as a disturbance of the peace may prejudice the position of China in the eyes of the world.
>
> ...The Government of India attaches the highest importance to the earliest settlement of the problem of

---

[5]As we will see later, he had perfectly seen the strategic implications two years earlier when he wrote a note to New Delhi advocating the recognition of the independence of Tibet.

Chinese   representation   in   international organisations…"[6]

The memorandum goes on and on about the difficulties for India to sponsor the Chinese case, though it is nowhere clear or explicit that the Chinese even want to join the UN.

The memorandum ended on a rather strange note: *"In Tibet there is not likely to be any serious military opposition and any delay in settling the matter will not therefore affect Chinese interests."*[7]

It looked like a green light from Pannikar to the Chinese to settle the matter militarily.

In fact many observers felt that Pannikar was supportive of the Beijing government's plan to infuse a good dose of communism into the Tibetan feudal' regime in Lhasa and to 'liberate the serfs' from both the power of monks and the imperialists led by Richardson, the Indian Representative.

The note is dated 21st October, exactly two weeks after Liu's troops had entered Tibet. Obviously Pannikar knew about the invasion.

By this time, Ngabo Ngawang Jigme, the Governor of Kham had already been taken prisoner and was on his way to Beijing.

The Chinese could now sit back and watch. All the cards were in their hands. If they had wished to they could have continued their advance on Lhasa, but they wanted to show the world that Tibet could be liberated 'peacefully' and of course winter was setting in. Nineteen days after the Second Field Army crossed the Yangtse on October 26, *The Hindu* reported that: "The Indian Ambassador in Peking, it is understood, has been asked to ascertain full facts and report."

Was the 'picnic' still going on in Lhasa? On the same day in Kalimpong, a Tibetan Government spokesman said: "The Tibetan Government have so far no information from eastern borders about the movements of Chinese troops into Tibetan territory."

The spokesman added:

Tibet borders are covered by a network of wireless

---

[6]Memorandum of the Government of the Republic of India on the question of Tibet, delivered by the Indian Ambassador on 21 October 1950, to the Chinese Foreign Ministry in Peking.

[7]Emphasis added by author.

stations and Lhasa would have known if there had been any Chinese troop movements towards Tibet. We would be the first to tell the world if an invasion of Tibet had taken place, for it concerns our territorial integrity. Besides, a telegram which I have received from Lhasa clearly indicates that there has been no trouble or border incident in Tibet.[8]

Was it out of compassion for the Chinese feelings that Lhasa avoided announcing to the world the outrage committed by the PLA?

Tibet probably bent over backwards to not upset the Chinese feelings and provoke a stronger reaction. But what could have been worse?

During the next few years the same policy would be followed. It is particularly true of Ngabo, the chief negotiator during the 'talks' for the 17-Point Agreement in Beijing who accepted all the Chinese points for fear of over-reaction from the Chinese side.

In subsequent years, one of the only Tibetan leaders who would have the courage to be firm and stand up to the increasing demands of the Chinese is Lukhangwa, the future Prime Minister of Tibet. Unfortunately he was sacrificed on the altar of the same policy of appeasement. Thus Lhasa was silent; Delhi did not know anything; Kalimpong was kept in the dark and Pannikar in Beijing had 'only heard rumours'.

On 25th October, it was finally Beijing who decided to break the news to the world.

The Chinese communiqué had the merit of being frank: the Communist wanted to consolidate their border with India, and free Tibet from imperialist forces.

As for the 'imperialists', at that time there were only six in Lhasa. A couple of missionaries were living in Kham. One of them, George Patterson, had been staying with the Pandatsangs in Batang and had soon left for India "to inform the India and western government of the happenings in Eastern Tibet."

The first reaction of the Government of India was to assume that the Chinese were targeting them while speaking of 'imperialist forces'. After a Cabinet Meeting in New Delhi, it was officially announced that: "Official circles in New Delhi including the Prime Minister, Pandit Nehru are extremely perplexed and disappointed

[8]*The Hindu*, Madras, 26 October, 1950.

at the Chinese Government's action without a word of explanation in advance. To India which has been led to believe by the Chinese Foreign Office that the Chinese would settle the future of Tibet in a peaceful manner by direct negotiation with the representatives of Tibet, the latest development has naturally come as a shock."[9]

India could not see what had merited this action, but the future would reveal that she ought to have been more than just 'perplexed and disappointed'.

On the 27th a government note said: "The Government of India has read with considerable concern the report that the Chinese Government have ordered units of the Chinese army to advance into Tibet." Pannikar was asked to convey "their surprise and regret."

What is surprising is that the Government of India should have been so surprised, as the Chinese had announced again and again during the past year that they would liberate both Taiwan and Tibet.

And had Nehru forgotten that he himself wrote in September 1949 that the "Chinese communist are likely to invade Tibet"?

The next day, *The Daily Telegraph* in London summed up the point:

> The Indian Government had 'invited' China to open military operation on Tibet by her attitude. 'Regret possible, but why by surprise? From the very beginning of the year and at frequent intervals the liberation of Tibet had been proclaimed over radio as a task of the Chinese Communist Government.'
> The Indian Government made it equally clear that it had no desire to intervene militarily. This was a clear invitation to the Communists to proceed and the only reason for surprise is that they left it so late in the year.[10]

Soon after Pannikar had taken charge in Beijing, he had been informed by Zhou Enlai of the impending attack, so where was the surprise? But it was indeed regrettable.

On the 28th October, the second note from the Government of India was handed over to the Chinese Ministry of Foreign Affairs:

> We have seen with regrets reports in newspapers of official statements made in Peking to the effect that "people's Liberation Army units have been ordered to advance in Tibet.

[9]*The Hindu*, Madras, 27 October, 1950.
[10]Quoted in *The Hindu*, Madras, October 28, 1950.

We have received no intimation of it from your ambassador here[11] or from our ambassador in Peking.
... In an interview which India's ambassador had recently with the Vice-foreign Minister, while reiterating the resolve of the Chinese government to 'liberate' Tibet, he had expressed a continued desire to do so by peaceful means.[12]

The Note continues:

The decision to order an advance of China's troops into Tibet appears to us most surprising and regrettable.
...The Government of India do not believe any foreign influence hostile to China has been responsible for the delay in the delegation's departure.
The Government of India can only express their deep regret that in spite of the friendly and disinterested advice repeatedly tendered by them, the Chinese Government should have decided to seek a solution of the problem of their relations with Tibet by force instead by the slower and more enduring method of peace approach.[13]

In this note the Government of India decided to state her position in slightly stronger terms:

Now that the invasion of Tibet has been ordered by the Chinese Government, peaceful negotiations can hardly be synchronised with it and there naturally will be fear on the part of the Tibetans that negotiations will be under duress. In the present context of world events, invasion by the Chinese troops in Tibet cannot but be regarded as deplorable and in the considered judgement of the Government, not in the interest of China or Peace.

But what about the interests of India? Why was Pannikar so preoccupied by the interests of China?

On 26 October, the Tibetan delegation in Kalimpong declared that they could not understand what was happening and why Lhasa was still silent. Did Shakabpa know that one third of Tibetan territory had already fallen into the hands of the Communists? Did he know

[11]In Delhi.
[12]See Sen, op. cit., p. 69 ff.
[13]Note of the Government of the Republic of India on the question of Tibet delivered by the Indian Ambassador in Peking on 28 October, 1950.

that Ngabo was a prisoner on his way to China and that not a single Tibetan soldier was left between the advancing Chinese troops and Lhasa?

The Hindu of October 26 quoted a Tibetan source saying: "It cannot be possible. This news comes just when the Tibetan delegation is leaving for Peking for negotiations with the Chinese Government. If the Tibetan delegation had, after talks in Peking, been unable to reach a settlement, then... we could have understood Chinese taking military action."[14]

But this was the Chinese way! Some twelve years later, in September 1962, the Chinese Foreign Minister, Chen Yi, would put the too bright Indian Defence Minister to sleep by assuring him that a small skirmish at the border of two brothers like India and China was nothing: "we are first brothers, let us preserve this brotherhood." A few days later, they invaded India.

Mao Zedong was first and foremost a great and ruthless strategist and he was free from all moral considerations. He planned everything at all levels: diplomatic, military, strategic.

He had first got the clearance and support of Stalin. His lieutenants Deng Xiaoping and Liu Bocheng prepared the military front while Zhou Enlai played his diplomatic role to allay India's suspicions. Pannikar was not only easy to delude, he was always ready to espouse the Chinese cause and did his best to convince his bosses in Delhi of the New China's greatness and the good and pure intentions of its leaders. Different operations went as smoothly as Mao had planned them on the Tibetan front.

In the meantime, big brother in Moscow felicitated China. *The Pravda* of 26 October said: "The courageous sons of the Chinese people will wage battles at an altitude of four to five thousand meters above sea level and at the most rigorous time of the year." For Moscow, the Second Field Army was liberating "the last area of the continental part of the Republic of China - still under the oppression of foreign imperialists."

The American press took an opposite position, *The New York Times* ran the titles: "India disapproves invasion of Tibet in notes to Peking. Protests made. The Indian Prime Minister acted with misplaced sincerity".

[14]*The Hindu*, October 26, 1950.

The Indian public had reacted with shock at the news of the invasion of Tibet. Some Indian leaders suggested that the Government of India should take the matter to the UN.

Tibetan traders reaching Kalimpong said that everything was normal in Lhasa. They also declared that the Kashag was split over Tibet's relation with China. Probably, nobody in Lhasa knew how to handle the debacle on the eastern front and the advance of the Chinese troops towards Lhasa. The Regent, Taktra Rinpoche was too old and inexperienced, thus the only viable solution was to ask the gods to decide.

The Shakabpa delegation was totally at a loss. They left Calcutta for Kalimpong from where they announced that they would soon be proceeding to Beijing to reach the Chinese capital by the first week of November.

Meantime, the Chinese were in full control of the war propaganda. Their communiqués were the only news from the front. Lhasa remained silent. The monopoly of information being with Beijing, all sorts of strange news reports were announced. For example, it was said that the Geshe Sherab Gyatso[15], Vice-President of the Free Tibetan Government along with an army of 5,000 troops, was leading the People's Liberation Army in freeing Tibet of its 'olds.'[16] In India (and probably in Tibet) nobody had ever heard of this Free Tibetan Government.

On 30 October, Zhou Enlai replied to the two notes from the Government of India, making it very clear that India had no business to interfere in the internal affairs of the People's Republic:

> The Central People's Republic of China would like to make it clear: Tibet is an integral part of the Chinese territory and the problem of Tibet is entirely a domestic problem of China. The Chinese People's Liberation Army must enter Tibet, liberate the Tibetan people, and defend the frontiers of China. This is the resolved policy of the Central People's Government. The Central People's Government has repeatedly expressed the hope that the problem of Tibet may be solved by peaceful

[15]The teacher of the great scholar Gedun Choepell; he had been arguing with Gedun Choepell that the earth was flat.

[16]The 'Four Olds' during the Cultural Revolution were "old ideas, old culture, old traditions and old customs".

negotiations, and it welcomes, therefore, the delegation of the local authorities of Tibet to come to Peking at an early date to proceed with peaceful negotiations. Yet, the Tibetan delegation, under outside instigation, has intentionally delayed the date of its departure for Peking. ...But regardless whether the local authorities of Tibet wish to proceed with peaceful negotiations, and whatever results may be achieved by negotiations, the problem of Tibet is a domestic problem of the People's Republic of China and no foreign interference shall be tolerated.[17] "

The Note from the Chinese ended in a rather insulting remark for India;

Therefore, with regard to the point of view of the Government of India on what it regards as deplorable, the Central People's Government of China cannot but consider it as having been affected by foreign influences hostile to China in Tibet and hence express its deep regret."

Poor Pannikar, to say that he was influenced by foreign forces, someone who had written *Asia and Western Dominance* and who was so obsessed by the 'western influences' that he had refused to take up residence in the diplomatic campus in Beijing near the western legations!

The Chinese were master manipulators, they knew whom to hit and where. By accusing Nehru and his ambassador of being guided by foreign nations, they were certain that they would react strongly to disprove these statements and therefore fall in the trap of the government of New China. It was an excellent tactic that paid rich dividends for Beijing, but in the process Delhi lost its centuries-old peaceful border.

[17]Reply of the Central People's Government of the People's Republic of China on 30 October 1950, to the memorandum and note of the Indian Government on the question of Tibet.

21

The Appeal to the UN

The International Betrayal

The attention of the world is riveted on Korea where aggression is being resisted by an international force. Similar happenings in remote Tibet are passing without notice.

From the Tibetan Appeal to the UN

By the end of October 1950, things finally began to move in Lhasa. Though the young Dalai Lama had not yet taken over as the political and religious head of Tibet, the Kashag decided to emulate South Korea and appeal to the General Assembly of the UN against the Communist Chinese act of aggression.

Their best bet for support was the Government of India, since for the preceding months, the British had made it clear that they would follow whatever New Delhi decided.

During the last days of October Lhasa sent feelers to Delhi to see if India would be ready to sponsor the Tibetan appeal in the UN. The Tibetan Government was quite confident that Nehru's government, which had always taken the side of oppressed people against imperialist and colonialist powers, would cooperate.

India's reply was that it would certainly support an appeal from Tibet, but would not sponsor the appeal themselves.

On November 1, in an interview with United Press, the Indian Prime Minister declared:

I have received a 'suggestion' from Tibetan sources that Tibet would like to appeal to the United Nations against the Chinese Army's invasion. I have replied that India does not feel free to sponsor such a resolution in the United Nations, but Tibet is free to appeal directly, if it so chooses, through Secretary-General Lie. India has neither the resources nor the inclination to send armed assistance[1] to Tibet.[2]

The same day Nehru cabled B.N. Rau:[3] "Chinese military operations against Tibet have undoubtedly affected our friendly relations with China. But these developments do not affect our general policy or even our policy regarding admission of new China in United Nations."[4]

For the Tibetans, it was a terrible let down, but the Government of India felt that it could not do more without upsetting the Chinese. Shakabpa's orders to go to Beijing were cancelled and he was directed by the Kashag to remain in Kalimpong to help in preparing and sending the appeal to the UN.

On November 3, the Tibetan Government informed the Indian Government that as it was not ready to sponsor the appeal, they were going to request some other Buddhist nations to do so.

The Tibetan Appeal

The appeal by the Government of Tibet was cabled to the UN on November 7.

The well-drafted appeal stated that the problem was not of 'Tibet's own making' and that "the Tibetans were racially, culturally and geographically far apart from the Chinese." It compared their situation with Korea.

> ... As you are aware the problem of Tibet has taken alarming proportions in the recent times. The problem is not of Tibet's own making but is largely the outcome of unthwarted Chinese ambitions to bring weaker nations on her periphery within her active domination. As a people devoted to the tenets of Buddhism, Tibetans had long eschewed the art of warfare, practised peace and tolerance and for the defence of their country, relied on its geographical configuration and on non-involvement in the affairs of other nations. There were times when Tibet sought but seldom received the

---

[1]He cited the case of the Dogra War when the Sikhs of Zorawar Singh were decimated during the winter in Tibet.

[2]SWJN, Series II, Vol. 15 (2), p. 335. Tibetans Free to Appeal to the United Nations.

[3]Sir Benagal N. Rau, the Indian Representative to the UN.

[4]SWJN, Series II, Vol. 15 (2), p. 339.

protection of the Chinese Emperor. The Chinese, however, in their natural urge for expansion, have wholly misconstrued the significance of the ties of friendship and interdependence that existed between China and Tibet as between neighbours.

China's conduct during the expedition of 1910 completed the rupture between the two countries. In 1911-12 Tibet, under the thirteenth Dalai Lama, declared her complete independence, even as Nepal simultaneously broke away from allegiance to China. The Chinese Revolution in 1911, which dethroned the last Manchu Emperor, snapped the last of the sentimental and religious bonds between China and Tibet. Tibet thereafter depended entirely on her isolation, and occasionally on the support of the British in India for her protection.

Then the Appeal clarifies the position of Tibet vis-à-vis China from the beginning of the century to date. And it added: "This unwarranted act of aggression has not only disturbed the peace of Tibet, but is in complete disregard of the solemn assurance given by the Chinese to the Government of India, ...the problem is simple. The Chinese claim Tibet as part of China. Tibetans feel that racially, culturally, and geographically, they are far apart from the Chinese."

The Appeal concluded with:

We, ministers, with the approval of His Holiness the Dalai Lama entrust the problem of Tibet in this emergency to the ultimate decision of the United Nations and hope that the conscience of the world would not allow the disruption of our state by methods reminiscent of the jungle.[5]

The appeal was signed by the Kashag and the National Assembly on the 27th day of the ninth Tibetan month of the Iron-Tiger Year[6] and was dispatched from Shakabpa House in Kalimpong.

It was rumoured that the text was too well written to have been drafted by Tibetans and that an Indian officer at the Indian Mission in Lhasa had secretly written it for the Kashag. This was never proved

[5]For the text of the Appeal see The Dalai Lama, *My Land and my People* (New York: Potala, 1983), p. 249.

[6]November 7, 1950 of the roman calendar.

though it is obvious that the English language was checked by some one who spoke excellent English.[7]

The Tibetans immediately ran into the heavy bureaucracy of the UN. The first objection was that Tibet was not a member of the UN, but worse, the UN wanted to refuse the message because it had originated from outside the country of the appellant.[8] According to the UN rules, an appeal could not be received unless it originated from the country of the appellant. India, UK or the United States knew very well that for technical reasons[9], all official communiqués from the Tibetan Government had always been issued from Kalimpong in the past.

Meantime, the Tibetan Government continued to send personal appeals to a few Western governments such as Canada and the US, requesting them support the Tibetan appeal.

On November 15, it was finally the tiny state of El Salvador which requested the UN Secretary General to list the Tibetan appeal on the Agenda of the General Assembly.

Hector Castro, the head of the El Salvadoran delegation to the UN, asked that the Tibetan issue should come up for discussion in the General Assembly with reference to Article 1 of the UN Charter which states that it was the responsibility of the UN to maintain international peace and security.

Some have attributed El Salvador's stand to some pressure from the CIA; their argument being, why did a small Central American state take a matter to the UN which appeared totally unrelated to the normal preoccupations of that state?

Until the CIA papers are fully declassified, it will be difficult to know the complete truth. Whatever might have been the reasons or motivation which pushed El Salvador to take the initiative to help the Tibetans, the merit for having done what bigger and much better informed powers did not do,[10] remains with El Salvador.

[7]Tsering Shakya, *The Dragon in the Land of Snows* (London: Pimlico, 1999) cites British Archives to show that S. Sinha, the Indian Representative in Lhasa 'helped' to put the draft in proper English. Shakabpa did not speak English.
[8]Shakabpa, the Chief Negotiator, had cabled the appeal from Kalimpong.
[9]Mainly due to the poor transmission network.
[10]One of our informants, who had the opportunity to meet the leader of the Salvadorian delegation many years later, was assured that it was purely a Salvadorian initiative.

This example illustrates how very few states[11] stood by their professed ideal of defending the rights of small peace-loving, oppressed nations. But worse was to follow.

Meanwhile, on November 12, Shakabpa declared in an interview in Kalimpong: "I have received intimation from Lhasa about the Tibetan Government's appeal to the UN." And when asked, "What will be the Tibetan Government's case against China? Does Tibet seek independence?" he prudently answered that "Tibet is a peaceful and religious state. China attacked us from four or five directions while negotiations were going on regarding relations between Tibet and China. Our appeal to the UN is that the Chinese forces be made to withdraw to the Sino-Tibetan boundary demarcated by the river Drichu.[12] The second question does not arise at present since we have to settle the first question of withdrawal of the Chinese forces from Tibetan territory.'[13]

One can often note the Tibetan reluctance to state their objectives in a direct manner. Instead of declaring that Tibet was an independent country and that they wanted to remain independent, he said: "the second question does not arise."

Did the Tibetan government dream that the Chinese, at this point in time, would withdraw and begin the negotiations?

The Indian Reaction

On November 14 the Indian government announced in New Delhi that, "Tibet and Nepal, besides domestic problems will be raised in the two-day debate in Parliament beginning tomorrow on the Presidential address."

And on the same day *The Hindu* wrote:

> According to informed quarters here, India is expected to extend her general support to Tibet's case before the Security Council.
>
> India's support, it is understood, will mainly be based on the ground that the issue could be solved peacefully and without resort to arms and the extent to which there were military operations, world peace was endangered.

[11]Including India, UK and US.
[12]The Yangtse in Tibetan.
[13]*The Hindu*, Madras, 13 November, 1950.

The UK and the US, according to diplomatic quarters here, are also expected to support the Tibetan appeal.[14]

Two days later in New Delhi, *The Hindu* announced: "Mr. N. Gopalaswami Ayyengar, India's Railway Minister, said today that India would support before the UN, Tibet's case against China."[15]

Finally on November 17, in the midst of preparations for the proposed discussion of the Tibetan issue in the UN, the Gods spoke through the Nechung State Oracle in Lhasa: "Make him King".

And so Tenzin Gyatso was enthroned as the Fourteenth Dalai Lama.

In Lhasa, the Tibetan Foreign Office nominated a delegation including Zasag Surkhang, Ngawang Gyaltsen and Trunik Chhenpo Chhombay to plead the Tibetan cause at the UN. It is not clear what happened to the delegation, but they never reached the seat of the UN. If they had, it would have certainly made a difference, but who was interested to see Tibetan delegates in New York?[16] Their presence might have brought an unwanted clarity into the confusion.[17]

The British Position

The British had always managed to keep the status of Tibet quite nebulous. It had always been advantageous for them to keep the legal position on Tibet as vague as possible.

In 1914, the Government of British India had accepted a nominal suzerainty of the Chinese over Tibet with the explicit condition that Tibet would be fully autonomous.

The main objective of the Simla Convention had been to show that Tibetans were able to manage their own affairs. The British had only kept the Chinese 'suzerainty' aspect as part of the definition of the status of Tibet in order to have leverage with the Tibetans, in case they were tempted to lean towards the Russians.

The highly intricate thinking of the players of the 'Great Game' was sometimes so complicated that ordinary human beings could

[14]*The Hindu*, Madras, 14 November, 1950.

[15]*The Hindu*, Madras, 16 November, 1950.

[16]It was clear that nobody was ready to issue visas on their Tibetan passports at this point in time.

[17]It has to be noted that when Tibet sent delegations to the UN in 1959, 1961 and 1965, resolutions were passed in favour of Tibet; but it involved strong lobbying by the Tibetan delegates.

not follow the sequence of logic. It was certainly the case with the self-trained Tibetan diplomats who were totally ignorant of the vagaries of world diplomacy.

Vagueness had worked well for years, but times were changing. With the UN becoming an important world body, new rules were framed and the old colonial definitions had to be fixed in black and white: either a state was independent or it was not. No state could claim to be at the same time under the suzerainty or vassalage of another state and yet to be fully autonomous.

The problem for the British government was that a proper legal definition of the status of Tibet had now become necessary.

The place and status of the Land of Snows on the Asian chessboard and its appeal to the General Assembly depended on this issue because according to the UN rules, only a 'state' could make an appeal to the General Assembly.

Was Tibet a 'state' for the British Government?

Surprisingly, after consulting legal experts His Majesty's Government accepted the fact that Tibet was a separate state. One of the points of White Hall was that the British Government had concluded a Convention between China, Tibet and herself in 1914 in Simla. The other point was that the Chinese had been expelled from Tibet in 1911 and Tibet had declared her independence two years later. The fact that Tibet had kept control of her internal as well as external affairs from 1911 to 1950 certainly qualified it as a separate state under Article 35 (2) of the UN Charter.

However, the Foreign Office wanted to further study the meaning of 'suzerainty'. It was a complicated matter, as it had always been kept vague in the past.

The legal cell of the Foreign Office concluded that two factors had to be taken into consideration:

    1- Whether the treaties concluded by a suzerain state were ipso facto concluded for the vassal; and

    2- Whether war of a suzerain was ipso facto war of the vassal.

On both counts, it was obvious to the British Foreign Office that Tibet was an independent state.

The instructions to the British Representative at the UN were: "We are committed in a general way to India's support and this will doubtless extend to the line she adopts in Lake Success. Though we fully acknowledge preponderance of India's interests in this matter and recognize that initiative must lie with her, we consider it of utmost importance to have a preliminary exchange of views with her."[18]

The British Representative in the UN was requested not to mention the legal position taken by the British Government. The Representative's brief was that though they had to be prepared to accept that Tibet is a separate state in case the matter came to the General Assembly, the British strongly favoured a mild action: "The Council content itself with a condemnation of the Chinese action and not call on China to withdraw her forces from Tibet." But for London the question remained: what will India's position be?

India Vacillates

Till mid-November the position of the Government of India was clear: India would not sponsor the appeal but would support it if raised by any other nation. Then India's position began to vacillate.

Here we should remember that Nehru must have had the Kashmir issue in his mind; he had become quite disillusioned about the effectiveness of the UN.

> ... when Chinese troops marched into Tibet proper, we told Tibetan Government that if they so chose, they could prefer appeal to UN. We could not, however, sponsor such an appeal, though we might support it generally. We cannot go back on our assurance and have, therefore, to support inclusion of proposal for consideration by UN.
>
> ...We cannot, consistently with previous declarations, support Tibetan claim to independence, though we can and should favour recognition of Tibetan autonomy. We should support appeal on broad ground that problem of Sino-Tibetan relations should be solved peacefully and not by resort to arms.[19]

Nehru added a small sentence which speaks for itself: "Chinese Government has repeatedly expressed themselves in favour of Tibetan autonomy, but of course we do not know what their idea of autonomy is."

---

[18]Quoted in Goldstein, op. cit., p.717. Telegram from London to UK High Commissioner in Delhi dated 10 November 1950.

[19]SWJN, Series II, Vol. 15 (2), p. 347. Cable from Nehru to Rau dated 19 November 1950.

But the Prime Minister had began to have doubts, for in the same telegram to B.N. Rau[20], he replied: "We doubt whether a discussion of Tibetan problem in General Assembly or in Security Council will yield any useful result."

The change in policy seemed to be due mainly to B.N. Rau. According to a telegram sent by Henderson to Acheson:

Tenor telegram[21] as read me would indicate Rau has been endeavoring prevail on GOI take no action in UN re Tibet which might dispel Soviet Union and Communist China. Apparently Rau was under impression that by not criticizing Communist China in UN re Tibet he might play more helpful role in mediating between Communist China and western powers following arrival Communist Chinese delegates in Lake Success.[22]

According to Acheson's information, the change of stance of the Indian delegation was due to the receipt of the Note from the Chinese Government dated November 16: "Presumably change of position from that taken Nov 19 result of delay in receipt of Nov 16 note or reconsideration of policy."[23]

However, opinion was divided in India, as Henderson explained:

Bajpai told me Rau had telegraphed GOI that apparently no member SC desired take initiative re Tibet and therefore suggested matter be dropped in UN. GOI however could not agree to "letting Tibet down". There had been some sentiment among various members Indian cabinet opposing GOI taking any action UN. However overwhelming majority sentiment was regardless effect on India-China relations GOI could not afford take uninterested position re Tibet.[24]

[20]Rau stated that no member of the Security Council appeared to be inclined to sponsor the Tibetan appeal mainly on grounds of the 'doubtful' status of Tibet and a general lack of knowledge about the problem, and asked for instructions in case the matter was brought up.

[21]Bajpai showed Henderson a telegram from Rau dated 19 November.

[22]USFR, Telegram, 793B.00/11-2050 dated November 20,1950. The Ambassador in India to the Secretary of State.

[23]USFR, Telegram, 793B.00/11-2550 dated November 28, 1950. The Secretary of State to the Embassy in India.

[24]USFR, Telegram, 793B.00/11-2050 dated November 20,1950.The Ambassador in India to the Secretary of State.

In an internal note on November 18, Nehru had written down his position:

> I think that in no event should we sponsor Tibet's appeal.
> *I would personally think that it would be a good thing if that appeal is not heard*[25] in the Security Council or the General Assembly. If it is considered there, there is bound to be a great deal of bitter speaking and accusation, which will worsen the situation as regards Tibet, as well as the possibility of widespread war, without helping it in the least. It must be remembered that neither the U.K. nor the U.S.A., nor indeed any other powers, is particularly interested in Tibet or the future of that country. What they are interested in, is embarrassing China. Our interest, on the other hand, is Tibet, and if we cannot serve that interest, we fail.[26]

At that time, the Communist nations were lobbying for the inclusion of Beijing as a member of the UN and the Security Council[27]. Would Mao Zedong care if the General Assembly or the Security Council were to take a decision in favour of Tibet? It is not certain as, after all, the UN was for him an imperialist invention which had nothing to do with the true international socialist movement.

From New York Vijayalaksmi Pandit[28] announced on November 20: "India's view is that communist China should be given a seat in the UN". She said that she thought that "if this had been done earlier, some of the present troubles in Korea might have been avoided."

Mrs Pandit also expressed "the Indian Government's disquiet about the Communist military invasion of Tibet which might make it more difficult for the Peking Government to qualify as a 'peace loving' nation within the meaning of the Charter."[29]

Again and again, oblivious of India's interests and security, the Indian diplomats worried about only one thing: the entry of Peking into the UN.

[25]Emphasis by the author.
[26]SWJN, Series II, Vol. 15 (2) p. 345. Policy Regarding Tibet, note dated 18 November 1950.
[27]Pannikar, the Indian Ambassador in China, and some other Indian officials were pushing harder than anyone else.
[28]Sister of Jahawarlal Nehru and Indian Ambassador to the UN.
[29]*The Hindu*, Madras, November 21, 1950.

Rumours were rife in India. One news report from Kalimpong stated that: "Tsepon Shakabpa, Tibet's Finance Secretary and the leader of the Tibetan delegation to Red China, categorically denied on behalf of the Government of Tibet the reports that the Chinese-led Tibetan People's Army had entered Lhasa ... and that the Tibetan National Assembly had accepted the Chinese proposals on Tibet's future status'.

Though Shakabpa characterised all these reports as 'utterly baseless and malicious', they illustrate the prevailing confusion.

At Lake Success[30] a procedural battle was going on: the Secretariat of the UN informed El Salvador that the Tibetan problem should first be brought to the General Committee which had to decide if the issue could or could not be referred to the General Assembly.

Castro, the Salvadorian representative proposed that the following Resolution should be passed by the General Assembly:

Taking note that the peaceful nation of Tibet has been invaded, without any provocation on its part, by foreign forces proceeding from the territory controlled by the government established at Peking.

[The General Assembly] Decides

1. To condemn this act of unprovoked aggression against Tibet;

2. To establish a committee composed of (names of nations)... which will be entrusted with the study of the appropriate measures that could be taken by the General Assembly on this matter;

3. To instruct the committee to undertake that study with special reference to the appeal made to the United Nations by the Government of Tibet, and to render its report to the General Assembly, as early as possible, during the present session.[31]

In a cable to B.N. Rau, Nehru stated:

Draft resolution of El Salvador completely ignores realities of situation and overlooks fact that only result of passing such a resolution will be to precipitate conquest of Tibet and destruction of Tibetan

[30]Lake Success is the Headquarters of the UN in New York.
[31]Sen, op. cit., p. 93.

independence and perhaps even autonomy. We cannot possibly support it or even adopt merely negative attitude. We would therefore suggest that delegate of El Salvador should be induced to modify his resolution so as to limit it to expression of concern of General Assembly at recent developments in Tibet and call upon parties to come to a settlement by peaceful means and not by force. If he is unwilling to do so, you should try to have amendment moved on line suggested.[32]

In the course of the negotiations in New York, most of the representatives indicated that India was the nation most concerned and that they would follow India's lead.[33]

India was not very happy with the British who did not want to make the first step and include the Tibetan question on the agenda of the Security Council.

Who wanted to hold the hot potato?

India was clearly not ready to take all the responsibility, so the British suggested a draft beginning thus: "The situation in Tibet is one which primarily concerns the Government of India although His Majesty's Government is also interested."

But some British bureaucrats in New York considered this still too strong a position for the British government.

The logical outcome of the Foreign Office legal cell's opinion was that Tibet was a separate state and consequently an act of aggression had been committed. As a result pressures would have to be exerted by the community of nations to take an action in favour of Tibet. But, nobody wanted to act!

The telegram of the British Representative cabled to London concluded that: "I greatly hope therefore that I shall be instructed when and if the Indians raise this matter in the Security Council, to argue to the general effect that the legal situation is extremely obscure and that in any case Tibet cannot be considered as a fully independent country."[34]

---

[32]SWJN, Series II, Vol. 15 (2), p. 347. Cable from Nehru to B.N. Rau dated 20 November 1950.

[33]The same thing will happen in 1959, 1961 and 1965 when the Tibetan issue will again be brought up in the UN.

[34]Quoted in Goldstein, op. cit., p. 718. Telegram from the UK delegation in New York to London dated 14 November 1950, (FO/371/84454).

Because the British diplomats did not want to take action, the British Foreign office had to change its legal opinion on the status of Tibet! Vagueness should prevail.

The British government then asked for a fresh legal opinion from their Attorney General. Britain and the USA made their position known: they would support the stand of the Government of India.

At the same time, the American Government informed New Delhi that they were ready to help the Tibetans in 'whatever means possible', but in view of the geographical and historical factor, the main burden of the problem remained on India and India's collaboration was more than necessary in any attempt to help the Tibetan Government.

While the British were struggling with legalities, Nehru was rejecting them: "We do not think that legal arguments will be helpful or that Assembly should attempt more than appeal to two parties to come to a peaceful settlement."[35]

Deputy Prime Minister Sardar Patel, was dying and his departure from the Indian political scene sealed the fate of Tibet. With the passing away of the only person who could oppose Nehru and his utopian idea of friendship with China, Nehru was left alone to decide an issue which would have the most serious consequences in India for the next fifty years. Romantic idealism was to prevail over down-to-earth pragmatism.

At the last moment, Nehru backed out of the understanding India had given Tibet. He requested Washington to refrain from publicly condemning China for its action in Tibet for fear that such condemnation might lend credence to Chinese charges that Western powers had an interest in Tibet and that the Americans were exerting an influence over Indian policy. Nehru decided:

> We cannot save Tibet, as we should have liked to do so, and our very attempts to save it might bring greater trouble to it. It would be unfair to Tibet for us to bring this trouble upon her without having the capacity to help her effectively. It may be possible, however, that we might be able to help Tibet to retain a large measure of her autonomy. That would be good for Tibet and good for India. As far as I can see, this can only be done on

[35]SWJN, Series II, Vol. 15 (2), p. 347. Cable from Nehru to Rau dated 19 November, 1950.

the diplomatic level and by avoidance of making the
present tension between India and China worse.

Tibet was sacrificed!

The main reason behind Nehru's volte-face was that he was very
involved in the Korean issue and did not want to yield his role as
'neutral' mediator.

This is also clear from the fact that in his Beijing office, Pannikar
was spending most of his time on the Korean problem and was hardly
concerned by the invasion of Tibet.

On the eve of the debate in the General Committee, Nehru cabled
India's Representative at the UN:

We are entirely in favour of deferring consideration of
Tibet question because of various developments, more
particularly arrival of Peking representatives.[36] It is of
vital importance that every effort be made to lessen war
tension, more especially in Far East where situation is
dangerous.[37]

The Debate that Never Was

Thus, because the Chinese Representatives were 'arriving' at the UN
to discuss the Korean question, the issue of Tibetan was deferred.[38]
Nehru concluded:

Any particular reference to an Article of the Charter of
the UN might tie us up in difficulties and lead to certain
consequences later which may prove highly
embarrassing for us. Or a resolution of the UN might
just be a dead letter, which also will be bad.

It is clear the Korean affair was much more interesting to the
Indian diplomats than the fate of this small nation.

On November 24, the request of El Salvador came up for
discussion in the General Committee of the United Nations, India
and Great Britain moved for postponing the matter: Jam Saheb of
Nawanagar, the Indian Representative, said that "the Indian

[36]To the UN.

[37]SWJN, Series II, Vol. 15 (2), p. 351. Cable from Nehru to B.N. Rau dated
23 November 1950.

[38]It is interesting to note that a scholar has recently made a study of the
Tibetan issue in the UN and has found out that the matter was still pending
and could theoretically be taken again from where it was left in November
1950.

Government was certain that the Tibetan question could still be settled by peaceful means, and that such a settlement could safeguard the autonomy which Tibet enjoyed for several decades while maintaining its historical association with China."

The matter was adjourned.

The next morning the world press announced:

> The UN General Assembly's Steering Committee tonight unanimously decided to defer consideration of whether to place the Chinese invasion of Tibet on the Assembly's Agenda....
>
> Just before the vote was taken the Jam Saheb Nawanagar (India) had told the Committee: "In Peking's Government latest note to the Government of India, they have not given up the desire for settling the problem peacefully".
>
> Sir Keith Officer, Australia and Mr. Ernest Gross, US said they voted for deferment after hearing his statement.[39]

The American Representative explained that: "he had voted for adjournment in view of the fact that the Government of India, whose territory bordered on Tibet and which was therefore an interested party, had told the General Committee that he hoped that the Tibetan question would be peacefully and honourably settled."[40]

The poor Salvadorian Representative fought till the end, at least he wanted every member of the General Assembly to receive a copy of the Tibetan appeal. Though the Office of the Secretary General promised to do this, it never did.

The fate of Tibet was sealed and the consequences followed one after another, the first being the signature in Beijing in May 1951 of the 'Agreement on Peaceful Liberation of Tibet'.

Mao now had the green light for a free hand in Tibet. He knew that Nehru's India was little more than a Paper Tiger. It would do no more than send an occasional weak protest, and in the course of time the protests would become weaker.

Not everyone in India agreed with this policy of appeasement of Nehru and Pannikar and by the end of October many voices in the Government were protesting against the weak stand India had

[39]*The Hindu*, Madras 25 November, 1950.
[40]Sen, op. cit., p. 91 ff..

taken. Public opinion and many national leaders were outraged by the treatment meted out to Tibet and clearly saw its consequences for India.

One of these leaders, Jayaprakash Narayan, told *The Hindu* in Madras: "India is vitally interested in Tibetan affairs and she should do all that is possible to enable the Tibetan people to maintain her independence and their own way of life."[41]

The socialist Dr. Lohia spoke in even stronger terms:

To call the invasion of Tibet an effort to liberate three million Tibetans is to make language lose all meaning and stop all human communication and understanding. Freedom and slavery, bravery and cowardice, loyalty and treason, truth and lie, will become synonyms.

Our friendship and esteem for the people of China will never dim, but we must state our conviction that the present government of China will not be able to wash out the infamy of this invasion and baby murder.

The point remained, the Indian Government had shown that when the time came, it was neither able nor willing to defend a small weak nation. This stigma would remain.

On November 20, in a cable to his Ambassador in China, Nehru stated his policy which would continue for the following years:

I want to make it clear that I am convinced of importance of Indo-Chinese friendship both from short-term and long-term points of view. We have laboured to that end, but military operations against Tibet came as shock to us and to Indian opinion. During past two years or more we have consistently adopted policy in Asian matters, such as Indonesia, Indo-China, China, which has been opposed to Anglo-American policy. We would have thought that this was evidence enough of our independent policy. In regard to Tibet no country has influenced us in the slightest.

He added: "But, of course, India has special feelings towards Tibet". .

Yet his priorities were clear: "...Even now we are anxious to continue friendly relations with China...Our present policy is

[41]*The Hindu*, Madras 1 November, 1950.

primarily based on avoidance of world war, and secondly on maintenance of honourable and peaceful relations with China."

Mao had indeed calculated well when he decided to open two fronts at the same time. None of the Western powers were interested to fight on two fronts and India being the main nation concerned, all decisions and eventual actions were left to India.

Now that China had decided to enter the Korean war, a new situation had arisen. Nehru explained to Pannikar that:

> This realisation has made Western Powers appreciate dangers of situation and U.K. is trying hard to find way out.[42] We have indicated to you U.K. approach which seems to us reasonable. Bevin has sent special message to Chou En-lai through their Chargé d'Affaires. He has also addressed me and asked for our support. U.K. are anxious to have frank talks with Chinese delegation going to U.N.[43] and have deputed special officer Lamb to New York for this purpose.
>
> ... We suggest to you to clarify our position to Chinese Government both in regard to Tibet and wider issues in as friendly a manner as possible.

Tibet had been sacrificed for "wider issues". Mao's stroke in Korea helped to make the world silent on the invasion of the Roof of the World.

The efforts to revive the case in the UN continued for a few more weeks. On December 18, Bajpai told Henderson that the Government of India was still interested in Tibet's case before the UN but "had delayed action pending outcome its efforts assist in achieving cease-fire in Korea."

Bajpai assured the American Ambassador that the Indian Government "would probably re-examine whole problem of Tibet just as soon as it had done all it could in matter of cease-fire."

However on December 30, Henderson cabled Acheson to inform him that:

---

[42]On 20 November a British Foreign Office statement said that the British Government was consulting with the U.S., French and Commonwealth Governments to find a solution to the Korean problem.

[43]A Chinese delegation arrived in New York on 24 November to appear before the Security Council to support its Government's charges of USS aggression against Formosa.

Representatives GOI had repeatedly assured us it intended do so [support Tibetan appeal]. Now appears views B.N. Rau and other Indian officials who do not wish India make any move in present world context which might offend Communist China have prevailed and GOI continues postpone taking initiative re Tibet in UN. Seems likely Communist China will have taken over Lhasa and have fastened firmly its grip on Tibet before GOI prepared take lead in UN.[44]

He concluded:

We seem faced with choice supporting some power other than India taking initiative or of continuing postpone hearing Tibetan pleas until autonomous Tibet cases exist. We are wondering whether this would be to credit UN. Is it logical for UN which gave Indonesia which was under Dutch sovereignty hearing to ignore Tibet? Will India, for instance, have greater respect for UN if merely out of deference to it, UN gives Tibet no opportunity present case?

Fifty years later, the case is still 'pending'!

[44]USFR, Telegram 793B.00/12-3050 dated December 30, 1950. The Ambassador in India (Henderson) to the Secretary of State.

22

The Debate in India

*I attach great importance to India and China being friends.
I think the future of Asia and to some extent of the world
depends upon this.*

Jawaharlal Nehru, August 1950

A Letter of Sardar Patel

On November 9, 1950, Sardar Patel declared in New Delhi that: "In
the *Kali Yuga*, we shall return *ahimsa* for *ahimsa*. But if anybody resorts
to force against us we shall meet it with force."[1]

In the pages which follow, we shall go through the contents of
the letter that Patel had written two days earlier to Jahawarlal Nehru.
Could Patel have wanted something to be done at that time to
support Tibet and protect India's borders?

Nobody will ever be able to say, as in any case by mid-November
Patel was a sick man and too weak to oppose the Indian Prime
Minister on serious matters. In fact, a few days after writing his letter
he ceased all his activities and withdrew to his native Gujarat.[2]

One more chance was lost for the Tibetans.

We shall quote extensively from Patel's letter to Jawaharlal Nehru
because it marked a turning point in the foreign policy of India, at
least as regards its China policy.

During the months of October and November 1950 India had
the choice between two options: either to bend with the 'east wind'
and side with China, or to stand up and defend her own interests:
Patel's letter, which might be considered as his political testament,
was resolutely in favour of the second path.

The clarity of Patel's perception on the strategic implications for
India's foreign policy were masterfully summed up in following
lines:

[1]*The Hindu*, Madras, November 10, 1950.
[2]He passed away a month later on December 15.

My dear Jawaharlal,
Ever since my return from Ahmedabad and after the
Cabinet meeting the same day which I had to attend at
practically fifteen minutes notice and for which I was
not able to read all the papers, I have been anxiously
thinking over the problem of Tibet and I thought I
should share with you what is passing through my
mind.
I have carefully gone through the correspondence
between the External Affairs Ministry and our
Ambassador in Peking and through him the Chinese
Government. I have tried to peruse this correspondence
as favourably to our Ambassador and the Chinese
Government as possible, but I regret to say that neither
of them comes out well as the result of this study.[3]

As we have seen earlier, Notes had been exchanged between the
Governments of India and China between October 21 and November
1 and we have already dealt with these notes briefly. Patel continued:

The Chinese Government has tried to delude us by
professions of peaceful intentions. ...There can be no
doubt that, during the period covered by this
correspondence, the Chinese must have been
concentrating for an onslaught on Tibet. The final action
of the Chinese, in my judgement, is little short of perfidy.

Future events have borne out Patel's perception. It has now been
proved beyond doubt that Mao had planned and prepared the
invasion of Tibet for months in advance. But Patel further elaborated:

The tragedy of it is that the Tibetans put faith in us; they
chose to be guided by us; and we have been unable to
get them out of the meshes of Chinese diplomacy or
Chinese malevolence. From the latest position, it appears
that we shall not be able to rescue the Dalai Lama.
Our Ambassador has been at great pains to find an
explanation or justification for the Chinese policy and
actions. As the External Affairs Ministry remarked in
one of their telegrams, there was a lack of firmness and

[3]The letter has been published by *The Indian Monitor*, Bombay, November
2, 1968; also Durga Das, *Sardar Patel's Correspondance 1945-50*, Vol. 10
(Ahmedabad, 1974), p. 337.

unnecessary apology in one or two representations he made to the Chinese Government on our behalf. It is impossible to imagine any sensible person believing in the so-called threat to China from Anglo-American machinations in Tibet. Therefore, if the Chinese put faith in this, they must have distrusted us so completely as to have taken us as tools or stooges of Anglo-American diplomacy or strategy. This feeling, if genuinely entertained by the Chinese in spite of your direct approaches to them, indicates that, even though we regard ourselves as friends of China, the Chinese do not regard us as their friends. With the Communists mentality of "whoever is not with them being against them", this is a significant pointer, of which we have to take due note...

The best proof of this mentality came three or four years later when at the height of the Hindi-Chini-Bhai-Bhai euphoria, Mao began building a strategic road linking Tibet to Sinkiang, cutting through Indian territory.

It is also obvious that the policy of the Chinese leadership based on the motto "who ever is not with us is against us" paid very rich dividend with officials like Pannikar or Krishna Menon, for the last thing they wanted was to be seen as being on the side of the Western nations.

The western world was regarded as a symbol of imperialism responsible for the oppression of masses and the slavery of the Asian race. While advocating the principle of 'non-alignment' as the official Indian policy, many Indian politicians and diplomats felt much closer to the Communists in China or Russia than to the 'western imperialists.'

It was forgotten that the western world and especially the United States with all its imperfections was also the symbol of the struggle against totalitarian and fascist forces and therefore ultimately a symbol of democratic freedom.

The letter goes on:

I have doubt if we can go any further than we have done already to convince China of our good intentions, friendliness and good will. In Peking we have an Ambassador who is eminently suitable for putting across

> the friendly point of view. Even he seems to have failed
> to convert Chinese. Their last telegram to us is an act of
> gross discourtesy not only in the summary way it
> disposes of our protest against the entry of Chinese
> forces into Tibet, but also in the wild insinuation that
> our attitude is determined by foreign influences.
>
> It looks as though it is not a friend speaking in that
> language, but a potential enemy.

Twelve years later this last sentence would resound in the Indian mind. But was the China of 1950 so very different from the China of 1962? It was the same China which had already decided in 1949 who would be the new leader of Asia and was ready to use all available means to ruthlessly achieve its plans.

Foremost in Patel's mind was the future of India and he tried to look towards this future as objectively as possible.

> In the background of this, we have to consider what new
> situation faces us as a result of the disappearance of
> Tibet, as we know it, and the expansion of China almost
> up to our gates. Throughout history, we have seldom
> been worried about our northern frontier. The
> Himalayas have been regarded as an impenetrable
> barrier against any threat from the North. We had a
> friendly Tibet which gave us no trouble. The Chinese
> were divided...China is no longer divided. It is united
> and strong...

The significance of Patel's letter lies in the fact that the Tibetan issue was not seen from an ideological point of view, but from a very practical angle; it was seen from the point of view of Indian and not Tibetan or Chinese or Western interests.[4]

The letter goes on to analyse with great lucidity all the defence and other problems facing India. The following points give an example of the problems listed by Patel on which he thought immediate action had to be taken:

- a military and intelligence appreciation of the Chinese
  threat to India both on the frontier and the internal
  security.
- An examination of our military position and such
  redisposition of our forces as might be necessary,

---

[4]While Pannikar and sometimes Nehru saw it from the Chinese and anti-western point of view.

particularly with the idea of guarding important routes or areas which are likely to be subject to dispute.
- An appraisement of the strength of our forces...
- A long-term consideration of our defence needs...
- The question of Chinese entry into the UNO...
- The future of our mission in Lhasa and trade posts at Gyanste and Yatung
- The policy in regard to the McMahon line...

The letter concludes by suggesting that "we meet early to have a general discussion on these problems and decide on such steps as we might think immediately necessary...."

Unfortunately no meeting was ever held. Nehru did not even respond to the letter. Patel passed away on December 15, five weeks after having written the letter.

Patel's letter will remain in history for its great clarity of thought and prophetic tone. Up to November-December 1950, India regarded Tibet as a separate and independent nation, it only recognized a vague suzerainty of China over Tibet — the 'constitutional fiction' described by Curzon.

Nobody clear-headed and strong enough was left on the Indian scene to counterbalance Jawaharlal Nehru and his advisors. Some leaders like Rajendra Prasad, the President of India, Acharya Kripalani and Dr. Rammanohar Lohia tried to oppose Nehru but without success. They could not match the charisma and aura of the idealistic Prime Minister.

In October 1950, Dr Lohia even suggested a plebiscite:

China has invaded Tibet, which can only mean that the giant has moved to rub out the life of a child. Tibet's present rulers may or may not be reactionary and tyrannical but of her independence from foreign control there can be no doubt...

If the government of China takes its stand on some wholly inoperative but technical and doubtful issue of sovereignty, let the will of the people of Tibet be ascertained in a plebiscite. The Indian government will do well to advise the China government to withdraw its army...[5]

But the Prime Minister was not ready to listen to any dissent.

[5]*Indian Leaders on Tibet*, published by the DIIR, Dharamsala, 1998, p. 12.

The Debate in Parliament

The problem of India's borders to the north was discussed for the first time in the Lower House of the Indian Parliament on March 17, 1950, during the debate on foreign affairs. The government was requested to define its border with Tibet. The Anglo-Indian nominee, Frank Antony, cautioned the Government against the threat from Communist China: " I believe that it is not self-delusion but dangerous self-delusion, either to hope or believe, however exemplary our motives in the international planes, how genuine our desire for neutrality... that Communists will in the final analysis respect our neutrality and our loftiness of motives."[6]

At that time, nobody was ready to listen to such warnings.

The policy of appeasement would continue until October when the Chinese troops finally entered Tibet.[7]

On November 1, Nehru announced for the first time in the Parliament that the Chinese troops had entered Tibet and captured Chamdo, the capital of Kham. The next debate on Tibet occurred in mid-November, after the Presidential address.

On November 14, President Rajendra Prasad told the Parliament:

My Government has been consistently following a policy of friendship with our great neighbour country, China. It was a matter of deep regret to us, therefore, that the Chinese Government should have undertaken military operations in Tibet, when the way of peaceful negotiations was open to them. Tibet is not only a neighbour of India but has had close cultural and other ties with her for ages past. India must therefore necessarily concern herself with what happens in Tibet and hope that the autonomy of this peaceful country will be provided.

During the debate, many Congress MPs regretted the attack on Tibet and many felt that India should use her full strength to defend her weak neighbour.

Some members called for the reinforcement of Indian defence, especially in the Northeast. The Members felt that India should also fulfil her responsibilities vis-à-vis Nepal, Sikkim and Bhutan.

---

[6]The text of the quoted interventions in the Lok Sabha are available in Sen, op. cit., p. 109 ff. or *Parliamentary Debates*, Vol. 3, 1950, col. 1734.

[7]The Policy would continue till 1962 and some aspects of it remain even today.

The Indian Prime Minister replied on November 20 and stated that the McMahon Line was the border between India and Tibet and that it was clearly delineated. On the western side, Nehru had to admit that the border between Ladakh and Tibet was defined "chiefly by long usage and custom".

One member pointed out that the new map printed in China showed the entire area north of NEFA as part of the Chinese territory. Nehru reassured the House that the maps were old: "Our maps show that the McMahon line is our boundary and that is our boundary – map or no map. That facts remain and we stand by the boundary and we will not allow anybody to come across that boundary."[8]

The problem of maps would be a recurring one during the following years and the Indian Prime Minister constantly used the same argument — "the maps are old; the Chinese government had no time to print new ones". This continued until the day the Government of India discovered that the Chinese had built a road on Indian territory in Ladakh.[9]

While the Chinese Government had already started to claim, through the diffusion of these maps, a large chunk of Indian territory, the Government of India through its Survey Department maps was still showing the Western sector border as 'undefined.' Was it 'loftiness of motives' or plain folly?

The main debate in the Indian Parliament was held on December 6, 1950. It opened with a statement by the Prime Minister who stated that he had made it clear to the Chinese Government that India "had no territorial or political ambitions in regard to Tibet and that our relations were cultural and commercial."

Nehru said that the Government of India did not challenge or deny the suzerainty of China over Tibet, but it was anxious that "Tibet should maintain the autonomy it has had for at least the last forty years."

Quoting from the exchange of correspondence he explained the Chinese point of view and also said that China would "very much like to settle the question peacefully but that they were, in any event, going to liberate Tibet." He added the famous remark: "From whom they were going to liberate Tibet is, however, not quite clear."

[8]Statement in the Lok Sabha on 20 November 1950.
[9]In 1954 and 1955, but it was admitted only three years later in the Lok Sabha.

He concluded: "We had come to believe that the matter would be settled by peaceful negotiations and were shocked when we heard that the Chinese armies were marching into Tibet. Indeed, one can hardly talk about war between China and Tibet. Tibet is not in a position to carry on war and, obviously, Tibet is no threat to China."

The debate that followed was very heated. Congressmen as well as Opposition leaders, except the Communists, expressed their anguish at the happenings on the Roof of the World.

Professor Ranga[10] began by saying:

> Could we be indifferent to the fact that only the other day it was none else than the Chinese Government which had hinted that India was the foreign power in Tibet which is supposed to be queering the pitch? Could we be also indifferent to the fact that China, the modern China, the present-day China, was sending her own troops in order to assert the sovereignty over Tibet?

He pointed out that the term sovereignty in Asia was synonymous with "expansion and political, economic and social control over other people".

Prof. Ranga added "Are we not giving a blank cheque to be signed on our behalf by somebody else in order to spread their own imperialist tentacles?"

He had a dig at Pannikar for "professing the friendship not only to China's people, not only to the Chinese Government but to China's sovereignty[11] over Tibet. This beats anybody and everybody."

He ended by a warning: "Millions of people are supposed to have poured into Korea. It is something like an avalanchic sweep. Is it impossible for those people, under more or less similar circumstances, to pour into India too under the same pressure of ideological and imperialistic urges? Should we not keep these things in our mind?"

Acharya Kripalani[12] regretted that India had rushed so much to recognize the new regime in Beijing. About China, he said: "This

---

[10]A peasant leader from Andhra Pradesh, until recently with the Congress Party.

[11]It was Pannikar who had offered to the Chinese their sovereignty over Tibet; this is the same man who wrote so much about imperialism and control by a foreign power over another nation and who, in 1948, suggested that India should recognize the independence of Tibet.

[12]Acharya Kripalani, once Congress Party President and now the leader of the Praja Socialist Party in the Parliament.

nation that was struggling for its own freedom, strangulated the freedom of a neighbouring nation, in whose freedom we are intimately connected... In spite of this theoretical claim of China on Tibet, many of our politicians feel that our advocacy of China for the membership of the UNO was premature."

M.R. Masani expressed strong doubts about the relationship with a country 'avowedly Communist'. He reminded the House that to reward India for her friendliness, Mao had sent Ranadive[13] a message of greetings and good wishes "for the 'liberation' of India. Mao hoped that India would soon go the Chinese way."

He quoted from a statement of the New China News Agency (Xinhua) released few months earlier saying "the 'Anglo-American', imperialists and their running dog, Pandit Nehru, were plotting a coup in Lhasa for the annexation of Tibet."

He strongly objected to the implications in the recent Chinese Notes that India had been responsible for instigating the Tibetans to resist Chinese suzerainty. "If anything, our Prime Minister was trying to persuade the Tibetan leaders to accommodate the Chinese claims to suzerainty."

He concluded his intervention by saying: "While we might maintain diplomatic relations with the Chinese Government on a basis of reciprocity, there can be no longer any illusions about friendship, about cordiality and about comradeship in Asia."

Shyama Prasad Mookerjee[14] made a similar point especially in view of the incorporation of Assam and Ladakh in the Chinese maps. He warned the House that it was clear from the Chinese notes that "China will do everything necessary for the purpose of keeping intact what it considers to be China's border and when it refers to Chinese border, it includes Tibet as well and the 'undefined boundary' of Tibet so far as it touches Indian border."

As he would do several times over the next decade, the Congress leader Brajeshwar Prasad defended his Chinese and Russian comrades. In 1954, he would declare: "I am convinced that the destinies of India and China are intertwined. If China goes down

---

[13]The Secretary of the Communist Party of India was engaged in trying to overthrow the Indian Government by force.

[14]A member of Nehru's Cabinet until he resigned in 1950. One of the founder of the Jan Sangh. He was soon to die in Kashmir under mysterious circumstances.

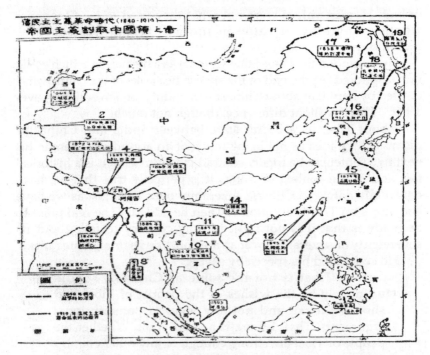

Chinese territorial claims as shown in a 1954 Chinese text book
(Liu P'ei-hua, A Short History of Modern China, Beijing, 1954).
The accompanying text says that Number 3, 4, 5 and 6
have been acquired by India through unfair treaties.

under the Americans, India will also positively go down, for the
Americans will not spare India."

In 1950, Brajeshwar Prasad went on about his favourite topic,
the great Axis Moscow-Delhi-Peking. He said: "I hold the opinion
there will be no war if we ally ourselves with China and Russia.
There will be peace and stability in Southeast Asia. From the point
of view of both military strategy and geo-politics, it will be physically
impossible for any alien power to land troops on Southeast Asia. If
we want peace, we must join hands with Russia and China."

Unfortunately for India, though she more and more closely
'joined hands' with China during the following years, war with its
physical and psychological destruction was unleashed against her
in any case.

Nehru did not want to take a clear stand. He said that there is a
tremendous change in Asia, though he could not say if it was good

or bad. Human values were not what they used to be: "I wonder whether anything of value in life will remain for sensitive individuals"

He reminded the House that China was a big nation which could not be ignored. At the end of the speech he spoke of the controversy created by Pannikar about Chinese 'suzerainty' or 'sovereignty' over Tibet. "There is slight difference, though not much."

About Tibet as a buffer state between India and China, he dismissed the idea as not being much of an argument. Then, in his next two sentences he totally contradicted himself: "It is a historical fact and in the context of things it is perfectly true that we have repeatedly admitted Chinese suzerainty over Tibet just as we have laid stress on Tibet's autonomy. Then he added: "The real point to be made is that it is not right for any country to talk about its sovereignty or suzerainty over an area outside its immediate range."

He concluded his speech by saying:

> ...since Tibet is not the same as China, it should ultimately be the wishes of the people of Tibet that should prevail and not any legal or constitutional arguments. That, I think is a valid point. Whether the people of Tibet are strong enough or any other country is strong enough to see that this is done is also another matter. But it is a right and proper thing to say and I see no difficulty in saying to the Chinese Government that whether they have suzerainty over Tibet or sovereignty over Tibet, surely, according to any principles they proclaim and the principles I uphold, the last voice in regard to Tibet should be the voice of the people of Tibet and of nobody else.

Two weeks earlier he had written in an internal Note: "We cannot save Tibet."[15] When he spoke in the Parliament, he already knew that the Tibetans would never have the 'last voice' any more with regard to Tibet.

---

[15]SWJN, Series II, Vol. 15 (1). Note on Tibet dated 18 November 1950.

23

The Pannikar Factor

Our Ambassador has allowed himself to be influenced more by the Chinese point of view, the Chinese claims, the Chinese maps and by regard for Chinese susceptibilities than by his instructions or by India's interests.

G.S. Bajpai, General Secretary of the Indian Foreign Ministry

One of the most important factors in the relationship between the Tibetan Government and the Government of India was the appointment of K.M. Pannikar as an Ambassador to 'two Chinas'.

Though it is very unusual to reappoint the same diplomat to the same country in a totally different context (after the Communist take-over), Pannikar's proximity to the Indian Prime Minister helped him to get a second posting to Beijing in Spring 1950. He himself remarked that it was not normal to be re-appointed to the same post under drastically different circumstances.

More interestingly, Pannikar's position changed diametrically between the time of his tenure as Indian Ambassador in Nanjing and his subsequent tenure with the Communist regime in Beijing.

Posted in Nanjing as the first Ambassador of Free India[1] to Nationalist China, Pannikar had been friendly towards the Nationalists but later when, in Beijing, his 'leanings' shifted so much to the East that Deputy Prime Minister Patel was obliged to remark: "My own feeling is that at a crucial period they managed to instil into our Ambassador a false sense of confidence in their so-called desire to settle the Tibetan problem by peaceful means."[2]

---

[1]Earlier, K.P.S. Menon was posted in Chungqing, then in Nanjing as the Agent-General for British India.
[2]Letter from Sardar Patel to Nehru dated 7 November, 1950.

Pannikar in Nationalist China

A confidential note from Pannikar to the Government of India written on 22 November 1948 makes interesting reading to grasp the 'political' evolution of Pannikar.

The doctrine of 'divide and rule' had always been mastered by the imperialist powers. At the Simla Convention, the British had divided Tibet into Outer Tibet[3] and Inner Tibet.[4] At one point the Chinese government had the idea to form a Chinese province called Xikang which would regroup the parts of Kham controlled by Lhasa and other parts under the administrative control of Sichuan province.

> In Sinkiang and Kham areas (the territories bordering on Tibet) also this policy is likely to be pursued. Kham is what is known as Inner Tibet, portions of which are under the effective control of the Central [Chinese] Government, while over a great part Tibet still exercises authority. The establishment of Kham republic will enable China to follow a forward policy in Tibet.[5]

Some Khampa leaders were not against the idea provided they were given full autonomy. However the Chinese government had very little control over these areas which were controlled by local warlords. In any case, they were not ready to concede any kind of real autonomy to the Tibetans from either Lhasa or Kham.

Later the Chinese further divided Kham into different counties and prefectures and attached these areas to the provinces of Yunnan and Sichuan.

Pannikar's note continued:

> All this can be claimed to be in conformity with Sun Yat Sen's doctrine of Five-Races, the Hans (Chinese proper), the Manchus, the Mongols, the Mohammedans and the Tibetans. The independence of the five races and their voluntary union was Sun's formula. The Communists can therefore claim that in establishing the republics of Manchuria, Mongolia, Sinkiang and Tibet they are only carrying out the teachings of Sun Yat Sen.

[3]More or less corresponding to what is today the 'Tibet Autonomous Region' or Central Tibet.

[4]The regions of Kham and Amdo which have been amalgamated in neighbouring Chinese provinces of Yunnan, Sichuan, Gansu and Qinghai.

[5]*When China goes Communist*, a report by K.M. Pannikar.

To this main body will be attached smaller autonomous republics and regions carved out of the territories occupied by the Mongols, Muslims and Tibetans, or what is now known as the border areas.

A China so organised will be in an extremely powerful position to claim its historic role of authority over Tibet, Burma, Indo-China and Siam. The historic claims in regard to these are vague and hazy, at different times China did exercise authority over Tibet, Burma, Tonkin and Annan and claimed suzerainty over Khmer kings of the present state of Siam.

Pannikar clearly acknowledged that Chinese suzerainty over Tibet and other neighbouring countries was 'vague and hazy'. Pannikar who was a great historian must have gone through the records and the Chinese annals before coming to that conclusion.

In 1948, he was still preoccupied with strategic considerations for India:

It is necessary to examine how Chinese policy in regard to these areas will work and how they will affect the interests of India.

The importance of South East Asia not only to the security but the economic life of India need not be emphasised. What India's policy should be in relation to the countries is a matter for most careful consideration.

As a good Ambassador, Pannikar then goes on to analyse the changing political and strategic situation to see in which way it will affect his country.

This was not the case a few years later when G.S. Bajpai, the Secretary General in the Ministry of External Affairs,[6] had to compare Pannikar's protests on Tibet closely with Neville Chamberlain's protest in Nazi Germany on behalf of Czechoslovakia. "Our Ambassador has allowed himself to be influenced more by the Chinese point of view, the Chinese claims, the Chinese maps and by regards for Chinese susceptibilities than by his instructions or by India's interests."[7]

[6]Bajpai was the direct boss of Pannikar, but obviously Pannikar had his direct entries to the Prime Minister (also Foreign Minister).
[7]Quoted in Gopal. Dr. S., *Jawaharlal Nehru – a Biography* (New Delhi: Oxford University Press, 1979), p. 107.

But in 1948, he was still motivated mainly by India's interests.
Let us come back to Pannikar's analysis of 1948:

> Tibet: A more vital area to us immediately is Tibet.
> Recent Chinese diplomatic action (e.g. the denunciation
> of the already invalidated treaty of 1908) shows clearly
> the direction in which a strong Central government of
> China may move. Not only the Macmohan [sic] line, but
> the entire boundary from Laddakh to Burma may
> become a new area of trouble. With the Tibetan republic
> established in the Kham area, the 15th century regime of
> ignorant lamas will crumble to pieces and new republics
> with different names will come into existence on the Roof
> of the Word.
>
> The authorities in Tibet, however, backward they may
> be in other respects, are said to be aware of these
> dangerous possibilities. Information available here
> points to the conclusion that if the Kuomintang
> Government falls Tibet will make a public declaration
> of her independence and request recognition from India,
> Britain and the United States. The British position has
> always been in favour of recognising the independence
> of Tibet and in the changed circumstances America may
> not also hesitate. *If Outer Tibet's claim of independence is
> recognised by Britain, America and India, there may be some
> hope of keeping the new Chinese Communist State away from
> the Indian border.*[8]
>
> Attempts will be made on the basis of recognised
> suzerainty to infiltrate into Tibet proper, and then the
> claims of Tibet in regard to the Indian border will be
> revived.

It is very unfortunate that the later reports of Pannikar have
remained 'classified', but one day it will certainly be of great historical
interest to study the evolving political thought of the ambassador to
'two Chinas'.

However, it appears clearly from the above confidential note
that Pannikar could foresee the danger to the borders of India of a
Chinese take-over of the Roof of the World.

[8]Emphasis added by author.

In 1949, the Communists were far from having 'liberated' all the parts of China but were in control of most of the mainland. Unfortunately for the corrupt regime of Chiang Kai-shek, the Americans were divided on their China policy and as a result, the Nationalists were left to fend for themselves. As soon as they moved to Formosa (Taiwan), India decided to recognize the Communists in Beijing. One of the reasons given by the Government was that the Chinese like the Indians had been fighting a war of liberation against an imperialist oppressor. India would be the second country outside the Soviet bloc and after Burma to recognize the new regime in Beijing.

In India, it was not the general opinion that Red China should be immediately recognized. Many like C. Rajagopalachari, the then Governor-General, Sardar Patel and others wanted to go slow on the matter. "They were supported in this attitude" wrote later Pannikar "by a powerful section of the Civil Service, including, I suspect, some of the senior officials of the Foreign Service," but Nehru and Pannikar prevailed and Communist China was recognized in a great hurry on December 31, 1949.

We should point out here the two different currents in the Indian Ministry of Foreign Affairs: one was led by Bajpai, the Secretary General who advocated a stronger stance vis-à-vis China. He wanted, for example, to support the Tibetan appeal to the UN and continue the supply of arms and ammunition to the Tibetan army even as late as October 1950. The other side, led by Pannikar and B.N. Rau, the Indian Representative to the UN, felt that nothing should be done because it would only "exacerbate [the Chinese] feelings and perhaps jeopardize efforts for agreement on more important issues [Korea]."[9]

Pannikar and B.N. Rau had direct access to Nehru[10] and most of the time the correspondence went over the head of Bajpai, their direct boss. Pannikar and Rau were able to inform and directly influence Nehru's choices.

The same sad story occurred in the early sixties when a Corps Commander could send files directly to the Prime Minister without taking into account the Army Chief's opinion and analysis. In both cases, India was lead to commit colossal blunders.

[9]USFR, Telegram 330/11-3050 dated November 30,1950. The Ambassador in India (Henderson) to the Secretary of State.
[10]Who was also holding the External Affairs portfolio.

Pannikar in Communist China

Less than six months later and after a few tête-à-tête dinners with Zhou Enlai and his wife, Pannikar became so enamoured of the Communist regime that he made it a point to convince everyone in Delhi of his new 'convictions'. Patel even remarked that Pannikar "has been at great pains to find an explanation or justification for Chinese policy and actions."

He began propagating his enthusiasm for New China in the corridors and offices of South Block. The contagion spread even to the Prime Minister's Office and a generation of bureaucrats and diplomats would see the future of India leaning towards the East.

Many have noted that during the course of the Chinese revolution, not once did the Indian National Congress or any other force struggling for the independence of India receive any encouragement or friendly message from their Chinese communist brothers. On the contrary it was the Nationalists who supported the Indian independence struggle. The only friendly messages from Mao were for the Communist Party of India, as if the Communists had been the ones fighting for Freedom.

One would have thought that Communist China would have been delighted to receive such an early recognition from India and that the exchange of Ambassadors would automatically follow. But nations would have to start learning that nothing was 'automatic' with Mao Zedong.

An Indian Chargé d'Affaires, A.K. Sen who had earlier worked in Nanjing with Pannikar, was requested to proceed to Beijing to start 'negotiations' on the exchange of Ambassadors. After difficult technical discussions, the Chinese Government accepted to have discussions with the negotiator and finally acceded to the exchange of Ambassadors. It was as if the Chinese were doing India a favour by accepting its envoy.

But Pannikar was not prepared to read the writing on the wall.

During the next few months, while waiting for his posting to be ratified by Mao Zedong. Pannikar was busy rewriting Indian and Asian history from "the point of view of Asians themselves". It was during this period that his book, *Asia and the Western Dominance* was revised. It would influence all Nehruvian foreign policy and still does, even today.

The point made in his book is that all the nations of Asia have been dominated by foreign imperialists, they have suffered the same ordeals throughout the centuries, therefore following their liberation from 'Western dominance' they should come together to fight unitedly against the return of any 'white' imperialism.

Unfortunately for India, though the theory was sound, the reality on the ground was different. To decide that the 'white man' had been an imperialist and would therefore always remain an imperialist is an assumption not always borne out by historical fact.

The reverse assumption — that because you have once been under the yoke of a foreign power, you can never be an imperialist in future — is equally erroneous. During the following years, China proved not only through its 'map policy' of engulfing neighbouring nations but also through the 'barrel of the gun', that one can be yellow and imperialist at the same time. It is strange that such a good historian as Pannikar should have made this fundamental error in judgement which would have such serious consequences for India.

As an Indian, Pannikar should have known the history of both India and China. During the five or six millennia of her history, from the time of the Indus-Saraswati civilisation, India had never been an imperialistic nation. India had never tried to convert or amalgamate other states.[11]

While just a single glance at Chinese history demonstrates that China has always been an imperialistic power, it is a historical fact that when the Chinese Empire disintegrated the so-called 'outer provinces' became 'autonomous'. But even when China was weak, Chinese regimes always continued to claim these 'outer' provinces.

As shown in his 1948 Note, Pannikar was not without knowing that for all purposes, Tibet was an independent country between 1912 and 1950. The Chinese had no power whatsoever over the internal and external politics of Tibet. Tibet had its own currency and its own postal system and Tibetan diplomats were travelling around with their own handmade paper passports. This was witnessed by every foreigner who visited or lived in Tibet during the last century, but China still claimed that Tibet was part of its empire.

What was worse for India was that the Tibetan Government had only to claim a portion of Indian territory as part of Tibet, for the

---

[11]In fact when India did try to create a great empire, it was at the time of the Buddhist emperor Ashoka, but it was a cultural empire rather than a military one.

Chinese government to automatically claim it back as a part of the Chinese empire. Tawang and NEFA are the best examples of these claims. Did any Chinese ever visit Tawang or Sikkim before 1950?

The Nationalists had also asserted that these areas were theirs. They even tried to take up the matter with the British government in the late 40's. It might have been understandable coming from Chiang Kai-shek's regime, which was corrupt and very friendly with the 'American imperialists', but the first thing the Communists did after coming to power was to claim the same territories.[12] Is this not imperialism?

These were the premises on which Pannikar influenced the policy of the Government of India. They were false from the start. This would become more and more evident in the course of time. The main problem was that such suggestions appealed to the idealist Indian Prime Minister who was keen to be seen as a defender of oppressed people. However, it is not clear how he could pretend to be a defender of the oppressed nations such Algeria or Indonesia and at the same time befriend neo-colonial China.

Nehru did not understand that in abandoning the Tibetans he could no longer claim to be the hero of the trampled and the downtrodden; the years ahead would prove that he had supported and defended one of the most totalitarian regimes of this century.

It should be noted here that Mao Zedong never spoke of 'Chini-Hindi Bhai-Bhai' and it was a known fact that Mao Zedong actually held India in utter contempt. Mao had respect only for the strong, for those who could oppose him and not for those who bent over backwards to please him.

Patel clearly understood the problem when he wrote that "even though we regard ourselves as friends of China, the Chinese do not regard us as their friends."

[12]Mao had changed his view after coming to power. In 1936 he told Edgar Snow: "When the People's Revolution has been victorious in China, the outer Mongolian republic will automatically become part of the Chinese federation, at its own will. The Mohammedan [Sinkiang] and the Tibetan peoples, likewise, will form autonomous republics attached to the China federation. The unequal treatment of national minorities, as practised by the Kuomintang can have no part in the Chinese programme, nor can it be part of the program of any democratic republic." Snow, Edgar, Red Star on China (New York: Penguin Book, 1937), p. 505.

Upon receiving the news of his second appointment as the Ambassador of India to Red China, Pannikar thought with an incredible pretension that he would be able to convert Mao Zedong to his views. Nobody could change Mao's views: he was what is called, in Indian literature, a great Asura (or Titan) for whom the death of millions of his countrymen did not matter.

Pannikar quoted Mao as saying that there can be only two camps and those who were not with the Communists were against them. "It was my mission, as I saw it, to prove it to him that a neutral position was also possible," he said.[13]

While on board the ship which took him to Beijing, Pannikar was thinking:

In fact except for the Soviet and the Eastern bloc diplomats in Nanjing, I had not known any communists at all. All my training has been in the liberal radicalism of the West and consequently ...I had no sympathy for a political system in which individual liberty did not find a prominent place.

I had a deep sympathy for the Chinese people, a desire to see them united, strong and powerful, able to stand up against the nations which had oppressed them for a hundred years, a psychological appreciation of their desire to wipe out the humiliations which followed the western domination of their country. And to proclaim the message of resurgent Asia.[14]

Soon after his arrival in Beijing in April 1950, he met with the new 'elected' Chinese leaders, most of them puppet leaders put in place to give a democratic face to the new regime of Mao Zedong in the first year[15] after the 'liberation'. It was clear for Mao that "from day one, they would never have a word in the affairs of China."

Pannikar commented:

These were among the first people I met in New China and generally speaking I gained the impression that the Central People's Government[16] was being run by men

[13]Pannikar, op. cit., p. 73.

[14]Pannikar, op. cit., p. 72.

[15]They will be removed after a few months by the Communists.

[16]Dr Li said, "The Chinese People's Political Consultative Conference (CPPCC) turned out to be a tragic joke for the Communist Party run everything... the CPPCC came to be referred to as a vase of flowers – pretty to look at but of no use at all."

and women who were efficient and honest, who knew their minds and were prepared to put their best into the service of the State. There was a dynamism in all of them, a desire to go forward, which is perhaps the characteristic of all new governments.[17]

Pannikar recalled at length his first encounter with Mao Zedong in May 1950.

Before meeting him, one question was in Pannikar's mind: was Mao "the chosen leader of a resurgent people, driving out those who had sold out the Chinese Revolution and pushing back to the sea, from whence they came, the western nations who had enslaved the nations of Asia?"[18]

The historian in Pannikar should have known that the 'foreign imperialists' had already been pushed back into the sea by March 1950. The Japanese had long since been defeated and sent back to their island and the 'imperialist paper tigers' had also left China long ago. But Pannikar had two constant psychotic obsessions — to take revenge on the imperialists and to not be seen himself as a defender of imperialism.

Chinese 'Grand Masters' like Zhou Enlai would use these obsessions to their advantage. As we have seen earlier, the Chinese had mastered the game and Mao knew the trick: by calling Nehru 'a running dog of the imperialists', he knew that Nehru would rush to show the world that he was a friend of China.

Another example illustrates the new ambassador's attitude: Pannikar was looking for a residence to house the embassy: "I had made up my mind from the beginning to select a residence for myself outside the Legation area. I had no desire to be associated with the quarter, which stood so much for European domination in the East."[19]

It is strange that a couple of years earlier, the same Indian Ambassador had been quite at ease with the western diplomats in Nanking and his contacts with them were more than cordial.

Ironically (Pannikar could not know at that time) Mao's main worry in these first months of 1950 was about Soviet imperialism and the bad experience he had had with Stalin in Moscow. Recent

[17]Pannikar, op. cit., p. 87.
[18]Pannikar, op. cit., p. 79.
[19]Pannikar, op. cit., p. 77.

historical research proves that Mao would not have minded 'leaning' towards the West, although his propaganda had to proclaim otherwise.

When Pannikar went to present his credentials, he gave a speech which was to be repeated by Indian leaders during the next twelve years on the importance for world peace of friendship between China and India. The first thing, Pannikar noticed that day was Mao's wife: he was very impressed by Chiang Ching, a 'very good looking woman.' Some twenty years later she became the leader of the 'Gang of Four' and was responsible for the death of more the ten million Chinese during her mad Great Proletarian Cultural Revolution.

Describing Mao, Pannikar said: '"The impression which his face conveys is pleasant and benevolent and the look in his eyes is kindly. His personality is impressive but not intimidating and he has a gift of making people at home."[20]

To make Pannikar 'feel at home', Mao told him of an old belief: "If a man lives a good life, he would be reborn in India." It is very doubtful if Mao believed a word of what he told Pannikar, because as a good Communist, would he have believed in reincarnation?[21] One can safely presume that if Mao Zedong did believe in rebirth, he would have prayed to be reborn only in a Marxist (or Maoist) paradise of permanent Revolution and certainly not in India.

And Pannikar continued: "There is no cruelty or hardness either in his eyes or in the expression of his mouth. In fact he gave me the impression of a philosophical mind, a little dreamy... Mao Zedong in his epic life must have experienced many hardships and endured tremendous sufferings. Yet his face showed no sign of bitterness, cruelty or sorrow."[22]

Pannikar had fallen under Mao's charm.[23] So had India and her Prime Minister. Was he not already the expert on China, the person who knew, and who could give a direction to India's foreign policy in Asia?

[20]Pannikar, op. cit., p. 81.
[21]In 1954, Mao told the Dalai Lama in Beijing that all these religious beliefs were 'poisonous'.
[22]Ibid.
[23]One long term member of the Indian Parliament who had been closely associated with China in the 50's told us that Pannikar was 'bribed' by the Chinese through tête-à-tête dinners with Chinese officials and many other facilities and good treatment offered to him by the Communist regime.
We have not been able to verify this information.

Pannikar was no more 'neutral' thereafter. He had failed to convince Mao about his so-called 'middle way' position. Zhou would continue to listen to him politely and smile during their many tête-à-tête dinners, but by now Mao knew that the Indian idealists would not block his plans for the 'liberation' of Asia.

Pannikar went so far to please the Chinese that, in a telegram of October 25, the Prime Minister, his only defender in the Government, had for once to rebuke him:

> We cannot help thinking that your representation to the Chinese Government was weak and apologetic. In fairness to the Chinese Government as well as to ourselves our views regarding threatened invasion of Tibet and its probable repercussion should have been communicated to them clearly and unequivocally. This has evidently not been done.
>
> We have not even had any information from you regarding the Chinese Government's directive to the 'Liberation Army' to advance into Tibet. A full copy of this order was transmitted to us by the U.K. High Commissioner; and it was embarrassing for us not to have received intimation from our own Ambassador regarding such serious developments.[24]

The communication from Pannikar to the Chinese Foreign Office dated October 2, tends to confirm that he had prior knowledge of the Chinese intentions to invade Tibet. Pannikar is reported to have said that the Tibetan Delegation would be leaving India shortly for Peking. He expressed the hope that further military action would, therefore, not be necessary. "It will help the peaceful settlement of the Tibetan question if the Chinese troops which might have entered territory under the jurisdiction of the Lhasa authorities could restrict themselves to western Sikang."

Pannikar's 'Oversight'

The following incident more than anything else demonstrates Pannikar's character.

---

[24]On 27 October, Pannikar telegraphed that the "official release issued on the 25th afternoon contained merely the news of the official orders to the army to advance into Tibet first heard over *All India Radio* on the 25th morning."

On 26 August 1950, in an *aide memoire*,[25] Panikkar defined India's policy vis-à-vis Tibet as "autonomy within framework or Chinese sovereignty".[26] Following this note, discussions with the Chinese authorities were based on the same terminology which was a radical changed in India's Tibet policy. In fact, many believed that it helped China justify its military action in Tibet.

Though an Indian note of I November 1950 tried to rectify the 'oversight', it was too late and hereafter China kept on using 'sovereignty' for 'suzerainty'. It went a step further when Beijing attributed the rectification (of November 1) to 'outside influence'.[27]

The Statesman in Calcutta reported its own version of the incident: according to them, it the result of a careless slip in transcribing a coded message in the diplomatic communication from New Delhi to Beijing in 1950:

> A corrigendum did follow after the mistake (or mischief) had been detected, and was traced to inadvertence in transmission of a coded message. It was K.M. Pannikar, then Indian Ambassador to China, who held back the correction on the ground that it would mean discomfiture for the Indian Government. As the matter stands now because of this blunder, (a permanently sad commentary on the functioning of the foreign service), India remains committed to 'Chinese sovereignty' over Tibet.
>
> ... For all that Nehru wondered from whom Tibet was being 'liberated', it passes understanding how his government could write 'Chinese sovereignty' when it meant 'Chinese suzerainty' in a reply to Beijing, and then not bother to inform the Chinese formally that the mistake had been spotted and corrected.[28]

The Statesman may have not known that a- 'correction' was eventually sent, but the fact that more than two months passed before the Chinese received it, was translated by Beijing more as an encouragement to go ahead with their 'liberation' of Tibet.

[25]SWJN, Series II, Vol. 15 (2), p. 349. Cable from Nehru to Pan.ikar dated 20 November 1950.

[26]Instead of 'suzerainly'!

[27]Pannikar did not even want to issue a rectification for the 'oversight'. He felt that it would not serve any purpose.

[28]Quoted in *The Tibetan Review*, March 1988, p. 7.

But the truth is that it was certainly not an 'oversight'.

John Lall, a former Diwan of Sikkim (1949-1954) and ex-ICS officer, wrote in his book the *Aksai Chin and the Sino-Indian Conflict* that he had been told by a 'senior member' of the Indian Embassy in Beijing that the word change to sovereignty had been deliberately put by Pannikar.

A few months later, the deliberate 'lapsus' landed in the Indian Parliament with Nehru stating in a light vein: "Prof. Ranga seems to have been displeased at my occasional reference to Chinese suzerainty over Tibet. Please note that I used the word suzerainty, not sovereignty. There is a slight difference, though not much."

It is certain that Pannikar had a lot of influence on Nehru with regard to Chinese affairs. We were told by the then Indian Ambassador to Nepal[29] that he had sent to Nehru, at the same time, an assessment of the situation which was diametrically opposed to that of Pannikar, but Nehru chose to go by Pannikar's advice, perhaps since it fitted better his image as a man of peace.

It is clear that this policy was not agreed upon by all, as we have seen from Patel's letter, and there were divergent views inside the Indian Government. One can only say that it is such a pity that two great leaders like Nehru and Patel had not been able to work together: Patel with his clarity of thought, the strength of his will and his determination; and Nehru with his political charisma, his very high ideals, could have made India a very great nation. And surely the 'Himalayan Blunder' of 1962 could have been avoided and the fate of Tibet different. And India could have had an entirely different position in the world today.

China and India might have been ideologically very close or they might have suffered the same ordeals under the same imperial power, but that did not automatically mean that the liberated nations would behave the same or be the same after their 'liberation'.

Historically, one state has progressed through revolutions and upheavals, while the other has developed through evolution and assimilation. A big difference!

[29]C.P.N. Singh.

24

Appeasement and Ahimsa

*I attach great importance to India and China being friends.
I think the future of Asia and to some extent of the world
depends upon this.*

Jawaharlal Nehru, August 1950

Once Swami Rama Thirtha, a great self-realized sage of the beginning
of the century told a Muslim audience in Lucknow:

> The policy of appeasement is never successful. It
> increases the demands of the bully and encourages his
> unreasonableness. He will never listen to you. On the
> contrary, he will further insult you, by heaping
> imaginary allegations on you and finding baseless
> aberrations in you, because he is too proud of his
> transitory wealth, status, power, position and authority.[1]

In India, Vedantic or Buddhist philosophy always taught that
fearlessness is inseparable from non-violence. Ahimsa or the absence
of violence is not a concept which can be practised in a separate
manner. Truth, fearlessness and the principle of responsibility have
to be associated in the practice of Ahimsa.

Swami Tirtha continued: "Vedanta, therefore, does not allow
you to shirk your responsibility, to be inactive or to bow down before
tyrant if your cause is right and just. Your inertness, indolence or
tolerance will further encourage the tyrant in his acts of terrorism
and despotism."

It is a distortion of this ageless principle which led some british-
educated leaders of modern India to mix the notion of Ahimsa with
a policy of appeasement which has unfortunately been used by the
Indian Government, with tragic consequences that can be seen even
today.

---

[1]David Frawley, *Awaken Bharata* (New Delhi: Voice of India, 1998), p. 57.

We shall see in the following pages how the principles of Ahimsa were turned into a policy of appeasement.

Non-violence

"Rubbish. Total Rubbish. We don't need a defence plan. Our policy is non-violence. We foresee no military threats. Scrap the Army. The police are good enough to meet our security needs."[2]

Thus spoke Nehru, India's first Prime Minister in 1947.

Shortly after Independence, the Indian Army Chief of Staff had drafted the first paper on the threats to India's security. The paper contained recommendations for dealing with the newly independent nation's security and asked for a government directive on defence policy.

When General Sir Robert Lokhart took this paper to the Indian Prime Minister, the latter made the above incredible remarks.

The new Indian government had decided to be the champion of non-violence; they would prove to the world that problems and crises could be solved without recourse to force. The first casualty would be Kashmir. Nehru lost Kashmir while trying to stick to his principles.

Gandhi, the apostle of non-violence, was in many ways more realistic than Nehru. For example, it has been reported that Gandhi had said in September 1947 that he was not against sending in Indian troops to defend Kashmir. He stated that while he had always been an opponent of warfare, if there was no other way of securing justice from Pakistan, if Pakistan persistently refused to see its proven error and continued with it, then war would be the only alternative left for the Government. He added that "war was not a joke, that way lay destruction but he could never advise anyone to put up with injustice."[3]

According to military circles, the Indian Prime Minister needed the Pakistani raids on Indian territory in fall of 1947 to begin thinking about India's security. When the Pakistani raiders attacked Kashmir leaving behind a trail of destruction, he could no longer say "Rubbish, scrap the Army". He would see the problem with China, however, only after the 1962 debacle.

For their part, the Chinese were certainly not feeling threatened by the land of non-violence. The Chinese leaders knew their Indian

[2]Quoted by K. Subrahmanyam in an article in *The Times of India* (8 May 1997) "Arms & the Mahatma." This is extracted from the biography on Maj. Gen. A.A. Rudra written by Maj. Gen. D. K. Palit.
[3]Ibid.

interlocutors perfectly well. They may not have known that the Prime Minister wanted to scrap the army in 1947, but they were aware that there was no danger from such an idealistic leader.

An interesting anecdote is recalled by A.P. Venkateshwaran, a former Foreign Secretary of India who was posted in the early 80's as Indian Ambassador in Beijing. It demonstrates that the pacifist approach adopted by the Indian leaders was never understood by the Chinese. One day the Ambassador was requested by the Politburo of the Central Committee of the Party for a subtitled copy of the movie 'Gandhi'. It was loaned by the Embassy for a private screening for the Party leadership. When a Chinese official returned the copy to the Embassy, the Ambassador asked him how it was received. The official thanked the Government of India for its generosity and "replied enigmatically that it was a splendid and moving account of Gandhi's life. But no one had been able to understand what this non-violence is about!"[4]

When this incident occurred in the 80's, the Chinese leadership led by Deng Xiaoping was already 'soft' compared to that of his old comrades of the Long March. One can imagine the reaction of old revolutionary leaders in the 50's when Nehru preached non-violence to them.

Appeasement

Soon after Pannikar was posted to Peking, he held discussions on the fate of Tibet with the Chinese leadership. On 18 August, Nehru admitted in a telegram to Krishna Menon, then Indian High Commissioner in London: "Tibet is a very ticklish issue. We have to proceed rather cautiously in regard to it and we did not want it stated in public that we have been addressing the Chinese Government on this subject. They are sensitive and this itself might create an undesirable reaction in them."[5]

The policy of appeasement had begun.[6]

[4]*India's China Problem* by A.P. Venkateshwaran, in *India, Tibet and China* (New Delhi: Tibetan Parliamentary & Policy Research Centre, 1996).

[5]SWJN, Series II, Vol. 15 (1), p. 429. Cable from Nehru to Krishna Menon dated August 18, 1950.

[6]At the time of the above quoted letter to Krishna Menon, the Tibetan delegation was shuttling between Kalimpong, Calcutta and Delhi, begging for support for Tibet's cause.

Each time the views of the Government of India would differ from those of the Chinese, the Indians would end up appeasing the 'sensitive' Chinese, even at the cost of India's security.

A few examples will show how appeasement worked.

The day after having been recognized by India, the Chinese government announced its plan to 'liberate' Tibet: India did not react. On the contrary, India decided to intensify her efforts to get the admission of China into the UN.

In August 1950 the Government of India was informed that the Chinese were massing troops on the other side of the Yangtse river. No reaction.

Finally, in October, China moved in to 'liberate' Tibet. Pannikar and his government began bending backwards "not to upset the Chinese". It was for Mao the green light to go ahead with the 'liberation'. The more his troops penetrated Tibet, the more the Indian government (and the Tibetans) repeated that nothing should be done to upset the Chinese.

On October 18[th,] Pannikar cabled Nehru that he had met Chang Han-fu, the Chinese Vice Foreign Minister. Though the Chinese troops had already entered Tibet, Chang pretended that the Communist leaders were still waiting for the Tibetan delegation to arrive to 'liberate' Tibet. He added that some interested party was 'opposing and obstructing' a negotiated settlement.

A few days later, even though the Government of India was denying that they had any information about the entry of the Chinese troops into Eastern Tibet, it appears from the correspondence between Pannikar and Nehru that they knew about the Chinese troops having crossed the Yangtse and the fall of Chamdo.

> Our information from Lhasa is that Chinese forces are still advancing and Riwoche, Dzokangdzong, Markhan and Chamdo have fallen. Also that Lhodzong is expected to fall soon. Unless it is clear that these forces are halted and there is no imminent danger of invasion of Tibet, there is little chance of Tibetan delegation proceeding to Peking. We have been pressing them to go but cannot continue doing so in view of military movements threatening invasion.[7]

[7]SWIN, Series II, Vol. 15 (1), p. 437. Cable to Pannikar dated 22 October, 1950.

However, Panikkar believed that "a fresh representation to China was not called for" because of the 'lack of confirmation' of the presence of Chinese troops in Tibet.

He further argued that it could create an "interference to India's efforts on behalf of China in the UN" and would suggest "ulterior considerations".

Nehru clarified the next day:

We have no ulterior considerations in this matter as we have pointed out our primary consideration is maintenance of world peace and reducing tensions so that all questions can be considered in a more normal atmosphere. Recent developments in Korea have not strengthened China's position which will be further weakened by any aggressive action in Tibet.[8]

The appeasement policy continued till 1962, when the Government of India suddenly decided to practice a forward policy. Unfortunately, the Indian Army which had been neglected for so many years by the Defence Minister and his favourite generals, was not ready for the new forward policy which gave an excuse to Mao[9] to attack India.

Vagueness

In the telegram to Krishna Menon quoted earlier, Nehru also admitted that he wanted things to remain vague:

I have been asked questions about Tibet at press conferences. I have answered them rather vaguely and tried to avoid any direct commitment.

We do not intend any such clear declaration [regarding Tibet] because whatever we may say may be embarrassing either from Chinese or a Tibetan point of view.

From the start, even before the Chinese had 'officially' entered Tibet, Indian policy had been decided: "we should not be embarrassing the Chinese, they are our friends." The future of Asia depended on this friendship!

[8]Ibid. Reply to a telegram No. 263 dated 21st October from Pannikar to Nehru.

[9]He himself was in a difficult internal position inside China after the catastrophic Great Leap Forward.

It should be pointed that vagueness was also characteristic of the British policy on Tibet. It was the best method to avoid antagonizing the Russians or the Chinese. Vagueness would remain the hallmark of Nehru's policy on Tibet until 1962. The difference between Britain and newly independent India was that while the British had the muscle to impose their 'vagueness' by force, India did not have the strength to impose anything.

Friendship at Any Cost

In August 1950 Nehru already had information that Chinese troops were massing on the Sino-Tibetan border. How could he force the Chinese to respect Tibetan autonomy while Pannikar had just accepted Chinese sovereignty over Tibet? How could his pacifist approach prevent China from using force?

For Mao there was never the question of 'Chini-Hindi Bhai-Bhai' — Nehru was an enemy. In fact Mao must have been at a loss to understand this enemy who was giving concession after concession. Mao must have wondered, "Where is the catch?"

Here we see the difference between the Indian attitude with its declared one-point policy of friendship and non-violence, and the multi-faceted guerrilla tactics learned by Mao during the years of the Long March and constantly applied by the Chinese leadership.[10]

While preparing the onslaught on Tibet, Mao would send his soft-spoken Prime Minister to the Indian Ambassador to charm him with sweet words and succulent dinners. He stopped his military advance whenever it was necessary and gave his enemies the time to 'cool' down. He calculated that this way his enemies would not be forced to react militarily. After the Chinese entry into Tibet, Mao waited a few months before progressing further towards his target. He stabilized his front, using the waiting period to reinforce his strategic position. Nehru should have learned much from Mao, the strategist but unfortunately he was too blinded by his idealism.

The two leaders never spoke the same language: one was a pacifist wanting to play a role on the world-stage; the other a strategist used to guerrilla warfare and ready to sacrifice millions of his own people to bring about a new socialist world.

---

[10]These tactics were even applied to the internal leadership struggle within the Politburo.

On 23 October 1950, three years after India had become independent, when the news of the invasion of Tibet was still a well-kept secret, Pannikar cabled Nehru to say that since a few days Chinese troops had begun entering Tibet: "The Chinese effort to extend their authority in Tibet seemed to be actuated by their concern to make their rear secure against Anglo-American influence in case of war." [11]

The Indian Prime Minister could sincerely not understand the problem; he replied: "It is difficult for us to understand, how any intelligent person can consider Chinese security to be threatened along Tibetan frontier, whatever might happen, including world conflict."[12]

In another telegram sent to Pannikar, the policy of the Government of India was made very clear: "We have based our policy on the full recognition of the People's Government of China and her admission in the United Nations."[13]

The Prime Minister further explained to his Ambassador:

We are anxious to proceed in a manner friendly to China and to cooperate with her as far as possible. You have informed us that President Mao has strong feeling for Asia. It is from this point of view especially that I have tried to consider this question. We should like a number of Asian countries to cooperate with us in our attempts to maintain peace and to prevent the conflicts of the major Powers from pushing the world towards destruction. China can play a vital role in this.[14]

But was China interested either in this cooperation or in this idealist perception of Asia as the custodian of world peace? Did Nehru sincerely believe that Mao would follow the policy of non-violence initiated by him?

Certainly Mao had strong feelings for Asia, but only a socialist Asia, with 'Chinese characteristics', and under Chinese leadership.

The one-pointed policy of the Government of India would remain the same for the following twelve years: friendship at any cost.

[11]SWJN, Series II, Vol. 15 (1), p. 436. Cable from Pannikar to Nehru dated 23 October 1950.
[12]Ibid., p. 438.
[13]SWJN, Series II, Vol. 15 (1), p. 431. Cable from Nehru to Pannikar dated 19 August 1950.
[14]Ibid.

The underlying assumption was that if India remained friendly to China, China would help India. Nehru went a long way in this direction first with Formosa: "We recognize China's claim to Formosa and the strong desire of the Chinese Government and people to take some steps in regard to Formosa".[15]

However, as a true and sincere pacifist, he always preferred a negotiated agreement, even with regard to Tibet.

We should also quote from another telegram from the Indian Prime Minister to Pannikar dated 25 August[16]: "If Chinese Government distrust and disbelieve us in spite of all that we have said and done, then there is nothing further that we can say."[17]

Larger Issues Only

Nehru's greatest error was that he was only concerned by 'larger issues', such as the decolonization of Asia and world peace. In August he wrote to Pannikar: "This invasion of Tibet might well upset the present unstable equilibrium and let loose dangerous forces. Some of our border States will be affected. But I am more concerned with the larger issues which this involves."[18] Apparently the threat building up on the Indian border was not part of the 'larger issues', to his mind!

When the Tibetan Minister, Tsepon Shakabpa, met Nehru in Delhi in September 1950, the Indian Prime Minister advised him to go to China.

Nehru and Pannikar were so much enamoured of the Chinese that they did not foresee that if the Tibetans were to go to Beijing to negotiate with the Chinese, they would fall into a trap and as a result, India stood to lose as much as the Tibetans.

Shakabpa wanted India to help Tibet in the same way the British had done at the Simla Convention in 1914. He wanted the three interested parties to sit together at a negotiating table, and take a fair decision on the future of Tibet. If this was not possible, at least he wanted India to facilitate the negotiations in Delhi.

---

[15]Ibid.

[16]Pannikar stated "Chinese have been talking of security of their Tibetan frontier and whenever I have pointed out that we are the only State on that boundary, they have remained silent."

[17]SWJN, Series II, Vol. 15 (1), p. 438. Cable to Pannikar. New Delhi, 25 October 1950.

[18]Ibid. Cable to Pannikar dated 19 August.

Nehru did not want to give "the impression that they were taking part in the talks",[19] therefore they did not want to propose Delhi as the venue.

Nehru's main problem was to show China and the world that he had no vested interest in Tibet. To prove that he was ready to go to any extent to appease the Chinese leadership, in a telegram to Pannikar, Nehru said:

> We know very well what China's claims have been in Tibet in the past. We are not entering into their merits. It is quite clear to us that any invasion of Tibet by Chinese troops will have serious consequences in regard to their position in the United Nations. It will strengthen the hands of the enemies of China and weaken those who are supporting China's cause there. Easy success in Tibet, which can be had at any time later, will not counterbalance loss in international sphere.

The merit of the case clearly did not interest Nehru. The only point he was interested in was that it would make it more difficult to help China's admission to the UN.[20]

Another Argument

In the *Selected Works of Jawaharlal Nehru* one argument appears which is quite flabbergasting: Nehru compared the case of Tibet to the cases of Pondicherry and Goa. This extraordinary argument created an opportunity for the Chinese to twist India's arm on Kashmir and blackmail successive governments with the argument, "if India speaks for the Tibetans, the Chinese would speak for the Kashmiris".

Here are Nehru's precise words:

> We might remind you of our position in regard to French and Portuguese possessions in India. Their legal position is, we know, different from that of Tibet, but, to the world at large, Tibetan autonomy is a reality not to be swept aside by force of arms. We are convinced that Goa and Pondicherry must come to us and it is easy for us to seize them by military means. But we have deliberately refrained from doing so because of larger considerations.

[19]Cable to Pannikar dated 2 September, 1950.

[20]SWJN, Series II, Vol. 15 (1) p. 236. This telegram was sent on 19 October, 12 days after the Chinese troops had crossed the Yangtse and a day after they entered Chamdo.

382   *The Fate of Tibet*

We do not understand the occasion for urgency and immediate military action in Tibet, when international situation is so delicate and no harm can result by delay in an attempt to seek settlement by negotiation.[21]

Pannikar is bound to have brought the argument of Pondicherry to the Chinese leadership who must have taken good note of it.

To conclude it is interesting to quote a remark made by Sri Aurobindo in *The Foundation of Indian Culture*, which shows that the foreign policy of a state such as India needs to be balanced. It is here that the presence of Sardar Patel was so dearly missed. If Nehru, the Idealist, had been able to work with Patel, the Pragmatic, the destiny of the Indian nation would have perhaps been different:

The political system of a society has to be judged, no doubt first and foremost by the stability, prosperity, internal freedom and order it ensures to the people, but also it must be judged by the security it erects against other States, its unity and power of defence and aggression against external rivals and enemies. It is not perhaps altogether to the credit of humanity that it should be so and a nation or people that is inferior in this kind of political strength, as were the ancient Greeks and mediaeval Italians, may be spiritually and culturally far superior to its conquerors and may well have contributed more to a true human progress than successful military States, aggressive communities, predatory empires. But the life of man is still predominantly vital and moved therefore by the tendencies of expansion, possession, aggression, mutual struggle for absorption and dominant survival which are the first law of life, and a collective mind and consciousness that gives a constant proof of incapacity for aggression and defence and does not organise the centralised and efficient unity necessary to its own safety, is clearly one that in the political field falls far short of the first order.[22]

India would pay dearly for not having organized her own safety.

[21]SWJN, Series II, Vol. 15 (1), p. 437. Cable to Pannikar, New Delhi. 22 October, 1950.

[22]Sri Aurobindo, *The Foundations of Indian Culture* (Pondicherry: Sri Aurobindo Ashram, 1972), pp. 362-63.

25

Nehru and the Tibet Policy

We cannot save Tibet.
Jawaharlal Nehru, 18 November, 50
*From whom they [the Chinese] were going to liberate Tibet
is, however, not quite clear.*
Jawaharlal Nehru, 6 December, 50

It is not an easy thing to speak about the role of Nehru in the Sino-Tibetan-Indian conflict (or any other matter in fact). Even today, he is considered by many Indians as one of their greatest leaders and by some, even as something of a god. To criticise him can prove costly. We can nevertheless try to point out some historical facts.

At the outset we face one major difficulty in making an objective study of Nehru's role and contribution because most of the documents relating to Nehru are not yet accessible to researchers.

In the course of our research, we were told that these documents belong to the Nehru family and are locked up in the vaults of the Jawaharlal Nehru Memorial Fund in Teen Murti Bhavan and only the heir of the Nehru family can give permission for access to them.[1]

In the National Archives all the files related to Tibet and the North-east border are still classified, even today. When we enquired, we were told (and shown the Rules) that all documents related to the above areas were classified after 1913.[2]

When we pointed out that there was no problem to access the files up to the time of India's independence at the India Office of the British Library in London, no comment could be given. The

[1]Some other documents, we were told, are kept unindexed in dusty almirahs of Ministry of External Affairs.

[2]The Government of India was more 'generous' with the North-west, referred to as the 'Gilgit area': these documents were declassified before 1923.

bureaucrats perhaps have not noticed that the British had walked away with all the archival material in 1947.

To assess Nehru, we are left only with the voluminous series of *Selected Works of Jawaharlal Nehru* published by the Jawaharlal Nehru Memorial Fund and edited by Dr S. Gopal. This can be considered as a partial 'declassification' though only Nehru's letters, notes or speeches are published; the letter or event which provoked Nehru's reply are only briefly mentioned in footnote. For example the opinion of Patel who held diametrically opposite view on the strategic importance of Tibet do not appear anywhere in the *Selected Works*.

Keeping these limitations in mind, we shall try to examine Nehru's role during this Fateful Year.

Nehru: a Complex Personality

Nehru had a complex personality with many contradictory facets. We shall not insist on the well-known qualities of Nehru as a statesman, but will deal more with some other aspects. One of these traits of character is the very high opinion he had of himself.

To give an example, in a cable to Ambassador K.M. Pannikar on 22 August 1950, Nehru wrote:

> The situation changes so rapidly that one can only deal with it by telegram, and anything one may write might well be out of date. You must have received copies of the speeches I delivered in Parliament here during the foreign affairs debate last month. I tried to explain and clarify what our foreign policy has been and is. On the whole, I created an impression on most people. There are, of course, some who just cannot understand anything but a crude lining up with this or that Power."[3]

Though the transcript of the debate shows that many members of the House were not happy with the way things were going on the Kashmir or Northern front, Nehru assumed that he had impressed most of them. Other examples could be given.

Another aspect of Nehru's personality which has been widely attested to, was poor judgement in the choice of his friends and collaborators. His two main collaborators and advisors on the Indo-Sino-Tibetan relations were K.M. Pannikar and V.K. Krishna Menon.

[3]SWJN, Series II, Vol. 15 (1), p. 432. Cable from Nehru to Pannikar dated 2 September 1950.

In his book *Aksai Chin and the Sino-Indian Conflict*, John Lall wrote:

> After India attained Independence in 1947, two persons
> came to exercise an influence on Indian affairs that had
> far-reaching consequences on India's relations with
> China and, in a deeper sense, on India's place in the
> world. One was K. M. Pannikar who, as the title of one
> of his many books describes him, was Ambassador to
> Two Chinas. The other was V. K Krishna Menon who
> was appointed India's High Commissioner in London
> and, in 1957, Minister of Defence in the Union
> Government. Neither of them had any established
> political base in the country. Pannikar's glittering
> intellectual attainments were matched by a remarkable
> gift of seizing the occasion. He had caught Nehru's eye
> as early as 1924; that was enough.[4]

We have earlier given some details of Pannikar's position and
influence on Nehru and of his capacity to 'seize' the occasion.

Krishna Menon had also a great influence on Nehru after India's
independence, although he came later on into the Sino-Indian picture.

However Menon typifies the poor choice of advisors that Nehru
did. Whoever had worked with Menon knew of his arrogant
character, his utter contempt for those who disagreed with him and
his impulsive ways with his collaborators.

The fact that Menon as Defence Minister interfered directly with
the preparedness of the Indian troops to man the northern Indian
borders in the early 60's is beyond doubt. His own erroneous and
motivated choice of 'favourites'[5] lowered the morale in the army.

Both characters (Pannikar and Menon) had many similarities:
they were intellectually very bright, they knew it and wanted
everyone to know it. They had the full confidence of the Prime
Minister and their Marxist leanings made them closer to Mao's China
or Stalin's Soviet Union than to Western democracies or even a
theocratic state like Tibet for that matter.

In an interview, we asked the Dalai Lama if he agreed that Nehru
believed that a small dose of communism was not bad for 'feudal'
Tibet." He replied "I think so, I think so! A big dose!" and then he
laughed and laughed in his characteristic way. When we further

---

[4]Lall, op. cit., p. 232.
[5]Such as Lt. Gen. B.M. Kaul, the Corps Commander on the Eastern front.

asked him if he felt that Nehru had been very much influenced by advisors such as Pannikar or Krishna Menon who had leftist leanings, he replied, "No doubt!" But in his compassionate way he added that it was not the only factor. "From the Buddhist point of view, there was the inner factor, the karmic factor, some kind of very forceful negative karmic movement. Even when some positive movements came, somehow we had to face some obstacles."

The fact that many Indian leaders who had, like Nehru, been educated in England, were atheists and had leftist leanings, deeply influenced India's internal and external policies. At the same time, it should be pointed out that it was the socialist leaders such as Acharya Kripalani, Dr Lohia, Jayaprakash Narayan and more recently former Speaker Rabi Ray and George Fernandes who strongly defended Tibet's autonomy.

Difficulty to Work with Others.

Apart from the poor choice of advisors, Nehru had difficulties to work with others as equals. We have seen that he had been chosen as the first Prime Minister of India by Gandhi on the fallacious argument that Patel would be able to work with Nehru, while the opposite would not be possible.

The fact that very often Nehru dealt directly with his ambassadors without informing his Foreign Secretary (or the Secretary General of the Ministry of Foreign Affairs) certainly created resentment within the Foreign Ministry.

To take another example: at the end of his letter of November 7, Patel requested Nehru to call a Cabinet Meeting to discuss the implications of the Chinese entry in Tibet. The meeting was never held; instead Nehru prepared a personal Note[6] in which he enunciated his China policy. His pronouncements would become the official China (and Tibet) policy for the subsequent years with all their disastrous consequences for India.

Yet another example was the hurried recognition of the Communist regime in Beijing. Many opposed Nehru and questioned his haste in recognizing Mao's government, but Nehru had the certitude that India should immediately recognize Communist China and become friends with her. Thereafter, all the energies of India's

[6]Dated 18 November.

diplomacy concentrated on getting China into the UN and the Security Council. If India had put as much energy in to getting her own admission through, she would certainly have been a member of the Security Council today.

It is as if India had resolved from the beginning to play 'second fiddle' to China, to view the world from a Chinese perspective and to put her own interests on one side. If she finds herself disregarded in world affairs today, she has only herself to blame.

Acharya Kripalani said in the Parliament in December 1950: "Soon, this nation [China] that was struggling for its own freedom, strangulated the freedom of a neighbouring nation [Tibet], in whose freedom we are intimately connected."[7]

He added that the situation would be ridiculous if China continued to advance in Tibet and Nepal and at the same time the Government of India continued to sponsor Beijing at the UN. This is precisely what Nehru's government did later.

It was not only the politicians — in the government and in the opposition — who felt it was premature for India to rush to recognize China when China was not ready to offer anything in return, but the general public was also uncomfortable. Many people wrote about it. In a Bombay fortnightly, the historian K.D. Sethna wrote: "In recognizing Red China the Indian Government has committed a mistake whose gravity beggars description. We have made a New Year's gesture which would rank as one of the stupidest in our history if its stupidity were not surpassed by its perniciousness."[8] Sethna's guru, Sri Aurobindo, had seen this article and approved of it.

But, nothing would stop Nehru from going ahead with his policy of friendship with China. Over the years, the myth of the Indo-Chinese friendship would grow larger and larger; becoming a 'brotherhood' until that day in October 1962 when Lin Biao and his PLA burst the bubble on the Thagla Ridge in the West Kameng Division of NEFA.

Even today India suffers from the 'China syndrome', an inferiority complex vis-à-vis China after the humiliation of 1962. And

[7]Sen, op. cit., p.113.
[8]K.D. Sethna, *India and the World Scene* (Pondicherry: Sri Aurobindo Institute of Research in Social Sciences, 1997), p. 1.

it was not as if Nehru had not been warned. Unfortunately the autocrat in him had decided to brush aside all warnings.

Such examples could be multiplied.

Nehru and the UN

One of the problems of Nehru was that he had earlier burnt his fingers on the Kashmir issue. In 1948 he himself referred the problem of Kashmir to the UN; by his own will, from a bilateral issue he made it into an international one. There is no doubt that at that time the matter could have been solved on the ground. It would have avoided fifty years of misery to the people of the State, not to mention loss of thousands of lives and a cost of thousands of millions of rupees to the Indian and Pakistani exchequers, but Nehru decided otherwise and put India's security into the UN trap. The Kashmir issue, like the Tibetan one is still pending today.

We were told by the Dalai Lama that, when he first came to Delhi to meet Nehru in September 1959, the Prime Minister told him that an appeal to the UN was a waste of time.[9] However, Nehru did not try to stop the Dalai Lama from going ahead.[10]

Is it not paradoxical that an internationalist like Nehru did not believe in United Nations body anymore?

In what is known as the last letter of Nehru,[11] the Indian Prime Minister wrote to Dr. Gopal Singh: "It is not clear to me what we can do about Tibet in the present circumstances. To have a resolution in the UN about Tibet will not mean much as China is not represented there. We are not indifferent to what has happened to Tibet. But we are unable to do anything EFFECTIVE about it."

Though the situation had changed since 1950, Nehru still had the same perception that nothing could be done as long as China was not represented in the UN. But was it not a convenient excuse to choose to do nothing?

In the course of our research, we interviewed a retired Tibetan official, Rinchen Sadutshang who was one of the Dalai Lama's envoys to the UN when the Resolutions were passed. Sadutshang told us

[9]Eventually resolutions were passed in favour of Tibet in 1959, 1961 and 1965. Under the courageous leadership of Lal Bahadur Shastri, India voted for the first (and only) time in favour of the Tibet Resolution in 1965.

[10]The Dalai Lama told us that he really appreciated the fact that Nehru, though opposed to a Tibetan Appeal to the UN, did not stop him from proceeding with it.

[11]Dated May 24, 1964 from Dehra Dun.

"We discussed with the Indian delegation, but they would always say: 'It is no use, it will not help you, it may even aggravate the attitude of the Chinese.' It was always their attitude, they tried to be detached from it as far as possible. The Indian attitude was our biggest obstacle."[12]

We shall see later in this chapter that this policy of doing nothing in order not to upset the Chinese or to aggravate the sufferings of the Tibetans was decided by Nehru in November 1950; it would be blindly followed by his successors, except Shastri.

Sadutshang continued:

> Since it was India's attitude, many of the Asian and Middle East countries (those who were uncertain) said: "India should support, India is the most interested party, the Dalai Lama is the guest of India, you have so many refugees in India, you have given them asylum, why is it that India is not supporting the case, if India supports, we will support. If India does not, then we have to think about it, and find out more, we have to talk to the Indian delegation." We do not want to upset the Indian delegation. And the Indian delegation was afraid that the Chinese might be upset or offended.

Though the Indian leaders did not realize it at the time, the double standards of India's foreign policy marked the beginning of the decline of India as a power on the world stage. The lack of courage and self-confidence of its leaders, demonstrated by their need to please the Chinese at any rate, cost India her chance to be a leader of the so-called Third World nations.

The Kshatriya (warrior) spirit had gone out of India.

The future proved that to base her foreign policy only on her friendship with China or Russia was not a viable path for India. When the Chinese Bhai blew up the bubble of friendship in 1962, it was to the 'imperialists' — Kennedy and United States — that India turned.

Nehru and the Chinese Mind

One recurrent trait in Nehru's character was his naivety vis-à-vis the Chinese. Perhaps because he was naïve and because he was a good man, he always wanted to see the good of others, too often

[12]Interview with Rinchen Sadutshang, Dehra Dun, December 1997.

ignoring the reality. He never really understood how Chinese mind was working.

From the beginning of the Fateful Year, Nehru received repeated warnings: India was accused of being a foreign imperialist power trying to grab Tibet, but each time India ignored the insults; after all, China was 'our friend'. Nehru and Pannikar chose to be fooled by the references which were repeated at the end of the Chinese notes, to "China desiring the friendship of India". This was enough to make the heart of the Indian ambassador[13] in China melt.

The fact that winter was coming and Lui Bocheng and Deng Xiaoping needed some months to consolidate their base in Tibet was never thought of.

It is also true that Zhou Enlai played his role perfectly; the soft-spoken 'old China' diplomat had only sweet words and politeness for his interlocutors. The Indian diplomats (including the Prime Minister) were completely charmed by his class and kindness. However, there was another side to Zhou too. Dr Li, Mao's Physician told the following story:

> As he [Zhou] was talking to Mao in room 118, trying to explain his idea, Zhou got out a map and spread it on the floor, kneeling on the carpet to show Mao the direction his motorcade would take. Mao stood, smoking a cigarette, watching Zhou crawl on the floor. For Zhou to kneel before Mao seemed to me humiliating, and I was deeply embarrassed to see a man of Zhou's stature, the premier of China, behave that way. Mao seemed to take a sardonic pleasure watching Zhou crawl before him. Nowhere were the contradictions of Mao's dictatorship more pronounced than in his relationship with Zhou. Because he was so subservient and loyal, Mao held the Premier in contempt.[14]

Dr Li's book showed again and again that Mao had utter contempt for those who crawled in front of him.

We should never forget that the so-called friendship between China and India was built on nothing more than the rapport

[13]B.N. Rau, the Indian Ambassador to the UN also melted and changed India's policy to support the Tibetan case in the UN and decided to keep the matter 'pending'.
[14]Li, op. cit., p. 510.

between Nehru and Zhou and on some dinner parties offered to Pannikar.

Zhou was the perfect instrument of Mao when his adversaries needed to be pacified. He could take the strongest action and at the same time use the services of Zhou to reassure India and the world of China's friendly intentions.

The naivety of Nehru was fully used.

To give another example: Zhou came to India several times in 1956-57[15], at the time when the strategic road between Sinkiang and Tibet[16] which passed through Indian territory was opened to traffic.

Did Nehru know what the Thirteenth Dalai Lama had said to Charles Bell about the Chinese in the early twenties? He said: "The Chinese way is to do something rather mild at first; then to wait a bit and if it passes without objection, to say or do something stronger. But if we take objection to the first statement or action, they urge that it has been a misunderstanding, and cease, for a time at any rate, from troubling us further."[17]

It was exactly the plans used by the Chinese during the Fateful Year. The problem was that Nehru was thinking and planning with his own mentality and vision: he never tried to think with Mao's mind. Nehru did not know and could not understand Mao. The Great Helmsman was fighting for a revolutionary cause; he had told his men during the Long March that the Revolution was not a tea party.

To take the example of Korea, Mao knew that he would face difficulties; most of his lieutenants had recommended that China should not enter the Korean war against the much better equipped UN troops of McArthur, but for Mao such a decision was not a question of losing a few million of his troops, but of losing face.

An anecdote involving Nehru shows how wrong Nehru was in his understanding of the Chinese psyche and motivations.

According to Dr. Li, the private physician of Mao, when Nehru visited China in 1954, the Chairman flabbergasted Nehru during their meeting:

[15]The Communist and atheist Premier even brought relics of Lord Buddha on the occasion of the Buddha Jayanti's celebrations.
[16]Cutting across the Aksai Chin, the Sinkiang-Tibet highway was opened on October 6, 1957, though this fact was admitted only a year later by India.
[17]Sir Charles Bell, *Portrait of a Dalai Lama* (London: Wisdom Publication, 1987), p. 112.

I did not immediately understand, because it was so hard to accept, how willing Mao was to sacrifice his own citizens in order to achieve his goals. I had known as early as October 1954, from a meeting with India's prime minister Jawaharlal Nehru, that Mao considered the atom bomb a 'paper tiger' and that he was willing that China lose millions of people in order to emerge victorious against so-called imperialists. 'The atom bomb is nothing to be afraid of,' Mao told Nehru. 'China has many people. They cannot be bombed out of existence. If someone else can drop an atomic bomb, I can too. The death of ten or twenty million people is nothing to be afraid of.'[18]

This was in 1954, but even this did not make Nehru rethink his Bhai-Bhai policy.

Nehru's Note on Tibet Policy

We have seen that Nehru did not respond directly to Patel's letter, but a few days after the letter, he dictated a Note[19] that would become the corner stone of the China Policy until the Prime Minister's death. We shall study in detail this Note to try to understand Nehru's fears and motivations.

Apart from Patel's letter which was not even cited in the Note, what prompted the drafting of a new Tibet-China policy was the Tibetan Appeal to the UN. It was coming up for hearing in the General Committee of the General Assembly: "We have to send immediate instructions to Shri B.N. Rau as to what he should do in the event of Tibet's appeal being brought up before the Security Council or the General Assembly," wrote Nehru.

In a previous Note, the Beijing Government had concluded their long communication by saying:

> ...as long as our two sides adhere strictly to the principle of mutual respect for territory, sovereignty, equality and mutual benefit, we are convinced that the friendship between China and India should be developed in a normal way, and that problems relating to Sino-Indian diplomatic, commercial and cultural relations with

[18]Li, op. cit., p. 125.
[19]Text of the Note in SWJN, Series II, Vol. 15 (2), p. 345. Policy Regarding China and Tibet.

respect to Tibet may be solved properly and to our mutual benefit through normal diplomatic channels.

The Prime Minister noted that the Chinese do "appear to be toning down and [making] an attempt at some kind of a friendly approach."

We have to point out here that the Chinese had not in fact cooled down at all. But as Charles Bell had explained to the Thirteenth Dalai Lama, after any action, the Chinese always prefer to wait a bit and see the reaction of their foes. Having secured their military position in Tibet, with the Tibetan Appeal in the UN still pending, the Chinese were 'waiting' before taking the next step.

This was enough to melt Pannikar's heart, even though after having said these sweet words, the Chinese note reasserted Chinese sovereignty over Tibet.

They told India that they [India] had already acknowledged China's sovereignty over Tibet and that "outside influences have been at play obstructing China's mission in Tibet". It was why the Chinese had to liberate Tibet: "the liberation of Changtu [Chamdo] proves that foreign forces and influences were inciting Tibetan troops to resist."[20]

Once again the message was loud and clear: the Chinese army would go ahead and this on account of India's imperialist designs over Tibet. But Nehru's comment was "All this is much the same as has been said before... and there are repeated references in the note to China desiring the friendship of India."

Nehru also felt that the China policy had to be decided keeping in mind the short term as well the longer term view of the problem. For him it was a *fait accompli* that "China is going to be our close neighbour for a long time to come. We are going to have a tremendously long common frontier."

In November 1950, Nehru had accepted that the frontier between India and Tibet had *de facto* become the border between India and China. It was a surprising statement as the Chinese troops had not gone further than Chamdo at that time and were still several week's walk away from Lhasa, and several months walk from the McMahon Line. Nehru added: "I think it may be taken for granted that China will take possession, in a political sense at least, of the whole of Tibet."

[20]Was it the 'lonely Briton', Robert Ford who was threatening the mighty China?

He further admitted that for the Tibetan people the "autonomy can obviously not be anything like the autonomy, verging on independence. which Tibet has enjoyed during the last forty years or so."

It is beyond comprehension how Nehru who wanted to be the hero of the oppressed nations could at the same time accept that a nation 'verging on independence', should lose its independence. The only reply he could give was: "it is reasonable to assume from the very nature of Tibetan geography, terrain and climate,[21] that a large measure of autonomy is almost inevitable."

In all probability one reason which motivated Nehru into this easy acceptance of the disappearance of Tibet from Asian maps was that he thought that it was in the interest of Tibet to have a socialist regime. For Nehru, the old theocratic system had to be reformed and a more 'democratic' set-up had to be installed; the 'liberation' was Tibet's chance. We should not forget that at the same time, he was himself trying to introduce democracy in Nepal and Sikkim.[22]

Another point made by Nehru was that "it is exceedingly unlikely that we may have to face any real military invasion from the Chinese side, whether in peace or in war, in the foreseeable future."

It is not clear what was meant by 'real' invasion. However, Nehru came to the conclusion that China would not take the risk to have too many new enemies; for that would weaken China.

He indirectly replied to Patel's view when he wrote that "there is far too much loose talk about China attacking and overrunning India. If we lose our sense of perspective and world strategy and give way to unreasoning fears, then any policy that we might have is likely to fail."

His only conclusion on the subject was that possible 'gradual infiltration' should be checked and 'necessary precautions' should be taken to prevent this. Unfortunately, even there nothing was done and less than three years later, the Chinese began building a road on Indian territory. It would take five more years for the Government of India to 'officially' discover it.

At that time, the main thorn in India's side was Kashmir. One can understand that the Government of India was not keen to open

[21]The future would show that adapting to the Tibetan plateau it posed little problem for the Chinese troops, who had participated in the Long March.
[22]And in Kashmir through Shaikh Abdullah.

a second front in the Himalayas. It meant a lot of human and financial resources which were hardly available. From the time of independence, Pakistan had been designated as the enemy Number One and for many strategists and politicians, it was out of the question to open 'a second front.'

Over the years, China fully played up the Indian difficulties in Kashmir.[23] Nehru admitted that: "Pakistan is taking a great deal of interest, from the point of view of the developments in Tibet. Indeed it has been discussed in the Pakistan press that the new danger from Tibet to India might help them to settle the Kashmir problem according to their wishes."[24]

However, we have to point out here that Pakistan systematically took the opposite position to India's in its dispute with China. Whenever India voted against a resolution in the UN, Pakistan voted for and vice-versa. We were even told by an informant that when Pakistan saw that India was abandoning Tibet in the UN in 1950, Pakistan informally made it known that they were ready to help to support the Tibetan cause.

The motto was "We cannot have all the time two possible enemies on either side of India". The only problem was that Nehru forgot that sometimes one cannot choose to have enemies or friends. India had two enemies but refused to accept the existence of one of them, and the Mantra 'Bhai-Bhai' was woefully insufficient to solve the problem.

On the problem of Communism, Nehru said: "The idea that communism inevitably means expansion and war, or, to put it more precisely, that Chinese communism means inevitably an expansion towards India, is rather naïve."

Future events revealed just how naïve Nehru was. Nehru thought that in introducing his own brand of socialism in India, he could counter Communist propaganda. But this did not work either.

[23]A Chinese Premier (Li Peng) even came to Delhi to threaten the Indian Government that if they did not muzzle the activities of the Tibetan refugees in India, China would support the Pakistani stand on Kashmir. India immediately obeyed.

[24]The editor of the *Selected Works* cited an article in the Pakistani newspaper *The Dawn* of 12 November which published a poem 'Tibet and Kashmir', and commented: "The passion which has inspired his (poet's) muse to sing a poem of praise to liberators of Tibet' and to let his despairing mind dwell wistfully on thoughts of some such 'liberation' for his own overrun and beleaguered. motherland cannot but touch one's heart...."

Now comes the corner stone of the China policy between 1950 to 1962: "In a long-term view, India and China are two of the biggest countries of Asia bordering on each other and both with certain expansive tendencies, because of their vitality. If their relations are bad, this will have a serious effect not only on both of them but on Asia as a whole."

This sentence contradicts the previous one when Nehru had stated that it was rather naïve to think in terms of expansion for Communist China, now it is admitted that China (and India) have 'tendencies'.[25]

The 'Ambassador of China' as Pannikar is sometimes referred to, had himself admitted, in 1948, that "a China so organized will be in an extremely powerful position to claim its historic role of authority over Tibet, Burma, Indo-China and Siam. The historic claims in regard to these are vague and hazy."

Vagueness and ambiguity or constitutional fiction never prevented China from asserting her claim when she was weak or from grabbing back 'her' territories when she was strong.

Nehru's Note concluded that what "we should seek is some kind of understanding of China" and he added, "China desires this too for obvious reasons."

"We cannot save Tibet", was the final conclusion.

The strange argument popped up again: if we do anything to help Tibet, it will upset the Chinese and the fate of Tibet would be worse than it is now. This argument was repeated again and again during the following decades. After having lost more than one million of their countrymen, having had more than 6,000 of their monasteries destroyed and their thousand-year old culture erased, the Tibetans can certainly question the validity of this contention!

Would it have been worse if India had supported Tibet the way she came out in support of other colonized nations?

About the Tibetan Appeal to the UN, Nehru finally decided to do as little as possible:

"We may say that whatever might have been acknowledged in the past about China's sovereignty or suzerainty, recent events have deprived China of the right to claim that. There may be some moral basis for this argument. *But it will not take us or Tibet very far. It will only hasten the downfall of Tibet.*"[26]

---

[25]However it was historically incorrect to assume that India had expansionist tendencies like China.
[26]Emphasis added by author.

The facts showed that Tibet was an independent nation, it was clear that China, as the aggressor, was in the wrong and that it was India's moral duty to defend this position, but under the pretext that it would not 'take us very far', the moral stand was dropped. The conclusion was clear: "Therefore, it will be better not to discuss Tibet's appeal in the UN."

Reply to the Debate

A few days later, Nehru spoke in the Parliament and gave what was a typically Nehruvian speech. After a vague and moralistic lecture on a totally unrelated subject, he finally came to the topic of the debate. Were these unrelated words a tactic to show himself as a humanist? Here are some of his pompous words:

> People have become more brutal in thought, speech and action. All the graciousness and gentleness of life seems to have ebbed away. The human values seem to have suffered considerably. Of course, plenty of human values still remain. ...We are being coarsened and vulgarised all over the world because of many things, but chiefly because of violence and the succession of wars. If this process continues, I wonder whether anything of value in life will remain for sensitive individuals.[27]

But this can be viewed as merely demagogical rhetoric aimed at cooling down the opposition and the general public who had been very upset by the entry of the Chinese troops in Tibet.

The fact remains that ten months before the Chinese troops entered Lhasa, Nehru had already accepted that Tibet could not be saved and that what was formerly the Indo-Tibetan border had already become the Indo-Chinese border.

A year later, the Tibetans would use the same argument as Nehru: "Chinese should not be contradicted otherwise they may become more upset and our position would become worse." It then resulted in the 17-Point Agreement signed in May 1951.

Nehru did not realize that though it is good for a nation to speak about principles, if these principles are not followed up by actions, the nation becomes merely a Paper Tiger.

[27]Sen, op. cit., p. 118.

Conclusion

To conclude and to be fair we have to give back to Nehru what belongs to Nehru. After 1959, when the Tibetan refugees started pouring into India following the flight of the Dalai Lama, Nehru did his best to provide rehabilitation and education for all the Tibetans.

We were privileged in the course of our research to meet three persons who met Nehru during the last month of his life, in 1964. All three reported that Nehru was a broken and sad man. Dapon Jampa Kalden, who was responsible for the Special Frontier Forces[28] in 1964, told us that one month before he passed away, when Jawaharlal Nehru visited Chakrata, the headquarters of the Tibetan Force in Uttar Pradesh, Nehru admitted that he had committed a mistake and that he had let down Tibet. "I have been betrayed by a friend," he told the Tibetan troops.

Rinchen Dolma Taring, the aristocratic Tibetan lady who started one of the first Tibetan refugee schools in India, also met Nehru just before he passed away. Invited by Indira Gandhi who was to visit her school in Mussoorie, she travelled on the plane which took the Prime Minister to Dehra Dun. She remembered that "Mr. Nehru was very sad and worried [before he passed away] because he felt that he had done a mistake. Some people said he died of that," she added: "it was the last week before he passed away, he was a very sad man."

The Dalai Lama told us that he had the last 'official' meeting with Nehru in May 1964. He remembered that "after he got the stroke, I had a last meeting, I was later told that it was the last meeting of any other persons. At that last meeting, he had to keep his hands on the armrest, because he was shaking. Mentally he seemed fine. I think he realized that he had made a mistake of trusting the Chinese too much. But there were no signs of regret."

The Dalai Lama always full of compassion added that "it was quite obvious, quite clear, it was quite wrong [what Nehru did]. Yet that wrong thing happened due to many factors, so it was something quite unavoidable. It happened."[29]

[28]The Tibetan Commandos working under the Cabinet Secretariat.
[29]Interview with the Dalai Lama, March 1997.

26

The Avalanche

It is on the Roof of the World that our friendship with China will flourish or flounder.

Acharya Kripalani

A geologist thus described the emergence of Tibet:

"This area, formed about 200 million years ago, was a site of a calm and regular sedimentation...It used to be a placid shore hemmed by a large continental shelf where great reptiles frolicked in the shallow waters. There were no erupting volcanoes or devastating earthquake. Peaceful rivers deposited their mud in the vast deltas."[1]

From these earliest days of placidity and peace until the beginning of this century, Tibet had gone through a tumultuous history, both geological and human. However, one can assert correctly that from the time the Thirteenth Dalai Lama returned to Tibet in 1912 until the Fateful Year, Tibet experienced one of the most harmonious phases of its history.

It is only after 1950 that Tibet has suffered sheer hell. Tibetans often explain away their suffering in philosophical terms and use the concept of 'Karma'; nevertheless, hell is hell, karmic or otherwise.

Nobody in Tibet with the possible exception of a very few, such as the Thirteenth Dalai Lama, Tsarong or a couple of young Tibetan reformers such as Gedun Choepell foresaw the coming avalanche. The Roof of the World lived a peaceful and independent life, oblivious of world events, similar perhaps to that of the days of the Tethys Sea.

In the course of our research one Tibetan Lama told us: "We had a good life, perhaps a too good life and we did not see anything coming."

[1] Paul Taponnier, *Indo-Asian Collision Created Tibet* (New Delhi: Tibetan Review, April 1987).

This Shangri-la was another world, a world of picnics and brocades, a world of great harmony despite the difference in living standards between different sections of the society. The monasteries still believed that it would be enough to increase the number and intensity of their daily prayers to avert the looming crisis.

We also remember what an Indian Army General, who went on a secret mission to Tibet in 1949, told us how shocked he was to see ordinary people living in poverty while high Lamas or aristocrats lived such a wealthy life. He could hardly believe his eyes each time he saw people prostrating in the dust when some officials passed by. But what surprised him even more was the fact that these poor people were so joyful and smiling. There was no envy in them; they were happy where they were and with what they had.

The Dalai Lama explained[2] the traditional belief of 'Luck.' He says that it can be seen shining on someone's forehead:

> Somehow, the shining of our forehead had vanished at one point. [Earlier] there was some kind of ray or shine which means a 'force of good karma' or 'luck' (which had now disappeared). Somehow, it was not there anymore [in the fifties].
>
> ...at the time India became independent in 1947 or even before, something went wrong, Even from the purely spiritual field, many believed that in 1920's or 1930's if some puja had been done in time, this tragic thing would not have come. In the world politics also, if the Tibetan Government had continuously sent Tibetan students from the first batch amongst our civil servants then, at least a few hundreds would have been speaking English and naturally they would have been able to deal with foreigners. It was important to safeguard Tibetan independence and the Tibetan rights. I think that for the last forty years from a hopeless situation we regained some footing.
>
> [*Showing his forehead and laughing*] Some shining is coming again on the Dalai Lama's head, little, little with the help of the [Tibetan] people.

---

[2]Interview with the Dalai Lama.

When the Shining Goes

In December 1950, Tsepon Shakabpa, Tibet's Chief Negotiator in Delhi was recalled to Chumbi Valley to discuss the situation with the Kashag.

It was decided to send a delegation to Beijing to negotiate with the Chinese. One after the other all doors for help had closed (Western support, Indian mediation, appeal to the UN, etc.).

In February 1951, a fifteen-man delegation left for China via Chamdo to pick up Ngabo Ngawang Jigme, who had just been released after a short period of indoctrination. He was now Vice-Chairman of the 'Chamdo Liberation Committee'.

Another group led by Zasag Khemey Sonam Wangdi, joined them later in Beijing. The 'negotiations' with the Chinese leaders began on April 29.

Though the Indian Government had initially advised the Tibetans to negotiate with the Chinese in Beijing, they later warned them that with the military conquest of Tibet in progress, it would be difficult for them not to be forced to sign an unwanted agreement.

The Dalai Lama did not give his Representatives any plenipotentiary powers. They were asked to refer any important decision back to the Kashag in the Chumbi Valley.

In Beijing there were no negotiations. Soon after they reached, the Tibetans were presented by the Chinese with a draft agreement which was not acceptable to them[3]. After several days of debate, each party sticking to its stand, the Tibetan delegation finally rejected the draft proposal. To 'unlock' the situation the leader of the Chinese delegation introduced an 'amended' draft which was in fact more or less the same as the previous one. This time the Chinese made it clear to the Tibetan delegation that they had no choice but to sign it.

In the words of the Dalai Lama, "It was not until they returned to Lhasa, long afterwards, that we heard exactly what had happened to them."[4]

The Dalai Lama added:

This was presented as an ultimatum, our delegates were

[3]We owe most of our information on the 'negotiations' in Beijing to late P.T. Takhla, brother-in-law of the Dalai Lama and translator for the delegation (who unfortunately passed away when this manuscript was being completed) and Mr Rinchen Sadutshang, the English translator.

[4]The Dalai Lama, *My Land and my People* (New York: Potala, 1977), p. 87-88.

not allowed to make any alterations or suggestions. They were insulted and abused and threatened with personal violence, and with further military action against the people of Tibet, and they were not allowed to refer to me or my government for further instructions.

This draft agreement was based on the assumption that Tibet was part of China. That was simply untrue, and it could not possibly have been accepted by our delegation without reference to me and my government, except under duress. But Ngabo had been a prisoner of the Chinese for a long time, and other delegates were also virtual prisoners. At last, isolated from any advice, they did yield to compulsion and signed the document. They still refused to affix the seals which were needed to validate. But the Chinese forged duplicate Tibetan seals in Peking, and forced our delegation to seal the document with them.

Neither I nor my government were told that an agreement had been signed. We first came to know of it from a broadcast which Ngabo made on Peking Radio. It was a terrible shock when we heard the terms of it.[5]

In signing this 'Agreement on Measures for the Peaceful Liberation of Tibet' known as the '17-Point Agreement', Tibet lost her two-thousand-years old independence.

The preamble stated: "The Tibetan nationality is one of the nationalities with a long history within the boundaries of China, and like many other nationalities, it has done glorious duty in the course of the creation and development of the Great Motherland."

Then India and the Western powers were targeted —.the Agreement said that the People Liberation Army entered Tibet.

...in order that influences of aggressive imperialist forces in Tibet might be successfully eliminated, the unification of the territory and the sovereignty of the Chinese People's Republic (CPR) accomplished, and national defence safeguarded; in order that the Tibetan nationality and people might be freed and return to the big family of the PCR.[6]

[5]Ibid.

[6]Text of the 17-Point Agreement is available in many publications, one of them being Richardson, op. cit., p. 290.

The preamble repeats twice that the Tibetan delegation had full powers to negotiate, but we have seen from the Dalai Lama's quote that this is not correct. The delegation was supposed to refer back to the Kashag and the Dalai Lama for further orders and they never did so.

One sometimes wonders if the Chinese themselves really believed in imperialist influences in Tibet, but repeating the argument again and again, it gained the strength of a mantra and mere allegations became reality. It certainly had an effect on the Indian Government and in particular on Pannikar, who would soon repeat it himself: "I do not think that there is anything wrong in the troops of Red China moving about in their own country."

The Agreement further authorized the entry of Chinese forces into Tibet and empowered the Chinese Central Government to handle the external affairs and the defence of Tibet. The Tibetan Army was also to be integrated in the Chinese forces and a Committee was appointed in Lhasa to implement the Agreement.

One should note that no mention was made of India, even though many parts of the Agreement contradict certain articles of the Simla Convention which was still in force at that time.

After hearing the news of signing of the Agreement, the Dalai Lama telegraphed his delegation in Beijing that the agreement was not acceptable. Nevertheless the Agreement itself was not immediately repudiated, as the Dalai Lama wanted to obtain a full first-hand report of the delegates. Unfortunately for Tibet, when the report finally came, it was too late; the Chinese had already started to implement it.

It was only after crossing the Indian border to take refuge in India in April 1959 that the Dalai Lama was free to repudiate the 17-Point Agreement.

But in point of fact, when Tibet lost control over its defence and foreign affairs in 1951, it lost its independence.

Did the Kashag know that under international law, what qualifies a state for an independent status is its ability to conduct a separate and independent foreign policy and to sign treaties on its own?

Michael van Walt van Praag, in his *The Status of Tibet*[7], argued that the Agreement was not legally valid because the Chinese used war to settle the Tibetan issue and under the General Treaty for

[7]van Praag, op. cit., p. 165.

Renunciation of War to which the Chinese government was also a signatory, no dispute should be settled 'except by pacific means.' Another point in international law was that an agreement, treaty or contract is valid only if both contracting parties sign by free and mutual consent, which was hardly the case for the 17-Point Agreement. However, the legal position did not change the physical situation in Tibet and the occupation by the PLA.

The Government of India did not react to the 'Agreement', even though it was in clear contradiction of the Simla Convention, in particular the dissolution of the Tibetan Army into the PLA and the establishment of the Army headquarters at Lhasa.

On June 11, three weeks after the Agreement was signed, Nehru admitted at a press conference:

> I do not know much more about it than you probably know. The story about an agreement being reached between the People's Government in China and the Tibetan authorities has reached us too. That is all; no further development has taken place to our knowledge. It is not proper for me to react to something which is not complete, which is not fully known.[8]

The Agreement meant an obvious loss of the autonomy which India had wanted to preserve for Tibet. It is at this point in time that the first Chinese incursion into Indian territory was reported.[9]

Western governments were quick to react: on June 6, 1951 Kenneth Younger, the spokesman of the British Government, commented that although the Agreement guaranteed Tibetan autonomy, he had grave doubts about the value of the guarantees. The British Government was convinced that India was bowing to 'communist blackmail'; however it decided to go along with the policy of the Government of India.

The United States government sent secret communications to the Chumbi valley and urged the Dalai Lama to repudiate the Agreement, to leave Tibet and take asylum in a 'friendly' country like the United States or Sri Lanka.

After considering the possibility of leaving Tibet and taking refuge in India, the Dalai Lama bowed to the advice of some of his ministers and to pressure from the great monasteries. On 17 August,

[8]SWJN, Series II, Volume 16 (1) p. 446. The Sino-Tibetan Agreement.
[9]Near Rima on the Indian side of the McMahon Line in Walong sector of NEFA.

after the visit of the Chinese General Chang in Chumbi Valley, the Dalai Lama finally decided to return to Lhasa in the hope of renegotiating the 17-Point Agreement.

India Begins Leaning Towards China

The main problem at that time was that India was much too preoccupied with more pressing and 'important' problems such as mediating in the Korean war. In the exchange of Notes with the Chinese government India had never insisted on her rights in Tibet, which she had inherited from the Simla Convention. Nor were these rights mentioned in her submission to the UN when the Tibetan issue came up for discussion.

In February 1951, on a resolution in the General Assembly of the United Nations India along with the Soviet Union voted against condemning China for its aggression in Korea. Later on in May, India refused to participate on a vote for an arms embargo on Korea and China. In September 1951, India refused to participate in the San Francisco Conference to sign the Japanese Peace Treaty, as it did not incorporate a clause for restoring Formosa to China.

For months and years to come India would champion the cause of China and try to promote the entry of China into the United Nations in every possible fora. In spite of friendship between Nehru and Chiang Kai-shek, India refused to recognize Nationalist China in order not to displease the Communists leaders.

Up to the time of 1962 attack on India, Nehru's Government tried to appease China in every possible way, in what was known as the Hindi-Chini Bhai-Bhai policy. Pannikar being the chief advisor to Nehru on Chinese matters took the lead in defending the Communists. The Communist revolution in China was, for him, part "of the great Asian Resurgence." 'Asian Solidarity' and 'Sino-Indian friendship' would soon become the two most popular slogans for many Indian politicians. The 'cultural exchanges' between two 'friends' became very fashionable.

It is said that one of the Indian leaders of such a delegation remarked that he "felt like kneeling down, kissing the Chinese earth and like giant Antaeus, gaining faith and strength from common Mother."[10]

[10]R.K. Karanjia, *China Stands Up, and Wolves of the Wild West* (Bombay: People's Publishing House, 1952), p. 76.

Some delegates described Kuomintang China as "an inferno more horrible and hellish than anything conceived in the nightmares of Dante and Milton", but Communist China is a land of "super heroes and heroines, steadily and sturdily marching towards a planned goal of scientific perfection".[11]

The Chinese had planned their campaign with scientific perfection. After having forced the 17-Point Agreement on the Tibetan government, they consolidated their military position in Tibet. The next step was to lull the Indian government to sleep by a well-orchestrated propaganda on the brotherhood of the two Asian giants.

On September 9, 1951, several thousand Communist troops entered Lhasa under the command of General Wang Chi-Mei. They were followed during the next months by 20,000 PLA troops who started occupying strategic points on the Tibetan Plateau. For the first time in Tibet, troops used motor-vehicles and were air-lifted to reach their destinations.

The planned strategy of the Chinese was clear: now that the matter had been 'legalized' and since there had been no objection from the Government of India, the supremacy of the PLA had to be established on the ground.

The Strategic Roads

Very important construction work began immediately. Priority was given to motorable roads: the China-Lhasa via Nagchuka and the western Tibet road which would later become the Tibet-Xinjiang Highway. The first surveys were done at the end of 1951 and construction began in 1952.

By 1955, the road was already cutting through Indian territory. Air-strips were also laid in many strategic places.

An interesting account about how the Indian army already knew in 1955 that the Chinese were building a road across Indian territory, has recently been published in the UK.[12] In 1955, Wignall, a British mountaineer went on an expedition inside Tibet with the knowledge

---

[11]Quoted, by P.C .Chakravarti, *India-China Relations*, (Calcutta: Firma Mukhopadhyay, 1961), p. 51. From *The Hindustan Times* dated 10 November, 1961.

[12]Sidney Wignall, *Spy on the Roof of the World* (Edinburgh: Canongate, 1997).

of Indian Military Intelligence. The Indian Army Chief, General K.S. Thimayya seriously suspected that the Chinese were building a road on Indian territory. Wignall was asked to get proof of it.

He was eventually caught by the Chinese Liberation Army, interrogated and kept as prisoner for several weeks. He was later released in the midst of winter in a high altitude pass. The Chinese thought he would never survive the blizzard or find his way back to India. After an incredible journey, he managed to reach India and was able to report about the road to the army authorities who, in turn, informed the Prime Minister and Krishna Menon, the Defence Minister.

The politicians chose not to believe him. He was later told by his army contact:

> Our illustrious Prime Minister Nehru, who is so busy on the world stage telling the rest of mankind how to live, has too little time to attend to the security of his own country. Your material was shown to Nehru by one of our senior officers, who plugged hard. He was criticised by Krishna Menon in Nehru's presence for 'lapping up American CIA agent-provocateur propaganda.' Menon has completely suppressed your information.
>
> 'So it was all for nothing?' I [Wignall] asked. 'Perhaps not,' Singh[13] responded. 'We will keep working away at Nehru. Some day he must see the light, and realise the threat communist Chinese occupation of Tibet poses for India.[14]

The matter would become public and be discussed in the Lok Sabha only after three years although the Government of India has never acknowledged that it had information about the Aksai Chin road as early as 1954-55.

The same Indian army chief was forced to retire in 1961, one year before the Chinese attacked India. In his valedictory address to the Indian Army Officer Corps, he is supposed to have said: "I hope that I am not leaving you as cannon fodder for the Chinese communists."

[13]Wignall's army contact.
[14]Wignall, op. cit., p. 250.

The Occupying Forces

But let us go back to Tibet.

The influx of fresh troops brought the first serious problem in the new co-habitation regime and it became the first test: how would the Chinese implement the 17-Point Agreement?

The military command started requesting the Tibetan government for food supplies for its troops and land for its army camp. Tibet had for centuries had a sustainable development and been self-sufficient in food and starvation was unheard of. The arrival of the PLA provoked a breakdown of the Tibetan economy and it became very difficult for the Tibetan Government to deal with the problem. An interesting side-effect of the invasion was that China had to request food from India.

Earlier Lukhangwa, the courageous Tibetan Prime Minister had tried to protest to the Chinese authorities by saying that it was unfair to put such a burden on the poor Tibetan people and that the troops around Lhasa were not necessary. He tried to point out that the actions of the Chinese military command were against the 17-Point Agreement. But when a petition was sent to the Chinese General Chang he immediately asked the Dalai Lama to remove Lukhangwa who "was obstructing their welfare program".

The Dalai Lama was told by General Chang Chin-wu that the Tibetans had signed an agreement which mentioned that "Chinese forces should be stationed in Tibet, and we were therefore obliged to provide them with accommodation and supplies." He added that the Chinese "...had only come to help Tibet ... to protect her against imperialist domination and that they would go back to China.... when you can stand on your feet, we will not stay here even if you ask us to."[15]

The Dalai Lama had no alternative but to dismiss Lukhangwa:

> ... to oppose and anger the Chinese authorities could only lead us further along the vicious circle of repression and popular resentment ...Our only hope was to persuade the Chinese peaceably to fulfil the promises they had made in their agreement. Non-violence was the only course which might win us back a degree of freedom in the end, perhaps after years of patience. That

[15]The Dalai Lama, *My Land*, op. cit., p. 92.

meant co-operation whenever it was possible, and
passive resistance whenever it was not.[16]

It was the first breach of the Agreement in which it was stipulated
that the Chinese would maintain the existing political system and
the status and powers of the Dalai Lama. Removing the Prime
Minister as an intermediary between the Dalai Lama and the Cabinet
resulted in the young Dalai Lama having to deal directly with the
Cabinet and the Chinese thereafter.

The last resistance had fallen, but could it have been otherwise?
Non-violence and passive resistance had no meaning for the Chinese
invaders.

In the meantime and despite the newly found 'Eternal
Friendship' between India and China, China started putting other
kinds of pressure on India. India had a Consulate General in Kashgar
in Eastern Turkestan. Suddenly Eastern Turkestan (Sinkiang) was
declared a 'closed area' and India was forced to close down her
Consulate, thereby ending her trade with Central Asia.

In the early fifties, India still enjoyed some rights in Tibet; apart
from the privilege of its Mission in Lhasa, there were two Indian
Agents in Gyantse and in Yatung who were both entitled to an escort.
The Post and Telegraph Service and a chain of rest-houses were also
under the Indian Government's control.

Soon after the Chinese entered Lhasa, it was rumoured that the
Communists had asked for the withdrawal of Indian officials from
Tibet. However Richardson wrote, "it is improbable that the Chinese
made any such suggestion. They still found it convenient to have
communications and a supply route available to them from India
and it would have been imprudent to jeopardise Indian goodwill at
that stage. It suited their book to preserve official silence and leave
it to the Indian Government to make the overtures."[17]

In Tibet, the Indian government was finding it more and more
difficult to keep the advantages they had inherited from the British
and the Simla Convention. The visitors and traders from India were
harassed and put to hardship. The Indian government was pressed
to withdraw its Political Representative in Lhasa and in September
1952, the Indian Representative was re-designated as a Consul-
General under the Indian Embassy in Beijing.

[16]The Dalai Lama, My Land, op. cit., p. 97.
[17]Richardson, op cit., p. 196.

Pannikar was proud that "the main issue of our representation at Lhasa was satisfactorily settled".[18] He said that Zhou Enlai "suggested that the political agency at Lhasa, an office of dubious legality, should be regularized by its transformation into an Indian Consulate-General in exchange for a similar Chinese office in Bombay." In this clever move, the Chinese gained on both fronts: they got a foothold in Bombay and the Mission in Lhasa was downgraded to a Consulate-General.

Pannikar said at the time of his departure from Beijing that: "there was no outstanding issue between us and the Chinese".[19]

This was not true as the border issue had been avoided during bilateral talks and the first intrusions in the Indian territory had already started.

Richardson saw this development differently: "'That decision adroitly transformed the temporary mission at Lhasa into a regular consular post. But it was a practical dimension of the fact that Tibet had ceased to be independent and it left unresolved the fate of the special rights acquired when Tibet had been in a position to make treaties with foreign powers and enjoyed by he British and Indian Governments for half a century."[20]

At that point in time the Government of India decided to renegotiate some of the arrangements it had with Tibet.

When Panchsheel Would Shine Over the Universe like a Sun

Though Pannikar had boasted that there were no outstanding issues, Delhi took the initiative and proposed negotiations in Beijing to resolve certain issues such as the trans-border trade. In December 1953, talks began; they were expected to last six weeks, but went on for six months. In the Indian Parliament after many enquiries by anxious members, the Government had to admit that the Chinese were insisting on matching trade agency for trade agency. India had three trade agencies in Tibet. China now wanted three trade agencies in India in addition to her embassy in New Delhi and consulates in Calcutta and Bombay. The suggested new locations for Chinese trade agencies were Almora and Simla.

This was not acceptable to the Indian government and finally it was decided to have an extra Chinese trade agency in Delhi. On 29

[18]Pannikar, op. cit., p. 175.
[19]Ibid.
[20]Richardson, op. cit., p. 196.

April 1954, the representatives of the two countries signed the 'Agreement on Trade and Intercourse between the Tibet region of China and India'.[21] It was described by Acharya Kripalani as an agreement 'born in sin'.[22]

When the Panchsheel Agreement was signed it was considered by many as Nehru's final capitulation to China. It marked the opening of the doors of North India to the Chinese. But Nehru considered it the best thing he had ever done.

The 'friendship' or the 'foolishness' reached such a height that on October 20, 1954 it was announced that although China had enough rice, India had decided to supply rice to the PLA stationed in Tibet. It was a first in military annals that the government of a country supplied food to the enemy's troops. But of course, China was not an enemy.

As quoted in an article in *The Hindu*:

> Mr. Kung Yuan, leader of the Chinese trade delegation announced the conclusion of another agreement for the purchase of 1,500 tons of Indian rice by China for supply to Tibet and that the negotiations were in progress in regard to the purchase of one other 1,000 tons.
>
> ...Rice which China would buy was intended exclusively for Tibet and only difficulties of transport has necessitated this purchase by China.[23]

India was supplying rice to the Chinese troops, engaged in building a road on Indian territory![24]

[21]Known as the Panchsheel Agreement; couched in Buddhistic terms, the preamble of the Agreement stated the five principles of pacific co-existence.

[22]'Born in sin' said Acharya Kripalani, 'Born in Sind?' jokingly retorted the Indian Prime Minister.

[23]*The Hindu*, Madras, 21 October, 1950.

[24]In his book on Aksai Chin, John Lall recalled: "But suddenly all was sweetness and light. The reason became apparent when a request was made for shipment of Chinese rice through India and Sikkim to their troops in Tibet. This could, and indeed should, have been made the occasion for a settlement of the major problems with China as a prelude to the altogether unprecedented help requested from the Government of India It simply did not occur to anyone in Delhi, and which caution as I advised was brushed aside. Released from anxiety on accounts of supplies, the Chinese and local Tibetan labour were able to press ahead with the vitally important task of creating a network of communications to defend frontiers of China with India." Lall, op. cit., pp. 235-36.

The same month the Indian Prime Minister went to Peking to celebrate the new 'friendship'. One newspaper wrote: "The meeting of Nehru and Mao may change history." During the banquet Nehru "spoke in Hindustani was applauded at the end of each sentence," though nobody understood Hindustani.

It was the height of the friendship. During the same visit Nehru had an occasion to meet for the first time the young Dalai Lama. Though the press reported that "the Dalai Lama, temporal leader of Tibet, saw and spoke with Mr. Nehru for the first time yesterday and immediately commented that he was surprised that the 65-year old Indian Prime Minister looks so young", the Dalai Lama later told us that no words were exchanged:

> We had heard his name and also India as a country is very close to our mind, and also had personally heard about Nehru. When we heard that we will meet him, there was a bit of excitement.
>
> Pandit Nehru led by Zhou Enlai and many Chinese dignitaries were lining up when he reached the place where I was. Zhou Enlai said: 'This is the Dalai Lama.' Nehru remained motionless, no speech, not looking in the eyes.
>
> He just stands in front of me, without speech, without moving, motionlessly he remained like that. I was a bit embarrassed. I told through the Chinese interpreter: 'I have heard a lot about you, and today I am very happy to meet you'. Then, Nehru did not give a particular response, he seemed happy, then he went to the next person. That was my first experience [with him].
>
> I thought and felt that from Nehru's side, there will be no support for Tibet and no support for the Dalai Lama. During a short moment, many things that occurred from 1949 till 1954 [passed] in his mind, like lightning.[25]

Tail End of the Avalanche

Events continued to flow in the same direction during the following years. After his long visit to China in 1954, the Dalai Lama was happy to receive an invitation to visit 'Aryabhumi' at the end of 1956. The celebration of the 2,500[th] birth anniversary of the Buddha was a good occasion to make a pilgrimage and meet the Indian leaders.

[25]Interview with the Dalai Lama.

During the few months of his stay, the young Tibetan leader (who was accompanied by the Panchen Lama) had many occasions to discuss the Tibetan issue with Nehru who advised him to return to Tibet.

Zhou Enlai, anxious perhaps that the Dalai Lama could strike a deal with Nehru, was often seen in Delhi during these months.

He had several meetings with the Dalai Lama who recalled one in the Chinese embassy in Delhi: "I was having a frank discussion with Chou [Zhou]. He told me that the situation in Tibet had deteriorated, indicating that the Chinese authorities were ready to use force to crush any popular uprising."[26]

The Dalai Lama 'bluntly' replied that the Chinese were "forcing unwanted reforms, despite explicit reassurances that they would do no such thing". The Dalai Lama said that the clever Foreign Minister used his charm and promised that the words of Chairman Mao who had announced that "no reform should be introduced in Tibet for at least the next six years" would be implemented. Generously, he even added that it could be postponed for "fifty years, if necessary".

The Dalai Lama was not convinced, especially when Zhou Enlai asked him not to go to Kalimpong where he was scheduled to give Buddhist teachings to the local population.

When the Dalai Lama next met Nehru, the Prime Minister made it clear that he had to return to Tibet and work with the Chinese on the basis of the 17-Point Agreement. "There is no alternative," said Nehru, "India could be of no assistance to Tibet". He even added that he should obey Zhou and return to Tibet without stopping in Kalimpong. However, after the Dalai Lama had explained the purpose of the stop, he suddenly changed his mind and said,: "India is a free country after all. You would not be breaking any of her laws." And eventually Nehru made all the arrangements for the Dalai Lama's visit to Kalimpong.

After the Dalai Lama's return nothing really changed in Tibet; on the contrary the pressure increased, especially due to the revolt of the Khampas. All the problems became more acute.

The end of the avalanche came when the Dalai Lama had to flee Tibet after an uprising of the entire population of Lhasa in March 1959. This part of the story has been well documented and described,

[26]The Dalai Lama, *Freedom*, op. cit., p. 133.

we need not insist on it. Over the next forty years, more than 100,000 refugees would be forced to live in exile in India, Nepal or in the West.

The Blow

The last straw for India—and the first one to open Nehru's eyes—was China's invasion of India in October-November 1962. The blow has been well described by many good authors[27], and we shall not go into the details of the military operations. However a few points should be mentioned.

Some have argued that the forward policy of the Government of India in 1962 provoked the Chinese attack on the Indian border, but this argument cannot withstand closer scrutiny. The Chinese leadership had decided many years earlier 'to teach India a lesson' for giving refuge to the Dalai Lama and his people. The fact that the 1962 Chinese border attack occurred at the same place where the Dalai Lama had crossed over to India was an indication that shows that the two were directly related. The Chinese are always attached to this sort of details.

Moreover it took months for the PLA to get ready for the onslaught on the McMahon Line while the Forward Policy of Krishna Menon began in September 1962 only.

Another aspect which has not been well studied is that Mao was facing a lot of internal problems after the three or four years of implementation of the Great Leap Forward during which more than thirty millions of Chinese are said to have been starved to death by the Chairman's agricultural policies. There were a lot of questioning within the Party and Mao was under attack by a new generation of leaders such a Liu Shaoqi and Deng Xiaoping. The war with India was certainly an 'adventure' which distracted the cadres of the Party from challenging Mao's leadership.[28] We should not forget that Lin Biao, his protégé at that time was also the Defence Minister and nothing serves to divert the people's attention as well as a short war.

---

[27]One of the remarkable book is by Brig. J.P. Dalvi, *The Himalayan Blunder* (Delhi: Hind Pocket Books, 1964); another interesting one from the point of view of military operations is by Maj. Gen. D.K. Palit, *War in High Himalaya* (London: Lancer International, 1991); see also by Maj. Gen. K.K. Tewari, *A Soldier's Voyage to Self Discovery* (Auroville: Tewari, 1992).

[28]It came two years later and Mao responded by initiating the Great Proletarian Cultural Revolution which left more than 10 millions of Chinese dead.

Mao also knew that India was not prepared and that at the same time China could not have sustained a long war with the coming winter and the lines of supply passing through an 'occupied' territory. The short 'blow' was definitively the best strategic and political solution for Mao and it was perfected executed by his faithful lieutenants.

After the war, Nehru was physically and psychological a broken man when he realized that he had been taken for a ride by Mao, the strategist Chairman of the People's Republic of China and Zhou, his Machiavellian Premier.

The Government of India's policy towards China changed after Nehru's death. Lal Bahadur Shastri the new Prime Minister decided to take a tougher stand on Tibet and his government voted in favour of the Resolution for Self-determination of Tibet in the UN in 1965.

The Indian Representative to the UN declared:

> The naked truth — which all of us must face — is that the Chinese Government is determined to obliterate the Tibetan people, but surely no people can remain for long suppressed. I have faith in the world community. I believe it will be able to help restore the Tibetans all the freedom which we have enshrined, with such dedication, in the Universal Declaration of Human Rights.
>
> For our part, we assure the United Nation that — as In the past — we shall continue to give all facilities to the Tibetan refugees, and do our best to alleviate their sufferings and hardships. The Dalai Lama has been living in India for some years now, and is carrying on his religious humanitarian activities without any restriction from us. We shall continue to give the Dalai Lama and his simple and peace loving people these facilities and all our hospitality.
>
> It is for these reasons that we support, fully and wholeheartedly, the cause of the people of Tibet. Our hearts go out to them in their miserable plight and the terrible suppression that they are suffering at the hands of the Government of the People's Republic of China.
>
> My delegation will, therefore, vote in Favour of the draft resolution.[29]

---

[29]*Indian Leaders on Tibet*, op. cit., p. 84.

The Dalai Lama told us that one day in 1965, Shakabpa[30] came down to South India[31] to meet him. He was very excited, he had just had a meeting with Shastri who told him that India had decided to recognize the Tibetan Government-in-exile after his return from Tashkent. Unfortunately for the Tibetans and perhaps for India, Shastri never returned from Tashkent.[32]

After the shock treatment of 1962, it took many years before India could sit with China at the negotiating table.

In the beginning of the seventies, the next Indian Prime Minister, Indira Gandhi took the initiative but China was still in the throes of turmoil following the Great Proletarian Revolution and Mao Zedong was still struggling with his heir-designate Marshal Lin Biao who would soon die mysteriously in an air crash while fleeing out of China. Soon afterwards President Nixon would pay his historic visit to Beijing and a new era of détente would be opened between the United States and China. India had no place in the new scheme. Mao had no respect for a weak India.

In 1978, two years after Mao's and Zhou's deaths, Deng replaced the Great Helmsman, but the scene was not very different.

In 1979, the Janata Party government which had just taken over in India tried again for an opening with Communist China by sending Vajpayee, its Foreign Minister to Beijing. It is still not clear why the Chinese leaders chose to time the invasion of Vietnam to coincide with Vajpayee's visit. Whatever might have been their reasons, Prime Minister Morarji Desai immediately recalled his Minister and negotiations were broken off. Speaking of Narasimha Rao's visit to China in 1991, Vajpayee said:

> Myself I went to China in 1979, the talks were good, but during that time they [the Chinese] attacked Vietnam and that spoiled the whole trip. This time there was nothing of the sort, I am happy about it. But how many minutes this leader's hand remained in that leader's hand, this cannot be the touchstone of the success of a foreign tour.... Whether the Prime Ministers, the

[30]Shakabpa was then the Tibetan Representative in Delhi.

[31]During the 1965 Indo-Pakistani war the Dalai Lama had been sent by the Government of India to South India 'to avoid the shelling'.

[32]He had gone to Tashkent for a conference arranged by the Soviet Union with the President of Pakistan to try to find a 'peaceful' solution to the Indo-Pakistani war of 1965.

Presidents of two countries address each other by their
first names, cannot be a criteria of the fruitfulness of the
relations. As if I would say: Narasimha Rao, how are
you? And then Narasimha Rao would say: Atal, I am
all right. How are you?[33]
Indeed, it was not enough.

When Indira Gandhi returned to power in 1980, she was not
ready to take any new initiatives: perhaps she was too involved with
the internal politics of the Congress.

Another factor which was making the normalization of the
relations difficult was the close relationship between India and Soviet
Union, while China had become closer to Pakistan. China became
the main military supplier of Pakistan, more consistent than the US,
as well as a source of nuclear weapons technology and sophisticated
missiles.

In July 1986, the People's Liberation Army once more intruded
into Indian territory in Arunachal Pradesh. They tried to occupy the
Wangdung IB observation post which is used in summer as a yak
grazing hamlet. The Indian army this time without waiting for orders
from Delhi stood firm on the ground. As described by former Indian
Army Chief, General V.N. Sharma, "We were on our territory and
any withdrawal orders by government or army headquarters would
be considered illegal as the army was tasked to defend India's
border." And the former Chief added: "It was with renewed
confidence that Rajiv Gandhi could plan his visit to China."[34]

It was the first time that India took a strong stand and showed
the Chinese that they could not bluff their way through into Indian
territory.

It was perhaps a turning point because until then the Chinese
leaders had always considered India as a weak nation.

Finally in 1988 Rajiv Gandhi became the first Indian Prime
Minister to visit China since his grandfather, Jawaharlal Nehru who
had gone to Beijing in October 1954, at the peak of the Hindi-Chini
Bhai- Bhai relationship. Though Rajiv once again conceded that Tibet
was considered by India as an autonomous region of China, his visit

[33]I am grateful to my colleague Christine for the English translation of the
beautiful speeches on Tibet delivered by Atal Bihari Vajpayee in the Lok Sabha
between 1959 and 1991.
[34]General V.N. Sharma, *India's Defence Forces: Building the Sinews of a Nation*
(New Delhi: USI National Security Papers, 1994), p. 20.

had the merit of reopening the dialogue at the highest level after decades of mistrust and hatred.

Later on and in spite of a number of high level rounds of talks initiated during that visit, the question of the status of Tibet could not be resolved. Though India still acknowledges Tibet as an autonomous region of China and has not succumbed to Chinese pressures to take action against the Dalai Lama and his followers, very little has been done to remove the stumbling block.

It would have been too damaging for the image of India as 'a liberal democracy committed to free expression' if India were to fully accept the Chinese take-over of Tibet. Furthermore India would have lost the last card in her hand.

As analysed by Surjit Mansingh, a China watcher at the Nehru Memorial Museum and Library:

> Tibet will always be of vital importance for India because of its location, and because of its historical role in creating the Himalayan border. Tibet may well take on greater international importance because of the unpredictable dynamics of change in Central Asia as a whole as well as the still growing prestige of the Dalai Lama. It would be well for the Indian Government to formulate a long range policy taking into account contingent factors.[35]

Indeed the major problem or irritant if seen from the Chinese angle remains Tibet.

The world situation is changing fast. Were Mao Zedong to come out of his mausoleum, he would not recognise the China of today. Where has the beacon of socialism gone? Jiang Zemin or Zhu Rongji are what the Red Guards would have called 'capitalist-roaders'.

Is there a way to come out of the impasse reached after the round after round of talks between India and China?

Lord Buddha taught that everything is impermanent and the wheel of time turns faster and faster. Is it not time for all governments to look into the future?

---

[35]Surjit Mansingh, *An Overview of Indo-China Relations: From Where to Where?* (New Delhi: The Indian Defence Review, 1992), p. 70.

27

A Possible Solution

The solution — whatever it may be — will need boldness and courage from all the concerned parties. Perhaps it may lie in a proposal the Dalai Lama made one year before Rajiv Gandhi's visit to China. It is known as the Five Point Peace Plan.

On September 21, 1987, the Dalai Lama addressed the members of the United States Congress in Washington D.C. and presented his *Five Points Peace Plan for Tibet*. The plan was well received all over the world and many countries saw it as a very positive step towards the solution of the Tibetan problem and a chance for a more durable peace in Asia, but the Government of India kept quiet.

It has been rumoured that the Plan was shown to South Block, and the Foreign Ministry was not against its formulation. Nevertheless, during an interview, the Dalai Lama assured us that the Indian diplomats had nothing to do with the drafting of the Five Points, which are as follows:

1. Transformation of the whole of Tibet into a zone of peace.
2. Abandonment of China's population transfer policy which threatens the very existence of the Tibetans as a people.
3. Respect of the Tibetan people's fundamental rights and democratic freedoms.
4. Restoration and protection of Tibet's natural environment and abandonment of China's use of Tibet for the production of nuclear weapons and dumping of nuclear waste.
5. Commencement of earnest negotiations on the future status of Tibet and of relations between the Tibetans and Chinese.[1]

[1]Text in *Government Resolutions and International Documents on Tibet* (Dharamsala: Office of Information, 1989), p. 3.

The Dalai Lama's immediate motivation in proposing this peace plan was to be found in the second point: the 'new' invasion of Tibet by a 'vast sea of Chinese settlers'. Beijing had decided to out-number the Tibetan population by bringing in Han settlers: this was the method they had used in Manchuria, in Eastern Turkestan (Xinjiang) and Inner Mongolia.

But the point which interests us here is the first point of the Plan. The Dalai Lama said:

> We wish to approach in a reasonable and realistic way, in the spirit of frankness and conciliation and with a view to finding a solution that is in the long term interest of all: the Tibetans, the Chinese, and all people concerned.
>
> ... It is my sincere belief that if the concerned parties were to meet and discuss their future with an open mind and a sincere desire to find a satisfactory and just solution, a breakthrough could be achieved. We must all exert ourselves to be reasonable and wise, and to meet in a spirit of frankness and understanding.[2]

Definitively it would be in the interest of India to have a 'Zone of Peace or Ahimsa' in between her own territory and that of China. It seems to be the only solution if Nehru's great dream of eternal friendship between the two Asian giants, China and India, is to be achieved.

History has proven this point beyond doubt. Is it unreasonable to think that the Government of India could approach its Chinese counterpart with the request, "Let us sit together with the Dalai Lama's representatives and see how we could make of the Himalayas a model for the world"?

The process could include simultaneously or at a later stage the Himalayan states of Bhutan and Nepal. It would certainly be easier for the Chinese to accept such a proposal from India which, in spite of her differences (and one war with China) has always had a non-aggressive relation. India has no business interests to defend with China. India has never been a bully in her relationship with China and has never imposed an unequal treaty on China or on any other nation.

The technicalities and the time frame of the demilitarization of the Roof of the World could be discussed through tripartite

[2]Ibid., p. 7.

negotiations. China would certainly not be the loser: strategically, the terrain on the Tibetan high plateau naturally favours the Chinese. It is far easier and faster to rush men and weapons from Sichuan to the border in case of an emergency on the Tibetan side than from the plains of Assam on the Indian side. The difficulties in holding the lower ridges and the long supply lines must be taken into account. The development of good roads for the past forty years on the Tibetan side allows for quick supply for the nearby Sichuan province and there would be nothing to fear from India.

The other points (No. 2 to 4) of the Dalai Lama's plan could be discussed by the Tibetan and Chinese sides in due course through negotiations as soon as the first issue is settled and a time frame for its implementation is agreed upon.[3]

It is certainly in the long-term interests of Asia that the differences between India and China are amicably resolved and that the energies of these countries be directed towards eradicating poverty and bringing about a decent life and happiness to all.

In China's last Five Year Plan, President Jiang Zemin proposed that the main goal for the People's Republic of China should be the establishment of what he called 'a spiritual society'.

The creation of a zone of Ahimsa and Peace at the heart of the Himalayas would go a long way towards this goal. And at last the energies of India, China and Tibet could be turned towards the highest spiritual values preached by the Buddha more than 2,500 years ago and shared by so many Asian nations since that time.

In an interview the Dalai Lama said:

> I have dedicated the rest of my life to demilitarisation on a global level. As a first step, Tibet should be a zone of peace and completely demilitarised, so that in the future we can help not only China and India but also the world community. This is my vision and hope for the future.[4]

---

[3]It is also worth highlighting Point No. 4 about the environment which is of vital interest both to the Chinese and Indians. All the major rivers of Asia have their source on the high Tibetan plateau and it has now been demonstrated that the environment of Tibet has an influence on the pattern of floods in China and the seasonal monsoon in India. It was even officially accepted by the Chinese Prime Minister after the devastating floods of 1998 and logging has since been banned in many places of western and southern Tibet.

[4]Interview with the Dalai Lama, Auroville, December 1993.

Politically, the issue is more complicated and it will require more 'creativity' to be resolved. One of the main problems since the advent of the United Nations is that a nation has to be de facto independent or this nation cannot be recognized by the UN. Traditionally, there used to be so many other forms of relationships between nations. Without going back to the imperial age where the 'big insects' would always eat the 'small insects', a more creative collaboration could be found whereby a nation could keep its autonomy and its right of self-determination without being a fully independent nation. Some nations could choose to be guided and protected by other nations without being eaten by them.

A nation could have such an 'association' with one or more than one nation. One can take the example of Andorra, a principality with two Coprinceps: the French President and the Spanish Bishop of Urgell who provide protection to the tiny nation. At the same time Andorra is fully autonomous and governed by an elected Council.[5]

Similar solutions could be found for other nations such as Tibet which could have an association with China and India (and eventually Nepal), which would ensure the stability and the sustainability of the Tibetan nation which would be free to put again its energy to 'look inside'.

To conclude, we believe that no permanent and durable solution can be found if negotiations do not include India. The 'Tibetan issue' cannot be seen as a problem only between the People's Republic of China and the people of Tibet. It is a global problem influencing the stability of the whole Asian continent and therefore the future of Asia. It has to be remembered that the Simla Convention, a treaty which is still in force between India and Tibet, has pointed out that any negotiations with Tibet should involve all three parties, namely India, China and Tibet.

Tibet, during the last two thousand years of her history, has been geographically, spiritually, culturally, and often politically very close to India and to ignore this fact in global negotiations would hardly lead towards a permanent solution for Asia.

[5]Article 44 of the Andorran Constitution reads: "The Coprinceps are the symbol and guarantee of the permanence and continuity of Andorra as well as of its independence and the maintenance of the spirit of parity in the traditional balanced relation with the neighbouring States. They proclaim the consent of the Andorran State to honour its international obligations in accordance with the Constitution".

We should not forget, and it is the best proof of the above point, that when Tibet was passing through difficult periods in her history, particularly in 1910 and again in 1959, it was to India that Tibet turned for help and it was India which provided help and support.

In an interview the Dalai Lama related the following:

> I feel that Tibetan culture with its unique heritage — born of the effort of many human beings of good spirit, of its contacts with Chinese, Indian, Nepalese and Persian culture, and due to its natural environment — has developed some kind of energy which is useful, and very helpful, towards cultivating peace of mind and a joyful life. I feel that there is a potential for Tibet to help humanity, and particularly our Eastern neighbour, where millions of young Chinese have lost their spiritual values.[6]

This could be the preparation for a larger unity, the unity of the human race as envisaged by Sri Aurobindo:

> The unity of the human race can be achieved neither through uniformity nor through domination and subjection. A synthetic organisation of all nations, each one occupying its own place in accordance with its own genius and the role it has to play in the whole, can alone effect a comprehensive and progressive unification, which may have some chance of enduring. And if the synthesis is to be a living thing, the grouping should be done around a central idea as high and wide as possible, and in which all tendencies, even the most contradictory, would find their respective place.[7]

Today, like yesterday, the key to peace in Asia lies on the 'Roof of the World.'

"It is on the Roof of the World that our friendship with China will flourish or flounder," said Acharya Kripalani in 1950.

We must also keep in mind that the world is going through a 'whirlwind' of changes.

What may look improbable or impossible today, may be a reality tomorrow.

[6]Claude Arpi, Ed. *The Dalai Lama in Auroville* (Auroville: Pavilion of Tibetan Culture, 1994).

[7]The Mother, *On Education* (Pondicherry: Sri Aurobindo Ashram, 1978), p. 40.

Bibliography

Official Sources

Aitchison, C.U., *A Collection of Treaties Vol XIV* (New Delhi: Mittal Publications, 1983)

Bureau of H.H. the Dalai Lama, *Constitution of Tibet* (Delhi: Bureau,1963)

Bureau of Parliamentary Research, *India-China Border Problem* (New Delhi: Congress Party, 1960)

China Handbook Editorial Committee, *History* (Beijing: Foreign Language Press, 1982)

Chopra, Ed., *Collected Works of Sardar Vallabhbhai Patel* (Delhi: Konark Publishers, 12 Volumes)

Collective, *Indian Public on Tibet* (Dharamsala: Tibetan Youth Congress, 1997)

Dalai Lama, The, *Collected Statements, Interviews & Articles* (Dharamsala: DIIR 1986)

    Five Point Peace Plan (New York: 1987)

    Framework for Sino-Tibetan Negotiations (Strasbourg: 1988)

    Nobel Peace Prize Address (Oslo: 1989)

    Tibet, China and the World (Dharamsala: Narthang Publications, 1989)

DIIR, *Dharamsala and Beijing* (Dharamsala: 1994)

    International Resolutions and Recognitions on Tibet (Dharamsala: 1994)

    The Legal Status of Tibet (Dharamsala: 1989)

    Tibet, Under Chinese Communist Rule (Dharamsala: 1976)

    1959 Tibet Documents (Dharamsala: 1987)

Foreign Language Press, *The Sino-Indian Boundary Question* (Beijing: Foreign Language Press, 1962)

    The Boundary Question between China and Tibet: A Valuable Record (Beijing: 1960)

International Commission of Jurists, *Tibet and the Chinese People's Republic* (New Delhi: Sterling Publishers, 1966)

Kumar, Anand, *Tibet: a Source Book* (New Delhi: Radiant Publishers, 1995)

Ling Nai-Min, *Tibetan Sourcebook* (Hong Kong: Union Research Institute,1964)

Mao Zetung, *Selected Works of Mao Zetung, Vol 1 to 5* (Beijing: Foreign Language Press, 1975)

Ministry of External Affairs, *Notes, Memoranda and Letters Exchanged and Agreements signed by the Governments of India and China*, known as White Papers (New Delhi: Publications Division, 1954-61)

Ministry of Information & Broadcasting, *China Aggression in War and Peace* (New Delhi: Publication Divison, 1962)

China's Betrayal of India (New Delhi: Publication Division, 1962)

Nehru, Jawaharlal, *India's Foreign Policy* (New Delhi: Publication Division, 1961)

Letters to Chief Ministers (New Delhi: Oxford University Press, 1986)

Selected Works of Jawaharlal Nehru, Series II (New Delhi, Jawaharlal Nehru Memorial Fund, 22 Vols. already published)

Sen, Chanakya, *Tibet Disappears* (Bombay: Asia Publishing House, 1960)

Tibetan Youth Congress, *Political Treaties of Tibet: 821 to 1951* (Dharamsala: Tibetan Youth Congress, 1990)

Xinhua News Agency, *China's Foreign Relations: A Chronology of Events - 1949-1988* (Beijing: Foreign Language Press, 1989)

China's White Paper on Tibet (Beijing: Xinhua News Agency, 1992)

Newspapers and Journals

Beijing Review (Beijing)
China Reconstruct (now China Today) (Beijing)
China's Tibet (Beijing)
Journal of Royal Asiatic Society (Cambridge)
Mother India (Bombay)
The Hindu (Madras)
The Indian Defence Review (New Delhi)
The New York Times (New York)
The Statesman (Calcutta)
The Tibetan Review (New Delhi)
The Tibet Journal (Dharamsala)
The Tibet World News (Ottawa)
USI National Security Papers, USII (New Delhi)

Books

Abrol, Mridula, *British Relations with Frontier States (1863-1875)* (New Delhi: Chand & Co, 1974)

Andrugtsang, Gompo Tashi, *Four Rivers, Six Ranges* (Dharamsala: DIIR, 1973)

Aris, Michael & Aung San Suu Kyi, *Tibetan Studies in Honour of Hugh Richardson* (New Delhi: Vikas Publishers, 1980)

Aris, Michael, *Hidden Treasures and Secret Lives* (Simla: Indian Institute of Advanced Studies, 1988)

Avedon, John F., *Current Conditions and Prospects* (New York: The US Tibet Committee, 1987)

    In Exile from the Land of Snows (New York : Alfred A. Knoff, 1984)

Bandyopaddyaya, Jayantanuja, *The Making of India's Foreign Policy* (Delhi: Allied Publishers)

Banerjee, Lt. Col., D.K., *Sino-Indian Border Dispute* (Delhi: Intellectual Publishing House, 1985)

Barber, Noel, *The Flight of the Dalai Lama* (London: Hodder & Stoughton, 1960)

Barnett, Robert, *Resistance and Reform in Tibet* (London: Hurst & Co, 1994)

Bell, Sir Charles, *Portrait of a Dalai Lama* (London: Wisdom Publication, 1987)

    Religion of Tibet (Delhi: Motilal Banarsidass, 1994)

    The People of Tibet (Delhi: Motilal Banarsidass, 1994)

    Tibet, Past and Present (Delhi: Asian Educational Services, 1992)

Bidya Nand, *British India and Tibet* (New Delhi: Oxford and IBH, 1975)

Burman, Bina Roy, *Religions and Politics in Tibet* (Delhi: Vikas Publishing, 1979)

Chakravarti, P.C., *India-China Relations* (Calcutta: Firma KL Mukhopadhyay, 1961)

Chatterjee R.K., *India's Land Borders— Problems and Challenge* (New Delhi: Sterling Publishers, 1978)

Chattopadhyaya, Aloka, *Atisa and Tibet* (Delhi: Motilal Banarsidass, 1996)

Chaube, Shibani Kinkar, *Politics and Constitution in China* (Calcutta: KP Bagchi, 1986)

Chitkara, M.G., *Tibet: a Reality* (New Delhi: Ashish Publishing House, 1994)

Chris Mullin & Phuntsok Wangyal, *Two Perspective on Tibetan-Chinese Relations*, (London: Minority Rights Group, 1983)

Collective, *Tibetan People's Right of Self-Determination* (Delhi: Tibetan Parliamentary & Policy Research Centre 1996)

Collective, *India, Tibet & China* (Delhi: India Tibet Friendship Society, 1996)

Craig, Mary, *Tears of Blood* (Delhi: Indus, 1992)

Dalai Lama, The, *Freedom in Exile* (London: Hodder & Stoughton, 1990)

   My Land and my People, (New York: Potala Corporation, 1977)

   The Dalai Lama in Auroville (Auroville: Pavilion of Tibetan Culture, 1994)

   The Spirit of Tibet: Vision for Human Liberation (Delhi: Vikas, 1996)

Dalvi, Brig J.P., *The Himalayan Blunder* (Delhi: Hind Pocket Books, 1964)

Das, Sarat Chandra, *Indian Pandits in the Land of Snow* (Delhi: Asian Educational Services,1992)

David, M.D., *Rise and Growth of Modern China,* (Bombay: Himalaya Publishing House, 1986)

De Filippe, Filppo, *An Account of Tibet, the Travels of Ippolito Desideri* (London: Routledge, 1937)

Dhondub Choeden, *Life in the Red Flag People's Commune* (Dharamsala: DIIR, 1978)

Dhondup, K., *The Water-Bird and other Years* (Delhi: Rangwang Publishers, 1986)

   The Water-Horse and other Years (Dharamsala: Library of Tibetan Works and Archives, 1984)

DIIR, *The Mongols and Tibet* (Dharamsala: 1996)

   Tibet: Proving Truth From Facts (Dharamsala: 1993)

Domenach, Jean-Luc, *La Chine 1949-1985* (Paris: Imprimerie Nationale, 1987)

Dutt, Subimal, *With Nehru in the Foreign Office* (Calcutta: Minerva Associates, 1977)

Dutt, V.P., *India's Foreign Policy* (New Delhi: Vikas Publishers, 1994)

Fleming, Peter, *Bayonets to Lhasa* (London: Oxford University Press, 1984)

Ford, Robert, *Captured in Tibet* (New York: Oxford University Press, 1990)

Francke, A.H., *A History of Western Tibet* (Delhi: Asian Educational Services, 1995)

French, Patrick, *Younghusband, the Last Great Imperial Adventurer* (London: Flamingo, 1995)

Gandhi Rajmohan, ed., *Patel: A Life* (Ahmedabad: Vallabhbhai Patel Memorial Society, 1991)

Gautier, François, *Rewriting Indian History* (Delhi: Vikas Publishers, 1996)

Bull, T. Geoffrey, *When Iron Gates Yields* (Chicago: Chicago Moody Press, 1960)

Ghosh, Suchita, *Tibet in Sino-Indian Relations 1899-1914* (New Delhi: Sterling Publishers, 1977)

Goldstein, Melville, *The Fall of the Lamaist State* (University of California Press: 1989)

   Tibet, China and the US - reflections on the Tibet Question (USA: The Atlantic Council of the United States, 1995)

Gopal, Ram, *India China Tibet Triangle* (Lucknow: Ram Gopal, 1964)

Gopal, Sarvepalli, *Jawaharlal Nehru: a Biography*, Vol. 2 & 3 (London: Oxford University Press, 1979)

Grunfeld, Tom A., *The Making of Modern Tibet* (London: Oxford University Press, 1987)

Gupta, Karunakar, *Sino-Indian Relations 1948-52* (Calcutta: New Book Centre, 1987)

    Spotlight on Sino-Indian Frontiers (Calcutta: New Book Centre, 1982)

Harrer, Heinrich, *Seven Years in Tibet* (New York; Granada, 1983)

    . *Return to Tibet* (London: Penguin Books, 1983)

Hede, H.C., *Dalai Lama and India* (New Delhi: Institute of National Affairs, 1959)

Heruka, Tsang Nyon, *The Life of Marpa the Translator* (Boston: Shambala, 1986)

Hopkirk, Peter, *The Great Game* (London: Oxford University Press, 1990)

    Trespassers on the Roof of the World (London: Oxford University Press, 1983)

Hsu, Immanuel C.Y., *The Rise of Modern China* (London: Oxford University Press, 1995)

Huthcesing, Raja, *A White Book: Tibet fights for Freedom* (New Delhi: Orient Longmans, 1960)

Ingram, Paul, *Tibet: the Facts* (Dharamsala: Tibetan Young Buddhist Association, 1990)

Jain, Girijal, *Panchsheela and After* (Bombay: Asia Publishing House, 1960)

Jain, R.K., *China, Pakistan & Bangladesh Vol II* (Delhi, Radiant Publishers, 1977)

Jasbir Singh, Amar Kaur, *A Guide to Source Materials in the India Office Library* (London: British Library, 1988)

    Himalayan Triangle (London: British Library, 1987)

    How the Tibetan problem influenced China's Foreign Relations (London: Unpublished)

Jetly, Nancy, *India-China Relations 1947-1977* (Atlantic Highlands: Humanities Press, 1979)

Joshi, Dr. L.M., *Review on Some Alleged Causes of the Decline of Buddhism in India* (Allahabad, Journal of the Ganganatha Jha Research Institute, Vol XXII, 1966)

Jung Chang, *Wild Swans* (London: Flamingo, 1991)

Kadian, Rajesh, *Tibet, Indian & China* (New Delhi: Vision Books, 1999)

Karan, Predyumne P., *The Changing Face of Tibet* (Lexington: The University Press of Kentuky, 1976)

Kaul, P.N., *Frontiers Calling*, (New Delhi: Vikas, 1976)

Kaul, T.N., *India, China and Indochina* (Delhi: Allied Publishers, 1987)

    Reminiscences Discreet and Indiscreet (New Delhi: Lancers Publishers, 1982)

Kewley, Vanya, *Tibet: Behind the Ice Curtain* (London: Grafton, 1990)

Kristof Nicholas D. & Sherryl Wudunn, *China Wakes* (New York: Times Books, 199)

Kuleshov, Nikolai S. *Russia's Tibet File* (Dharamsala, Library of Tibetan Works & Archives, 1996)

Kunsang Paljor, *Tibet, The Undying Flame* (Dharamsala: DIIR, 1977)

Lahiri, Latika, *Chinese Monks in India* (Delhi: Motilal Banarsidass, 1995)

Lall, John, *Aksai Chin and the Sino-Indian Conflict* (New Delhi: Allied Publishers, 1988)

Lamb Alastair, *The China-India Border* (London: Oxford University Press, 1964)

    The McMahon Line, 2 Vol. (London: Oxford University Press, 1964)

Li Xiao Jun, *The Long March to the Fourth of June* (London: Duckworth, 1989)

Li Zhisui, Dr, *The Private Life of Chairman Mao* (London: Arrow, 1996)

MacFarquhar, Roderick, *The Origin of the Cultural Revolution Contradictions among the People* (London: Oxford University Press, 1974)

Majumdar, R.K. & Srivasta, A.N., *History of China* (New Delhi: SBD Publishers, 1994)

Majumdar, R.C., *Ancient India* (New Delhi: Motilal Banarsidass, 1952)

Majumdar, R.C., *The History and Culture of the Indian People*, 11 Volumes (Bombay: Bharatiya Vidya Bhavan, 1957)

Malaviya, H.D., *Peking Leadership: Treachery and Betrayal* (New Delhi: New Literature, 1979)

Maraini, Fosco, *Secret Tibet* (New York: Grove Press, 1952)

Maxwell, Neville, *India's China War* (Delhi: Jaico Publishing, 1971)

McKay, Alex, *Tibet and the British Raj: The Frontier Cadre 1904-1947* (London: Curzon Press, 1998)

    Tibet 1924: a Very British Coup Attempt? (Cambridge: Journal of Royal Asiatic Society, November 1997).

Mehra, Parshotam, *Negotiating with the Chinese 1846-1987*, (New Delhi: Reliance Publishing House, 1989)

    The McMahon Line and After, (Delhi: Reliance Publishing House, 1974)

    The North-Eastern Frontier 1914-1954 — Vol. 2 (Bombay: Oxford University Press, 1980)

Menon, K.P.S., *Memories and Musings* (Bombay: Allied Publishers, 1979)

Mishra, A.N., *The Diplomatic Triangle China -India – America* (Patna: Janaki Prakashan, 1980)

Mishra T.P., *The Taming of Tibet* (Jaipur: Nirala Publications, 1991)

Mitter, J.P., *Betrayal of Tibet* (Bombay: Allied Publishers, 1964)

Moraes, Frank, *The Revolt in Tibet* (New York: MacMillan Co, 1960)

Mullik B.M., *My Years with Nehru — The Chinese Betrayal* (Delhi: Allied Publishers, 1971)

Mullin, Glenn H., *Path of the Bodhisattva Warrior* (New York, Snow Lion, 1988)

Murty, T.S., *Path of Peace: Studies on Sino-Indian Dispute* (New Delhi: ABC Publishing House, 1983)

Namkhai Norbu, *The Necklace of Gzi* (Dharamsala: DIIR, 1984)

Neterowicz, Eva M., *The Tragedy of Tibet* (Washington: The Council for Social and Economic Studies, 1989)

Norbu, Dr. Dawa, *Red Star Over Tibet* (Delhi: Sterling Publishers, 1987)
    The Road Ahead (New Delhi: Harpers Collins, 1997)

Norbu, Thubten Jigme, *Tibet is my Country* (London: Wisdom Publications, 1986)

Palit, Maj. Gen. D.K., *War in High Himalaya* (London: Lancer International, 1991)

Panjabi, K.M., *The Indomitable Sardar* (Bombay: Bharatiya Vidya Bhavan, 1990)

Pannikar, K.M., *Asia and Western Dominance,* (New York: The John Day Company, 1943)
    In Two Chinas (London: Allen & Unwin,1955)

Pant, Apa, *A Moment in Time* (Bombay: Orient Longmans, 1974)

Patt, David, *A Strange Liberation* (New York: Snow Lion Publications, 1992)

Patterson, George N, *Peking vs Delhi* (London: Praeger, 1963)
    Tibet in Revolt (London: Faber & Faber, 1960)

Prema Addy, *Tibet on the Imperial Chess Board* (Calcutta: Academic Publishers, 1984)

Raghu Vira, Prof., *Tibet: a Souvenir* (New Delhi: Bureau of Afro-Asian Convention on Tibet, 1960)

Rahul, Ram, *The Dalai Lama: the Institution* (Delhi: Vikas Publishing, 1995)
    The Himalayas as a Frontier (Delhi: Vikas Publishing, 1978)

Richardson, H.E., *Tibetan Precis* (Calcutta: Indian Political Service, 1945)
    Tibet & Its History (Boulder, Shambala, 1984)

Riencourt, Amaury de, *Lost World: Tibet* (Delhi: Sterling Publishers,1987)

Rockhill, W.W., *The Land of the Lamas* (London: Longmans, 1891)

Rowland, John, *A History of Sino-Indian Relations — Hostile Co-Existence* (Princeton: D Van Nosrand Co., 1967)

Sacks, Howard C., *The Quest for Universal Responsibility* (Dharamsala: DIIR, 1983)

Saigal, Lt. Col., J.R., *The Unfought War of 1962* (Bombay: Allied Publishers, 1979)

Salisbury, Harrison E., *The New Emperors China in the Era of Mao and Deng* (New York: Little Brown, 1991)

Sandberg, Graham, *The Exploration of Tibet* (Delhi: Cosmo Publications, 1986)

Schurmann, Frantz & Schell, Orville, *Communist China* (New York: Vintage Book, 1967)

Sethna, K.D., *India and the World Scene* (Pondicherry: Sri Aurobindo Institute of Research in Social Sciences, 1997)

Shakabpa, Tsepon W.D., *Tibet: a Political History* (New York: Potala Corporation, 1967)

Shakya, Tsering, *The Dragon in the Land of Snows* (London: Pimlico, 1999)

Shakya, Min Bahadur, *Princess Bhrikuti Devi* (Kathmandu: Pilgrims Book House, 1997)

Sharan Shankar, *Fifty Years after the Asian Relations Conference* (Delhi, TPPRC, 1997)

Sharma, Brig., B.N., *India Betrayed, the Role of Nehru* (New Delhi: Manas Publications, 1997)

Singh, L.P., *Portrait of Lal Bahadur Shastri* (New Delhi: Ravi Dayal Publisher, 1996)

Sinha, Nirmal Chandra, *Tibet - Considerations on Inner Asian History* (Calcutta: Firma KL Mukhopadhyay, 1967)

Smith, W. Warren Jr., *Tibetan Nation* (New Delhi: Harpers Collins, 1997)

Snow, Edgar, *Red Star Over China* (New York: Penguin Books, 1937)

Sondhi, M.L., *Non Appeasement — New Direction for Indian Foreign Policy* (New Delhi: Abhinav Publications, 1972)

Stein, R.A., *La Civilisation Tibétaine* (Paris: Dunod, 1962)

Stoddard, Heather, *Le Mendiant de l'Amdo* (Paris: Société d'Ethnographie, 1989)

Taring, Rinchen Dolma, *Daughter of Tibet* (New Delhi, Allied Publishers, 1970)

Tashi Tsering, *A Brief Survey of Fourteen Centuries of Sino-Tibetan Relations* (Dharamsala: DIIR, 1988)

Tewari, Maj. Gen., K.K., *A Soldier's Voyage to Self Discovery* (Auroville: Tewari, 1992)

Tewari, Udai Narain, *Resurgent Tibet: a Cause for Non-aligned Movement* (New Delhi: Select Book Service Syndicate, 1983)

Thomas, Lowell, *The Silent War in Tibet* (London: Secker & Warburg, 1960)

Thubten Kalsang, Lama (trans.) *Atisha,* (Delhi: Mahayana Publications, 1974)

Tieh-Tseng Li, *Tibet Today and Yesterday* (New York: Bookman Associates, 1960)

Tsering Tashi Gashi, *New Tibet* (Dharamsala: DIIR, 1980)

Turner, Captain Samuel, *An Account of an Embassy to the Court of the Teshoo Lama in Tibet* (London: G & W Nicol, 1800)

Uban, S.S., *Phantoms of Chittagong: the Fifth Army in Bangla Desh* (New Delhi: Allied Publishers, 1985)

van Walt van Praag, Michael, *The Status of Tibet* (Boulder: Westview Press, 1987)

Wignall, Sydney, *Spy on the Roof of the World* (Edinburgh: Canongate, 1997)

Williamson, Margaret D, *Memoirs of a Political Officer's Wife in Tibet, Sikkim and Bhutan* (London: Wisdom Publication, 1987)

Woodman, Dorothy, *Himalayan Frontiers* (London: Barrie and Rockliff, 1969)

Xinru Lui, *Ancient India and Ancient China* (New Delhi: Oxford University Press, 1988)

Younghusband, Sir Francis, *India and Tibet* (New Delhi: Asian Educational Services, 1993)

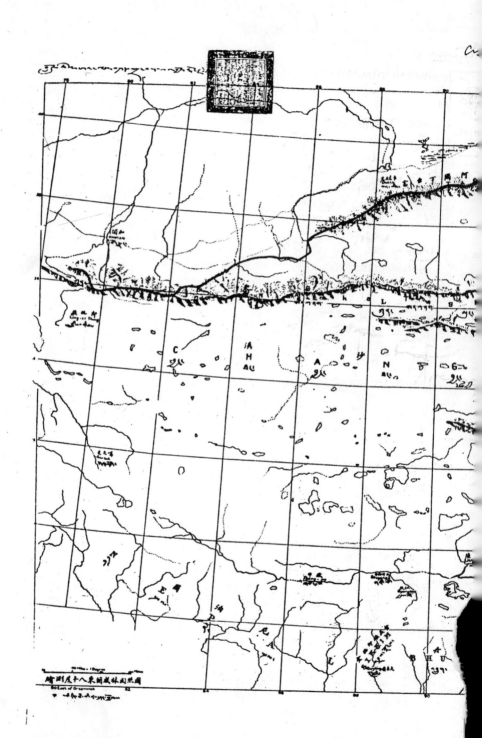